The
Royal Marines

1664 to the present

The
Royal Marines

1664 to the present

Richard Brooks

CONSTABLE • LONDON

Constable & Robinson Ltd
3 The Lanchesters
162 Fulham Palace Road
London W6 9ER
www.constablerobinson.com

First published in the UK by Constable,
an imprint of Constable & Robinson Ltd 2002

A copy of the British Library Cataloguing in
Publication Data is available from the British Library

ISBN 0-094-80390-0

Printed and bound in the EU

Acknowledgements

I T is a pleasant task to acknowledge the support and assistance of the following: Don Bittner, Ken Brooks, S.M. Buxton, The Diggers, Dr Eric Gruber von Arni, Sue Lindsay, Ken MacDonald, Matthew Sheldon, Dr James Thomas, Allison Wareham, Paul Whitehead, Brian Witts. I owe a particular debt to Matthew Little of the Royal Marines Museum, without whose expertise this book could not have been written.

The Trustees of the following institutions have kindly given permission for use of their original archive material: The National Maritime Museum, Greenwich, London; the Royal Marines Museum, Eastney, Portsmouth; The Royal Naval Museum, HM Naval Base, Portsmouth. The Council of the Navy Records Society has granted permission to reproduce passages from their invaluable printed collections of documents. The Society continues to add to its series of volumes, which form the starting point for any study of British naval history. It deserves every support.

Full references may be found in the Bibliography and Notes.

Contents

	Illustrations	ix
	Map	x
	Introduction	1
1	Overture and Beginnings	3
2	False Starts and False Musters	25
3	Action Under Sail	51
4	Raids and Expeditions	75
5	Sea Service and Barrack Life	105
6	The Marines and the Emperor	127
7	Pax Britannica	157
8	The Advent of Steam	189
9	Action Under Steam	205
10	Poor Bloody Infantry	231
11	Where Sea Meets Shore	251
12	Survival of the Fittest	275
	Appendix I – Marine Establishments 1690–2000	291
	Appendix II – Marine Regiments 1690–1747	293
	Notes	295
	Bibliography	323
	Glossary	329
	Index	331

Illustrations

Between pages 116 and 117

Soldier of the Lord High Admiral's Regiment (Richard Simkin)
The capture of Gibraltar celebrated on a contemporary playing card (RMM)
Destruction of the *Royal James* at Sole Bay 1672 (W.H. Overend)
Marine of the 1740s
Marine detachment on the poop of Liverpool privateer 1778
Marine Officer, Grenadier, Drummer and Private Marine of 1776 (Capt. J.S. Hicks RMLI)
Royal Marine sentinel of the Napoleonic Wars (RMM: I.C.Stadler)
Night attack on French invasion flotilla at Boulogne 15–16 August 1801
Marine walking out 1830
Paddle gunboats and wooden walls bombard Sidon 27 Sept 1840
Royal Marine Artillery, 1850s (Capt. J.S. Hicks RMLI)
Marines and Riflemen on Balaklava Heights
The Blue Devils at Tel-el-Kebir (Col. C. Field)

Between pages 212 and 213

Royal Marine Artillerymen in Overseas Service dress of the 1890s
Nile gunboats in action at al Matamma 1898
Betsy the international gun at the Peking Legations 1900 (RMM)
Royal Marine peacekeepers in Albania 1913 (RMM)
The Transmitting Station: (RMM: Charles Ingle)
Engaging the main force of the enemy (RMM)
HMS *Lion* after Jutland (RMM)
Landing craft trials in Langstone Harbour 1929 (RMM)
Buffaloes and Weasels disembark from an LCT at Walcheren (RMM)
HMS *Theseus* off Suez preparing to land 45 Cdo by helicopter (RMM)
1960s Marines in Borneo (RMM)
Marines of 42 Cdo in Port Stanley (RMM)
Marine foot patrol in Ulster 1987 (RMM)

Illustrations are from author's collection, except where shown as RMM, courtesy of the Royal Marines Museum, Eastney.

Major Actions and Campaigns of the Royal Marines

Landguard Fort 166?
Sole Bay 1672
Texel, Schooneveldt
Camperdown 1797
Heligoland Bight 191
Dogger Bank 1915
Jutland 1916

Loss of
HMS *Hood*   Iceland,
1941   Faroes 1940

Ireland Ongoing

Annapolis 1710
Quebec 1711/1759
Louisburg 1746/1758
Boston 1775
Halifax 1776–8
Great Lakes 1813–15

Camaret Bay 1694   Beachy Head 1
Vigo 1702   Dieppe 1942
Quiberon Bay 1759   Normandy 194
Belle Isle 1761
Glorious First of June 1794
Virginia 1676   North Spain 1815/1833–40
Chesapeake Bay,   *Bismarck* Action 1942
Washington 1814   Cockleshell Heroes 1942   Tangier 168
New Orleans 1815   Cadiz 1702/
                        Catalonia, Minorca 1705–08 Gibraltar 17
                        Algiers 1816   Trafalgar 18
Havana 1762   Lisbon 1810

Vera Cruz 1862   Goree 1758
                Leeward Islands 1759/1762   Gambia 1894
                                                   Dakar 1940
Cartagena 1741   Sierra Leone 200

                                                   Gold Coast 187
                                                   Brass River 189
                                                   Benin 1897

                                Ascension Island 1815–1
                                St Helena 1815–16

Buenos Aires 1806
Obligado 1846
River Plate 1939

Falkland Islands 1914/1982

rn Convoys & 1941–4
rhorst Action 1943

North Russia 1918–19

1940

Enzheim 1674
Walcheren 1809/1944
Ostend, Antwerp 1914

1854–5

France, Flanders 1916–18
Zeebrugge 1918
Calais, Boulogne, Hook 1940
Rhine, Weser, Aller and Elbe 1945

1827

ia,
943–4
2000

Crimea 1854–5

South Russia
1918–20

Vladivostok, Siberia 1919

Dardanelles, Gallipoli
1915–16, 1919

Peiho River, Peking 1858–60/1900

Kurdistan 1991

'98   Crete 1941

Afghanistan 2001–2

Acre 1799

Shanghai
1860–3/1927

Japan, Okinawa
1864/1870–2/1945

1940–3

Syria 1840   Persian Gulf

43

Palestine 1948   Ongoing

Canton
1838–42/1856–8

3–5

The Nile 1798

India
1857–9/

Sudan
1883–4/
1897–8

Alexandria, Tel-el-Kebir 1882
Suez 1882/1956

1941–5

Burma, Arakan
1852–3/1859/
1885/1942–5

Manila 1762

Aden 1960–7

Witu 1891
Mwele 1895
Somaliland 1904
German East Africa 1916–17
Tanzania 1964

Singapore, Malaya
1942/1949–52

Borneo
1962–4

Java
1811/1942

Madagascar 1942

Australia 1788

806/1879/1899–1900
South West Africa 1914–16

New Zealand
1845/1860–4

Introduction

THE history of the Royal Marines can be traced from the spacious days of King Charles II, who shared a mistress with one of the most distinguished soldiers ever to serve at sea, John Churchill, 1st Duke of Marlborough. Later Marines won their laurels in less agreeable circumstances: off the North Cape, at Trafalgar, at Gallipoli and Singapore. Recent exploits have been so celebrated as to obscure the links between the Admiral's Regiment of 1664 with today's Royal Marine Commandos. Yet modern Marines pursue a 350-year-old trade, employing expertise acquired painfully, in face of government neglect and inter-service hostility. Restoration sea soldiers served in every role associated with later Marines: as ship's detachments, as part of naval brigades alongside seamen landed from the fleet, and with the Army as self-contained battalions, participating in campaigns ashore. The Commando role predominates today, but few military organizations have proved so adept at re-inventing themselves as the Marines. In 1944, as the Corps transformed itself into its modern shape, a senior officer paraphrased the dying words of Earl St Vincent, only half in jest: 'If ever the hour of real danger comes to England the Royal Marines will be found busy reorganizing themselves.'[1]

This is the first single volume study of the Royal Marines' history as a whole. It seeks to provide the context missing from the wealth of books that focus exclusively on Commandos. Any student of the subject owes an immense debt to the de facto official history in four volumes, written by three authors working over the last hundred years:

- Colonel Cyril Field RMLI, *Britain's Sea Soldiers,* Vols i & ii (Lyceum Press, Liverpool, 1924).
- General Sir H.E. Blumberg KCB RM, *Britain's Sea Soldiers – A*

Record of the Royal Marines During the War 1914–1919
(Swiss, Devonport, 1927).
- James D. Ladd, *By Sea, By Land – The Royal Marines 1919–1997* (HarperCollins, 1998).

Length and all-embracing scope tend, however, to lose the overall picture. Fifty years ago, the reviewer of an excellent pocket history recognized the problem of summarizing nearly 300 years of active service in every continent: 'the story of the Marines from beginning to end must approximate to a history of the British at war.'[2] The present study focuses on the Marine contribution to that history, rather than seeking to chart every detail of its course. It does not provide detailed accounts of Trafalgar or Operation Overlord – there are plenty of them already – but it does discuss the specific part Marines played in such battles, and what they felt about it. Often I have returned to original material, unused since the pioneering days of naval and Corps history at the turn of the twentieth century, to uncover the true nature of the Marines' contribution to British naval supremacy in the age of sail, how steamships and rifled cannon changed their role, and what elements of it persist today, after the passing of that naval supremacy, and the technologies associated with it.

CHAPTER ONE

Overture and Beginnings

THE Royal Marines are among the oldest British regiments, and have seen more varied action than any purely land-based corps. Their colours bear a single battle honour, 'Gibraltar', its very uniqueness a reminder of their far-flung service. Specific in time and place, 'Gibraltar' celebrates a defining moment in the history of the Corps, and of British maritime power. The seizure of the Rock in 1704 began a 100-year struggle between the Royal Navy and the combined fleets of Bourbon France and Spain that culminated at Trafalgar, another high point in Marine history. Two hundred years after its capture a Royal Marine gunner wrote: 'No one may consider himself a fully fledged Marine until he has been to Gibraltar. . . See Gibraltar and die is a saying peculiarly applicable to the Marines.' An old saying claimed: 'he is not a Marine who has not been to Gibraltar.'[1] For over 300 years Gibraltar has been a landfall for Royal Marines on their way to conflicts in the Mediterranean, South Atlantic and beyond. Its capture and epic defence was the first significant success attributable to British Marines, an example of a type of operation that would provide the Corps' bread and butter for 300 years: the amphibious seizure and defence of a bridgehead against heavy odds.

The War of the Spanish Succession, 1701–14, ranged most of Europe against France and Spain. The death of the last Hapsburg king of Spain, Carlos El Hechizado, brought a grandson of Louis XIV to the Spanish throne destabilizing the European balance of power in favour of France. The German Empire, ruled by another Hapsburg, Leopold I, fought for family territories in Italy and Spain, while English and Dutch fought for commercial access to Spanish territories in the Americas. Any war between England and Spain must be a maritime affair, which Queen Anne's government recognized by raising infantry regiments specifically for service with the fleet. Detachments from three of these took part in an unsuccessful descent on Cadiz in 1702, a failure redeemed in part by interception of a Spanish treasure fleet at Vigo, on the way home. Each regiment present earned £561 10s 0d prize money, and the ensuing litigation occupied senior officers well into the following year.

The year 1704 saw renewed operations against the Spanish coast. An Anglo-Dutch fleet looked in on Barcelona in May, before moving south. In July watering parties landed in Malaga Bay, covered by Marines, where Spanish horse killed two sailors stealing onions, and nearly caught Admiral Dilkes fishing in a stream, but the Marines withdrew without loss, beyond four deserters from Luttrell's regiment. A week later their officers went aboard HMS *Boyne*, the flagship, to consult with Admiral Sir George Rooke on the prospects for an attack on Gibraltar. Its defences were strong, although the garrison was weak, 'but two Spanish regiments, of about forty men each.'[2] Rooke's council of war agreed to launch a bold combined operation: all the Marines of the fleet, some 2,300 men, would land north of Gibraltar to cut the isthmus joining the Rock to the Spanish mainland, while warships attacked the town more directly. Not only was the operation joint, it was international, the German Prince George of Hesse-Darmstadt commanding the mixed force of Dutch and English Marines.

The fleet came to anchor on 21 July, close enough to the Old Mole at Gibraltar for a cannonball to smash a water tub in HMS *Ranelagh*, and prepared to land the Marines. Prince George's men carried additional battle stores, in the expectation of severe fighting, although ammunition scales seem absurdly low:

> every Marine at his landing should have 18 charges of powder and ball, and two grenades with match proportionable to each grenadier. . . the officer commanding each company of Marines should have one of the largest cartridge cases filled up with musket cartridges of powder and shot; and . . . there should be a sufficient quantity of shovels and light crows and men with hatchets to cut fascines.[3]

Shallow-draft frigates drove off Spanish cavalry with naval gunfire, and the Marines consolidated around three mills. Dutch bomb vessels, specialist craft designed for shore bombardment, lobbed shells into the town, while heavier warships warped themselves closer, to begin a six-hour bombardment on the 23rd, firing bombs and incendiary carcasses. A fire broke out near the Governor's House, and the enemy were driven from their guns on the South Mole. While Hesse-Darmstadt led the

Marines within musket shot of the landward defences, seamen from the fleet manned and armed boats to gain the New Mole and Great Bastion, inducing the Spanish Governor to agree to a ceasefire:

> It being Sunday, all the women were at their Devotions in a little Chapel, about four Miles distant from the Town, so that our men were between them and their Husbands, which was a very great inducement to the Citizens to oblige the Governor to capitulate, whereupon in the Evening the Prince of Hesse, with the Marines, marched into the Town.[4]

The Admiral personally conducted the ladies out of town to protect them from the troops, who perpetrated the customary disorders, despite the General Officers' efforts to prevent them:

> continually patrolling, with their sergeants, and sending them on board their ships, and punishing the Marines; one of which was hanged after he had thrown dice with a Dutchman, who hove 10 and the Englishman 9.[5]

Sir George Rooke quickly hoisted the English flag over Gibraltar, despite the Allies' ostensible war aim of restoring Spain to the Hapsburgs. The defence of the Rock would depend more upon the efforts of the Royal Navy than the wishes of a distant Emperor. Early in August a strong French fleet bore down upon an Allied force, weakened by detachments ashore and short of ammunition. Rooke re-embarked 1,000 Marines to win one of the few decisive naval actions of the period at Malaga (12–13 August). Both fleets were badly mauled and the French put back to Toulon to refit. Rooke retired to Gibraltar, where he demonstrated the inherent flexibility of amphibious forces by once more landing his Marines before departing to winter in England. He left Prince George in command with 2,000 English Marines, over 100 naval gunners, armourers, and carpenters, six months' provisions and forty-two guns.

Holding the Rock

The reinforcement was none too soon. Some 10,000 Spanish troops appeared before the Rock, reinforced by 4,500 French soldiers and French warships. The besieging army broke ground on 9 October, covered by thirty guns ranging up to 48-pounders. The besiegers had the seven-to-one odds that the great French engineer Vauban calculated necessary to bring a siege to a successful conclusion, and they pressed the garrison hard. Rooke had left some of the more seaworthy 3rd and 4th rates at Lisbon, under Sir John Leake, which brought timely assistance on 29

October, catching several enemy ships in the Bay and driving them ashore:

> (but to my surprise) find the Town closely besieged and instead of Provisions
> and ammunition they want officers and men to defend the place, for the
> Enemy has approached very close, and have two strong Batteries, which
> I'm affraid will in a very few days level the Bastion that is the only security
> to that Part of the town. . .

But for the navy:

> the place had been stormed and taken for they [the enemy] had got a great
> number of boats together. . . to land 3000 men at the new Mole and had
> likewise on the East side by the help of Rope ladders got 500 men upon
> the top of the hill that overlooks the Town, but were timely discovered
> and attacked by Coll. Burr with the Granadiers who killed 200 of them
> and took the rest prisoners.[6]

Jacob Bor was a major in Fox's Marines, and a true fighting soldier. During
the next year's landing at Barcelona he would kill a fellow colonel in a
duel, as if amphibious operations were not difficult enough. Bor was a
key figure in the defence of Gibraltar, succeeding to the regiment after
Fox's death, and acting as second-in-command to Prince George. Under
their energetic direction the garrison palisaded the ditch, dug mines under
the covered way and blocked up breaches with the rubbish cast down by
Spanish guns. At night they threw fire barrels into no-man's-land to
illuminate enemy workmen sapping forward, behind racks of fascines
known as 'chandeliers'.

Gibraltar's situation remained desperate throughout November. Leake
reported to Sir John Methuen, the English Ambassador at Lisbon, 'the
Garrison is yet in our possession, but dare not promise it may continue. . .
The principal thing they want to make it defensible is men.' An anonymous
account of their numbers, claimed they were, 'but 1300 men in all, and
200 of them sick, so that half of that number is upon duty every night'.
Parties of seamen landed daily to fill up houses inside the curtain for a
second line of defence, but Leake had few men to spare. Prince George
had to beg medical stores and a 'Chyrurgeon to receive them'. Winter
gales threatened the garrison's lifeline, for sailing vessels blown down the
Straits could not return until the wind changed:

> the *Panther* and a Dutch Man of War were very near driving ashore. The
> Dutch having most of their cables cut by the foulness of the ground, and
> likewise several of ours, wee were oblig'd to retire to the East side this day.

Methuen reported over 600 casualties before Christmas, over a quarter of the original garrison.[7]

The balance of forces shifted before Christmas. Two thousand fresh infantry from the Coldstream Guards and two line regiments arrived on 13 December, allowing Leake to withdraw his battered ships, leaving the garrison with what extra muskets he could spare.[8] The besiegers now had only 7,000 against 3,000 defenders, but kept up the pressure. A month into the New Year Hesse was down to 2,000 men, including 900 sick, with twelve days powder, and the enemy only ten paces from a gaping hole in the Round Tower. In February they made a sudden rush with 600 picked men:

> Colonel Bor made a very good defence tho' the enemy got above the breach and threw great stones and granadoes down on his men: but those who had got in at the wall marching down to cut off his retreat into the town, obliged him and his men to get over the parapet of the line, and to retire into the covered way, where the English Guards were posted.[9]

Captain Fisher of Seymour's Marines dashed at the enemy with seventeen men, only to be captured. Colonel Moncall of Barrymore's Regiment collected 400–500 before charging sword in hand, 'so that he drove them from place to place, quite out of the Round Tower.' The gallant Fisher was retaken, only to be captured again, pursuing too closely. Luckily for him, the prisoners included a Spanish Grenadier Captain, and he was promptly exchanged. The failure of the attack puzzled an Allied 'Ingineer', the breaches wide enough for thirty men, and the assault trenches so close. He had great hopes of the defence, however:

> the Prince, our officers, and even our private sentinels are fully persuaded, that we shall beat the enemy; and I have often observed that persuasions of this nature go a long way.[10]

In early March the defenders opened fire from a new battery behind the breach. Hesse issued fifty gallons of punch to drink Queen Anne's health, which was done with such 'Huzzas' that the enemy took alarm. The attackers were correspondingly depressed, and began to saw up their guns in preparation for a retreat. Most of their ammunition was spent after throwing 'more than 8,000 Bombs and upwards of 70,000 Cannon Shot fired to very little purpose.'[11] Guns' vents were so enlarged from constant use they could only be fired safely by laying a powder trail to them. Trenches were so knocked about that the besiegers were up to their knees in mud and water, 'almost naked, ill-paid, and in great want of ammunition and other necessaries.'[12] A French squadron arrived early in February for a last amphibious effort, but bad weather delayed the operation. Before it could be carried out Sir John Leake returned from resupplying his ships, and on 10 March drove two French ships ashore and captured another three. The reassertion of Allied maritime superiority assured Gibraltar's communications and broke the siege.

Gibraltar's strategic importance can hardly be overemphasized. One of the last of Britain's imperial outposts, it lies between Africa and Europe at the intersection of key maritime lines of communication. It still provides the Royal Navy with a foothold in the Western Mediterranean, and a stepping-stone to the South Atlantic. Contemporaries quickly recognized its significance. Robert Harley, Speaker of the House of Commons, 'chewing this victory yet in the lump', described Gibraltar as 'the largest thoroughfare of trade in the world'.[13] Methuen had poured in supplies at his own expense: 3,000 grenades, 170 barrels of flour, a ton of candles, a surgeon to attend the Marines, and 'engines and all sorts of ammunition borrowed from the King of Portugal's arsenal.'[14] As soon as the siege was concluded he recommended, 'settling immediately a regular Government and order in that place. . . as likewise the strengthening of that place which seems capable of being made without great expense extreamly strong.'[15] Parliament showed its approval by voting £1,800, 'bounty money for the Marine soldiers that were in the action at Gibraltar the last summer.'[16]

Admiral Leake's biographer pronounced Gibraltar's defence, 'an act so great and glorious that it may well find a place amongst the many wonders of the reign'. Considering the insuperable difficulties of a weak and sickly garrison, confronting the united forces of France and Spain, and an undermanned fleet, forced to keep the sea for want of anchors, and in constant danger of attack, he felt the action might claim pre-eminence, 'with the greatest of our naval successes that the war produced.'[17] A pamphleteer proclaimed, with commendable bias, that the garrison had done more than could humanly be expected and 'the British Marines gained immortal honour.'[18] Not only had they held the Rock, they had ruined the best troops in Spain, inflicting at least 10,000 casualties in action or by disease. The élite Walloon Guards lost 900 men out of 1,300, while 2,000 French Marines landed in October suffered 75 per cent losses; the defenders of the Rock lost about 1,200 dead. Their stand altered the course of the war in Spain, allowing the Allies to go on the offensive.

Sadly, there is no extant account of the coup de main of July 1704, nor of the eight months' siege, from the pen of a Marine. Their viewpoints are lost, although petitions of wounded and impoverished officers record some of their names and sufferings: Captain John Henley of Holt's Marines received £182 10s 0d for losing his right arm; Lieutenant Robert Dove of the Queen's Own got a year's pay, 'in consideration of his having lost his right eye at the siege of Gibraltar'; John Mason of Will's Marines hoped for a Lieutenant Governorship, having lost his right arm and been much wounded besides: 'The company he has cost him a large sum, and his misfortunes render his service on board Your Majesty's ships very uneasie to him.' Less is known of the other ranks: John Curtis, a Marine in Holt's Regiment, petitioned for relief in 1711:

> He hath lost his left arm and part of his said shoulder at the taking Alligant [sic], he was likewise shot through the head by a Musquett Ball and several pieces of his Scull taken out such damage he received against Gibraltar.

He had received £7 from the Chatham Chest, 'stopt three years next Christmas, the Officers not paying towards the said Chest.'[19] A Derbyshire gravestone commemorated a more fortunate veteran. William Billinge enlisted under Sir George Rooke, was at the taking of the Fortress of Gibraltar, and later served with the Duke of Marlborough, before returning to his birthplace to die in 1791, reputedly 112 years of age.

More than a century passed before the Royal Marines received the privilege of wearing 'Gibraltar' on their colours, headdresses and accoutrements, by which time the true nature of events on the Rock in 1704–5 had been obscured. The Duke of Clarence, later William IV, glossed over the presence of other regiments at Gibraltar when awarding new colours to the Royal Marines in 1827, although four line regiments possessed a similar battle honour. The delay and error suggest that the undoubtedly glorious capture and defence of the Rock were something of an anomaly. The history of British Marine forces before 1704 was not at all distinguished. Their combat record was obscure, while their administration was a byword for corruption and ineptitude, even by the relaxed standards of the day. Queen Anne's Marine regiments were the latest in a series of attempts to provide soldiers for naval service. Many of their officers were 'reformadoes' – half-pay officers inherited from earlier Marine regiments disbanded in the 1690s. Three of the regiments at Gibraltar were disbanded at the end of the war, and the others transferred into the Army. Forty years would pass before the Admiralty hit upon a sound basis for a permanent corps of Marines.

These unpromising beginnings played an essential part in forming the distinctive esprit de corps of today's Royal Marines. The Corps is not an artificial élite, created overnight by robbing established corps of their best men. Its reputation, like that of the French Foreign Legion, has been earned through years of arduous, often ill-rewarded service in out of the way corners of the world. Their traditions are the more potent for having been hard won, in the face of many difficulties.

The Lord Admiral's Regiment

The customary starting point for historians of the Royal Marines is an Order in Council sealed by His Majesty King Charles II on 28 October 1664, directing:

> That twelve hundred land Souldjers be forthwith raysed to be in readinesse, to be distributed into His Ma[ts] Fleets prepared for Sea Service w[ch] said twelve hundred Men are to be putt into One Regiment Under One Colonell.[20]

The Order took practical shape with dramatic speed. Warrants of 5 November commissioned a Colonel, Lieutenant Colonel, Major and three Captains, responsible for recruiting the six companies, and authorized the Paymaster of the Forces to advance the men a week's wages. Enlistment proceeded at such a pace that the Regiment mustered on the 16th, allowing the officers to claim their first pay, and marking the start of the Regiment's effective existence.[21]

The prompt appearance of 1,200 men suggests a ready pool of manpower, perhaps old Commonwealth soldiers of the New Model Army. Several of the new Regiment's officers, including Colonel Sir William Killigrew, had seen service in Holland, but the most widely canvassed source of men were the 9,000-strong London Trained Bands, a seventeenth-century precursor of the Volunteer Movement. The Admiral's Regiment may have inherited its yellow coats from the Trained Bands, but yellow was part of the Stuart livery, and featured prominently on the horse furniture of the Duke of York's Horse Guards. More than one historian has suggested that the Marines' long-standing privilege of marching through the City of London with colours flying, drums beating and bayonets fixed derives from a Trained Bands connection, but the argument is circular, and the true origin of the custom lost. Colonel Lourenço Edye, the definitive historian of the early days of the Corps, found the question, 'wrapped in the profoundest obscurity'.[22]

In the autumn of 1664, the English Fleet was preparing for a descent on the Dutch coast, but the bare text of the Order in Council gives little clue to its immediate motives. It makes no reference to the nature of the new Regiment's duties at sea, or any particular training that might justify the attribution of the term 'sea-soldiers' uniquely to Killigrew's men. Other regiments contributed to the fleet: the Foot Guards and Coldstreams sent over a thousand to sea in spring 1665, while Treasury minutes of 1667 refer to two naval regiments, associating the Admiral's with the Holland Regiment as maritime infantry. The most obvious reason for regarding Killigrew's as a marine regiment is its association with James, Duke of York and Albany, the King's brother and Lord Admiral. As second man in the kingdom he had a good claim to the military patronage represented by a Regiment of Foot. The conspiracy theorist might see the Admiral's Regiment as an alternative focus of interest to the Coldstream Regiment, which George Monck, now Duke of Albemarle, had led into England to restore the King. Albemarle was also Sir William Killigrew's uncle, and as Lord General had special responsibility for supplying the Admiral's Regiment with its arms, drums and colours. The first of these provide the only material evidence for their maritime function. The Regiment was equipped throughout with flintlock muskets, or firelocks, and had no pikes, an anti-cavalry weapon of limited use in a ship. Flintlocks were more reliable in damp conditions than the matchlocks used by other regiments, and hence more serviceable at sea. A Warrant coinciding with the Admiral's first muster instructed the Ordnance Commissioners to supply them with 1,200 firelocks and bandoliers, 24 halberds and 6 drums, 30 barrels of bullets and 2 hogsheads of flints. The Admiral's was the first English regiment equipped throughout with firelocks, but, after the maritime emergency of the Dutch Wars, it reverted to pikes and matchlocks. It kept its link with the Duke of York, even when anti-Catholic hysteria drove him from public office in 1673. Sir Charles Littleton, third Colonel of the Regiment, gives us a glimpse of the informal operation of the small, closely knit Stuart government:

> I asked last night how the regiment should be styled, he being no longer Admiral. He went to the King about it, who then ordered that the commissions in future should be in the name of the Duke's or His Royal Highness' regiment.[23]

The maritime function of the Admiral's Regiment was therefore less permanent than its personal connection with the Duke of York, an affiliation that would prove disastrous.

First Blood

The Admiral's Regiment was a wartime creation, and its men were pitched

straight into some of the most stubborn battles ever fought by the Royal
Navy. The spring of 1665 brought renewed preparations for Anglo-Dutch
hostilities. Lieutenant Dennis marched 600 Irish recruits from Bristol to
Southwark to join the Admiral's Regiment, while Lieutenant Gardiner
arrested a press gang making off with some of his existing soldiers. The
provision of more formal detachments of men for sea service would be
an essential function of later Marine formations. The first documented
example of the Admiral's Regiment so doing was in May 1665: Wray's
and Griffiths' companies going aboard the *Loyall Subject*, a 42-gun
merchant ship, and the *Baltimore*. Another group of 300 refused to join
the *Loyal Katherine* at Greenwich until paid their arrears.[24] On 3 July,
the Dutch fleet suffered a great defeat at the hands of the Duke of York
off Lowestoft. A round-shot killed three officers on the quarterdeck of
the English flagship, but the Duke was safe, 'though he was so near the
noble persons killed by that fatal shot that his clothes were smeared with
their blood'.[25] The part played by non-royal members of the Admiral's
Regiment is less certain. *Baltimore*'s detachment is unlikely to have smelt
powder, the Captain declaring her, 'so miserably manned that there is no
venturing to sea'. Several hundred soldiers sailed from Harwich and Deal,
where companies of the Admiral's were quartered, but there is no evidence
that they arrived in time to make Lowestoft the Regiment's first fleet action.

The Four Days Fight of 1–4 June 1666 was one of the hardest-fought
fleet actions in British naval history, when the Dutch drove the English
fleet into the Thames. The Admiral's Regiment's share remains frustratingly
obscure, although 245 soldiers from that and another regiment had been
shipped off to the Nore in February, with '39 musketeers for their guard'.
Sir Chichester Wray had succeeded Killigrew in July 1665, and sixty of
his men were among those despatched to make good losses, their uneven
quality showing the strain of two years of fighting: '30 of them will pass
Moustir,' wrote the Captain of the *Rupert,* 'for the Rest are all new Raysed
first upon thare bringing hither and knowe nothing of being a souldgar
further then they have heard of souch a thing.'[26] More companies arrived
in time for the English riposte, off the North Foreland on 25 July: two
from the Tower and three more from Harwich. The whole country was
in arms, awaiting the movements of the Dutch Fleet. Land service had
proved more popular than the Navy: 'Men who fly from the press offer
themselves as soldiers', a contemporary observer leaving no doubt about
the military contribution to the St James' Day Fight:

> never was a braver fleet seen at sea than the English of 100 sail of frigates

and 25 fire-ships. The *Rupert* has sailed from the Rolling Grounds, bravely manned, as is the whole fleet, the soldiers going with great cheerfulness.[27]

The Dutch lost twenty ships sunk or burnt, against one English loss admitted. Afterwards, the recently embarked companies of the Admiral's Regiment were discharged ashore to guard Dutch prisoners, and recruit, 'for most of their men went aboard the ships before the last fight'. The following year would see the first single ship action to involve British Marines, and their first documented casualties: 'The *Paradox*, carrying over a company of the Duke of Yorke's yellow coates to Guernsey, had a hot dispute with a French flyboat of 14 guns, and drove her on the French coast.' Captain Herbert's company had sailed from West Cowes, when a French 'Doger' or privateer attacked them:

> but the winde blew soe hard & the sea was soe high cold not bord her, the Paradox had 100 soldiers besides their owne company & they plyed their small shot lustily, one of them was killed and 6 more wounded. [28]

The Regiment's first land action soon followed. The Dutch raid on the Medway in June 1667 inspired general alarm around south-eastern coasts. Four companies of the Admiral's Regiment concentrated at Harwich, and two more in Landguard Fort, between the harbour and open sea. Lord Oxford, Colonel of the Blues, collected militia and troops of horse, while the dockyard authorities moored colliers across the arm of the sea behind Landguard: 'all with jacks, ensigns, and pendant as though they were men of war, and with holes cut ready to be sunk in case of an attempt by the enemy'.[29] Localities from Lowestoft to Aldborough complained at being, 'left without defences, which are all drawn towards Landguard Fort',[30] but Government strategists had predicted Dutch intentions correctly. On 2 July seventy Dutch ships sailed into the Rolling Grounds, 'fired many guns at the fort and at the ships placed at the entrance of the harbour to be sunk for security'. Two thousand men landed below Felixstowe and maintained the lanes and hedges against the Suffolk militia:

> Meanwhile 300 or 400, covered by the smoke from the ships, made up to Landguard Fort, with scaling ladders of 20 feet, hand granadoes, drawn cutlasses, and muskets, and came up close to the fort; their reception was brisk when discovered, and they were repulsed after half an hour's assault. They got under the sand banks, but the *Lenox* and *Truelove* played upon them from the water. An hour after they tried again, but ran away, leaving some of their ladders and arms.

The Dutch had underestimated the garrison, and were confused by the blockships, 'not knowing whether they were men-of-war or fire-ships'.[31] Their own boats were hard aground, but the tide floated them off before the Suffolk men could drive them into the sea. 'They carried off their dead and wounded and culverins in the night, and by morning were all aboard again; one Fleming was killed with a cheese under his arm.'[32]

Casualty figures proved elastic. The *London Gazette* expanded reports that, 'only one man was killed in the fort, but four Dutch were killed before it', to 150 dead, 'at the least'.[33] The authorities were keen, after the Medway débacle, to make the most of what a modern historian has described as 'a particularly feeble affair',[34] although the Earl of Oxford was more positive. The dockyard at Harwich, 'was not now an enterprise for Dutch courage, and the disrepute of this enterprise moderates the grief for the loss at Chatham'.[35] One of the few English casualties was Captain Nathaniel Darell, commander of the victorious garrison, whose arm wound prevented his penning the first battle report by a Marine officer. The garrison were jubilant:

> The officers, seamen, and soldiers at Landguard Fort are well fitted, and heartily wish if the enemy's purpose is a further fight, that they would do it out of hand, being now far better provided for them, having thrown down the banks between the fort and sea to bring the small shot as well as great to bear upon them.[36]

But their preparations were unnecessary, for the war was almost over. Troops quartered at Harwich dispersed, leaving just four companies of the Admiral's Regiment under Darell, promoted to Major the following April. He remained at Landguard until 1672 when, on the eve of another Anglo-Dutch War, Colonel Wray died 'of a long ague and Feaver contracted at Sheerness'. Darell followed him at that unhealthy station, while Sir Charles Littleton succeeded to the Regiment, which he would command for the rest of its existence.

The Admiral's Regiment plainly fought in fleet actions during the Second Dutch War of 1664–67, but contemporary reports lack even basic details of ships and companies engaged, let alone numbers and casualties. 'This,' grumbled the painstaking Edye, 'is unfortunately the case with so many documents of the period, which are either mutilated by the ravages of time or are deficient in the very essentials which render them so interesting to the modern student.'[37] The Third Dutch War, which began in March 1672, affords the first hard evidence of Marines in action at sea. Three officers of the Admiral's Regiment left accounts of the main engagements, in which their corps suffered heavy casualties, and won its first official recognition as Marines. Three companies, Captains Bennet, Bromley and Vaughan, were at sea on 28 May, when the Dutch fleet surprised an Anglo-French fleet in Sole Bay, destroying the *Royal James* complete with the Earl of Sandwich, commander of the Allied rear squadron. An eyewitness ashore, who 'saw almost every broadside, and was in hearing and whistling of the shot' described his epic stand:

> A whole squadron of the Dutch came down on her like a torrent, having only the *Edgar*, *York*, and *Henry* for his succour, but they so oppressed by numbers as could not help him. So brave Montague (I shall ever honour him), being all in fire and smoke, that nothing but his flag was to be seen from seven till about one, was fired by a pitiful fire-ship, having sunk a great Dutch ship and three fire-ships before, and let the whole squadron taste of his valour.[38]

More fireships nearly put an end to the *Henry*, which fought until 'there was not an officer left on board alive, and half their men killed'. Her Captain, Francis Digby was another of Littleton's company commanders, and the first Marine officer known to fall in action:

> having destroyed two fire-ships, and seeing a third come on, stepping forward to the fire boom to encourage his men to put off the fire-ship, was shot in the breast, and died.[39]

Captain Roger Vaughan was killed in the *Katherine*, 'very much torn and disabled' by the fifteen fireships consumed around her and the *Royal James*. Two more of Littleton's captains fell, Thomas Bromley in the *Royal James* and Thomas Bennet in the *Henry*, whose companies must have been practically annihilated. Four captains and three subalterns were killed, although Bromley's Ensign was saved after 'swimming at least an hower and more was taken up and is well; only his head a little burnt and his mouth hurt'.[40] Flocks of seabirds revealed the scorched body of the Earl of Sandwich, 40 miles from the scene of the action. Littleton knew him by the rings in his pockets, and had the regimental surgeon embalm the corpse in Landguard's chapel. Two companies of the Admiral's Regiment acted as guard of honour, an appropriate gesture after their own losses in the *Royal James*: 'wee fired some volleys of small shot & after 21 great Guns from the Fort. I thought it undecent to part w[th]out some such.'[41]

After Sole Bay, it becomes possible to speak of 'Marines' without anachronism. Captain Silas Taylor, a dockyard official at Harwich, reporting the casualties among the Admiral's Regiment, wrote of: 'Those

marines of whom I soe oft have wrote to you behaved themselves stoutly.'[42]
Edye believed this the earliest use of the term in its modern sense. He felt
soldierly satisfaction 'that the first use of the name was associated with
words of praise and respect for the regiment'; while the term's appearance
in so official a communication justified its subsequent use, considerably
simplifying discussion.[43]

Commanded Detachments

The Dutch spoiling attack at Sole Bay disrupted plans for a descent upon
their coast in 1672. Next year 12,000 English troops went to sea, as part of
a mysterious plan known as 'Zealand – the Design'. The second item in the
programme was for 'The Admiral's Regiment to march to Deal, and there
be taken into the ships now in the Downs.'[44] French support evaporated,
and the scheme fizzled out after unsatisfactory naval battles off Schooneveldt
and the Texel. In future the Admiral's Regiment would serve ashore, and
be known as the Duke's Regiment, their patron having lost the title of Lord
Admiral. Active service consisted of participation in expeditionary forces,
alongside drafts from the Army's other regiments: First Foot Guards,
Coldstream Guards and Holland Regiment. Civil disorder in the colony of
Virginia drew a mixed battalion there in November 1676, including 200 of
the Duke's under Captain Charles Middleton. The expedition was bloodless,
but only seventy men returned next May, those remaining as nucleus of a
colonial defence force only accounting for twenty of the missing.

Another provisional battalion took part in the Rescue of Tangiers in
1680, including 120 of the Duke's under command of Captain James
Fortrey. Service at England's outpost in Morocco was not popular. Troops
of horse attended the embarkation of drafts, 'for preventing any
disturbance or suppressing any mutiny'.[45] A tipsy Ensign declared: 'Hang
Tangiers. . . we resolve to pay no money to pay the whores at Whitehall
and arbitrary government.'[46] Nevertheless, the expedition gave a good
account of themselves. Men from the Duke's may have served in two
formations: Fortrey's company, and a battalion of seamen and marines
landed from the fleet. Admiral Herbert gave the latter sound advice on
tactics to be used against the elusive Moors:

> we are not to run here like furious Lyons, as enraged (bereaved of their Whelps)
> to our own destruction. . . since we have an enemy of great subtlety to deal
> with, let us counterpoise their cunning with conduct, and not be surprised by
> them; let us be guided by true resolution more than furious boldness.[47]

The troops followed Herbert's advice, winning a pitched battle on 26 October. The Moors lost 2,000 men and three guns, two to the King's and one to the naval battalion, and offered terms. Captain Fortrey had the doubtful honour of remaining in Moorish hands as a hostage against conclusion of the definitive peace treaty. As with the Virginia battalion, the rank and file were lost to their regiments, staying at Tangiers with the new King's Regiment.

The least likely of these expeditions is associated with John Churchill, later Duke of Marlborough. He received Vaughan's vacant company after Sole Bay, as a reward for outstanding bravery, although the cynic might think an extra-mural entanglement with Barbara Villiers, Duchess of Cleveland and one of Charles II's mistresses, not unhelpful. Churchill's company was made up to 100 men, 'completely Cloaked with Clothes, Hatts, Shooes, and Stockings', and shipped over to France to serve Louis XIV, under overall command of one of Charles II's natural sons, the Duke of Monmouth. The regiment came to 'push of pike' and took five guns at the Battle of Enzheim (5 October 1674), near Strasburg, the last action to involve British Marines so far inland upon the continent of Europe until 1945. Monmouth's saw further action in the Rhineland, 'though that regiment was in the heat of all that service, not many of it was slain'. Wounded prisoners were repatriated to Harwich, 'so poor that not one in ten has a penny',[48] but Churchill did rather better, rising to Lieutenant Colonel in the Duke of York's in January 1675. He would serve longer in that corps than any other which, with his apprenticeship under the master strategist Turenne in Alsace, formed the professional basis for his subsequently glorious career.

The Duke of York's saw service as a formation only once in its quarter century of existence. In January 1678 the diplomatic merry-go-round brought the English into alliance with the Dutch, against the French. The Stuart army showed its remarkable capacity to meet an emergency, rapidly expanding to three times its peacetime strength. The Coldstream, Duke's and Holland Regiments recruited existing companies to 100 men and raised additional companies, enough for each regiment to form two battalions of 1,000 men. The Duke's received extra small arms in the same proportion as the other infantry regiments: 930 muskets to 464 pikes, the mixture of weapons underlining the loss of their distinct naval function. They were shipped over to Spanish Flanders to garrison Ostend, Bruges and Louvain, Sir Charles Littleton taking command of English troops in the coastal area. Sixty thousand French lay nearby at Ghent, but diplomatically avoided action, which was just as well: 'We are in a mighty mist with our business here,' wrote Sir Charles, 'this place is not to be defended nor worth it.'[49] The main enemies were malaria and boredom, the Duke of Monmouth receiving 'advice every post that the men contrive to fall sick, and that the battalions are already very much diminished'. Absenteeism was rife, prompting orders for Littleton to proceed, 'according to the law martial for a terror to the others, and to cure that infinite scandal the troops at present lie under of deserting in great numbers.'[50] The Duke's came home at the end of the year, returning their tents to store, and officers to their old places, while newly raised companies were paid off. The Regiment had been cheated of action again, except for religious disturbances between the Anglo-Dutch forces and the townspeople they had come to defend. Multiple fatalities included the Flemish tailor responsible for the quarrel, who was hanged.

A Garrison Regiment

The Restoration Army, of which the Duke's Regiment formed part, was a peaceful institution that rarely operated in force. It occupied strategic fortresses such as Portsmouth or Berwick, maintained law and order in a half-hearted manner, and above all ensured the king never had to go on his travels again. Regiments spent most of their time dispersed by companies, acting as a gendarmerie. The distribution of the Admiral's Regiment in spring 1665 was typical:

- Sir William Killigrew's company at Southampton, with detachments at Winchester and Romsey;
- Wray's at Southwark;
- Littleton's at Dover and Canterbury;
- Griffiths' at Rochester and Gravesend, with a detachment across the Thames at Tilbury;
- Legge's at Harwich, less fifty men at Norwich;
- Darell's on the Isle of Wight.

After the Third Dutch War the Duke's remustered as twelve companies of sixty: two at Berwick; two more at Hull; one at Landguard; two at Plymouth; three at Portsmouth; and one at Sheerness; 'besides one company now in France not computed'.[51] This geographical distribution hardly supports the claims of Alexander Gillespie, the first Royal Marine historian, that early Marines 'were always quartered in the vicinity of our principal seaports, where they were regularly trained to the different methods of ship fighting'.[52] How regimental staffs administered such fragmented units, let alone carried out any coherent training, is a mystery.

Garrison duty was not necessarily comfortable. Major Darell took advantage of a royal visit to Harwich in 1668 to represent to the king, 'That his Company. . . doe daily fall sick for want of Bedds, Blanketts, and other accommodation, which he humbly prayed may be forthwith provided.'[53] Transferred to Sheerness, he complained of 'being left naked to defend a place of the greatest importance in England, his company being but 60 and those worn out & sickly by over-watching the last winter & killed by the severity of a harsh spring'.[54] Darell was agitating for an increased establishment, with corresponding chances for self-enrichment, but two companies of sixty (including one at Queenborough) with ten matrosses do not seem excessive protection for the country's main naval dockyard against a recurrence of the embarrassing Dutch raid of 1667. A month before Darell's plea a Dutch frigate had appeared off Sheerness and fired on the fort. Malarial swamps weakened the garrison, and Darell suggested recruiting his company from units elsewhere, 'who can complete their numbers better than we can, because this place is terrible to men'.[55] Darell was himself confined to his chamber for nineteen weeks, 'tortured by the gout', and in 1676 lodged 5 miles from Sheerness, 'curing myself of an ague'.

Sheerness, like Harwich, was in the front line of the Dutch Wars, and both garrisons were kept busy. Captain Anthony Buller at Landguard Fort had orders to arrest two Dutch boats. 'I clapped a guard on both, and now I am bringing their sails and rudders ashore. These things and guards for pressed men and prisoners all fall on my company, which is but sixty.'[56] Officers impounded neutral fishing boats, a good cover for spies, but even in wartime required a search warrant. Faced with boatloads of rotten shellfish, Darell pressed Lord Arlington 'to finish the business of the Dutch ships I seized, for four or five hundred pounds worth of oysters being on board, they will be spoiled'.[57] Direct naval support included assisting maimed vessels after Sole Bay, pursuing shell-shocked seamen who deserted by the boatload, or guarding the ferries the sailors used to escape the Isle of Sheppey.

Restoration England was the product of revolutionary disturbances in the 1640s and 1650s, and society remained dangerously divided. The king and the Duke of York officered their regiments with men of undoubted loyalty, as insurance against another revolt by the gentry. Old Royalists like Killigrew and Wray had been ruined in the Civil Wars and looked to the Crown for wealth and preferment. Sir Charles Littleton, the most conspicuous Colonel of the Admiral's Regiment, first saw service during the siege of Colchester, and held a variety of posts under the Restoration: Governor of Rochester during 1672's invasion scare, Prize Commissioner in 1673, Governor of Sheerness after Darell's death in January 1680, and Deputy Lieutenant of Kent. These men surrounded themselves with their own dependants: Wray's two sons followed him into the Admiral's, while three Littletons appeared among the officers in 1688, as Colonel, Major and Lieutenant.

The military were often the only reliable instrument of government. After the Duke of Monmouth's disgrace in 1683, Lieutenant Philemon Powell complained how the Sergeant of Queenborough:

> having by the Mayor's orders set up the proclamation for apprehending the Duke of Monmouth, etc, tore it down again saying it was a pack of lies. . .
> I am now informed that the Mayor continues him in his place, and that he acted as Sergeant yesterday, so you may judge what the Mayor is.[58]

Fanatical Protestants saw Popish Plots under every bed. Captain Darell spent the tense days before the attack on Landguard providing himself with a certificate that he 'attended Church, kept the fasts, was charitable to the poor, and not at all suspected of popery'.[59] The 1673 Test Act compelled public office-holders, including members of the Army, to take oaths demonstrating their Protestantism. Lieutenant Henry Cornwall's pay was respited for eight months, until he did so. The Duke of York's conversion to Catholicism further poisoned the atmosphere. Matthew Forster of Berwick attempted to suborn men of the Duke's Regiment, 'swearing he would lead them up to the mouth of a cannon', but 'furiously threw away all the drink in the cup' when a private soldier, aptly named Thomas Jolley, pledged the Duke's health. A notorious layabout, Forster was thrown into jail, but Berwick remained a trouble spot for 'the townspeople had undertaken to cut the throats of the soldiers quartered with them', which they could easily do as there were no barracks to lodge the soldiers together.[60] An informer denounced John Edser, a Queensborough house carpenter, for conspiring to lay fire balls privily in Sheerness dockyard: 'so that they should fall about the powder house. . . so that it should blow up and down among the timber there to fire that also'. Meanwhile, a hundred pretended fire-fighters would enter the fort, 'and when the men are all busy to fire every one on his man, and so kill every soul in the fort'. The Secretary of State was sceptical, but requested Littleton to investigate Edser and his landlady the Widow Evans, being 'of the same religion with her neighbours, that is Whig all over'.[61]

Police work and dispersal undermined discipline and training. When Monmouth attempted to overthrow his uncle, King James II, in 1685, 'Sir Charles Littleton's men were in so bad condition that His Majesty did not think proper to let them march towards you so soon as he had designed'.[62] The Guards and veterans of Tangiers crushed the revolt at Sedgemoor before the Duke's arrived. Their only recent fighting had been with Excise men, or among themselves. John Churchill duelled with Henry Herbert, who 'ran Churchill twice through the arme, and Churchill ran him into the thigh, and after Herbert disarmed him'. Lieutenant William Morris quarrelled with Colonel Piper, Deputy Governor of Plymouth, about a horse:

> before Piper cou'd draw his sword Morris ran him through the thigh, and making a second pass at him, putting by with his hand, is soe wounded in ye hand it is thought if he recovers, he will loose ye use of his fingers.

Morris was court-martialled, but resurfaced as Adjutant to the provisional battalion sent to Virginia, where he remained, remote from sources of pleasure and profit.[63] Morris' outrageous behaviour had been inspired by drink, a frequent cause of disciplinary problems. Landguard Fort's garrison ran their own brewery in the 1660s, and sold the surplus to passing ships duty free. The remote location encouraged smuggling – when Excise men seized twenty hogsheads of contraband wine at Bardsey Island, a great number of persons, including the fort's gunner and four of Littleton's men, attacked the guard, bound the constable of Felixstowe neck and heels and carted off the wine.[64]

The Glorious Revolution

On the Duke of York's accession as James II in 1685, the Duke's Regiment became known as the Hereditary Prince of Denmark's Regiment of Foot, beginning a long association between James's son-in-law, Prince George of Denmark, and English Marine regiments. They also changed their yellow uniforms to red, as worn by other Regiments of Foot. The accession of an admitted Catholic, intent on undermining the Restoration settlement, heightened political tensions, which were reflected in the Regiment's history.

The king turned to loyal officers like Littleton to help him. Royal Warrants overthrew existing municipal charters, allowing the king to select civic corporations, and hence Members of Parliament. Sir Charles and two of his family became burgesses for the Worcestershire town of Bewdley.

A warrant increasing military establishments in September 1688 coincided with moves to pack Parliament with royal supporters, including Littleton, his Lieutenant Colonel and Major: 'The King thinks fit you should stand for the borough of Bewdley and desires you will lose no time in doing what shall be necessary for your election.'[65] The king's evident intention to establish absolute rule drove the English political establishment to invite William of Orange, James II's other son-in-law and Stadthouder of the United Provinces, to intervene. Prince George's Regiment formed part of the army collected against the threat, although Littleton was left disconsolate at Sheerness. He comforted himself with the thought that 'Yesterday was so dead a calm, he [i.e. William] could make no way; so is today, and so thick a fog withal he can't stir.'[66] A Protestant east wind, however, had already helped the Dutch fleet down the Channel to land William at Torbay. James' two daughters and many English officers, including John Churchill and Littleton's own son Henry, joined William, but Sir Charles remained loyal to the end:

> I told the king I could not see his majestie without some confusion, that so much of my blood had forfeited his duty in my son's defection, which he was very graciously to return: 'he could not wonder that my son had done so since his own children were so disobedient.'[67]

'Mightily broken', King James fled to France, while his leaderless army surrendered. Prince George's Regiment went into quarters around Huntingdon, until ordered to Holland in February 1689. Embittered at their bloodless defeat, and fearing transfer to the ill-paid Dutch service, Prince George's Grenadier Company refused to go further than Brentford, where a quarter of the Regiment deserted overnight. The official response was unforgiving:

> I am yet in suspense how my regim^t will be disposed, for we are treated so hardly, both in words and deedes, ab^t it, that, tho' we are not broke, I can't hardly think they care to keep us.

John Churchill had received a Dukedom for his treachery, and Littleton appealed to him, 'as being the regim^t, whose officers have stuck best together in ye service of any in the army', but that astute politician did nothing for his old corps, to Littleton's disgust:

> I doe so despize the opinion I hear is had of me, that I did privately contrive the meeting and deserting at Brandford, &c as ye playing such a 2^{ble} game, when I had taken this King's comm^n, that I am quite wearie of serving any

longer and am very willing to resign to those they can be better assured of.[68]

The decision to break the regiment had been taken. Other regiments suffered similar disorders, without being disbanded, fathering the suspicion that the new regime wanted to be rid of a unit particularly associated with the outgoing monarch. Confusing warrants have inspired claims that the Coldstream and Holland Regiments incorporated elements of the old Duke's Regiment, but Edye exploded such wishful thinking in the 1890s. The first English experiment with sea-soldiers came to a definitive end on 28 February 1689, although Sir Charles Littleton continued to receive his subsistence money, in recognition of long and devoted service. He settled at Hagley in the West Midlands, where he died in 1716 aged eighty-seven years, outliving all his royal masters.

His regiment had long been indistinguishable from other marching regiments in armament, organization and function. There was little justification in so small a force as the Restoration Army for a distinct Marine regiment dedicated exclusively to service at sea. When emergency threatened, all regiments contributed drafts, whether for sea service, or expeditions ashore. The Nine Years War that followed the Glorious Revolution saw an escalation in the military effort demanded of the English. The needs of a greatly enlarged Royal Navy and protracted operations overseas impelled statesmen to seek new ways to man the fleet, and enhance its fighting potential. New Marine regiments appeared, with stronger links to the Royal Navy and explicit naval functions.

CHAPTER TWO

False Starts and False Musters

THE scale of warfare changed dramatically at the end of the seventeenth-century. New financial devices like the Bank of England and the National Debt supported professional standing armies and fleets, which fought interminable wars of attrition on a global stage. The War of the Spanish Succession lasted thirteen years, and saw regular deployments of English battle fleets to the Mediterranean and West Indies. The War of Jenkins' Ear (1739–48) brought the first circumnavigation by a Royal Navy task force. Anson's voyage around the world enriched at least one Marine officer, Mordaunt Cracherode, who set off to make his fortune at the unlikely age of sixty, and yet more implausibly lived to collect his prize money. The Royal Navy's tonnage doubled between the 1690s and 1750s, while its manpower trebled. The Stuart system of small home defence forces, capable of rapid expansion in an emergency, was no longer adequate. Fleets that wintered in the Mediterranean could no longer rely on borrowing a few soldiers from a convenient coastal garrison, as they had during the Dutch Wars.

A 'Memorandum in favour of raising two marine regiments' was drafted in 1690, creating the first true Marines. It specified regular alternation of sea, land and dockyard duties, 'thus securing the training of the marine soldier in both the naval and military branches of his work'. Each regiment of 1,500 men had three battalions: 'the first of each regiment to be left on board the fleet or to be disposed into such quarters near the sea as shall appear most convenient for their speedy embarking on board their Majesties' ships of war'. They were expected to be 'equally fitted both for the sea and land, and answer all the purposes as well of the navy as of land forces'. The unknown seventeenth-century civil servant even prefigured the rapid reaction capability of modern amphibious forces: 'always. . . in readiness to be embarked upon any sudden emergency'.[1]

Unfortunately for officers and men concerned it was easier to raise regiments and send them to sea, than to feed, pay and clothe them. Slow and uncertain communications and arcane financial procedures resulted in administrative disaster. Early Marine regiments suffered a vicious cycle of hasty deployment and administrative collapse, followed by scandal and disbandment. Only in the 1750s did the Admiralty, under Anson's sure hand, establish the sound administration that allowed Marines of the later eighteenth century to establish their reputation as a fighting force, rather than simply struggle to stay alive. The operational fragmentation of Marine regiments that frustrated their administration also hampers the Corps historian. Marine forces went through four incarnations between disbandment of the Duke of York's and the formation of three Grand Divisions in 1755 that provided administrative stability for almost two centuries. Their growing establishments reflected the military effort demanded of a nation fighting for a global empire. Two regiments became six, rising to ten in the 1740s.[2]

The passing of the Duke of York's Regiment deprives the reader of a single narrative focus, as future Marine formations were dispersed at sea, with separate administrative and combat organizations. Except for untypical concentrations like the Cartagena expedition of 1741, most Marines were scattered in penny packets around the fleet. It is impossible to reconstruct their fragmented and ill-recorded service without first understanding its administrative foundations.

Hark Now The Drums Beat Up Again

The formation of Marine regiments was always a panic measure, taken after the outbreak of hostilities. The 1690 Memorandum appeared eight months after English naval forces clashed with a French squadron in Bantry Bay. Queen Anne's Marine officers were commissioned twelve months after French troops had occupied the barrier fortresses in the Netherlands, precipitating the War of the Spanish Succession. George II announced his Marine regiments three months after Admiral Vernon had set off to attack Spanish possessions in South America without any trained infantry at all:

> I could wish indeed we had each of us a company of Foot of regular
> troops sent on board each ship we would have strengthened us in numbers
> as well as had their expertness in handling their arms to have excited our

raw men to an imitation of them. If we should come into a general war with France as well as Spain I believe your grace [the Duke of Newcastle] will have clearly perceived from the difficulty of manning these ships, as they are, the necessity there may be for having most of the marching regiments converted into Marines.[3]

Vernon was too inclined to subordinating the Army to the Royal Navy, but his letter puts the reasons behind the formation of Marine regiments in a nutshell: their skill at arms and the Royal Navy's chronic manpower shortage. Market forces limited the number of prime seamen trained from boyhood in the merchant navy. Skilled top-men could not be improvized overnight, while lower-deck conditions of service deterred volunteers, who could earn more as privateers. One of the many jobs of Major Darell's company at Sheerness in the 1670s had been to flush out Kentish seamen avoiding the press. The situation was worse in the 1740s, when the Government failed to initiate an early press. Cabinet strategists earmarked the six Marine regiments mustered in October 1739 for expeditionary purposes, but soon had to raise an extra Lieutenant and thirty men per company, 'to serve on board the fleet', besides four more regiments at the end of the year. So scarce were seamen that even fishermen faced losing their exemption from the press.

There were always unskilled hands ready to enlist as Marines. In 1739 Walpole hoped to recruit men:

> rejected or turned out of our men-of-war because they were found not to be expert seamen, nor in any way fit for their business. These men will immediately list as Marines, though they could not be accepted of as good seamen.[4]

In 1702 the Admiralty planned to make up half its predicted shortfall of 10,000 men with Marines, equivalent to the crews of nine second-rate ships of the line. Most work aboard ship required muscle, not seamanship; captains immobilized for lack of men were glad for any sort of labour:

> I assure you, Sir, I have not a man on board that is a seaman; soe I hope my Lord High Admiral will be pleased to order me 15 Marenes and 10 seamen which I can make shift with till I meet with some homeward bound ships.[5]

Commodore Charles Cornwall spent the winter of 1709–10 badgering the Admiralty for more men: 'The several ships of the squadron under my command are in so great a want of men, that I must take leave again to remind their Lordships of sending the Marines.'[6]

Recruitment of Marines, as of soldiers generally, was the responsibility of regimental officers, on receipt of a Royal Warrant: 'that by beat of drum or otherwise volunteers are to be raised for recruiting and completing his marine regiment according to the establishment'.[7] Wartime Parliaments permitted conscription, instructing JPs and Land Tax collectors to:

> make a speedy and effectual levy of such able bodied men as are not younger than 17, nor more than 45, nor papists, nor less than 5 foot 4 inches high, and having no vote for parliament men, and, who do not exercise any lawfull calling or employment.[8]

Not everyone was happy to infringe the rights of freeborn Englishmen. A party from Bor's Regimental Headquarters at Southampton was assaulted 'in a riotous and rebellious manner', while bringing in one Joseph Cooper, 'who was taken up and listed by three Justices of the Peace. . . according to the late Act of Parliament as an idle and disorderly fellow'.[9] Some JPs were less helpful, remanding insolvent debtors who preferred jail to falling into the hands of Marine recruiting officers.

Outside short periods of limited compulsion, recruiting officers depended on volunteers, driven by hunger, or lured by bounties. The bounty paid to recruits during the War of the Spanish Succession doubled from forty shillings to four pounds, several months wages for an agricultural labourer. John Howe enlisted in 1778 for six guineas, to escape an irksome apprenticeship. He was a healthy sixteen year old, but many recruits were less desirable. A newspaper described a deserter from the Duke of York's in 1688 as 'a squat, bow-legged squinting fellow and almost blind of one eye, aged about 30'. An advertisement in 1709 reads like a casting list for the pirates in *Treasure Island*:

> John Grindle, a lusty black man, having a bushy Head of Hair, very much pitted with the small pox, somewhat round shouldered, Richard Hill a lusty man of a fair complexion, having lank hair, he goes creeping with his Feet. Jacob Ferry a well set man of fair complexion having a bushy head of hair, his face full of Pock holes, and John Arthur, a fair man, having a great cut on the back of one of his hands and another in his Face.[10]

Squints and pock marks were common enough afflictions, but the 1745 desertion of an alehouse keeper: 'of indifferent appearance. . . but one eye and. . . past middle age' suggests a recruiting process in real trouble.[11] Recruiting officers faced a choice between recruiting full-grown but decrepit adults, or healthy but undersized teenagers. Some Kentish recruits posed a problem for an officer of Cottrell's Marines:

> six of them are very pretty boys for the appellation of men they will not be intituled to some years. The tallest of the six is 5 foot $4^1/_2$ & the shortest 5 foot $3^1/_2$. They are very strait & well limbed but Colonel Wolfe's return has almost frightened me & really I am in a dilemma about them. . . I would not have such a flock under me as to fear the approach of the Wolfe nor would I refuse such men as our neighbours might jump at. Men are very scarce & we are behindhand.[12]

Later in the century, the physical standard of Marines still fell below conventional infantry. Major John Pitcairn was mortified in 1775 to find his Marines shorter than men of marching regiments at Boston, Massachusetts, and asked the Admiralty to impose a minimum height requirement of 5 feet 6 inches.

Recruits went to sea with a promptitude reflecting the urgency of their raising, or perhaps the chances of desertion. Torrington's Marines went aboard HMS *Victory* within two months of the officers receiving their commissions in January 1690. Throughout the 1690s Marines seem to have been continuously at sea, going aboard port guard ships until required by some sea-going vessel. Marine regiments mustered on the Isle of Wight in 1739, convenient for embarkation, but less so for desertion. Sea officers were not always sure what to make of Marines. The Captain of HMS *St Andrew* in 1690 queried whether his detachment counted as part of his complement, or as supernumeraries. The Admiralty settled on the former, compelling him to replace scarce seamen with less skilled Marines. In 1713 the Admiralty directed HMS *Dove*'s Captain 'to discharge men so as to make room for the Marines'.[13] Some officers resisted. HMS *Rochester*'s Captain objected to thirty-one Marines appearing on his complement of 240: 'I entreat you will be pleased to move that I may have orders to leave the said marines who can better be spared than so many mariners when the company is so small.'[14] The Admiralty continued to insist on effective use of manpower, reminding Admiral Keppel in 1778 of 'the rules of the service, that every ship should have the full establishment of marines, and should discharge seamen if she has a greater proportion of that class'.[15]

The Restoration Army had embarked relatively small detachments. A list of soldiers 'appointed to ye shipps now goeing out' in 1668 showed 337 among twenty-eight ships, barely enough for the Captain's personal guard.[16] A squadron at Jamaica forty years later averaged fifty-eight

soldiers per ship, excluding fireships and bombs, which carried none.[17]
By the 1740s ships' detachments had stabilized at roughly one Marine
per gun carried, with officers in proportion.[18] They contributed
significantly to naval complements: 62 out of 402 in HMS *Bedford* (1703),
80 out of 510 in HMS *Lancaster* (1709), or 47 and one washerwoman
out of 257 in HMS *Jamaica* (1710). *Port Glasgow's* Captain even
complained at losing 24 Marines out of his complement of 113: 'And
now my soldiers being ordered from me I hope you will take care that
there be more men allowed.'[19] Setting sail without his full force of Marines,
Admiral Sir Hovenden Walker wrote: 'there is no taking any Marines
from any ship without disabling her in action should she meet the enemy.'[20]
Marines had become an indispensable element of naval manpower.

A Devilish Expensive Service

Colonels and captains of Marines, like military officers, ran their
regiments and companies on a commercial basis. Sir Harry Goring paid
£6,450 for Joshua Churchill's Marines, and complained bitterly when
regimental renumbering threatened both prestige and business prospects.
Officers recruited, clothed, paid, and in emergencies fed their men on
credit, hoping to recoup their outlay from the Treasury, or from the
men themselves. Nobody seems to have considered what effect prolonged
periods at sea might have upon Marine administration, or upon the
men and their equipment. The physical limitations of sailing ships and
the attempt to apply pseudo-commercial principles of military
administration, proved disastrous to the individual Marine's health, his
officer's pocket, and their regiment's efficiency and well being.

The Lord Admiral's was paid in the same way as other regiments of the
Restoration Army, except the money was channelled through the Treasurer
of the Navy. Private sentinels were due eight pence a day, a barely adequate
income equivalent to the lowest agricultural wage. In theory, soldiers received
three-quarters of their wages as 'subsistence', to pay for food and lodgings,
and two pence a day was withheld as 'off reckonings', to pay for their
clothes. Any balance remaining was paid after the officers had cleared their
accounts with the Treasurer, and received the arrears of their own pay in
excess of subsistence, plus any off-reckonings spent on the soldiers' behalf.
In practice officers simply assumed men had received clothing due to them,
whether they had or not, and kept no records of stoppages.

The Treasury controlled the number of men paid through officials
known as Commissaries. Every two months they mustered regiments to

check men and equipment against the company rolls, in the presence of
the Captain and an impartial observer, such as a JP. The system was
open to numerous abuses, such as hiring 'faggots' to stand in for
imaginary soldiers whose pay went into the Captain's pocket. Collusion
between muster-master and regimental officers was common, despite
regulations: 'No Fee, Reward, or Gratuity to be taken for allowing a
false muster upon Penalty of Loss of Employment, and as he will answer
it at his utmost Perill'.[21] Officers' pay suffered disproportionately if
companies were under strength, which drove them to circumvent such
instructions. A Captain of Marines, unable to reconcile private and public
duty, wrote to his Colonel in 1743:

> I would be glad to know whether I am *absolutely* obliged to tell they are
> all Deserted who are so, or to call them absent on Furlow or Recruiting. I
> should be extreamly glad to know your orders for unless he [i.e. the
> Commissary] can do us a favour by allowing us to have more men on
> shoar than we can produce I believe he is not to expect a farthing.

The Colonel's response confirms the routine nature of corruption: 'I know
no way of making a tolerable muster,' he wrote in the margin, 'but to
muster all such men as we have raised. . . and unless he does not give
some *douceur* he can't be entitled to any gratuity.'[22]

Memories of the Civil Wars, when unpaid soldiers overthrew Parliament
and imposed military rule, ensured subsistence was paid promptly. The
Duke of York's Regiment seems to have received its subsistence regularly
every two lunar months, 'according to the muster rolls delivered'. Clearings
were more protracted. Sir Charles Littleton complained in 1680 that his
regiment received subsistence only, forcing officers to clothe their men
from their own pockets, or to stop the off-reckonings from the soldiers'
6d a day. However, the men could not be left entirely destitute, 'for if
they touch no money few but the very scum of England will enter that
regiment.'[23]

Sea service piled confusion on delay, for ship's detachments never tallied
with shore-based administrative units. Captain Darell's company, one of
the earliest documented examples, was 'divided into three parts, and sent
aboard the *Success*, *Drake*, and a galliot hoy'.[24] Officers were alive to the
problems of sending detachments to sea. Lt Gardiner wrote to Samuel
Pepys on the embarkation of his men, requesting 'an account of what
ships they go aboard, that I may be the better able to satisfy the
Commissary on Muster Day'.[25] In 1706 a naval officer suggested exchanging his Marines for those in another ship: 'This I presume may be

the same to her, and of service to the men in having one intire company aboard.'[26] The exigencies of the service ensured that fragmentation was the normal state of affairs. Regulations set minimum detachments: fifteen in 1702, or twenty-four in 1740, but had to allow exceptions 'in Cases of Necessity'. Of ninety-two Marines at Jamaica in 1710 no more than twelve came from any one company, one ship's detachment drawing on thirteen companies.

Keen officials interpreted the Mutiny Acts as requiring that regimental musters precede payment. The Marines' scattered deployment at sea, however, made it impossible to muster them at all, as the Admiralty recognized in 1707:

> The Marines being dispersed by separate Companies and Detachments into most parts of the World whereby the return of the Muster Rolls is necessarily rendered very Tedious and Delatory.[27]

Regiments went unpaid for years. Marine officers commissioned in January 1690 received no personal pay until March 1691, while their men starved. The Lieutenant Governor of Portsmouth advanced £1,000 from garrison funds, 'to save the soldiers of the Marine Regim[ts] from perishing'. The Admiralty admitted the Marines 'were in a starving condition and must have perished if they had not been supplied as aforesaid',[28] but would pay nothing except on petition. It seems the only reason the entire Corps did not starve to death was that at sea the men were paid and fed as seamen.

The Admiralty had authority 'to receive all the money for the pay of the said Regm[ts] and the contingent charges thereunto belonging',[29] but spent the budget elsewhere. Some £10,000 was still owed for the Marines' first clothing, when the officers' 'unparallel'd hardships' drove them to petition Queen Mary in March 1693 'for the payment of their arrears before they go on ship board. . . being already reduct'd to the last extremity, they are without the aforesaid payment totally incapacitated to performe that service.'[30] In 1696 the government was bankrupt, with debts of £2,911,340 against projected revenue of £3,000,000. As the eighteenth century began, the subalterns of the 2nd Marines faced ruin, their creditors, 'out of patience from the delayes and uncertaineties of the payments dayly threatening them wth imprisonment which will be impossible to avoid without yo[r] Lo[ps] Commiseration of this their deploreable case'. Threats of jail were not idle. A Lieutenant's wife petitioned for £100 back pay to release him from imprisonment, for debts contracted in the Service.[31] Officers were men of credit, accustomed to living on their debts, but they needed every last shred of their creditors' goodwill.

Rank and file resentment reached such a pitch in 1695 that the Navy Board reported, 'y^t said soldiers are so very Mutinous, that they fear they will soon pull down their Office, if some speedy care be not taken to satisfy them.'[32] Marines became the most persistent mutineers in an Army plagued by strike action against unendurable neglect of the common soldier. Disbanded Marines again threatened to pull down the Navy Board Office in 1699, driven by the 'Miserable Condition', described in a petition from Captain Plunkett's company as 'sum in prison sum a begging and sum that has wives and children and has not a penny to buy them bread'. Petitions to the House of Commons alleged Regimental Agents deliberately defrauded Marines by means of:

> Receipts in full of all Accounts, which they must sign, or receive nothing; and many through necessity, and others being illiterate, and not knowing what they did, signed the same, by reason of which the said Agent says, there is nothing due to the Petitioners.[33]

Protests continued in the following reign. Unpaid Marines refused to leave quarters during the 1708 invasion scare, as would a detachment of Villiers' Regiment a year later:

> They marched to the End of the Town, and then wheel'd about, Clubb'd Musquetts, and swore they would not move one step further, till they had their pay to a farthing: And also swore they would be the death of any that should oppose them. [34]

Changing quarters was a notorious flashpoint, with landlords anxious to collect debts. Embarkation was another boundary not to be crossed without eliminating some arrears of pay. Churchill's Marines mutinied at Exeter in 1710: 'upon marching a Detachment. . . for Plymouth to embark on board the Fleet, in which the townspeople have been very active and give great encouragement'.[35] Ten of Wolfe's Marines refused to go on board ship in 1742, Captain Shafto, the regimental paymaster, not having settled their accounts. All parties suffered courts martial: the men for disobedience, and the Captain for bringing 'Reflections upon Colonel Wolfe's Character, and. . . Injury to the Regiment'.[36] Embarkation pay was especially important as the Navy did not introduce dependants' allowances until the 1790s. Families of other ranks sent overseas faced starvation. Jane Dyer, 'under sentence of death for a bare felony', petitioned for her life in 1705, being the only support of two children, their father Cornelius Dyer 'serving at Gibraltar in one of the Marine Regiments commanded by the Honourable Colonel Borr'.[37]

Those responsible for Queen Anne's Marines appreciated the dangers posed by the confusion of the 1690s. Prince George of Denmark, the Queen's husband and Lord Admiral, noted in May 1702: 'several inconveniences having happened in manning the Fleet by those Regiments not being compleat and under the same command as the men employed there'.[38] A Paymaster of Marines was appointed to ensure prompt payment, and a year later the Queen directed 'that the six marine Regiments designed only for service at sea be henceforth under the sole control of the Lord High Admiral.'[39] Queen Anne's consort has a poor historical reputation, but under his control the worst abuses were held in check, until the financial pressures of a European war overwhelmed the Treasury. A vellum-bound notebook, 'Found with Colonel Edye's papers March 1923', but evidently compiled much earlier, summarizes the measures taken: 'Short Allowance Money' for Marines placed on reduced rations at sea; orders for the Sick and Hurt Board to subsist convalescent Marines, and certify the disabled; public funding for 'buying Arms to supply those broke or lost on Shipboard, and in the Expeditions on Shore'; suspension of Marine officers 'that shall neglect their duty or go on shore under pretence of leave'. The most fundamental reform, however, were bi-monthly returns of ships' detachments to the Commissary General, signed by the Captain, Marine Officer or Sergeant, and Purser. Combined with relaxation of the mustering regime ashore, this at last gave Marine companies some hope of being paid.[40]

The realities of eighteenth-century service life undermined such good intentions. Many officials were unfit for their posts. The Muster Master at Portsmouth in 1703 was 'a poor superannuated man. . . rolled about in a wheelbarrow, fitter much to be amongst the invalids than to be a commissary'.[41] Vital records were lost. HMS *Chichester*'s returns for February–July 1707 went down with Admiral Sir Cloudesley Shovell off the Scilly Isles.[42] The Marines who took Gibraltar were never mustered 'by reason of disputes arising between the commanding officers at Gibraltar and other accidents', and were paid by Royal Warrant five years after the Rock fell into British hands.[43] Prince George sought to treat all parties fairly, proposing Commissaries muster Marines as they came ashore, and pay two-thirds of the accrued wages, 'the other third remaining to satisfy the necessary Deduction of Chest at Chatham and reimburse the Officer what he has been out of pocket on his men's Account.'[44] Apart from common humanity, prompt clearing rendered men fit for sea duty again, whereas turning them over unpaid to another ship 'has occasioned several Mutinies and will be the cause of more'.[45] Administrative and operational efficiency went together.

Prince George died in 1708, and, although Marine accounts were cleared to the end of that year, scarcity of money kept them in arrears throughout the last years of the war. Colonel Bor represented the 'state of his Regiment in their quarters and the present necessities they are under for want of subsistence', but the Treasury response suggests this was business as usual: 'Is there anything particular in the circumstance and hardship this Regiment is alleged to lie under different from the rest?'[46] In lieu of cash public creditors received 'tallies' redeemable against future taxation, such as the 'orders on the Continued Impositions' used to clear Holt's and Wills' accounts in 1708.

Such expedients are not surprising, when the country had still not paid for the previous war. Throughout Queen Anne's reign old Marine lieutenants, or their widows, petitioned for arrears of pay 'by which most of them are in a miserable condition and are not able to appear abroad'.[47] Twelve years after Shovell's Marines disbanded, the Treasury finally authorized payment of two lieutenants whom the Navy had incorrectly certified as dead. Captain James Plunkett of Carmarthen's Marines was still owed £153 13s 4d in 1709, more than a year's pay. His petition demonstrates the commercial and other risks faced by Marine officers:

> he was two years in the Streights [of Gibraltar] where he was extremely troubled with the flux; was eighteen months in the West Indies with Admiral Nevil and was there seized by the plague and in his absence the Lieutenant who had management of the petitioner's company received levy money for recruits and made away with the same, ran himself much in debt and went off, so that at his [the petitioner's] return he was obliged to raise the company anew at his own charge and being oppressed with debts and sickness he was obliged to part with his company to discharge his impatient creditors and has been for eight years under the hands of physicians.

The Treasury reacted with unusual speed, instructing the Navy Treasurer to pay half Plunkett's claim, 'out of the remains in Exchequer from the rent of Hackney Coaches. . . until a regimental state be drawn up'.[48] They had become suspicious of Samuel Whitfield, the Marines' Paymaster, who was lining his pockets with some incomprehensible scheme called Quarter Respites. On his death Whitfield owed £6,798 0s $1^{1}/_{2}$d, deposited safely with a scrivener, secure from its proper owners, the officers of Marines, their widows and orphans.[49]

Two Steps Forward and One Back

Marine regiments in the 1740s were placed under the Army, despite an earlier Navy Board's opinion, 'that there appears no hopes of reconciling the Methods of the Land Service to those of the Navy.'[50] *Rules and Instructions for the Government of the Marine Forces* duly appeared, as they had done regularly throughout the 1690s, but standards of administration fell below those of Queen Anne's reign. Officers of detachments at sea, 'omitted to send Lists of the Men under their Command, as they ought to have done', while the Deputy Commissary General of Marines doubted his authority to see lists returned by Ships' officers, but never bothered to ask. Ships' books, which might have clarified matters, failed to identify regiments and companies, or to distinguish between NCOs and private Marines, who appeared, 'promiscuously with the seamen'.[51] Ships' captains prevented Marine officers checking their men were entered correctly, and transferred individuals between ships 'without leave of the Commanding Officer of the Marines, and without taking any Officer at all with them, in which case it is impossible there should be any Returns, the men sometimes not being heard of for a twelve month together.' One Marine, serving in the Mediterranean, 'was removed to another Ship, and no Return made of him for six Months; whereupon he was supposed dead, till by Accident he was found in a return from Southampton.'[52] Survivors of a twenty-month cruise in the Mediterranean were turned over after three weeks at Portsmouth, 'without any Pay or Cloaths; at which the Men were much dissatisfied.' Some of them spoke to their Lieutenant, 'who thereupon represented the Hardship of the Case to Admiral *Stuart*, by whose Order they were turned over; but that all the Answer he made, was, that he wanted Marines, and must take the first he could get.'[53]

This type of irregularity and a series of military and naval disasters provoked a Parliamentary enquiry in 1746. A mass of corruption emerged – regiments had not cleared their accounts since Christmas 1740. Officers, 'in a very bad way through the want of their clearings', were reduced to selling them at 50 per cent discount, although no one could imagine who might buy them. Marines who had been at sea for up to twenty-nine months went unclothed, unless they got slops on credit from the Purser, sergeants 'taking advantage of the Necessities of the Men', to cheat them of their pay. Agents with thousands in the bank refused to satisfy officers' bills until taken to court, amply sustaining their reputation as 'the biggest rascals living off soldier men in an age of very keen competition'[54]. Wolfe's agent Thomas Paterson made repeated difficulties over Captain Shafto's accounts after his court martial, despite holding £3,000 against moneys Shafto had spent as Paymaster to Wolfe's Marines:

> Mr Paterson objected to the Certificate, because the amount was in Figures, and not in Words at length, whereupon the Account was re-examined again, and approved, without any Variation; and then another Objection was raised, because the Certificate was not upon the back of the original Order, the Officers [with good reason] having some doubt about sending the Original.[55]

The evidence for Jeffreys' Marines is particularly extensive as Colonel and agent fell out during the inquiry, and blackened one another's faces in public. Jeffreys was broken for false musters, but they were not his only fault: he employed a servant as Quartermaster, and kept the pay himself, as he did for other vacancies, 'there being a great clamour made about it by the officers'; he demanded one man's pay from each company, placing his captains 'under a necessity of paying so much money, or of disobliging the Colonel'; he also refused to sign a prepared receipt for Quartermaster's expenses, throwing it into the fire, 'saying his own Receipt was sufficient', which was clearly not the case with so slippery a customer. Jeffreys' shameless defence of a colonel's right to cheat Government and Marine alike reveals the profits open to the military entrepreneur: advanced £4,500 for supplying clothes costing £1,900, he claimed another £365, alleging:

> it had always been the Custom upon raising of new Regiments, to Allow twenty months Off-reckonings for the Cloathing; and that the Application was founded upon that Custom. . . not upon any Estimate of the [actual] Charge of Cloathing.[56]

Such swindles were not confined to Marines, but the *Gentleman's Magazine* thought their officers suffered greater temptation, 'As the Marine regiments are larger than in the Foot, and their cloathes worse, it appeared that the Colonels gain more cheating them.'

Reclothing Marine detachments was difficult enough without malpractice. They were meant to receive new clothing every year, on 11 June, but were prone to, 'being out on a Cruise when it arrived'. Their location could not be predicted precisely enough to ensure supplies got through, although Marines' sea pay was regularly stopped 2d a day towards new clothes, just as they paid 4d a month towards a Chaplain, who never served at sea. Admiral Russell reported from the Mediterranean in 1695 'that the Marine Soldiers of the 1st Marine Regiment are in a manner naked for want of Cloaths.' Captain Spicer's company had received one suit of clothes in six years service, for which 'all their money is stopt', implying they paid £18 5s 0d each for some £2 worth of clothing, long reduced to rags.[57] Captain Butler of HMS *Devonshire* forwarded a petition signed by eighteen of his Marines in November 1706, 'setting forth their case which I think is very lamentable, and they are made incapable of doing their duty for want of being lookt after'. They had been at sea for four years, including service at Gibraltar, but: 'Since the raising of the Regiment and our listing [in 1702] wee have recd but one whole mounting of clothes, being now almost naked for want'. The official response shows the difficulties posed by uncertain ship movements. Prince George had sent an officer to Gibraltar with 350 suits of clothing,

> but before it could reach thither those men were sailed from that garrison, and the clothes left there ever since till about a month ago when the Town Mayor of that garrison brought what was left to England.

They finally received a second clothing on their return to England: 'Viz[t] – Coat, Shoose, Hose, 2 Shirts, 2 Cravats, and little Capps', with a further issue of shoes, hose, and shirts 'at their Embarqueason' in HMS *Dorsetshire* in February 1706.[58] Regimental agents added unnecessary uncertainty to the supply of ships in home ports. Colonel Lowther's agent ignored repeated requests from HMS *Norwich*'s Lieutenant of Marines for clothing against an intended voyage, compelling her Captain to ask the Admiralty for directions, and incidentally explaining the delays suffered by major expeditions.[59]

If a ship received a consignment of clothes, it might never be properly issued. A Court Martial into clothing gone astray in 1745 found witnesses knew nothing of any clothes, but had 'often heard it said that Sergeant Russell had clandestantly [*sic*] sold and made away with some of the said slops, which were in his custody.' The Court, under the presidency of the officer financially liable for the missing stores, reached the comforting conclusion that the now deceased Sergeant was to blame, and in any case, the detachments 'must have been supplied with their equal proportion of said Slops', and should therefore pay for them. Eighteenth-century courts martial were notoriously haphazard, but these proceedings strained even the Colonel's tolerance, his counter-signature below the record of proceedings bearing the note: 'I am of opinion that I ought not to have signed the above.'[60] Not all officers were so feeble. Numerous sea officers passed on petitions from their Marines, representing their miserable condition. The Captain of HMS *Augusta* even sent the Admiralty a sample of the shoddy clothes issued in the 1740s, when men like Jeffreys enhanced their profits by using cloth 3d a yard cheaper than that issued to the land forces, despite the wear and tear of sea service.[61]

Inadequate clothing was a serious problem. The Admiralty attributed the high wastage rate of Marines to:

> their being ill supplied with necessaries from the Agents of their Regts when the ships they serve in are ordered out on Foreign Voyages, and the Pursers will not supply their wants out of the slops as they do seamen, because there is no security for their repayment.[62]

The Surgeon of Duncombe's Marines reckoned he never had less than 200 sick a year, but Marine surgeons received no government allowance for medicines, 'as there is in marching Regiments, though the Number of Sick in the former is much greater.[63] 'I have 24 Marines of Colonel Borr's Regiment,' wrote the Captain of HMS *Tilbury*, 'and those of them that are not lame have the scurvy.'[64] Colonel Wolfe's agent reckoned on 150 new recruits every year to keep the unit up to strength, but loss rates at sea could be far higher. Captain Sir Thomas Hardy took forty-five of Churchill's Marines to sea on 25 May 1706, but a year later the detachment was down to eight.[65] The Captain of HMS *Antelope* lost half his Marines between the Nore and Plymouth, and placed little dependence on the survivors:

> of the forty marines that were put aboard me at the Nore, what by death, putt ashore sick, and unfitt for service, I have but 22 left. There were pickt out, as I'm told by the Lieutenant out of 11 of the 12 companies of the Reg^t of Wills, and not three of y^m y^t had ever clapt a musquette on his shoulder before he came on board my ship, but all raw recruits, and the very scum of the party y^t were in quarters at Canterbury. There are so many wanting now & I believe this cruize will end the days of half the remainder.[66]

Service in the West Indies was catastrophic. The Cartagena and Santiago campaigns of 1741–42 reduced companies from seventy to thirty men. Survivors were amalgamated, and surplus cadres sent home to recruit. Captain John Murray of Cochrane's Marines brought twenty-two men home out of his original seventy, 'some being sent back as incurable (of whom four or five. . . got home) and the rest either dead or having deserted.'[67] Colonel Cottrell might be forgiven an ill-tempered outburst on hearing from HMS *Chichester*'s perennially unlucky detachment:

they have dammed ill luck to lose so many men in so short a time, and where to get more by God I don't know, for what with the ill will of the Generaliztie. . . and the Idleness and Corruption of the Constables we shall never be completed. . . it frets me to the soul that I lose men faster than I can gett them, but the Marine Service is a Devilish expensive one for men.

Under such pressure Marine officers were not particular where they got recruits. In the 1690s they were accused of taking men pressed for the Navy, and pocketing the 40s levy money. Enemy deserters had the advantage of being trained already, like the Frenchmen who 'came over to the English at Barcelona where they were well entertained under Coll Parks of the Royal Regiment of Marines', and then shipped aboard HMS *Boyne*, 'as Marines in Major General Holt's Regiment'.[68] Cottrell knew but one way of completing his establishment: 'if his Majestie would approve it, and that is to send to Ireland and list Irish Protestants, I'd engage to raise 500 as good men as ever went to sea.'[69] Some officers defied the Test Acts, and recruited Catholics, with unhappy consequences at Genoa in 1698:

Last week giveing leave to some of the Marine Soldiers to goe ashore. . . two Irish men the one a protestant and the other a papist quarrelled about their Religion in so much that the papist challenged the other to fight him which he did & the protestant Run the other into the brest of which he imediatlye dyd.[70]

Demand for men in the 1740s drove down recruit quality, and inspired a flood of naval invective: 'very indifferent weak poor creatures, some being boys and the others decayed old men unfit to serve their country'; 'lads not seventeen years of age and not one of them that I should have entered for the ship'; 'so infected with the Itch that it would be madness to send them aboard'; 'the dregs and refuse of the Reg^ts, and I think of all mankind . . . amongst them all the distempers incident to human nature . . . of little service to us, but . . . a pest and a nuisance'. Admiral Cavendish feared their effect upon the fragile health of the fleet: 'We shall be undone with these new marines, being devoured with the Itch, Pox, and other distempers.' The Captain of HMS *Dolphin* (20) substantiated the generalization: 'Yesterday I sent ashore to the Hospital here thirteen Marines. . . of which 8 had the Itch, a distemper of bad consequence in a Ship, 4 of them the venereal disease to a great degree, and one so old he could not eat biscuit.'[71] Cavendish accused Marine officers of picking their worst men for embarkation, but they had no others to send. War

Office returns for April 1742 show 350 Private Marines ashore in quarters, of whom only seventy-seven were fit for service.[72]

Far from relieving the Navy's manning crisis in the early 1740s, the Marine regiments threatened its operational viability, and jeopardized national security. Captains sailed short-handed rather than compromise their seamen's health by embarking Marines known to be 'Bursten, Lame, Sick or Disabled or such as are infected with the Itch or Leprosy'. 'When we reflect,' wrote their Lordships:

> on the sickness which has prevailed to an unusual height in the Fleet for some time past, whereby many ships have been reduced to lie useless in port, to the great obstruction and disappointment of His Ma[ties] service, we can impute it to nothing so much as to the rawness and ill health of body of many of the Marine Soldiers.[73]

The Admiralty asked Marine colonels to send healthy men aboard, and supply weekly returns of the numbers available in quarters, but had no power to intervene directly. They could 'only represent these things humbly for His Majesty's information', until in February 1746 a Royal Warrant 'put under the immediate and entire Command of this Board, all His Majesty's Marine Regiments'.[74] It empowered the Admiralty to draft regulations for their administration at sea and ashore, but these appeared too late to save the Marines. At the end of 1748 the ten regiments went the same way as their predecessors, into the hands of Commissioners appointed for their Disbandment.

Disbandment

Disbandment was the common fate of junior wartime regiments. Only the most senior formations were secure against the clamour for retrenchment that followed every eighteenth-century war. Marine formations became political footballs, as king and Parliament pursued the old Civil Wars by other means. Queen Mary's death left William III isolated, and at odds with a Parliament dominated by his Tory enemies. The Treaty of Ryswick in 1697 encouraged them to impose defence cuts regardless of the provisional nature of the peace with France. William attempted to preserve seasoned cadres of officers by amalgamating under-strength units. The two Marine regiments merged in July 1698, forty-three of their officers going onto half pay. Rank and file were discharged, or used to fill up three Regiments of Foot, which joined the Marine establishment in August, to reach the 3,000 men laid down in 1690. This sleight of hand provoked the king's opponents in the Commons, who had already attacked the Marine regiments as 'an indirect establishment of a greater force than they intended'. Several officers sitting in the Commons defended them, arguing, 'we had found great disadvantages at sea for want of men bred to the use of firearms', but in December the Tory majority slashed William's military headcount to 10,000, including Marines. Such straitened force levels had not been seen since Charles II's reign, and bore no relation to the circumstances of the late 1690s.

An anonymous pamphlet, 'Concerning the Four Regiments Commonly Called Mariners', betrays the Tories' obsession with domestic politics. The Marines were 'a useless charge to the People, a Nuisance to the Navy, and dangerous to the kingdom's liberties'. They were not required ashore, where 7,000 men sufficed for the guards and garrisons, nor at sea, 'where they receive as much Pay, eat as much Meat, lie in as many Hammocks. . . as if they were better seamen.' The latter resented being 'clogged and hindered by any conjunction with landsmen'. Marine officers 'introduced pernicious Notions . . . such as Misratings, False Musters, and other Abuses, which the Sea Officers were formerly ignorant of', a sweetly naïve view of seventeenth-century naval administration. The pamphleteer revealed his true agenda by associating Marines with the political scarecrow of the Standing Army: 'a dangerous and dreadful Force . . . sufficient to have enslaved the Nation'. As for amphibious warfare:

> we have no need nor any occasion to make Insults upon our Enemies' Coasts; and must we be at a great Charge and Hazard to keep them up until the Lord knows when, to be sent the Lord knows where, to do the Lord knows what?[75]

Five years before the capture of Gibraltar, the operational case for amphibious forces could not have been put more succinctly.

A reply to the anonymous correspondent exposed, 'the scurrility, inconsistency, and falsity so conspicuous in every page of his book'.[76] The author, probably an old Marine officer, had little difficulty demonstrating the value of Marine detachments, at three-quarters the cost of seamen's wages:

> And for being equally useful at least, I have often heard it said by the Flag Officers, as well as private Captains, they had rather have one fourth of the men Marines, than be wholly manned with Seamen, for that they always found them more obedient to command in time of Action, whether quartered at the Great Guns or Small Shot, or put centrys over the Scuttles; whereas

the seamen at such times are not so Governable, being accustomed to greater Liberties and Disorders, from their frequent discharges and vareity of service, when the Marines are kept to a constant and severe discipline.

Marines had been instrumental in preventing mutinies at sea, for which reason, 'their arms are always lodged in the aftermost part of the ship', perhaps the first evidence of the practice of berthing Marines between naval officers and their seamen. Marines would perform such disciplinary functions as long as press gangs supplied the majority of men-of-war's men. In the immediate future, however, party politics took precedence over operational efficiency. William III's underhand attempt to maintain land regiments as Marines had substantiated the Tory conspiracy theory that 'courtiers design them only for Land Regiments, and call them by a new name to deceive unthinking men.' The four regiments ceased to exist on 20 May 1699, any Marines still at sea appearing on the ship's books as seamen.

Political skulduggery hung around the disbandment of Queen Anne's Marines also. A thin House of Commons voted through a surprise motion, 'the first Instance of any Parliament's concerning themselves in breaking any particular Regiments', that left eleven younger regiments standing. A letter to the *Flying Post* suggested the Marines had been victims of Tory attempts to obstruct the accession of George I, as their officers had shown 'an entire Abhorrence of the Shamster at Bar-le-Duc [James Stuart, the Old Pretender]; and all his Adherents, with a most sincere and inviolable Attachment to the Protestant Succession'.[77]

The Admiralty had already reduced Marine companies to the same establishment as marching regiments. This was a standard demobilization measure 'for easing the Public Charge', while maintaining regimental cadres, but it did not help the heroes of Gibraltar. Queen Anne accepted the House of Commons address on 26 June 1713, and commissioners repaired to Marine headquarters along the south coast to disband them. They had to make up the accounts of the officers and soldiers mustered, taking care 'that they be mutually satisfied and paid what is due to them respectively', while doing justice by other creditors, such as clothiers, detachments still at sea, and landlords, 'so far as the subsistence due to the men will go'. Particular care was taken to disarm the men, who in 1699 had refused to hand over their weapons until paid. A generous government left the men the uniforms, belt and knapsack, which they had just finished paying for, but paid three shillings for each bayonet, to reduce the temptation to become a footpad.[78] The rank and file also received an extra fourteen days' wages, and passes 'to the place of their former Residence allowing them a convenient time. . . to return thither'. Disbanded soldiers were often unfit for any trade, and rarely welcome. The Justices of Upper Rawcliffe in Lancashire ordered the parish to provide food and shelter for Thomas Hoole, late of Sir Cloudesley Shovell's 2nd Marines, but 'they think it no sin to slyte a poor man Neither have they either Pity Charity [or] Hospitality for it is ye worst town in ye County for its poor.' The Guardians allowed him 'but Thirteen pence A week' to keep a wife and three small children, 'having spent ye haszd of my Life limbs and Fortune in ye Nations service & defence of our kingdoms', and 'now not able to do any manner of work but in teaching of Petty Scolars'.[79]

Bor's and Holt's Regiments were paid off at Southampton and Chichester respectively, 'after struggling with many difficulties too long to enumerate'. The commissioners then separated, one to disband Churchill's and Goring's in the West Country, the other to deal with Shannon's and Wills' Regiments in Kent. Officers' accounts would be settled later at the Pay Office in London, but the rank and file needed cash. Regiments received an average of £14,000, two-thirds of which was subsistence or other moneys paid to the soldiers. Goring's 330 men at Exeter shared £10,200, evoking visions of commissioners on horseback struggling along roads heavy with winter mud, loaded with a fortune in small change.[80]

The two western regiments went quietly, but Wills' at Canterbury were less docile. On Christmas Eve, after two days of armed demonstrations, the whole body of sergeants demanded their accounts be stated as they, not the Commissioners thought fit:

> Soon after the other 11 Companys almost to a man, having gott together, forced the Colours out of the Major's house, and marched in a body out of Town, with Drums beating and their Bayonets in their Musquets, and as we are informed design for Rochester, if not for London.[81]

Four fifths of Wills' Regiment were implicated including fifty-eight Sergeants, Corporals and Drummers. Their behaviour was orderly, marching in proper military fashion to lay down their arms at the Tower of London in protest at their treatment. Their petition to the Admiralty, which none of them were fool enough to sign, underlines their concern for due form. They complained of 'such reductions made by Mr Wm Daws, Sub-Agent. . . all together so large and unjust that one Third of the Pay [the balance remaining] is thereby sunk'. They excused their actions, 'having been driven to great extremity. . . seeing no likelyhood of being justly relieved at Canterbury', and ended with great formality:

Therefore humbly beseach Your
Lordship's Protection and Enquiry into
their Hard Case in order for their being
relieved in such manner as your
Lordships in your great goodness and
Wisdome shall think fitt.[82]

Their courtesy cut no ice. The authorities ordered troops of Horse and a battalion of Foot Guards to, 'suppress and appease the said mutineers. . . by force of arms if it cannot be done otherwise',[83] and suggested trying the officers by court martial for neglect of duty. Lt Col Markham of Shannon's Marines, quartered at Rochester, harangued the passing mutineers as 'rebells and traitors to the Nation', but 'took care to secure our men so that they had no opportunity to joyn with the mutineers, which they certainly would have done had they been posted in any place of opposition.'[84] The mutinous battalion developed cold feet at Greenwich, politely asked the Governor of the hospital if he would take care of their arms, and drifted back to headquarters, 'more disorderly than ever, threatening to pull down houses and commit other violencys'. To get rid of them, the commissioners paid them up to the day of the mutiny, less three days subsistence to compensate the Mayor, 'for the Mischief they threatened to do before the Guards came'. Three sergeants, blamed as ringleaders, remained in custody until May, not deserving 'to be discharged from their bail, or have any orders for their payment'.[85]

The authorities had blamed the NCOs from the beginning, but the root problem was a system that shifted the cost of maintaining soldiers onto the communities responsible for quartering them, encouraging them to contract debts greater than their pay would answer for. Facing ruin, the inhabitants of Canterbury had been instrumental in stirring up trouble, but Wills' men were hardened offenders. The commissioners wrote plaintively: 'We find this Regiment has been used to Mutiny this being (as we are informed) the 6th or 7th time.'[86] The men's impatience is understandable in face of the great irregularities and imperfections of the records, and the need to draw up accounts, under forty different headings, for each Marine, tracing their service through muster rolls and ships' books. After all the trouble they had caused, it seems somewhat unfair that Wills' was one of three Marine regiments revived to see off the 'Shamster of Bar-le-Duc' in 1715. They transferred to the Irish establishment, safe from parliamentary scrutiny, as the 30th Foot. Like the 4th, 31st, and 32nd they would carry Gibraltar on their colours, but no longer expected to serve at sea.

The administrative termination of the ten regiments at the end of 1748 compares favourably with the politically motivated purges of 1698 and 1713, and what the *Naval Chronicle* would describe as, 'the age of prejudice 1715–1739, when the very name of a Marine Soldier carried with it hostility to British liberty.'[87] The ten regiments, however, were the last experiment with regimented Marines, and the administrative confusion it entailed. Future Marines would belong to a single integrated Corps, under unchallenged naval control, with an elastic organizational structure that resolved once and for all the problems that had dogged previous attempts to supply soldiers for the fleet.

Grand Divisions

The Royal Marines of today descend directly from a corps of 5,700 Marines, established by Order in Council on 3 April 1755. They were under unequivocal Admiralty control:

> appointed to serve on board Your Majesty's ships and vessels at such times, in such proportions, and under such orders and regulations as Your High Admiral or Commissioners of the Admiralty shall judge proper.

Clothing ceased to be a source of profit for colonels and their agents, being provided directly by the Admiralty, and inspected by a board of naval and Marine officers. The Navy took control of pay, specifying:

> That the marines be mustered, the muster rolls made up, and the respective companies cleared in such manner, and at such times, as Your Lord Admiral or Commissioners of the Admiralty shall judge to be most convenient, and best for the service.[88]

Operational needs took priority over pettifogging bureaucracy. The Board of Ordnance kept responsibility for arms and ammunition, but for the first time was to replace defective firearms without charge to the officers of the combat unit. The Admiralty had assumed control of the Marines before, in the hope 'that greater care will be taken for their subsistence and the keeping them under good discipline'.[89] Those hopes had been disappointed, but Anson was now First Lord of the Admiralty, imposing business-like efficiency throughout the Royal Navy. He had witnessed the folly of sending men to sea to serve as Marines, who were 'fitter for an infirmary than for any military duty', beginning his famous circumnavigation with a mixture of invalids, and raw undisciplined men from the new Marine regiments, 'for they were just raised, and had nothing more of the soldier than their regimentals, none of them having been so far trained, as to be permitted to fire.' Once in authority, Anson ensured that no future First Lord could be fobbed off with the excuse that 'persons, who were supposed to be better judges of soldiers than he [Sir Charles Wager] or Mr Anson, thought them the properest men that could be employed.'[90]

Anson was the true father of the Royal Marines, his signature appearing alongside Lord Barrington's on the covering memo that accompanied the 1747 Draft Regulations. He was the first of a series of distinguished naval officers, including Earls St Vincent and Mountbatten, who would act as patrons of the Corps, at key moments of its history. The 1747 Draft addressed the problems that had prevented the effective functioning of earlier Marine regiments. The essential change was to break away from the regimental model, where colonels and captains owned their commands, rather as doctors owned their practice until the advent of the National Health Service in 1948. From 1755 Marines belonged to a single Corps, like the Ordnance Board's Gunners and Sappers. Its structure reflected that of the Royal Navy, with headquarters or Grand Divisions at the three home ports: Chatham, Portsmouth and Plymouth. There had been Marine depots at all three (and Deal) since 1695, when each regiment had detached an officer and NCO 'to take care of such soldiers as are or shall be put sick on shore. . . as also to secure any deserters, with orders to put them aboard again as occasion offers'.[91] Concentration within the home ports improved on the 1740s when Marines had been quartered as far away from Portsmouth as Alresford, near Winchester, and ensured a critical mass of Marines fit for sea: 'As Nurseries are now established for training Marine Soldiers,' wrote Lieutenant Terence O'Loghlen in 1766, 'there may be a sufficient Number of disciplined Men always ready for his Majesty's Ships of War upon any unforeseen Emergency.'[92] In wartime it proved relatively simple to expand the Corps, either by forming more companies, or increasing the company establishment. The Marines numbered 18,092 in 130 companies by 1763, a quarter of the Navy's manpower.

A field officer resided at each headquarters, as Divisional Commandant, along with any captains and subalterns not at sea, the latter all ranking as lieutenants. The new Corps had no colours, so did not need ensigns to carry them. The 1747 Draft also required two Marine colonels to reside in London 'to receive any orders which the service may require', but in 1760 the Royal Navy celebrated its victory over the War Office by awarding senior posts in the Corps to itself. 'Blue Colonels' replaced divisional field officers 'to the unspeakable mortification' of Marine officers, who complained loudly of the destruction of 'that laudable spirit of emulation, which is the soul and life of a soldier'.[93] O'Loghlen protested the need for an officer of rank and experience to inspect the divisions and prevent:

> Misapprehension and Blunders, which must inevitably happen, while those Matters remain under the Direction of People who cannot possibly be supposed to know any Thing of the Business of a Soldier.[94]

Blue Colonels lost their administrative responsibilities after 1763, but continued to collect forty shillings a day, besides naval pay, until their abolition in 1833, 'a wound that rankled at the very heart of the service'.[95] The Corps seems to have had no professional head, until General John Mackenzie's appointment in 1783, 'to reside constantly in London to attend the Board of Admiralty in the Nature of Adjutant General'.[96] Colonels Commandant in Town became the principal focus for Admiralty communications with Divisional Headquarters, evolving through the Deputy Adjutant General's office instituted in 1825, into the Commandants General of the late twentieth century.

Major John Pitcairn drew the attention of Chatham's Divisional Commandant to the patchy results that arose from lack of central supervision:

> It is the Devil to come out with Marines, for what with the ignorance of Admirals of our business, and the inattention of our Commanding Officers at Quarters I am exceedingly distress'd: Some of the Marines from the other Divisions are sent out in a most shameful manner, not a greatcoat from Plymouth, and some of them not a Coat to put on their Backs, all these things I conceal like murder here, nor do I intend to say anything about [it] to anybody but you, it would hurt the Corps.[97]

The fifty-five unregimented companies each belonged to one of the headquarters, No. 1 to Chatham, No. 2 to Portsmouth, No. 3 to Plymouth, and so on in rotation. A Marine enlisted in a particular company, remaining there until promoted or discharged. Companies were purely administrative units, ship's detachments taking officers and men from the top of the list for sea duty, ensuring that only trained, rested and paid Marines went to sea. On return they went back to their own Division, to be paid and deloused, to remove the 'Bugs and other Vermin' inseparable from shipboard life, reclothed, and brought up to scratch as soldiers. Marines thus avoided the trap into which seamen fell, of being constantly turned over from one ship to another, which may explain the willingness of recruits to volunteer for the Marines, but not the Navy.

The passing of proprietorial Marine regiments ended the buying and selling of Marine commissions. Marines had always lacked the social cachet of those in more prestigious regiments. A father marooned at Fort St George in India grumbled at his son's guardians: 'I wish you had bought him a very good employ in the English Guards, though it had cost three times the money, for being in the Marines will oblige him to have a great deal at sea ports, where the associations are none of the best.'[98] Frequent disbandment further reduced the value of Marine commissions. A Lieutenancy in the 1740s cost £200–250 compared with £350–400 in an old marching regiment, and many Marine subalterns received free wartime commissions directly from the King. Nevertheless Marine officers were often scarce, hampering the provision of ships' detachments. Officials in Whitehall raised a hue and cry over the late arrival of HMS *Devonshire*'s Marine detachment in 1711, threatening to cashier the absentee officers. Colonel Bor replied that he had 'but two Lieutenants in England and they are in the North a raising of men, besides one madman and two who are officers at sea [i.e. naval officers]'. Even the Quartermaster was away with a detachment.[99]

The end of purchase brought new abuses. Patronage, the polite term for favouritism, became the route to a commission. Purchase had ensured officers were gentlemen, but even the butler of a retired Commissioner of Chatham Dockyard mustered enough interest to get his son a Marine commission. One young hopeful, 'of respectable connections, and of the best morals', advertised in *The Times* for the patronage of anyone with enough interest to procure him a Lieutenancy. Promotion depended upon seniority, as it did in the Royal Artillery and Engineers. High casualties and expanding establishments made this acceptable in wartime, but dispiriting in peacetime, especially as Admiralty control removed the safety valve of exchanging into a line regiment, making it impossible for a Marine officer, were he to serve fifty years, to attain a higher rank than that of Lieutenant Colonel: 'a dismal Prospect for a young Man who has Ambition, and perhaps Capacity, to distinguish himself in the Service of his King and Country.'[100] A young man with influence but little money might still find a career in the Marines attractive. Earl St Vincent felt 'the requests of fatherless children and widows cannot be parried', and limited patronage to 'sons and near relations of Officers'.[101] Family connection became the recognized way to a Marine commission. Generations of Marine officers shared such names as Adair, Collins, Elliot, Halliday,

Oldfield or Pitcairn, reinforcing bonds of regimental loyalty forged by their minority status within an overwhelmingly naval environment.

CHAPTER THREE

Action Under Sail

THE Admiralty's commitment to Marines, despite repeated dis-appointments, indicates they saw them as an essential part of the service. Not only did Marines supplement the perennially insufficient prime seamen, they possessed different skills. Marines were a force multiplier that allowed the Royal Navy to do more than it could have done had it consisted solely of seamen.

Marines were an essential part of a man-of-war's complement as long as seamen lacked the unfailing discipline that came from continuous service. Until the 1850s Marines were the Royal Navy's only permanently established personnel. The majority of wartime crews consisted of pressed merchant seamen, or untrained landsmen, 'a loose collection of undisci-plined people, and (as experience shows) sufficiently inclined to mutiny'.[1] The Captain of HMS *Ruby* completed his crew in 1709 with a draft of French prisoners of war, and humbly prayed for 'some marines to dissapling them'.[2] In action the steadiness of the Marine complemented the Seaman's dash, handiness and resource, to make the Royal Navy a uniquely successful battle-winning force. Marines' military training fitted them to carry out tasks that required discipline and regularity more effectively than seamen, whose reckless individualism made them unsuit-able for delivering controlled volleys of musketry, or standing sentry through long night watches. Marines were uniquely equipped to fulfil three main functions: provision of directed group small-arms fire in naval actions; participation in amphibious operations; and assuring shipboard security as part of a general group of activities, loosely known as sea service, representing the less glamorous majority of a Marine's life at sea.

The primary function of military forces, other than Praetorian Guards, is to fight. How they do this reflects the physical nature of their weapons, and their mental conditioning, or training. Marines' tactical function aboard ship is their obvious raison d'être, thanks to the gleam of their red tunics through the powder smoke of innumerable romantic battle paintings. The exact nature of the Marine's role in battle is rarely explored, however, beyond misleading references to 'marksmen', or a catalogue of battles that belongs to naval history in general, rather than in a Corps history. Detailed accounts of Marine detachments in battle are scarce. Hard-pressed naval officers rarely had time, in the aftermath of an action, to expand on details their professional peers could take as read. Ships carry their crew along with them, as cogs within an integrated fighting machine. Individual combatants tend to go unrecognized. Contemporary documents are more likely to reveal the names of defaulters, rather than those of the well-behaved majority who did their duty. A ship's Marine detachment was usually submerged in the mass of her complement, appearing in the official record only as casualties, or subsumed within the customary praise of the gallantry of officers, seamen and Marines in general. Captain Pole of the *Success* went further than most when he acknowledged the contribution to the capture of a Spanish Frigate, of Lieutenant Pownall of Marines, who, 'by the greatest Attention and good Example, formed a Party that would do honour to veteran Soldiers'.[3]

The constant and unpredictable movement of naval units limited individual opportunities for observation. Anti-climax is commonplace in Marine diaries. Captain John Robyns RM escorted reinforcements to the West Indies, only to find 'Guadeloupe surrendered eight days since, much to our mortification.'[4] Colonel Richard Swale's early career was a catalogue of missed opportunities. In June 1800 he spent a week 'expecting every moment to make a landing on Belle Isle. . . but on the 21st in the morning to our great surprize and disappointment were ordered on board of our respective ships and the enterprize given up.' Chasing a French squadron off Sicily, Swale's ship received orders, 'to engage the enemy as we came up with them, but next morning to our great mortification could see nothing of them.' She then arrived off Alexandria too late to contribute to the Marine battalion landed there. Swale missed Trafalgar by a continent, reading 'the glorious news of Lord Nelson's action' in newspapers obtained from a Danish ship at Table Bay, and suffered the embarrassment of watching his own ship engage a French frigate without him: 'the Signal was made for the enemy, *Diomede* got under way and I left on shore.'[5] Marines who did see action often lacked the imagination or literary skill to make anything of their experiences. The Lieutenant of Marines in Nelson's flagship at the

Nile noted the barest outlines of an occasion that made him the professional envy of his contemporaries:

> August 1st. Fought the French fleet at anchor off Alexandria, consisting
> of 13 sail of the line and several frigates; took 10 sail of the line and burnt
> one three-decker and one frigate and sunk one frigate. Capt Faddy of the
> Marines and six privates killed and seven wounded.[6]

Despite the inadequacies of the evidence, it is possible to reconstruct how Marine detachments supplemented the very different combat skills of the seamen. Contemporary descriptions of naval actions define the context in which Marines operated, while Captain's order books and early drill manuals reveal the logic behind the scraps left by eyewitnesses, enabling us to reconstruct the Marine experience of action at sea in the age of sail.

Close Hauled Line

The conditions of naval warfare between the 1650s, when Sir Charles Littleton began his military career, and the introduction of steam in the 1840s remained broadly constant. Square-rigged sailing warships with batteries of smooth-bore guns on each broadside dominated the oceans. The technical limitations of these ships and their weapons created a tactical requirement for well-directed small-arms fire, provision of which remained the primary function of Marines until the appearance of steamships and rifled cannon.

Sailing warships depended entirely on the wind for their motive power. Its force and direction imposed strict limits on ships' ability to manoeuvre. They could not sail less than five or six points from the wind, and if the wind dropped might not be able to move at all. Lieutenant John Robyns took part in the pursuit of a French corvette through the Malacca Straits:

> we had an evident superiority and by eight o'clock was nearly within gun
> shot range, when a dead calm arrested our Progress, the Corvette taking
> advantage of this got 24 sweeps out, and rowed from us like a Long Boat.[7]

Too much wind from the wrong direction, on the other hand, could be disastrous. A British squadron, replenishing water and firewood, found itself on a lee shore in Gardiner's Bay, NY:

> the wind came on to blowe very hard from the east and with Great
> Difficulty the *Russell* and *Adament* got Safe out. But the *Bedford* had her

fore and Main Masts Carryd away and the *Culloden* was Drove on Shore among the rocks at the east end of Long Island and was beat to Peaces but her men all Saved and her Masts and yeards.[8]

The position of opposing naval forces relative to the wind was of crucial tactical importance. Ships to windward of the enemy held the initiative and could launch attacks more easily than ships to leeward, which could however avoid action by running downwind. This tactic is commonly associated with the French, but British ships did the same when outclassed. Lieutenant Mortimer Timpson of Marines was in HMS *Mermaid* (32) when she had the worst of an encounter with the *Loire* (40), losing her mizzen and main topmast:

> Captain Newman, then, finding his ship dreadfully cut up in the action, and that he would be unable to board the French Frigate, on account of the number of troops on board her, thought it prudent to put the *Mermaid* before the wind and crowd as much sail as possible on the Foremast. The Frenchman still stood after, but did not gain on us: finding he made no progress he brought his broadside to bear on the *Mermaid's* stern, but the shot went over us: he then stood away, and gave over the chase about Sunset.[9]

John Howe was Corporal of Marines in HM Sloop *Serpent* (14) when she chased a suspected French merchant ship off Cape Francois in the West Indies:

> made sail after her till Six oClock in the evening when she was Joind by a Line of Battle Ship who Proved to be French this turnd the Scale and we were oblige to Runn from them as fast as we had before Runn after one of them.[10]

Thoughtful tacticians, like Anson in his engagement with the Acapulco galleon in 1742, tried to prevent such escapes, 'keeping to the leeward of them, with a view to preventing their putting before the wind'.[11] Ships of different navies were similar in point of speed, leading to lengthy chase actions, before the Marine detachment found themselves within musket shot: 'in the interim they are to be attentive to the orders they may receive in manoeuvring the sails, bracing the yards etc.'[12] HMS *Donegal* (74) chased a Spanish frigate for forty hours, 300 miles along the North African coast, before forcing her to surrender in ten minutes, her Captain killed by a musket ball.

The Royal Navy's aggressive tactics dated from the Dutch Wars, when the narrow waters of the North Sea and the importance of the issues forced the opposing navies to fight. Admirals had quickly appreciated the tactical advantage of possessing the weather gauge, which might allow their fleet to close on the opposing line and break it, as the Duke of York did at Lowestoft in 1664:

> His Royal Highness having got to windward of them, the engagement began, then the whole fleet passing and firing at every ship, and the fire returned. . . till at 1 p.m. weary of fighting at a distance, we divided their fleet. Opdam's ship blew up; a pell mell conflict ensued, when the Dutch fleet was driven into the Texel or Maes, thirty ships being burnt or taken.[13]

Sir Charles Littleton's analysis of Sole Bay, in which seven of his officers fell, left no doubt of the advantage of fighting upwind of the enemy:

> Our fleet yesterday fought upon great disadvantage, they having the weather gauge, and there was so little wind our ships could not work, which was the reason our fleet fought very scattering. The French engaged at a great distance to the southward of all the fleets, and the Dutch having the weather gage, would not come to a close fight with them, but fought all the time at a great distance.[14]

In a single ship action, the weather gage allowed a Captain to close with his opponent for boarding action, or to outmanoeuvre him as HMS *Success* (32) did to the *Santa Catalina*, when Lieutenant Pownall's detachment had acted like veterans:

> I wore and steered for his Lee bow, till we had a just Distance to weather him; then hauled close athwart his Forefoot, giving him our whole fire within half Pistol shot; passed close to windward engaging, while the Enemy, expecting us to leeward were firing their guns into the water; the Disorder which this threw them into they did not recover. We then wore and placed ourselves at great Advantage, which our superiority of sailing allowed us to do, supporting without intermission, a most astonishing close and well directed fire, at never more than half a Cable distance, till the enemy struck.[15]

The masts and rigging upon which such subtleties depended, however, were vulnerable targets, their loss converting the liveliest frigate into an inanimate log. An hour and a half into *Mermaid's* action with the *Loire* Captain Newman ordered her guns to be double shotted, preparatory to raking the enemy's bows, 'but unluckily just as the helm was put up, the Frenchman fired his Bow Guns, and cut away our Mizen Mast, and the Maintopmast came down with it', forcing her to flee for her life.[16] The

French made a deliberate practice of shooting away their opponents' masts and rigging, at least from the Battle of Toulon in 1744:

> the *Marlborough's* main mast (and mizen mast) was brought to by the Board as if it had been but a Twig, and the Admiral's Main Mast and Bowsprit were shot through and through. . . The Enemy fired chiefly at our Masts and Rigging, for though the Admiral engaged within Pistol Shot he had but nine men killed outright and forty wounded.[17]

The French aimed to cripple their opponents, so they could give them the slip and pursue some broader strategic aim. The British preferred to inflict crippling casualties and smash their opponent's morale. They usually fought at musket or pistol shot, i.e. 200 down to 20 yards, sometimes lashing the opposing ships' yardarms together. HMS *Buckingham* (64) began her attack on the *Florissant* (74) in November 1758 with 'a noble Dose of Great Guns and Small Arms, at about the distance of half Musket Shot'.[18] HMS *Magnanime* (74) ran so close behind *Le Hero* at Quiberon Bay that she lost her catshead, and snapped off the anchor suspended there. Closing with *Courageux* (74) in 1761, Captain Faulknor of HMS *Bellona* (74) restrained her people's impatience to return fire: 'let us see the whites of their eyes first, and take my word for it, they will never stand the singeing of their whiskers.'[19] One French Captain complained 'That it was cruel to engage so close', but such tactics were not the blind product of mindless savagery. Although naval guns were heavier than those used ashore, 12- to 42-pounders compared with 6- to 12-pounders, conditions at sea reduced effective ranges to half that of a field gun:

> the falling off of the ship from the wind, and bringing her to alters the line of fire; the rolling of the ship alters the elevation; either of these causes (and they are continually occurring) occasions a broadside, even at the distance of two cables length (or 480 yards) to have little effect, and this is diminished as the distance increases.[20]

At such close ranges iron cannonballs did enormous damage to wooden hulls. Ships rarely sank during an action, but like the *Santa Catalina* were often reduced to a sinking condition and had to be blown up later, the hull like a sieve, the shot going through both sides.[21] The brig sloop *Weazle* became a complete wreck after a twelve-hour fight with the gunboat escort of a convoy, which so reduced her complement that only the Marines and four guns continued in action:

> the whole of our running and the greater part of the standing rigging

gone, most of the sails shot from the yards, the masts shot through in several places, and many shot in the hull, five between wind and water, both our pumps shot away between the decks, with difficulty we could keep her free by constantly bailing at both hatches.[22]

The prospect of crippling physical damage and the ease with which ships could avoid action explains the scarcity of fleet actions during the eighteenth century. Long intervals separated Anglo-French trials of strength at Barfleur (1692), Malaga (1704), Toulon (1744) and Quiberon Bay (1759). Outnumbered squadrons usually sought shelter in a convenient harbour, as Rochambeau did at Rhode Island in 1780. John Howe was aboard the blockading squadron, and transcribed a ribald squib from a New York paper, neatly summarizing the difficulty of forcing an unwilling enemy to fight:

In truth my Good Sir ther has been nothing Like it
Tis easyer to threaten a blow than to Strike it
No Ship has been taken off frigate or Lugger
Or eane a Poor Frenchman for Jacktar to Bu.g.r[23]

Even when squadrons came to close quarters, contemporary tactical doctrine made decisive success unlikely. In early battles under sail, several ships might concentrate their efforts upon one opponent, as the Dutch did against Sir Edward Spragge's flagship during the battle of the Texel. Philip Bickerstaffe, aboard her as Captain-Lieutenant of Littleton's company in the Duke of York's, described what had happened:

Tromp was well seconded by several stout ships from which a gun was not fired at anybody but Sir Edward. . . which I conceive was the chief reason our ship was disabled so much sooner than any other in the fleet. . . our mainstay was shot in pieces, and almost all the rigging, and our main and mizen masts disabled, a great part of the fine cabins beat into chips, and many valiant men sent into the next world without any ceremony besides peals of thundering ordnance.[24]

Fighting instructions emerged to save ships from being defeated in detail, but also prevented admirals seizing momentary chances to crush disordered opponents. Fleets engaged in close line ahead, perhaps one cable between each ship, their broadsides overlapping to ensure a degree of mutual support. Against a similarly deployed opponent of comparable skill, the result was stalemate, as neither side could concentrate a decisive margin of fire against one part of the opposing line. Howe wrote dismissively of the

Second Battle of the Capes, which lost the American colonies: 'next Day adm[l] Graves Saild with the fleet Leaving us and the *Europe* to stay here, they returned in the begining of September having Don no good. General Cornwallis being taken and the *Terrible* blown up.'[25] Lieutenant William Ackroyd, a Marine with an interest in naval tactics, blamed Graves' obsessive attempts to maintain his line for the failure to catch the French fleet in disorder, but Ackroyd's own transcription of HMS *Cornwall*'s log of Rodney's action off Martinique shows how even a Rodney had trouble breaking the mould. Twenty-four hours of manoeuvres and signals petered out in an ineffective three-hour exchange of fire, punctuated by unavailing calls for closer action.[26] Occasionally Admirals might bring superior numbers to bear, as Suffren did at Providien off Ceylon (12 Apr 1782), when he overlapped either end of the British line and annihilated HMS *Monmouth*'s Marine detachment. Her Captain 'received two wounds in the face from splinters, two musket balls passed through his hat, his hair was on fire, his coat torn between the shoulders, and part of it shot away.' Having nailed his colours to the stump of the mizzenmast, he stood on the quarterdeck alone, except for the First Lieutenant and Master:

> every other person quartered there and on the poop having been killed or wounded, except Captain Pierce of the Marines and his second lieutenant Mr Minheer, who after their men had all been killed or wounded, nobly went and assisted at the guns on the main deck.[27]

Two circumstances combined in the 1790s to break the spell: improved signalling techniques and the French Revolution. Admirals, such as Earl Howe, learned how to impose their control over the course of a battle. The notebooks of Nelson's Marine officers are decorated with strings of signal flags, with which they, no less than their naval colleagues, had to be familiar. Restoration admirals had sent messengers, as when a youthful Cloudesley Shovell swam between ships with a note in his mouth, or even exchanged ships themselves, as Spragge tried to do at the Texel in a small boat, sunk by gunfire: 'He had often endeavoured but never attained any skill in the useful art of swimming.'[28]

While the French Revolution undermined the morale and infrastructure of the French Navy, the British developed a decisive edge in seamanship and gunnery, as demonstrated in HMS *Sybille*'s (44) capture of *La Forte* (54) in 1799. The British Captain took compass bearings on *La Forte*'s gun flashes, seen at dusk as she attacked a merchantman, put out all the lights in the ship that could betray his approach, and steered for the spot, closing 'so effectually that his main-yard-arm is said to have been between the enemy's main mast and mizzen mast, and in this situation poured into him a destructive broadside of great guns and musketry', firing three broadsides to his opponent's one.[29] The War of 1812 against the well-equipped US Navy set new standards of tactical decisiveness, on both sides. The *Shannon*'s successful attack on the *Chesapeake* 'ended in 13 minutes, one of the fairest, shortest, severest, and most decisive actions that ever was fought between two ships.'[30] At its peak, the Age of Sail approached the instantaneous combat resolution of the Missile Age.

Marine Tactics

Unlike modern warships, with their ability to engage over-the-horizon targets, sailing ships fought at very close ranges indeed. The weapons used were simple, but this does not imply that discipline and training were unnecessary. Lieutenant Terence O'Loghlen grumbled how 'Thousands in this great Metropolis that think an *English* Man of War ought to take or destroy any Enemy she might meet, without considering how the ship is manned', commenting reasonably enough that 'it is impossible for Officers, let them be ever so alert, to make Men fight who do not know how to load their Muskets.'[31] The economy-minded politicians who sent toothless geriatrics to sea in the 1740s, however, denied that Marines needed any particular training:

> Newly raised troops are as good on board a man of war as disciplined soldiers. In fighting a ship there is no part of the land discipline required but that of loading and firing a musket and a country fellow from the plough may be in three days taught to do this.[32]

Marine training was indeed simpler than that required in marching regiments, who had to manoeuvre in large formations, in the face of cavalry. However, fighting at sea required other skills not possessed by regular infantrymen. Marines had to keep powder dry and weapons serviceable in damp conditions, exposed to the corrosive effects of salt water. In action they had to bear in mind the continual alternation between firing to leeward or into the wind, which required different firing procedures and frequent changes of position. Like no other eighteenth-century infantry soldiers, outside North America or the Balkans, Marines were expected to take cover while reloading, and occupy alternative firing positions, 'springing sideways with Life and Spirit', halting of their own accord at the point directed, 'so that. . . a Detachment will occupy any Part of the Deck in a Moment, without being troubled by tedious Movements'.[33] A government critic claimed that Marines required more officers than land forces 'because they have more duties to learn, and a greater variety of difficulties to encounter'.[34] A Marine officer needed seamanship to anticipate his Commanding Officer's intentions, 'and be ready with his Detachment to throw in his fire, as Circumstances may require. . . . As a favourable Opportunity, if not immediately embraced, may often be lost.'[35] Marines had to synchronize their fire with the ship's motions, learning 'never to give Fire but when the Ship is rising with the Wave: If you fire when she pitches, you hit nothing but Salt-Water.' Regardless of official rhetoric, Marines needed as much training as line troops:

> An Encampment in the Neighbourhood of an Enemy, or a rolling Ship of War in the bay of Biscay, are very improper Places to teach Men their Firings and Evolutions; therefore they ought to know both perfectly before they are sent upon Service. It cannot be expected that Soldiers will perform in Action what they never saw in a Field of Exercise.[36]

The traditional role of Marines, as of all soldiers at sea, was to provide small arms fire. Warships became heavy gun platforms in the reign of Henry VIII, but still needed lighter weapons for close-in defence, or to engage targets of opportunity. Marines acted as a flexible reserve of fire-power to meet emergencies, or fill intervals in an action when a ship's main armament might not be effective. Heavy guns fired slowly, and could only engage targets within a narrow arc of fire, at right angles to the ship's line of movement. This limited a ship's ability to use her main armament, as shown in the 'prodigious fight' between the *Tyger* (36) and two Dutch privateers (42 and 36) off Dover in 1668:

> They began at 10 a.m., fought six hours, and killed above 100 Ostenders. . . Captain Herbert in the *Constant Warwick*, who was near when they fought, says they exchanged but two broadsides, the Ostenders having the wind, but both plied their small shot furiously.[37]

A Captain might begin an action with small shot only. HMS *Bienfaisant* (64) took a French privateer, flying false colours off Cork in 1780, after an initial exchange of musketry. This was almost certainly sustained by her Marine detachment, although their Captain failed to acknowledge them as such:

> As he larged within Pistol shot, some Conversation passed between us. In this mode we got so far forward on his Bow, that neither his Bow nor our

Quarter guns would bear. Being certain what this ship was, I then ordered the small Arms on the Poop to begin; she returned it, and hoisted her proper colours. It was some little time before I could regulate my Sail, and place my Ship.[38]

The close ranges of most engagements made it essential to suppress hostile musketry. A French warship habitually went into action 'with a great number of men at small arms in her tops, poop, quarter-deck, and forecastle'.[39] HMS *Namur* (90) lost fifteen killed and seventy-three wounded at the First Battle of Ushant, including the Lieutenant of Marines: 'As we engaged so closely, our officers and ship's company. . . were greatly hurt by the small arms.'[40] A well-handled detachment, on the other hand, could hasten the enemy's surrender, as when HMS *Blanche* (32) captured the *Pique* (38) on 5 January 1795: 'The Marines under Lieutenant Richardson keeping up so well-directed and constant a fire, that not a man could appear on the forecastle until she struck.'[41]

The ends of a ship were particularly vulnerable, if she were immobilized by a drop in the wind, or the loss of her masts. Marines provided end-on fire when ships became intermingled in a fleet action, exchanging volleys for broadsides:

> We were [given] the order to go on the Poop now the *Province* and the *Ardent* came down on us and Got on the Larboard bow whilst the *Ardent* went under our Stern and Did us a Deal of Damage one Shot Struck the mans firelock all to peaces that was in front of me and Cut away my Sidebolt and a Peace of my Coat. We were now drawn up a Cross the Taffrell to fire with our small arms into her.[42]

Coastal waters were particularly dangerous, as gunboats equipped with oars could cut up becalmed warships, as Danish craft did to *Melpomene* one night in the Kattegat:

> Her decks were strewed with slain men, many of whom had no covering but their shirts; and the poor Marine who had been sentry on the gangway, was cut entirely through the middle, with his musket and pouch lying alongside of him. . . Nothing could have been more unfortunate for an attack of the kind than the manner in which the frigate was placed; for being at anchor in a dead calm, the gunboats could take positions close to her, both ahead and astern, whilst not more than six, or at most eight guns could bear upon them.[43]

Before the Admiral's Regiment was formed, the Commonwealth had sent soldiers of the New Model Army to sea to fight the Dutch, in the 'Great and Bloudy Fight' in the Downs:

> the Musketeers on both sides, maintained the Dispute with great Gallantry and Resolution; till at last the English Red-coats, consisting of Colonel Ingoldsby's Regiment of Foot, plaid so fast upon them with Small-Shot and Granadoes, that they soon cleared the Decks, fired the Mistle or Main-sail, and afterwards boarded two of the Hollanders.[44]

The policy was maintained during the Second Dutch War. As the Dutch Fleet cruised off the North Foreland in July 1666, commissions for six additional companies of the Admiral's Regiment coincided with a report from the fleet 'that the small shot, which is double what was ever had before, will be landsmen, which will be a great ease to the seamen.'[45] The latter never appreciated the military discipline required for safe and effective use of small arms in action. Sea Officers in the 1690s complained: 'they could never bring one in ten of the Sailors so much as to endeavour at the exercise of the small arms.' The defender of 'The Four Regiments Commonly Called Mariners' ridiculed the claim of their anonymous Tory critic that seamen were 'properer to. . . annoy the enemy with small shot' as a result of their experience wildfowling, or that:

> to defend the decks, and make regular fires, to load and discharge with quickness, and order, preserving themselves carefully to advance and retire with that regard to command, as in companies well disciplined, may be learnt best by shooting Larks.[46]

Another apologist for Marine Regiments claimed, 'the Preservation of some Men-of-War has been in a great Measure being owing to their Small-Shot and the Want of them in others lost, has been very generously acknowledged by the Sea Officers',[47] and the documents bear him out. HMS *Greyhound*'s Commanding Officer requested, '20 Marrines, to serve under my command for small shot men, believing it to be very much for the service'.[48] HMS *Augusta*'s Captain preferred them to the product of the press gang: 'those men I had from the *Norfolk* and most of the others prest from Colliers being so very indifferent and ordinary I cannot depend on them for smal Armes.' Hostilities with Spain in 1719 drew a request from the Admiralty for every warship to be given an additional Lieutenant, 'particularly to train up and exercise the use of small arms; which is the more necessary to be done since there are not now any Marine regiments subsisting.' Their Lordships continued to impress upon captains the importance of training as many of their ship's landsmen as possible in the use of small arms, after the establishment of the Grand Divisions.[49] So valuable was musketry that Marine sergeants and drummers carried firelocks in action, rather than halberds or drums, and the wardroom muskets were brought on deck to provide a reserve of clean weapons.

Marines' action stations were the forecastle and poop, from where they had the best field of fire. A decorated punchbowl made for Sir Charles Douglas, Rodney's flag captain at the Battle of the Saints, and now at the National Maritime Museum, clearly shows HMS *Formidable*'s Marines drawn up in those positions. In 1776 HMS *Enterprise*, a 6th Rate Frigate with 28 guns and 34 Marines, stationed 24 on the quarterdeck with the senior Lieutenant, Sergeant and drummer, and another 10 on the forecastle, with the Lieutenant and Corporal. At the First Battle of the Capes John Howe, 'was Stationed on the forecastle with twelve Privates 2 Corporal 1 Serjent and one Lieutenant of Marines. . . they were all killed and wounded except myself and too Privats and the Lieu[t].[50]

The immortal memory of Nelson's death by a sniper's shot tends to associate musketry at sea with individual marksmanship, but this impression is misleading. Eighteenth-century Marines were not trained to pick off individual enemy officers, and they rarely went aloft. Small-arms men in the tops were also there to repair the rigging, a task for seamen. The tactical purpose of Marines before Trafalgar was to clear enemy decks with well-directed blasts of musketry. The emphasis was on volleys and tight fire control:

> see the Shot well rammed down; that the Men take a good Aim, level well, without trembling; direct their Fire where it is likely to do most Execution; pull the Triggers very strong, and look boldly into their Fire, without turning the Head; they must never be suffered to fire at random, or in a Hurry; for it is certain that the Discharge of one Rank, loaded methodically, and who take Aim, does more Execution than three Discharges of the same Number of Men, loading and firing at random.[51]

Even against small targets, Marines operated in groups: 'a platoon of the best Marksmen should be picked out, and ordered to take Aim, and fire at the Port-Holes: Two or Three expert Men killed at a Gun may silence it for half an Hour.'[52] At the critical moment of a frigate action (10 Aug 1805), 'one of the most brilliant and exemplary cases of the kind', *Le Didon* (40) ran on board HMS *Phoenix*'s (36) starboard quarter. The only gun either of the two entangled ships could bring to bear was a brass 32-pounder on the *Didon*'s forecastle, but as fast as the French gunners tried to fire it, HMS *Phoenix*'s Marines shot them down. Years later her

Captain wrote to Lieutenant Pleydell, the surviving Marine officer:

> 'Never can I forget the service you were to me', he wrote, '. . .when the
> success of the battle (. . .) depended, a good deal, upon your example and
> conduct, and prevented that large piece of artillery on the forecastle of
> Didon from sweeping the whole of our deck.'[53]

Marines learned three distinct ways of delivering fire: Parapet Firings to
leeward or windward, and, for more advanced students, the Marine Firing.
Sailing ships heel over before the wind, giving a clear view to leeward,
but exposing their deck to fire, so it was safer to engage to windward, but
more difficult, as the roll of the ship exaggerated the height of the bulwark,
obstructing the musketeer. Different drill formations emerged: two ranks
to fire to leeward, and three when firing to windward. The two ranks
kept as close as possible to the barricade, to exploit what cover it gave,
and fired together by successive platoons, from left or right as most appropriate. The three ranks fired one whole rank at a time, the other two
reloading under cover of the bulwark. The Marine Firing allowed soldiers
to reload kneeling down and fire in their own time. This was astonishingly
liberal in a period that usually reduced soldiers to mindless automata.
Raw Marines might blaze away aimlessly, but experienced men could be
trusted to take cover at random musket shot, standing up by platoons to
fire in their turn: 'Every man having an object in view, Fires, without any
Word of Command or waiting for the Rest, and kneels to load again.'
The aim of all three Firings was to deliver a continual hail of musket balls
to shake enemy morale. A detachment was not properly exercised until
they could deliver four rounds a minute: 'for nothing can gall an Enemy
so much as a constant Fire, which intimidates the common People, and
often puts it out of an Officer's power to re-animate them.'[54]

   Detachments only fired a full volley when raking an opponent's bow
or stern, to which the enemy could not reply, or when the enemy attempted
to board, followed by a brisk bayonet charge to deny them time to gain a
footing. Captain Robert Hughes recognized the value of foot soldiers in
such circumstances, when ordered to recruit his ship's complement in
1709: 'I humbly pray there may be 40 Mareens ordered amongst them
who are so serviceable in case of being boarded by an enemy.'[55] Marines
did not usually fix bayonets, 'very inconvenient in a Sea Engagement',
but:

> If the enemy, either by design or accident, fall on board His Majesty's
> ship, the officers will order their men to fix bayonets to repulse them, if

they should attempt to board, or to cover or protect our boarding party if they should be obliged to retreat.[56]

Marines and boarders associated the disciplined firepower of soldiers with the reckless agility of seamen – a powerful combination whether defending or attacking. HMS *Amelia* (38) fought the *Arethuse* (40) for three and a half hours (6 Feb 1813), before the latter's 24-pounder guns reduced her to an ungovernable condition: 'During the action we twice fell on board the enemy, in attempting to thwart his hawse, when he attempted to board, but was repulsed by the Marines. . . and the boarders.'[57] French and Spanish ships carried more men than their British opponents, threatening to swarm aboard unless held at bay by musketry. A Spanish three-decker ran her bowsprit over the poop of HMS *Revenge* (74) at Trafalgar, her fore-rigging packed with boarders:

> but they caught a Tartar, for their design was discovered and our Marines with their small arms, and the carronades on the poop, loaded with canister shot, swept them off so fast that they were glad to sheer off.'[58]

On the offensive, the Marines sought to clear enemy decks, as HMS *Buckingham's* detachment did for the *Florissant* (3 Nov 1756). 'An unlucky broadside. . . made some slaughter on the Quarter Deck', wounding the Captain and the Lieutenant of Marines. However, her Second Lieutenant fought the ship yardarm to yardarm, showing the combined effect of great guns, Marine musketry, and miscellaneous old iron:

> We silenced the French for some time, upon which she hauled down her colours, and after that fired about eleven of her Lower Tier, and gave us a Volley of Small Arms, which our people returned with great Fury, giving him three Broadsides, she not returning a single Gun. Captain Troy at the same time, at the Head of his Marines, performed the service of a brave and gallant Officer, cleared her Poop and Quarter Deck, and drove her Men like Sheep down upon their Main Deck. Our Topmen were not idle, they plying their Hand Grenades and Swivels to excellent purpose. It is impossible to describe the Uproar and Confusion the French were in.[59]

When boarding it was essential to drive the enemy away from their entangled boarding nets and pikes. At Trafalgar HMS *Temeraire's* Marines poured a murderous discharge of musketry upon the deck of *Fougueux* from the higher bulwarks of their own ship, 'which greatly assisted the boarders who entered her from the chains and main-deck ports'.[60] Not a man was left standing on *Chesapeake*'s quarterdeck when HMS *Shannon* boarded her in 1813. Once the boarders had gained the enemy deck, Marines consolidated the capture:

> Captain Broke and his first boarding party were almost immediately followed by between 30 and 40 Marines, who secured possession of the *Chesapeake*'s quarter deck, dislodged the men from the main and fore tops, that were firing down on the boarders, and kept down all who attempted to come up from the main deck.[61]

Marines did not usually man heavy guns during the eighteenth century. Although the first mention of Marines fighting as gunners dates from 1694, a witness told the 1746 parliamentary investigation that he never knew them put to the guns. Casualties in battle or from disease might demand emergency measures, as in HMS *Rippon* (60) at Guadeloupe in 1759:

> Of twenty eight Marines quarter'd on the Poop, eight were killed or wounded, and the Seamen so enfiladed on the Forecastle, that ten out of the twenty remaining were obliged to be sent forwards to assist in returning the Fire there; the rest of the Marines were employed at the guns, there being upwards of ninety Men sick in the Hold.[62]

The capture of *La Capricieuse* (32) by HMS *Prudente* (38) and *Licorne* (32) in 1780, required another exceptional redeployment that proves the rule. *Prudente*'s Marines, 'behaved with the utmost steadiness and bravery, keeping up a regular and constant fire from the beginning of the action, till necessity called them to the guns, when they shewed an equal share of spirit and good order.'[63] Only later did Captains systematically reduce the numbers of small arms men, moving them below decks to the big guns, where they left off their cartouche boxes, but kept their bayonets as a reminder of their military status. Thirty-nine of HMS *Egmont*'s Marines in the late 1790s had their action stations on the poop and quarterdeck, but all except four also had places assigned them with her main armament. A few years later HMS *Active*'s orders were similarly flexible:

> The Marines are to be quartered as well at the Great Guns as at the Small Arms and they will be frequently exercised at the former in order to their being expert thereat, when occasion requires their assistance.[64]

Reducing close-range defence may have gone too far at Navarino, the last great fleet action under sail (20 Oct 1827). Forty of HMS *Albion*'s Marines were below decks, and seventy on the poop, as small-arms men.

However, forty more went below to carry powder, and twenty manned quarterdeck guns, leaving only a handful to deal with a large and determined Turkish frigate:

> The Captain of Marines having been killed, the command had devolved upon the Marines' senior subaltern, who had enough to do to repel the Turk's attempt to board. A sergeant touching his left arm was shot through the head, and a private on his right hand was shot through the shoulder. He himself was obliged to use a double-barrelled pistol twice.[65]

The enhanced ammunition supply, however, may have contributed to the rapidity with which *Albion* then pounded her opponent into a hulk.

Weapons and equipment of early Marines made few concessions to their operational environment. The fuzils, or flintlock muskets, issued to the Admiral's Regiment in 1664, were a rare example of specialized equipment, whose value at sea had been recognised in the 1620s, 'For these may safely be laid down in any place upon any occasion, and as readily taken up.'[66] Replacement weapons delivered to Sir Charles Littleton in 1670, however, included 80 pikes, 34 muskets, and only 6 firelocks, suggesting his men used whatever arms were available. Later there would be little to choose between Marine and other muskets, except that the 1740 Sea Service pattern was shorter and lighter than its military equivalent.

Flintlocks became standard issue to all infantrymen during Queen Anne's reign, not always of best quality:

> The musquetts which belong to the 28 Marines we have on board being very defective and most of them unserviceable, and the officer who commands them having made several applications to his proper officers to have them exchanged without any answer, I desire they may be ordered to do it, otherwise those men designed for small shot will be in some manner useless.[67]

Matters had not improved by the 1740s, muskets issued to Duncombe's Marines 'being subject to split in the common exercise. . . the bores of the pieces being too small for the balls'. The Admiralty complained that 'many of His Majesty's ships are ill assisted by the Marines, who can contribute but little with bad arms to the defence of the said ships', and asked the Ordnance Board to exchange the firelocks of all four newly raised Marine regiments.[68] The soft hammers of Marine muskets were sufficiently notorious for manuals of the 1760s to suggest having them steeled while in harbour, to produce a better shower of sparks when struck by the flint. Half a century later, and well into the Industrial Revolution, HMS *Swiftsure*'s Captain of Marines had to give orders 'for shortening the shoulders of the flints, to try if by giving the flint greater impulse against the hammer, ignition may be more readily communicated.'[69]

Other shoddy material supplied to Marines included fragile wooden rammers. These frequently broke, their brass heads flying off, 'enough to disconcert the best Battalion of Infantry that ever went into the Field'. Undersized cartouche boxes that held a derisory nine rounds were 'almost intollerable on Shore Service, for which reason *none of the Land Forces make use of them*'.[70] Lieutenant John MacIntire devised canvas pouches for shipboard use, holding 'more Cartridges than a Man will have Occasion for in any Engagement'.[71] Waterproofed with black paint, they hung over the left Shoulder, with a flap over their mouth, to keep sparks out of the ammunition. Similar bags were issued to Marines during the Belle Isle landings of 1761, 'as their Cartouch boxes do not contain sufficient ammunition'.[72]

Wear and tear at sea had always reduced serviceability of Marine equipment. Charles II recognized that the Admiral's Regiment's maritime duties 'make it specially difficult to keep their arms in good order'.[73] The Admiralty addressed the problem in the 1740s, issuing instructions 'for Chests to be made to contain the Arms and Ammunition of the Marines serving on board each man of war, and a storeroom to be built on the Orlop to contain the spare Cloathing, accoutrements, etc.'[74] Admiral Matthews stood on such a chest at the Battle of Toulon, 'making use of his Spy Glass as cooly as a Bear in a Playhouse even while a double headed shot carry'd away the place he leaned on.'[75] Lashed to the grating abaft the mizzenmast, arms chests kept a detachment's arms in good order and supplied ammunition in action. For safety, one chest held cartridges and another the muskets, put away with fixed bayonets, 'the Inside of the Lock oiled, the Cock and Flint screwed fast. . . the Rammer fitted tight, so as not to fall out'. Officers were to ensure cartridges were, 'put into the Boxes, with Tops downwards, so that the Sparks that drop from the Flint may fall upon the Ball, and not upon the Powder'. Great care was required to prevent loose powder spilling on the deck, and cartridge boxes had to be 'fixed in such a Manner, that they cannot overset'.[76] Such precautions were necessary. A chest containing 900 cartridges exploded on HMS *Rippon*'s poop at Guadeloupe in 1762, setting fire to the ship, as did a cask of musket cartridges in *Chesapeake*'s ammunition chest, at the critical moment of her action with HMS *Shannon*. Low serviceability seems to have remained a problem, despite the assignment of armourers' mates to HM ships, 'in order that the Marine arms as well as all other arms on board the Ship, may be kept in constant good condition.' Almost a third of of HMS *Blenheim*'s Marine muskets in 1796 were out of service, their stocks broken or parts missing.[77]

Early Marines learned their business on board ship, as lack of military preparation in the 1740s and 1750s left no time for training ashore. Two years into the War of Jenkins' Ear, sixty Marines hastily embarked in HMS *Rupert*: 'the greater part of them had never been once exercised, as they were inlisted the very night before they were sent on board.'[78] The Grand Divisions made no immediate difference, O'Loghlen served in two line-of-Battle ships during the Seven Years War, and was grateful he met 'no Enemy of Force either Cruize':

> in the first. . . we embarked Ninety-two raw Recruits, who never burned a Grain of Powder before they came on board; in the second, we got Seventy-six, who came from *Ireland* but a few Days before, and were still more aukward, if possible.[79]

Ship's detachments faced the prospect of action whenever they left harbour, and were 'obliged to pay no regard to the usual Method of Drilling Recruits, but begin with the Practical Part of Discipline. . . without entering into the minute Points of Exercise'. Marine officers concentrated on essentials:

- Load and Fire, with fixed bayonets;
- Charge and Halt;
- Disperse and Reform;
- Recover arms, Unfix bayonets, and Dismiss.

When perfect in the Motions, recruits practised loading and firing ball against a mark, 'hung for the Purpose at the Extremity of the Fore-Yard Arm'. There was little scope for 'Complication of Manoeuvres, and Evolutions, which would be ridiculous in an Officer to attempt at sea.'[80] O'Loghlen thought shipboard training should be restricted to the Firings, as: 'It can answer no Purpose whatsoever to puzzle Men with Impracticabilities.' Officers struggled to keep their men up to the mark in cramped shipboard conditions: 'Marines should be exercised often, to keep them in Practice, that they may not forget the Whole of what they have been taught on Shore.'[81] The weather was a major constraint, although John Howe's Captain drilled his crew through a North American winter: 'Proved Cold and seveare. Nevertheless we exercised Great Guns and Small Arms twice every Day Sundays excepted.'[82] Marines spent much time working about the ship, so officers had to use what free moments were available, always keeping some arms ready upon deck in good weather, to exercise the recruits of the watch.[83]

In the absence of formal physical training, drill and sham fights provided valuable exercise, 'of great service to Young Soldiers, as it warms their Blood, and rouses them to Ardour and Intrepidity'. Bayonets were best unfixed, 'especially when young Soldiers are roused by the Noise of Drums, and the Idea of their being opposed.'[84] A boatswain's mate from HMS *Minden* almost drowned after the over-enthusiastic repulse of imaginary boarders. Another training session nearly caused general disaster:

> Exercised the party in the manual and platoon, fired three volleys of blank cartridge. Fired also by divisions. Fired ball at a target suspended from fore topsail yard. Well hit by men. At 11 a.m. ceased firing. In a few minutes after the ship was discovered to be on fire on the booms. Supposed to have arisen from the wadding of one of the pieces having combusted with some hay in a boat for the stock.

Fortunately the officer of the watch promptly hauled the mainsail out of the flames, so the only casualties were the wardroom cow, and a sailor's traps thrown overboard in the panic. *Minden*'s Captain took training seriously, for three days later he exercised the crew again, the Marines firing three rounds of ball without further accident, 'The Captain much pleased by their firing so well.'[85] Other naval officers showed less care for the good of the service. The subversive *Symptoms of Advice to the Oxxxxxxs of an Amphibious Corps* (dedicated 'without permission' to the First Lord) alleged one Captain, 'ordered the Marines to be exercised to leeward on the forecastle, with their faces towards the galley; so that they were compelled to go through the motions with their eyes shut, to prevent being blinded for ever.'[86]

The Shock of Battle

Drilling downwind of the crew's dinners was a minor unpleasantness compared with going into action. Fleet actions generated dense clouds of powder smoke, spreading miles downwind. The Battle of Sole Bay, where the Admiral's Regiment earned the title of Marines, plunged Harwich into premature darkness: 'they believed that never were so many guns fired in one day before. What was strange to me, the smoke, in a vast cloud, darkened us like a fog about seven in the evening.'[87] John Howe was deafened and blinded by his own ship's guns: 'a Whole broad Side which quite Deprived me of my hearing and the Smoke almost rendered my sight useless.'[88] HMS *Victory*'s lower decks at Trafalgar evoked comparisons with the abode of Old Nick:

> A man should witness a battle in a three decker from the middle deck for it beggars all description it bewilders the senses of sight and hearing, there was the fire from above, the fire from below besides the fire from the deck I was upon the Guns recoiling with violence, reports louder than thunder the decks heaving. I fancied myself in the infernal regions where every man appeared a devil. Lips might move but orders and hearing were out of the question.[89]

Meanwhile the hail of shot across the decks reduced them to a state that witnesses regularly describe as a slaughterhouse, wallowing in blood. Bodies were routinely mutilated beyond recognition, such as this Royal Marine Artillery officer, killed aiming one of the first shells of the bombardment of Algiers (27 Aug 1816):

> I never could imagine what sort of missile it was that ended his mortal career. He was cut in three pieces. One leg went forward on the gangway, and the other, and part of his body remained nearly where he had been standing; and his upper works went overboard – certainly on that day the Algerines threw about some queer articles.[90]

Crowbars and glass bottles might be expected from such people, but the French had a taste for unconventional projectiles, known as 'langridge', to the inconsistent fury of British Captains accustomed to double load guns with case and round-shot:

> No rascally Picaroon, or Pirate, could have fired worse Stuff into Us than they did, such as square bits of Iron, old Rusty Nails, and in short, everything which could tend to the Destruction of men.[91]

It was enough to try the resolution of veterans, let alone the raw recruits hurried off to face the enemy at Quiberon Bay:

> A draught of 30 Marines taken in about a month ago, and who very lately came from Ireland behaved with uncommon Bravery and resolution in such a scene of horror, for so it must appear to them who never saw a gun fired before.[92]

Not everyone passed the ordeal. Captain Henry Ruffane and a corporal of Frazer's Marines were condemned to death for their part in HMS *Lyon*'s interception of the *Elisabeth*, en route to Scotland with supplies for the

Jacobite Rebellion of 1745. The engagement lasted five hours within pistol shot, and 'was remarkably bloody and obstinate':

> Thirteen cannon shot entered upon the quarterdeck, betwixt the mizenmast and bulkhead, besides grape and musket shot, and everyone quartered at those guns were killed, except two men and a boy. The Captain was wounded in the left arm at the first broadside, and soon after in the left foot, and was knocked down several times with splinters, so that he was black and blue all over, yet he moved up and down the deck all the time. . . covered with blood and brains. He called upon his Captain of Marines several times, but he could not be found; at last he was discovered by the Chaplain between two trusses of hay, but refusing to fight. The Chaplain took his arms from him, and headed the Marines himself till he fell bravely fighting.[93]

The crew showed what they thought afterwards, making Ruffane 'walk the main deck with one of his own soldiers behind with a broad sword, uttering among other taunting expressions, Here is the fellow that would not fight.'[94]

Captain Wemyss, of HMS *Bellerophon* at Trafalgar, stood at the other end of the scale. He received eight musket balls in his body and had his right arm shot off before going below. 'Tis only a scratch,' he said to the First Lieutenant, 'and I shall have to apologise to you bye and bye for quitting the deck on so trivial an occasion.'[95] Officers were expected 'to shew a good Example and appear cheerful, it being remarked that the private Soldiers, when they go into Action, form their Notions of the Danger, from the outward Appearance of their Officers'. Recommended leadership styles are at odds with the usual draconian image of eighteenth-century military discipline. Officers were not to abuse the men:

> but encourage them by Fair Means, teach them to despise Danger; and in delivering their Orders. . . address themselves to the Soldiers in a manly affectionate Manner. When the Soldiers have a good Opinion of the military Capacity of their Officers, they will always acquit themselves with Honour.[96]

Marines' exposed stations on the ship's superstructure entailed heavy losses. Thomas Mitchell's 116 men of the Earl of Pembroke's 2nd Marines first saw action in the Anglo-Dutch defeat off Beachy Head in 1690. They lost 68 muskets and 114 bayonets implying between 57 per cent and 98 per cent casualties. HMS *Flora* (42) lost all her Marines killed or wounded in her desperate engagement with *Nymphe* (36) in 1780, except for Lieutenant Busigny and his servant. Busigny himself fell at Trafalgar twenty-five years later, in HMS *Temeraire* (98). HMS *Amelia* must have lost at least half her detachment in her unequal action against *L'Arethuse*: 8 killed and 26 wounded, including one of her Lieutenants RM.[97] Marine sergeants were 'always to keep two Ranks constantly compleat, by filling up immediately the Vacancies made by the dead and wounded', but it is hard to see how they can have done so faced with such casualty rates.[98]

Naval surgeons first received instructions to care for sick or injured Marines in 1694. The fate of soldiers wounded in action at sea, before then, is not clear. A surgeon's commission was issued for the Admiral's, as for other Regiments of Foot, but there is no evidence that he accompanied the troops to sea. The fate of Captain Roger Vaughan at Sole Bay was uniquely horrible. Severely wounded, 'which the confusion during the battle would not give them leave to inquire into', he was placed in the *Katherine*'s hold, while she was first taken by the Dutch, then recaptured:

> They had some hogs aboard, which the sailor, under whose care they were, neglected to feed; these hogs, hungry as they were, found out and fell upon the wounded person, and between dead and alive, eat him up to his very skull, which after the fight was over . . . was all that could be found of him.[99]

The massive iron projectiles used by naval guns inflicted terrible wounds leaving little alternative to amputation of injured limbs. Several Irish recruits at Quiberon lost a leg or an arm to the 2-feet-long bars of iron fired by the French. Perhaps, in the absence of effective anaesthetics, shock reduced the pain for hopeless cases such as Captain Wilson of the *Leander*, who lost both legs to an Algerian double-headed shot. Between amputations he spoke calmly with his Sergeant, who had lost an arm: 'Ah, Brabazon, are you here? I am sorry to see you thus. There is glorious work above – we are not unavenged', remaining in high spirits until shortly before he died. At Navarino one of HMS *Genoa*'s detachment had an arm shot off, which he coolly placed along the shelf-piece above the gun-port saying, 'There's an example to you all!'[100] The Chaplain of HMS *Venerable*, flagship at Admiral Duncan's victory off Camperdown (1797), alternately acted 'as Sailor, Chaplain, and Surgeon's Assistant, when the battle might too truly be said to bleed in every vein':

> A marine of the name of Covey was brought down to the surgery, deprived of both his legs; and it was necessary, some hours after, to amputate still higher. 'I suppose', says Covey, 'those d—d scissors will finish the business

of the bullet, master Mate?' – 'Indeed, my brave fellow', cried the Surgeon, 'there is some fear of it' – 'Well never mind', cried Covey, 'I've lost my legs, to be sure, and mayhap may lose my life; but we beat the Dutch! D— n me, we have beat the Dutch! This blessed day my legs have been shot off, so I'll have another cheer for it – huzza! huzza!'

Covey was credited with an awful reputation for swearing, though his language seems mild enough in the circumstances. He lived on until 1806 as cook in a ship in ordinary at Portsmouth Harbour, his last recorded words being, 'Hallelujah! Hallelujah!'

CHAPTER FOUR

Raids and Expeditions

THE strategic value of European navies in the eighteenth-century arose as much from their ability to influence events ashore as from their purely maritime skills. The veteran Thomas Hoole served eighteen years during the wars of William III and Queen Anne, a thoroughly amphibious experience:

> At yᵉ taiking of all yᵉ towns in Spain by sea this last Warr as Gibralter Alegent Calary Portemahon St Philipps Casstall & Majorca Minorka & Basselona & other places of smaller a Count And in yᵉ Raigne of King Willᵐ being with Corrˡˡ Gibbson at the taiking of Sᵗᵗ Johns in Newfoundland and Taking Pettyvovas in the West Indies and in yᵉ peace Along with Sʳ Wiˡˡm Norriss Ambusedor to yᵉ great Magull & with a pardon to yᵉ piratts att Madagasker[1]

Amphibious operations were an essential expression of naval power. Continental strategists raided hostile coasts to pre-empt invasion, or divert resources that might be used against Britain's allies. Blue water enthusiasts chased after sugar islands, or trading posts in India and Canada.

Marines were part of this amphibious capability, although they were rarely the largest body of troops engaged, and were frequently given the least glamorous role. They were present on every eighteenth-century landing beach, whether as a formal battalion, a tactical umbrella for a watering party, or a beach party unloading stores. Amphibious operations allowed Marines to appear on a wider stage, outside the tutelage of a jealous Navy. Ashore they formed larger, more visible units, led by field officers usually denied command in the interests of absolute naval control of operations at sea. Amphibious operations gave Marines their first opportunities to distinguish themselves, gaining their symbolic battle honour at Gibraltar, and the laurel wreath that still adorns their badges and colours at Belle Isle in 1761. They suffered their worst trial during the amphibious assault on Spain's West Indian possessions in the 1740s, when 10,000 Marines died of disease, the Corps' highest casualties in any single campaign. From such fiascos emerged a coherent British approach to amphibious operations, with specialized equipment, standard operating procedures, and a recognized place for Marines.

Viva Marines!

The hired detractor of King William's Marines made out they had only once been employed on land service during the entire Nine Years War. He could perpetrate such falsehoods, as contemporary reports rarely distinguished between seamen and Marines landed together, as what would later be termed a Naval Brigade. Sea officers compounded the confusion by holding parallel commissions in Marine regiments, as did Captain Keigwin, killed at St Christopher's in 1690 leading a so-called Marine regiment of 230 seamen.[2]

The distribution of Marines among ships of the Royal Navy makes it certain that they took part in conjunct expeditions during the 1690s. Marines joined the Siege of Cork in 1689 by Admiralty warrant. Three boatloads of assault troops, who silenced a battery near the harbour entrance, appear likely to have been Marines: 'Stout fellows who, by thick firing, obliged the enemy to quit their guns.' Others worked alongside the seamen, 'employed to draw the cannon along, & to mount them before the town, which they did with great cheerfulness and bravery.'[3] Both Marine regiments contributed 100 men to an expedition against Placentia under Sir Francis Wheeler in 1692, that showed the importance of good intelligence in combined operations, for they 'found the Enemy much stronger there than he expected. . . with at least 2,000 Soldiers and Inhabitants, well disciplined, and most of them old Buccaneers'. Thomas Hoole took part in the 'Destruction of that Nest of Pirates, Petit-Goave' (27 June 1697), acclaimed by a neutral analyst as 'one of the greatest Services done during the War', except that 'the Seamen, and at last (through their example) the Landsmen, began to plunder and drink so hard, that when the Rear-Admiral altered his Sentiments, and resolved to burn it, there were not above fifty sober Men under his Command.'[4]

Two Marine battalions and ten Regiments of Foot attacked Camaret Bay in June 1694, an example of how not to conduct an amphibious assault. John Churchill, Duke of Marlborough, betrayed the plans, to keep in with his old colonel-in-chief, the exiled James II, destroying the vital element of surprise. Marshal Vauban, foremost engineer of the age, fortified the landing beaches with mortars and trenches, occupied by regular troops outnumbering the attackers. The expedition dithered off the Breton coast, while the French 'alarmed the country by firing many guns, and making great fires at night'. An inshore squadron under the Marquis of Carmarthen tried to clear the landing beach with naval gunfire, but suffered heavily. One mortar bomb burst over the flagship: 'a great piece of it striking through the Poop, and two Decks more, flew out again into the Water, near one of the Stern Ports, and killed two of the Marquis's Marine Company and wounded a third, who stood close by him on the Poop.'[5] The 'Well boats' used as landing craft ran aground in waist-deep water, while the 'sudden and prodigious appearance' of the French defences, 'made our men not very forward to land'. A few hundred got ashore, along with General Talmash, who was shot 'about the middle of the thigh with a poisoned shot'. His staff paid a boat crew £5 to take him off, and 'by the time they were six or eight boat lengths from the shore the horse came down and cut off all that were left.'[6]

Amphibious operations are uniquely difficult. Subject to all the usual friction that affects military operations, they present additional problems, patrticularly 'the Uncertainty of Winds and Tides, not always adapted to Man's Occasions'.[7] Long voyages wear out men and ships, reducing numbers and fitness. Against the transient advantage of surprise, the attacker must set greater difficulties of intelligence gathering, while troops rarely arrive on the beach in the good order conducive to tactical success. Away from the beach amphibious forces lack transport and mobile troops, whether horsed cavalry or tanks, and have limited artillery support.

A council of war before Placentia in 1703 enumerated most of the difficulties that could scupper an eighteenth-century amphibious operation:

1) Ill state of [the] ships
2) Ill state of [the] seamen who can scarcely [work the] ships with the help of the soldiers now aboard
3) Ill state of the provisions
4) Difficulties which arise by the winter fast approaching
5) Condition of Placentia
6) Weak condition of the Regiments
7) The Enemy appears not inferior to these Forces in number – stores wanted to get guns up to the battery

Lastly that the season of the year wch falls out contrary to expectation is the unfittest for such attempts and the French at the same time being at their full strength.[8]

Placentia was last resort for squadrons worn out attacking fever-ridden islands in the West Indies, and anxious to return home before autumn gales overpowered crews too feeble to navigate their rotten ships. It was not the only location to witness amphibious setbacks for English forces. HMS *Lowestoft* and *Deptford* abandoned a night attack, with a company of Seymour's Marines, on the French slaving post of Goree in 1703, in face of bad weather, inadequate lift and loss of surprise: 'proving a fresh gale and a sea, the boats not being able to carry all the men ashore at once the islands being alarmed and firing several shot.'[9]

In the less hostile Mediterranean, Queen Anne's Marine forces played a variety of roles familiar to later generations of Marines. When fleets replenished their water supply ashore, Marines protected unarmed seamen against attack and shot at would-be deserters. The smooth handling of such an operation at Althea (31 Aug 1703) suggests considerable expertise:

> the *Flamborough* was sent close to the shore to cover the descent of their Regiments of Marines, who landed without any manner of confusion, and were actually drawn up in Battalia on the shore, before half the Fleet was come to an anchor. Brigdr-Genl. Seymour landed with the 1st Detachment, and gave such orders that a more orderly descent could not have been made in an enemy's country.[10]

A surviving example of such orders shows how a formed body of men might land with operable weapons and dry ammunition:

1. That all officers on board take care to look over their men's arms every day and see that they be well fixed and have good flints.
2. That before they land they take care to have six cartridges fixed in their hats and to tie their cartridge boxes and pouches about their necks so as to keep them dry.
3. That when they land no officer or soldier shall stir out of the ranks on any pretence whatsoever on pain of death which shall be immediately executed upon them.[11]

The victorious garrison of Gibraltar, including the Marines, took ship on 4 August 1705 for Barcelona, arriving 600 miles away less than three weeks later, moving four times faster than land forces. The officers 'unanimously declared the taking of Barcelona to be impracticable considering the small number of our forces and the strength of the garrison',[12] but the Earl of Peterborough, the Allied task force commander, was of another mind. In September, after deceiving both sides with false orders to break up the siege, he launched a surprise attack on Fort Montjuich, west of the city:

> executed on the 14th with great bravery and success in taking all the outworks and the Castle had been delivered by the Spanish within it if the Marquis de Risburgh had not gott in from the town with French soldiers.

The Prince of Hesse, who had played so important a part in the defence of Gibraltar was shot in the thigh, and 'having no surgeon at hand to stop the great flux of blood he unfortunately dyed in less than three hours.' While Hesse lay in state, with Wig and Hat, an Allied shell burst in the fort's magazine, 'blowed up a great part of the wall and buryed the Governor in the ruins.' Bor's Marines stormed the breach 'with such Bravery that they entered the very first assault upon which the garrison (consisting of 400 men) surrendered at discretion.'[13] Barcelona itself surrendered on 3 October 1705, after a five-day bombardment by guns landed from the fleet.

The fall of Barcelona provided a firm base for amphibious operations against the Spanish coast. English and Dutch Marines landed at Cartagena (July 1706), 'to give encouragement to the inhabitants to declare for King Charles III'. The Admiral recognized the vulnerability of raiding forces, particularly when re-embarking:

> in case you do not find the inhabitants inclinable to declare for His Royal Highness, and that it may be hazardous to force them to their obedience, you are then to return with the forces to the fleet taking particular care to avoid any ambush that may be laid.[14]

Alicante required a combined land and sea attack (July/August 1706). Warships brought up additional Marines, silenced defending artillery and breached the seaward defences. Seamen assaulted the breaches in boats, while Marines fought their way through the suburbs, 'notwithstanding the Spaniards had a continued Communication from one House to another, and fired upon our Men from the Windows and Holes made for that purpose.'[15] Alicante's surrender reduced all Aragon to the obedience of Charles III, the Allies' claimant to the Spanish throne, and when Marine garrisons withdrew from other Spanish towns, those at Alicante remained.

Exploitation into the Spanish hinterland was not an amphibious role, but shortage of manpower drew Wills' and Bor's Regiments inland. A third of the 1,500 Allied troops at the Battle of San Estevan (15/26 Jan 1707) were Marines. Both sides fought muzzle to muzzle, Major Burston of Bor's Marines receiving four bayonet wounds in the body. Outnumbered three to one, the Marines imposed upon the French by beating the Grenadiers' March, being mistaken in their mitre caps for the Grenadiers of half a dozen regiments somewhere in the background. The two Marine regiments escaped lightly from the disastrous Battle of Almanza (14/25 April 1707) where half the Earl of Galway's infantry were captured, losing one officer each taken prisoner. Wills' subsequent defence of Lerida 'so weakened and soyl'd the Enemy's Army. . . as rendered them incapable of further Action that Season, about 1200 Marines making the better Half of that Garrison, which Marines at the Capitulation were reduced to scarce Four Hundred Men.'[16]

Spain was a poor country, lacking transport and medical facilities. Regiments incurred considerable expenditure, fending for themselves, as shown by a petition, 'setting forth the great expense of the several Officers of Marines who served in Spain in 1705 and 1706 in buying and main-taining mules both for themselves and the baggage of the troops under them'. General Wills paid hospital expenses, presumably because the British Government did not. Conditions at Denia, Alicante and Catalonia, all Marine stations, were so bad that medical staff risked infection from their patients:

> For want of medicines and necessaries the sick can get no relief and the wounded cannot be dressed: and for want of sheets, blankets, and other things (which cannot be purchased for money in that country) the poor men cannot be kept clean or warm, which creates so nauseous a smell and leaves them exposed to the cruelties of the weather that the consequences are most infectious and render the sick and wounded irrecoverable.[17]

Not all the patients died. Major Burston survived his wounds to inquire into HMS *Devonshire*'s missing Marines. Galway requested assistance for a Captain, who:

> had the misfortune to have his leg broke at the attack of the breach of Valenca [*sic*] where he commanded a party of Grenadiers and did very good service, he has suffered much and cannot perfect his cure without going to the bath.[18]

Marines, being part of the Navy, may have suffered particular neglect.

The Board of Ordnance refused tents for Churchill's Marines, asserting: 'this Office never did furnish the Marines with Tents, nor have we any Money given us by Parliament for that Service.' At length the Colonel bought tents out of his own pocket, 'the same to be stopt out of the men's growing pay.'[19]

While Major-General Wills and Brigadier Bor found promotion in the mountains of Catalonia, other Marines saw more strategic employment against Sardinia and Minorca. The latter was strictly Spanish, but the English commander thought Port Mahon too useful to hand over to Charles III:

> For this reason I will leave an English Garrison here, and hope I have so disposed it as not to give any jealousy or uneasiness to the King of Spain for Troops being mightily wanted I shall make rather a merit to myself by carrying back thither all I brought out and borrow Marines of the Ships to leave here.[20]

The low political profile of Marines, easier to commit or withdraw than land forces, made their presence more acceptable. Allied successes in the Mediterranean showed the potential of cooperation between Army, Navy and Marines against isolated targets on remote coastlines. The age of prejudice, however, was sadly unmindful of the *Flying Post* enjoinder not to 'forget over the Bottle the usual toast in Catalonia, "Viva Marines!"'[21]

Darkest Hour

The Treaty of Utrecht that ended the War of the Spanish Succession promised Britain a share in trade with Spain's South American colonies. This proved less lucrative than expected, Spanish obstruction culminating in the incident of Captain Jenkins' ear. Public indignation dramatically reversed government policy on Marine forces, after twenty-five years without them. Six new Marine regiments set off for the West Indies as part of the 'most formidable Fleet and Army that ever visited those shores', in hopes of intercepting the annual treasure fleet, and forcing Spain to submit.[22] The operation was the largest commitment of Marines to a single operation before the First World War, but nine-tenths of the troops died, having failed in all their objectives. Inter-service relations fell to an all-time low.

The expedition began badly. The Government's opponents claimed an unwilling Cabinet 'intended only to amuse the Nation with the Appearance of an Expedition, without any design of weakening our Enemies'. The new regiments were 'a dangerous Tendency to the Constitution of this Kingdom', and a political job 'to get more places for some Members of Parliament'.[23] Bad weather and manning problems caused repeated delays. Troop transports sat off Portsmouth for weeks, denied fresh food and contracting scurvy without ever losing sight of home. The fleet of 170 sail left Portsmouth on 26 October 1740, convoyed by twenty-seven ships of the line, besides frigates, fireships, bomb ketches and hospital ships. Store ships carried 'all sorts of Warlike Implements and every kind of Convenience',[24] although the entrenching tools proved fragile and grenade cases were too thick to burst. Before the expedition reached Jamaica (9 January 1741) its naval commander reported, 'The Fleet in general has been very sickly, and particularly the Marines and soldiers on board the men-of-war of whom many are dead.' Six hundred had died by January 1741, including Lord Cathcart, the military Commander-in-Chief, 'dyed the 20th instant of a Bloody Flux'.[25] Cathcart's replacement, General Wentworth was not the man to deal with Admiral Vernon, the overbearing naval Commander-in-Chief in the West Indies.

Ostensibly the force numbered 15,000 seamen and 12,000 soldiers: two battalions of Foot (15th and 24th), six of English Marines, and four from the North American colonies, known as Gooch's Marines, and a labour corps of black Jamaicans. The Americans were meant to survive the Caribbean climate better than Europeans, but did not. Their discipline was poor, 'for what they call their Serg[ts] and Corporals are as ignorant as their Men', while the Government omitted to pay, victual, or clothe them, giving them, 'nothing but their coats to cover them'.[26]

Delays at Spithead had left the narrowest window for action before April's rain made operations impossible. Vernon did not leave Port Royal until the end of January, only reaching Cartagena, the Spanish landfall in South America, on 5 March. His objective was heavily fortified, the garrison reinforced by ships of the line. Swamps, shoals and low sandy islands limited approaches to the Boca Chica passage, covered by outworks on both sides, and several warships. Beyond Boca Chica lay the shallow harbour of Cartagena, separated from the city by a peninsula on which stood the heavily gunned Castillo Grande. On the landward side, if such a term applies to so watery a location, stood Fort San Lazar. Cartagena's most dangerous defenders were the yellow-fever mosquitoes of the surrounding marshes. Even today, with specialized equipment and tropical medicine, an amphibious operation against Cartagena would be complex. In the 1740s it was a nightmare.

The task force began by landing a combined Grenadier battalion on the island of Tierra Bomba, behind Fort San Luis, overlooking the Boca Chica passage; the remainder of their regiments joined them next day, with naval carpenters to cut a path through the woods to the planned site of a Grand Battery. The Marines camped near the beach, overs from the fort knocking a good many on the head. The novelist Tobias Smollett, a naval surgeon at Cartagena, suggested it was done 'with a view of accustoming the soldiers to stand fire, who were not as yet much used to discipline, most of them having been taken from the plough tail a few months before'.[27] In the stupefying heat Europeans, debilitated by dysentery and scurvy, were unable to support the least fatigue, while the black labourers downed tools whenever a shot came near them. The battery was ready on 16 March, a week after landing, which does not seem long to emplace twenty 24-pounders, on immobile naval gun trucks, except that so much time had been wasted already.

For the first time we are able to follow a land action from the words of a Marine officer, Lieutenant Colonel Macleod of Moreton's, a brave old veteran of Marlborough's campaigns, who described operations in a letter to his wife. A three-day bombardment breached the 40-foot walls of the fort, and Macleod received orders to parade the Grenadiers preparatory to storming. He left his keys and pocket book with a friend and marched off, preceded by a forlorn hope of twelve men and a sergeant, who was promised a commission if he behaved well:

> The Dons being at Dinner did not shew themselves 'till my Vanguard was within 200 paces of the Breach; and then I ordered my Men to close up, and marched directly towards it without any Confusion; though indeed we expected to be cut to Pieces by the Fire of four large Ships that could all point their Cannon upon us, as well as by the Fire of the Fort, on the Wall whereof there appeared to be more Men than I had with me: However, as soon as my Forlorn Hope began to mount the Breach, the Spaniards struck their Colours and began to retire.

This was just as well as the breach only admitted one man at a time, and the first ladder collapsed under the weight of men. Macleod systematically secured the batteries, until he found his men:

> had got to some Spanish Wine, and were drinking very hard; upon which I made one among them, and stav'd all I could meet with, set my Guards, and placed Centinels over all the Magazines. And thus ended an Affair which every Body thought would have cost much more Blood, and many Lives.[28]

The Spaniards, 'in a sort of Despondency', sank the rest of their ships in the mouth of the inner harbour, while the Navy felt their way across the uncharted shallows outside. Critics make much of Wentworth's methodical caution, but Vernon took ten days to bring up ships for a landing inside the harbour. Vernon deprecated likely resistance, telling Wentworth, 'We think if you push with vigour, you cannot fail of success', and urged him to land with only 1,400 out of the 4,500 infantry available.[29] Wentworth landed a mile from Cartagena on 5th April. Spanish infantry disputed the path through the woods, but cleared out when the British began their 'street-firing', a complex drill that suggests nothing much was wrong with the troops' training. Wentworth pressed on towards Cartagena, but stopped before Fort San Lazar. His 1,400 men, without ladders, artillery or grenades, were insufficient to bounce the Spaniards off a 70-foot hill topped by 25-foot walls behind a wet ditch. The follow-up waves did not get ashore until next day, when the opportunity had gone. The troops slept in the open for want of tents and were soon too sickly to clear a camping ground, let alone construct siege works. The impossibility of commencing a formal siege before the rains persuaded Wentworth to launch a night attack, a hazardous job even for fit and well-trained troops.

Five hundred Grenadiers led the way, supported by two bodies of 500 Marines, and some Americans carrying woolpacks, ladders and bags of grenades. They lost their way in the dark, and were caught in a cross-fire:

> But the bravery of our Soldiers surpass'd all Credibility, who leaping into the Lines among the thickest of their Enemies, put them to flight in the greatest Consternation. They then retreated over the Drawbridge into the Fort, whence the Shot was poured down incessantly upon us without having it in our Power to hurt any of them, and still advancing forward in the Breast-works towards the Walls of the Fort, in hopes to find an Opportunity of scaling them in a proper Place, we were at last all penn'd up together, at an end of the Lines, and could neither advance, retreat, nor meet with our Ladders for scaling.[30]

There they stood, 'as Butts to the Spaniards', for the Americans, 'finding they were knocked down without any Arms to defend themselves', had thrown down their ladders to take cover:

> Three only were brought up to the Trenches, upon which about ten of our Grenadiers and a Serjeant mounted the Walls of the Fort; but being unsupported, were immediately cut to Pieces, except the Serjeant who saved himself by jumping down.

The attackers withdrew at daylight, having suffered over 600 casualties, a third of their number. Graves were now a more pressing consideration than trenches. The men had been exposed to malarial infection for over a month, and were 'so far from being in a condition to offend the Enemy, that they had scarcely Duty-Men sufficient for the ordinary Guards of the Camp, and many of them in a very languishing Condition'. Violent rain rendered life under canvas impossible, although drinking water was scarce, 'the Cisterns from which the Camp had been supplied, being near exhausted'.[31] Only 3,569 men re-embarked on 16 April, after getting away their guns and stores. Wolfe's Marines were down to 96 men fit for duty, out of 1,000.

The withdrawal brought tension between Navy and Army to a head. Vernon took the credit for the opening moves, 'entirely began, carried on and concluded by his Sea Engineers. . . and the indefatigable industry of the Seamen without any Aid or Assistance from any one of the Train', alleging 'it was done with the more Expedition, because they had nothing to do with it.' The Army believed the Navy had deliberately starved them of water, provisions and reinforcements, although the fleet had fresh supplies of turtle and beef. At the culminating point of the Army's efforts at San Lazar, the Navy withheld support, although a Spanish officer declared, 'they waited only for the coming in of their Great Ships to have surrendered.' Vernon was evidently sensitive on this point, as he ordered a futile demonstration by *Galicia*, converted into a floating battery. Casks of rammed earth between her gun-ports kept out shot, but increased her draught, preventing her from closing to effective range, although 'but a little to the left, he might have stationed four or five of his largest Ships a-breast, within Pistol-shot of the Walls.'[32]

Violent quarrels among senior officers were not uncommon. The Marquis of Carmarthen had pursued a vendetta with Captain Nash, of his own Regiment, suffering such severe wounds in the ensuing duel that he could not attend to routine business.[33] Disagreements between Hesse and his subordinates at Gibraltar had prevented their pursuing the retreating besiegers. Vernon and Wentworth were exceptional in the volume and bitterness of their expressions of mutual contempt, each proving 'more eager for the disgrace of his Rival, than zealous for the Honour of the Nation'. Vernon stormed out of the final Council of War at Cartagena, contenting himself with off-stage interruptions from the quarter-gallery of his flagship. The concatenation of such personal antipathies with the other difficulties facing the expedition suggest that 'nothing but almost a Miracle could have brought it to any other Conclusion than what it had.'[34]

Vernon was 'heartily sick of a conjunctive expedition with an Army',[35] but like some hateful couple doomed to dance together forever, he and Wentworth set off again from Jamaica in July 1741, for Santiago de Cuba. The 2,684 men available for landing were one-third of their establishment, but there were no replacements: 'those that remain in quarters, are for the most part so distempered that they find difficulty to get a proportion of Marines for a single ship.'[36] The Admiral addressed an 'exhortatory letter to the land officers, earnestly recommending Unanimity as the most certain Means of Success, and cautioning them particularly to avoid splitting on the Rock of Discord',[37] but the mood did not last. Wentworth had to request specific orders compelling naval captains 'to admit [Marine] officers to come on board them in proportion to their number of private men'.[38] Vernon landed the Army 60 miles from their objective, 'the way all covered with thick woods which would render the Attempt upon that Town too hard a Task for so small a Body of Troops'. It is difficult not to sympathize with Wentworth's inquiry, 'whether the Declarations of Gentlemen of Character in matters relating to their own profession, do not deserve at least equal credit with the reports of such as are entirely unacquainted with the land service'.[39] Nicholas, the sober historian of the Corps, suggested the incomprehensible behaviour of the British persuaded Cuba's inhabitants that the landing lacked hostile intent, and joked grimly that disease had so reduced British numbers before they departed in November 1741, 'that probably in another month there would scarcely have been anyone left to bring home an account of this disastrous expedition'. Marine officer casualties for 1741 exceeded the six regiments' initial establishment: one General Commanding, 21 field officers, 55 captains, and 130 subalterns or staff officers.[40] Nothing was left of some regiments but their name and the memory of their heroism: 'whenever they are suffered to attack their Enemies they are ready to march forward, even when there is no possibility of returning. . . they are only to be withheld from Conquest by Obstacles which Human Prowess cannot surmount.'[41]

The Dawn of Combined Operations

The formation of a permanent Marines Corps coincided with emergence of a more rational approach to amphibious operations. Thomas Molyneux's 1759 book on *Conjunct Expeditions* is the first systematic treatment of the subject, introducing the concept of littoral warfare that would take up so much of the time of later Marines. Molyneux analysed sixty-eight amphibious operations from Queen Elizabeth's reign to the middle of the Seven Years War. Less than half succeeded, and only a quarter of Great Armaments like Cartagena. He attributed this to the unique difficulties of amphibious operations, and what would now be described as inappropriate doctrine: 'an Insufficiency, and a not right Understanding of this Amphibious Kind of Warfare'.[42]

The author of the 1690 'Memorandum in favour of raising two marine regiments' had foreseen the need for senior Marine officers:

> to the end there may be a sufficient number of men of experience and reputation to carry on and manage any enterprise for the nation's service, in case of a descent on land.[43]

Marine regiments, hastily formed, and often disbanded, could not provide such expertise. Critics of Marine regiments in the 1740s denied them any amphibious role at all: 'When sieges are to be formed, or battles fought, there are always a proper body of Land Forces put on board who go upon these services, but the duty of Marines, properly speaking, is confined to shipboard.'[44] Commanders of naval task forces resisted attempts to give active commands to senior Marine officers. Colonel Rycaut 'expressly named by the King for this service', accompanied 800 Marines to the Leeward Islands in 1759, 'but upon the arrival of the squadron at Barbadoes, Commodore Moore refused his assent to land them in battalion, and did in effect take away all command from the Lieut-Colonel and Major.'[45]

Denial of Marines' amphibious role coexisted with failure to contemplate the problems of opposed landings, and a bland assumption that any troops could carry them out: 'we may at any time qualify Land Soldiers for such Service, by keeping them only on board until their Sea Sickness be over.'[46] The formality of eighteenth-century infantry tactics presented particular problems to the planners of assault landings. Soldiers armed with single-shot muskets needed to land in a more or less straight line of complete platoons. This appears to have been beyond the comprehension of naval personnel, who muddled them up, or the capabilities of the ships' boats used as landing craft:

> containing various Numbers, drawing several Depths of Water, consequently requiring different Time to gain the same Space; consequently almost sure of not arriving at the destined landing Place together.

The result was 'at our Debarkments, it is true, we Debark an Army, but we never yet debarked Regiments. At the very moment the Army is required to be in Regiments most, it is least.'[47]

Specialized landing craft appeared during the 1750s – flat-bottomed boats built in standard sizes. Troop transports, like modern landing ships, carried a number of these flats on their deck, hoisting them out in response to pre-arranged signals. Each flat took forty to sixty soldiers, drawn from the same formation to ensure troops landed in viable units. Admiral Sir Edward Hawke's orders for an opposed landing at Rochefort directed naval lieutenants responsible for conveying troops to the beach 'to be very careful to range their Boats in Divisions, and in such manner that every Regiment may be all together'.[48] As at Gibraltar, naval gunfire from frigates or 3rd Rates on the flanks of the landing craft would carry the troops onto disputed beaches.

The increasing numbers of Marines made them a regular part of amphibious operations. Appropriately, in view of the Corps' modern role, a Lieutenant of Marines summarized the eighteenth-century approach to such matters.[49] John MacIntire's definition of the tactical remit of Marine raiding parties is timeless, apart from the language:

> to dislodge a small Body of the Enemy, while a Sea Officer is burning some Vessels in a Creek or Harbour; to attack a small Fort on the Land-Side, when a Ship is battering it from the Sea; to secure an advantageous Post, till some Troops, landed in another Place, can take Possession of it; to burn a Village, attack a Battery, nail up the Cannon, carry off some Prisoners, to gain Intelligence from the Enemy, support a body of Troops already landed.

MacIntire emphasized flexibility and speed:

> by Reason of the Variety of Places and Positions, and the unforeseen Circumstances which a Skirmish may produce. The whole depends on seeing favourable Opportunities, and knowing how to benefit by them in a Moment; for an Attack often succeeds, according to the Velocity with which it is made.

He advocated careful preparation before landing, the men drawn up in fighting order on the quarter deck, where: 'They must be told at the same Time, the Nature of the Service they are going upon.' Soldiers cast onto a hostile beach could not be treated like mindless automata. Commanders were to check weapons were in good order:

> the Flints good and well screwed in; the Bayonets fixed properly, and the Rammers well fitted; taking Care that every Soldier carries with him a Screw-driver, a Worm, two good Flints, besides the one in his Piece;

forty Rounds of Ammunition, and a Day's dry Provisions, in Case of Accidents.

Field modifications included leather or cloth covers over priming pans, and equipment buckled over the shoulders, rather than around the waist, to keep it dry. Firelocks were slung getting into the boats, explaining the sugarloaf hats worn by early Marines:

> When the Boats are near the Shore, the men unsling at once, pull off the Lock Cover; and when they leap into the water, must hold their Firelocks high recovered, to preserve their Shot, keeping their Ammunition from the Wet.

Offensive action was essential: 'One invariable Rule is, that in Skirmishes of this Nature, you are to attack the Enemy, and not wait to be attacked; for if you will not act upon the Offensive, you had better stayed on board.' An old Sergeant of Marines recalled similar advice from the Captain of his ship, off Anholt in 1809: 'whatever you do, in God's name, no manoeuvring or soldier's tricks. . . but short and smart work of it. It must be a bold straightforward *coup de main* – all depends on that.'[50] Simplicity was especially important with eighteenth-century Marines, 'who (though as brave as any Men) cannot be expected to act in so regular a Manner as well-disciplined Soldiers on Shore'. Much of MacIntire's advice still makes sense, whether approaching prepared positions from the flank, or securing the exits from a village before entering it, while his views on night attacks could come from a modern manual:

> Without Silence and Resolution, nothing can be done in the Night. If you surprise the Enemy act with Vigour, Half the Battle is over; because they are only putting themselves in a Posture of Defence, when you are actually conquering.[51]

The Marines of the 1760s were no longer hapless victims of circumstance.

The Leeward Islands

The low-key contribution of the Admiralty's new Marine Corps to the capture of Guadeloupe and Martinique from the French in 1759 and 1762 was more indicative of the future than the unwieldy expeditions of 1740–42. Marines provided a small proportion of the troops committed to the Leeward Islands, fighting at sea and ashore. In the earlier operation, after some fumbling around Martinique (15–20 January 1759),

Commodore Moore and General Hopson took Guadeloupe (23 January–25 April). In 1762 Admiral Rodney and Lord Monckton captured Martinique rather more briskly (4 January–12 February). Two Marine officers recorded these operations, from complementary points of view: Captain Richard Gardiner's journal focussed on the amphibious side of the 1759 operations; while Lieutenant Robert Lloyd kept an Order Book, presumably as Adjutant to one of two Marine battalions that supported the Army during the 1762 siege of Port Royal.[52]

Gardiner was Captain of Marines in HMS *Rippon* (60), whose Marines operated as part of their ship's complement, providing shore bombardments and raiding parties. Marines covered the right flank of the main landings, nearest the French at Port Royal. HMS *Rippon* and *Bristol* (50) bombarded Fort Negro, between landing beach and town, and landed all their Marines in the deserted battery. Red-coated sentries on the parapet persuaded the French to withdraw into Port Royal: 'leaving the Beach without Defence, and by these means affording an opportunity for the different Brigades to land without any interruption.'[53] Next day was less successful, showing the limitations of wind and muscle power. The prevailing wind and currents set out of the bay, and stopped ships supporting the Army's advance on Port Royal, while enemy fire made it impossible to land field guns from catamarans towed by ships' boats.

The expedition re-embarked by moonlight and ran down to St Pierre. HMS *Rippon* attacked the town alone, dropping anchor half a cable length from the defences, optimum range for great guns and small arms. She silenced her allocated battery 'in a few Minutes', showing what *Galicia* might have achieved, properly handled, but came under fire from other positions: 'oblig'd from her Situation between the batteries to engage both sides at once; this continued for two hours pretty warm.' Even the stern chase guns came into action: 'a brisk Fire was likewise kept up by the Marines upon the Militia on Shore, many of whom were carried off.' Finally, the Captain, realizing something was wrong, ordered the boats to tow her off, the wind having dropped, and expecting every moment to go aground.[54]

After this second rebuff the expedition transferred its attention to the neighbouring island of Guadeloupe, attacking Basse Terre on 22 January. Gardiner's Lieutenant, 'having behaved with great Spirit, received a violent Contusion in his left Leg, which was cut off immediately'. French militia raked *Rippon* fore and aft with musketry, until HMS *Bristol*'s Marines flanked them, forcing them to slacken their fire. The action lasted all day, *Rippon* expending all the grapeshot on board, 'Marines and Seamen making Wadding of their Jackets and Shirts and Firing them away at the Trenches'. Altogether *Rippon* fired 1,300 great shot, and her Marines 2,000 cartridges, perhaps 40 rounds per man, more than a land soldier carried into action. British casualties were low, suggesting the over-powering effect of close-range broadsides. The batteries fell silent, allowing the bomb vessels to fire incendiary carcasses into the town; 'Houses and Churches were everywhere soon in Flames, the Magazines of Powder blown about the Enemy's Ears, and the whole at ten o'Clock blazed out one general Conflagration.'[55]

The squadron's fire had so crushed the defenders that the Army landed unopposed two days later, but French planters led bands of armed slaves in a guerrilla resistance in the island's interior, with unpleasant consequences all round:

> A party of the French descended from the Mountains, and firing under cover of the Bushes in the Shore, killed three Marines and a Seaman at the Watering Place for the Squadron; upon which in the Evening the Troops burnt all the Sugar Canes and Houses in it. At another time a Body of armed Negroes concealing themselves in the Canes and firing out of them, the Troops set Fire to the several Corners of the Field and burnt them and the Canes together.[56]

Marines and Black Watch took part in a joint expedition against Fort Louis: 'where after a severe cannonading which lasted six Hours, the Marines and Highlanders were landed, who drove the Enemy from their Entrenchments with Bayonets fixed, and hoisted the English Colours at the Fort.' They stayed for a month, suffering 'on Account of the Scarcity of Provisions and Water, and not being supplied with Tents like the Rest of the Army'.[57]

Rear Admiral Rodney, who settled the unfinished business of Martinique in 1762, viewed the amphibious employment of Marines more positively than his predecessor. Approaching the Leeward Islands on 30 December 1761, Rodney appointed Captain Samuel Prosser, 'Major Commandant to a Body of Marines to be landed from the fleet to Act upon the present Expedition in conjunction with the troops'.[58] Among the officers were Terence O'Loghlen, who wrote *The Marine Volunteer* and Robert Lloyd. Unlike Gardiner's polished narrative, Lloyd's Order Book records the routine of a battalion on campaign: its equipment, discipline and health care. Officers had less than a week to pick out their best men and prepare them for the field, 'to demand Trowsers from the Purser of the Ship &. . . see those Trowsers converted into Geaters and Breeches', to check their arms, and supply them with worms, turnkeys and pickers. Sailmakers fabricated tents: one per officer, one for the sergeants, and one to every five men, who would also have a blanket apiece.

Lord Monckton, Rodney's military colleague, had experience of amphibious operations at Quebec, and a much stronger force than Hopson in 1759: fifteen battalions or 14,000 plus the Marines. He established a bridgehead on 16 January, but stuck fast: 'The difficulty of bringing up the Artillery being great the General has thought it proper to postpone the attack till Batteries can be raised to cover the troops in passing the Gullies.' Close terrain demanded strict precautions against surprise: 'COs to keep their Men together & to consider their Corps to be under the Orders of Readiness upon the Shortest Notice. . . . No man to stir from Camp without the leave of the CO. . . the Battalion to be in constant Readiness for Action.' Small parties that repulsed enemy attacks were warned:

> not to pursue so far to Endanger their being drawn into any Ambuscade, all advanced Posts Detach'd and Covering Partys to be very alert and vigilant as the Enemy is in constant Motion in Expectation of Surprizing some of them.

Monckton pressed forward on the 24th, the Marines with the right-hand brigade. By dusk the British had occupied the high ground around Port Royal and settled down for a siege. Like other battalions, the Marines provided working parties of 50 or 100 men, for example to make brush-wood fascines, for which they were paid an unspecified allowance. One company of Marines was employed 'night and day to carry ammunition to the batteries', and another as additional gunners, who, 'for their encouragement. . . have their pay made up Equal to Matrosses'. Security remained tight: 'Centryes to be Doubled during the Night & Posted in Corners or Bushes if any Near them.' Sightseeing was discouraged: 'Nobody to come in the Battery in the day time but those whose duty calls them there that they may not draw the Enemy's fire.' Monckton's ever-tightening grip, emphasized by defeat of a French sortie on 27 January, induced honourable surrender on 5 February.

Operations against Port Royal presented more problems to the Provost than the tacticians. Battalions called the roll four times a day, and read the Articles of War twice weekly, but to little effect. Injunctions against straggling and looting became ever more savage, expressions of sorrow making way for bloodcurdling threats: 'any soldier found with Plunder in his tent or returning to camp with Plunder of any kind notwithstanding he may say it belongs to an Officer shall be sent in Irons to the Provost try'd for his Life & Condemned.' Sentries shot two looters following orders to fire upon 'all Plunderers Marauders & Persons without Arms whether Soldiers or Sailors that attempt to go beyond the advanced posts of the Army'. Logistics were not the problem they had been at Cartagena. A corporal and two men from each company went every three days to collect beef and bread, carried up from the beach by negroes, but 'three days rum is not ordered on shore for the Troops as the COs will send for it daily, and are accountable that it is mixed with water.' This did not prevent 'Great Disorders & Riots being committed in the Camp during the Night', necessitating 'the Quarter Guard to send Patroles Every Hour to see that proper Order is maintained in the Tents'.

Both expeditions suffered more from disease than enemy action: 'troops unaccustomed to the Climate suffered greatly from *Fever*, from the *Flux*, the *Scurvy* from the Use of Salt Provisions, and from an accidental Evil, the *Small Pox*, which broke out amongst the Transports.' French resistance was calculated to 'weary out the British troops and by such frequent Alarms to call them out to the Sun whose Meridian rays they knew were fatally powerful on European constitutions'.[59] In 1762 the Army had 1,800 sick and dead out of 5,000 by late February. So run down were the ships' Marines they had to be augmented by soldiers. Lloyd gives no statistics, but reveals how field hospitals were staffed, the Director allowing, 'any Num[r] of Nurses [i.e. Soldiers] he has occasion for. . . by applying to the Commanding Officers of Corps. Beer may be had for the Sick and Wounded.' Each Corps supplied clean linen for its sick and collected their weapons, 'otherwise they will be broke or Rendered unserviceable.' A proportion of wives accompanied regiments on active service, including Marines. Two women per company were 'to wash the Men's linen but no more & each Corps is to send 2 women to Mr Adair [the Hospital Director] for the service of the Hospital'.[60]

The Leeward Island campaigns were not just examples of obscure corners of military administration, they were an opportunity for Marines to establish their reputation. Fighting alongside distinguished units like the Black Watch they acquired a professional respect naval officers denied them:

> The alacrity of the Marines at this attack [i.e Fort Louis] and at all others where they were employed during the course of the expedition was very observable; and though little notice was ever taken in the Squadron either of them or their officers, yet justice was done them by the gentlemen of the Army, with whom they gained credit, and who ever spoke of them with candour.[61]

The Siege of Belle Isle in 1761 dramatically advanced this process of recognition.

The Laurel Wreath

Most English descents on the French coast failed. The French Army was the best in Europe, and had excellent roads to counter the mobility of sea-borne forces. Small forces capable of snapping up slaving posts or sugar plantations invited disaster on a 'Coast so populous and fortified as to require at least 16,000 soldiers'.[62] The Belle Isle expedition of 1761 was different. Its objective was an island, which Commodore Keppel's ships of the line could isolate, although it lay as close to the Breton coast as the Isle of Wight does to Portsmouth. General Hodgson had 13,000 troops for the operation, almost Molyneux's magic number, including 500 Marines, under Colonel James Mackenzie. To mark the new Corps' first battalion-sized deployment, the taxpayer paid £23 13s 0d for a pair of colours: a Union flag and a plain white with a small Union and fouled anchor embellished with roses and thistles.

Belle Isle's resources were more limited – perhaps 4,000 troops to defend an island 15 miles by 5, and no mosquitoes. Its main protection was Vauban's citadel at Port Palais and a difficult coastline. The few bays that break the surrounding cliffs were well fortified: 'the outward breastwork 18 feet thick; and to prevent our men getting over it, as well as to defend their heads. . . palisades on the top of it, drove full of iron spikes, and placed at such a distance as just to admit the mouths of their muskets.'[63] While the Marines took part in elaborate demonstrations off one end of the island on 8 April, French infantry shot down the leading echelons of the main landings at the other. Naval gunfire proved ineffective so the attack was called off, with the loss of most of the troops put ashore.

A fresh attempt on the 22nd exploited amphibious forces' ability to threaten several points simultaneously. Covered by sea mist a company of Grenadiers, intended as a feint, landed unopposed at the north end of Loc Maria beach, supported by another company of Marines. Not for the last time Marines gained surprise by attacking over the most difficult terrain:

> The enemy supposing that Fort d'Ansic [at the other end of the beach] would be first attempted, did not adopt measures for the defence of the stupendous rocks, which offered such natural obstacles to the invaders.[64]

An officer approached the crest on hands and knees, 'then made the signal for his men to advance upon the rocks, and had just time to draw them up, when the French began to fire from behind a breastwork; the English returned it every time, squatting upon their backsides to reload which saved them from the enemy's shot', a description suggesting they had transferred the Marine firing to land.[65] Keppel and Hodgson, from their joint headquarters in the Commodore's barge, fed in more Grenadiers and all Mackenzie's Marines, to drive the French back. Colonel Mackenzie was wounded, but Arthur Collins had a good day:

> I myself was the first Marine ashore, for which I am made a Major, and at present command 800 men, and have the pleasure to hear everybody speak of the Marines as heroes. I think we shall soon take the town with great ease; as now the landing is made good we think ourselves out of all danger, and as soon as we get our great guns on shore it will be completed.[66]

Collins' optimism was misplaced as bad weather delayed landing of tools and artillery, allowing the French time to surround Palais with outlying redoubts that had to be tackled before the Citadel. In the absence of any naval threat, 900 Marines from the fleet reinforced the battalion ashore, the whole organized in three 'Divisions' of some 350 each, with another 350 on outpost duty. Outposts were not just for operational security – General Hodgson wanted good relations with the local people, in order to buy their produce. The Provost had orders:

> to go round all the villages in the Neighbourhood of the Camp, to take up Marauders and all soldiers he finds straggling from the Camp, and the General directs him to hang upon the spot the first man he catches Marauding, without bringing him any Tryal whatever.[67]

The pace was too slow for some. Thirty Marines petitioned General Hodgson for leave to attack the most advanced redoubt of the enemy, receiving answer that he would soon give them an opportunity of showing their courage. Two days later on 13 May, 200 Marines rushed the redoubts south of Palais, after a brisk mortar barrage, running field guns round to fire into the redoubt's open rear: 'The Marines, as usual, behaved re-markably well upon this occasion. The detachment with the two field pieces consisted of 16 men, 7 of whom were wounded, and 2 killed.' A Major of the 69th reinforced the storming party, providing momentum to carry the attack into the town:

> The Marines entered the town pell-mell with the fugitives, who ran with amazing speed towards the citadel, but though its gates were opened as

opportunely as possible, yet the Governor was obliged to shut them. . . to prevent the Marines from entering the Citadel in the same manner they had entered the town.

This success brought British guns within 500 yards of the Citadel, which they bombarded unremittingly. The enemy fired back, giving one Marine Lieutenant a narrow escape: 'Being in his tent a shell fell under him and burst, which overturned his cot, and wrapt the tent quite round him; but he was not hurt, tho' his cot was blown to pieces.' Even Vauban's walls crumbled, the garrison capitulating on 7 June.

The Marines' contribution to the successful outcome they received was out of proportion to the 92 casualties they suffered out of the British total of 800. General Hodgson thanked them for their part in the victorious rush of 13 May, and 'as a further approbation and intention of shewing them all the distinguishing signs of honour, placed them on the right of his army.'[68] Keppel passed on the General's expressions of gratitude, 'that his Majesty may be informed of the goodness and spirited behaviour of that corps.'[69] The Admiralty endorsed Keppel's report appreciatively: 'The behaviour of the Marines has given their Lordships great satisfaction, and they may expect all the encouragement in the Lordships' power.'[70] Three officers who took part in the siege later became divisional commandants: Mackenzie, who rose to Adjutant-General, Collins, and Captain Carruthers who led the charge into Palais. Tradition has followed Nicholas in attributing the award of the laurel wreath that encircles the globe in the Corps' badge to the Marines' conduct at Belle Isle, although Gillespie associated it less auspiciously with Bunker Hill. The most convincing testimonial to Marine prowess at Belle Isle came from the enemy. Asked which of the attacking regiments had impressed them most, they replied, 'Les Petits Grenadiers', alluding to the Marines' white-fronted mitre caps, and diminutive stature. If they did nothing else at Belle Isle, the Marines had shown they could fight.

An Opportunity Missed

The east coast of North America, with its inlets and great rivers, provided an ideal setting for amphibious operations in the eighteenth-century. Land communications were poor and defending forces vulnerable to sea-borne attack. Marines operated in North America as part of larger expeditions or as a spearhead for locally raised forces. When those forces turned against the Imperial Government in the 1770s, British strategists wasted the Marines' amphibious potential.

After the bloodless show of force in Virginia in 1676, Marines next saw action in North America against French settlements in Canada. At Placentia in 1703 they were ill prepared for the weather: 'the soldiers being forced to drink water in so cold a climate, had their limbs benummed and were scarce fit for the Service.'[71] An attack on Annapolis Royal in 1710 was more successful. The six regiments each contributed 100 Marines to a battalion, which combined forces with New England militia. They reached Annapolis on 25 September, the Marines landing first, and leading the advance through the woods. The Marines dug in 400 yards from the French fort, the Royal Navy landed some heavy guns, the Americans made fascines, and the French surrendered after five days' lukewarm resistance. An Anglo-American garrison stayed throughout the winter, ill-fed and ill-clad, losing seventy men killed by Indians in an ambush. Such operations in uncharted waters ran terrible risks. Admiral Walker's expedition to Quebec in 1711 came to spectacular grief – 740 soldiers drowned, including 208 Marines and 20 of the Battalion's women. HMS *Eagle*'s Marines: 'at great risk and with much daring, took to the sea in small boats belonging to their ship and rowed to the shore where the transport *Colchester*. . . had been driven. . . saving the lives of 167 of the men.'[72]

Marines were the only British infantry present at Louisburg's first siege in 1746, supporting American provincial forces. Twelve years later, 500 Marines joined a larger force under General Wolfe and Admiral Boscawen, sent to terminate French rule in Canada, beginning again with Louisburg. The British had learned about forest warfare. Boscawen ordered the Marines, 'not to come in their coats, but cropped hats, short jackets etc, thirty-six rounds of ammunition, and a blanket each man rolled up on their backs'. They built batteries, and received extra pay for manning two 6-pounder guns: $7\frac{1}{4}$d a day for sergeants, and $3\frac{1}{2}$d for privates. Arthur Tooker Collins wrote to his wife:

> I was three weeks and three days without pulling my clothes off, or getting any sleep but on boards, and never more than two hours at a time; sometimes 48 hours without any sleep; and notwithstanding this may appear hardships, yet I never had my health better the whole time.[73]

More Marines took part in Wolfe's siege of Quebec the following year, mounting a diversion to distract the defenders from the main attack on the Heights of Abraham.

The expulsion of the French from Canada was disastrous for Anglo-American relations. Colonists refused further contributions towards

Imperial defence, while the London Government neither made concessions, nor took adequate steps to stifle rising discontent. A battalion of Marines under Major John Pitcairn sailed in October 1774, to reinforce the Army at Boston. Pitcairn's problems escaping the clutches of the Royal Navy illustrate the Marines' ambiguous status. Admiral Graves, 'a weak Man – with infinite Pride', would only release 400 of the 600 supernumerary Marines, despite Pitcairn's insistence that they would be unfit to act with the Army unless landed immediately.

Pitcairn, like Collins and Mackenzie, belonged to a new generation of Marine officers. He had the professional confidence to stand up for the good of the Corps, wishing, 'most anxiously to Convince both Army and Navy that we can do our duty with propriety both on board and ashore'. He complained directly to the First Lord of Graves's refusal to release his best men: 'This distresses me greatly, as I have a great desire to convince everyone of the utility of keeping a large body of Marines, who are ever capable of acting either by sea or land as the public service may require.' In spring he began route marches 6 or 7 miles into the country: 'The people swear at us sometimes, but that does us no harm.' The cheap local rum was more of a problem:

> We have lost Seven by Death, kill'd by Drinking the Cursed Rum of this Country. . . I never was so plagued and distrest with such a set of profligate Scoundrels in my life, the Plymouth people by much the worst, they sell the beds from under them to get this Cursed Rum.

Pitcairn flogged the chief culprits, but was no martinet: 'I assure you it gives me such distress to be obliged to act in this manner, that I would rather live on bread and water, than have command of such people.' The Marines were not the only offenders: 'the rum is so cheap that it debauches both navy and army. . . Depend on it, my Lord, it will destroy more of us than the Yankies will.'[74]

Tempers rose on both sides: 'the Army here will if they are ordered most willingly give the People here a severe Chastisement, they are heartely provocked at them.' Captain William Souter of the Marine Light Company reported the colonists 'laugh at the thought of *little* Great Britain sending out such small Numbers to oppose them, saying we are a Mouthful only for them, and calling the Soldiers Bloody-Backs.' Everywhere the rebels erected Liberty poles, drilling by night, and terrorizing anyone who disagreed with them: 'What they call Tarring and Feathering.'[75] Major Pitcairn has been credited with firing 'the shot heard round the world' during an attempt to seize an arms cache at Concord in April 1775, but

Souter makes it plain American minute-men fired first: 'From this unhappy Accident the Americans have plunged themselves into the Horrors & Miseries of a Civil War.' The British pursued their mission, but found the country alarmed against them:

> it not being possible for us to meet a Man otherwise than from behind a Bush, Stone hedge, or Tree who immediately gave his fire and off he went. . . . On our leaving Concord we were immediately surrounded on every Quarter, and expected to be cut off every Moment, sometimes we took possession of one Hill sometimes of another; at last it was determined to push forward to Lexington, which we did thro' a plaguey Fire, when we were joined by Lord Percy with the first Brigade [and the remaining Marines] with four pieces of Cannon, otherwise I do not believe one of us had got into Boston again.[76]

The British defeat was strategically deplorable, the rebels blockading Boston, the town's people being 'in the utmost Consternation, Distress & Confusion'. Supplies were short, but British reinforcements in May included another 600 Marines, enough for two full battalions, each of a Grenadier and light company, and eight battalion or centre companies.

Boston lay on a peninsula, secure from direct attack, but overlooked. When the rebels occupied the position known variously as Bunker or Breed's Hill, General Gage, the British commander, had to throw them off, before they made the British position untenable. He sent eight battalions across the harbour early on 17 June 1775, to do the job, among them both Marine battalions' flank companies, and all 1st Marines. Lieutenant J. Waller, the Adjutant, wrote to his brother, 'Amidst the hurry and confusion of a camp hastily pitched in the field of battle'[77]:

> Two companies of the 1st Battalion of Marines and part of the 47th Regiment were the first that mounted the breastwork; and you will not be displeased when I tell you that I was with those two companies, who drove their bayonets into all that opposed them. Nothing could be more shocking than the carnage that followed the storming this work. We tumbled over the dead to get at the living, who were crowding out of the gorge of the redoubt, in order to form under the defences which they had prepared to cover their retreat.

The usual image of the attack is of closed ranks of redcoats labouring up a glacis-like slope with shouldered arms, but the detailed picture is more confused. Marines left knapsacks and coats at the foot of the hill before climbing over the rails and hedges before the redoubt:

> but when we came immediately under the work, we were checked by the severe fire of the enemy, but did not retreat an inch. We were now in confusion, after being broke several times in getting over the rails, etc. I did all I could to form the two companies on our right, which I at last effected, losing many of them while it was performing.

They exchanged fire for a while, until Waller begged the Colonel of a neighbouring regiment to make a bayonet attack:

> I ran from right to left and stopped our men from firing, while this was doing, and when we had got into a tolerable order, we rushed on, leaped the ditch and climbed the parapet, under a most sore and heavy fire.

Officer casualties were heavy, as the Americans picked them out. Among the dead was Major Pitcairn. The Battalion's fire slackened as his son cried out, 'My father is killed – I have lost my father', the men echoing his words, 'We have all lost a father.' The Marines had been in support until the leading battalion faltered, when Pitcairn cried out, 'push on or the 18th will get the honour of the day', but the soldiers demurred: 'Then break and let the Marines pass through you.' Somehow the story became attached to the 88th, who were not present, causing fights whenever a Marine met a Connaught Ranger and called out, 'Lie down 88th, and let the Marines pass to the front.'[78]

The Marines suffered 123 casualties, although David Collins commented to his father, now Colonel Commandant at Plymouth, 'they die so fast of their wounds that nobody as yet has got a true state of our loss.' He had little sympathy for Pitcairn's successor Major Shorte, who seems to have become a psychological casualty, dying 'not of any wound but of an absolute Penury and narrowness of Soul, which brought on a Flux, he denied himself the Necessaries of Life and the company of his Brother officers only to gratify a stingy Method of thinking.'[79] The Grand Divisions felt the effects of the battle, as modern garrison towns would, with added uncertainty for rank and file dependants: 'as no accounts received in private specify the names of the soldiers of the Corps, all the wives and families of the common men are therefore sighing and weeping, lest their husbands and fathers should be among the killed.'[80]

Young Collins found it, 'difficult to say how matters will turn out. The Rebels are throwing up immense strong redoubts all over the country, resolved only to act upon the defensive, while we are fortifying equally strong this little Peninsula.'[81] Souter denied newspaper claims of victories: 'No such things have happened since the Battle of Bunker's Hill except a little Marauding Party of two hundred Light Infantry, who were longing for Beef Stakes [*sic*] which relished the better in not having a Man hurt.'[82] Collins had also been grumbling about food:

> The very thing that was my aversion in old England, is the only thing I can get to eat in New England. Pork, and to my comfort the fattest of all Pork. Vegetables we have none: I have not seen a Potato or Turnip since I have been here. The vileness of the Pork has bred the flux or as we call it the Yankey. . . Very few have escaped. . . It has proved fatal to our wounded people.[83]

Even salt pork ran short. Marines received half rations, with dried fish, flour and rice instead of the salt beef and pork they usually enjoyed at sea, plus a few potatoes, and vinegar to make 'sour crout'.

Firewood was a constant preoccupation. General Howe, who replaced Gage in October 1775, fulminated against 'The frequent depredations committed by the soldiers in pulling down the fences and houses', directing the Provost 'to hang upon the instant the first man he should detect in the fact'. No Marines appear to have been caught, but a Grenadier got 800 lashes for insolence and mutinous behaviour.[84]

Lack of provisions and the colonists' interception of a brig loaded with bombshells persuaded the British to withdraw in March 1777. Like many British evacuations it was brilliantly executed, although it more 'resembled the emigration of a nation than the breaking of a camp'.[85] Marines maintained security around the wharves, and once back at sea followed their usual trade as surrogate seamen aboard short-handed transports. The elder Collins, who had replaced Pitcairn, had every reason to assure the First Lord, 'that the Marines on this service have proved beyond a doubt that every soldier should be a marine.'[86]

Crammed aboard a transport in Nantasket Road, Major Souter was less impressed:

> A pretty Situation for an English Army & Navy this – Twenty thousand souls on an Average, including the Friends of the Government taken on board from Boston, stuffed on board the Ships with not room to stir. No Asylum on the Continent to receive us. No Provision to hold out till a Reinforcement arrives, nor Shipping to take us off.[87]

The British still held a naval base at Halifax, which the king himself had already suggested as a suitable station for the Marine Battalions. Marines' association with dockyard defence dated back to the 1690s, and was increasingly a diversion. In this case it stifled the amphibious potential revealed in the Boston evacuation. When Lord Howe sailed for New York on 5 June he left both Marine battalions behind, except the Grenadiers. They saw action at Long Island in August 1776 and accompanied Howe to Philadelphia, where their capture of an American vessel in the Delaware river suggests what two full Battalions of Marines might have done along American waterways.

Garrison duties at Halifax had compensations – soft bread and half a gallon of spruce beer a day, while rank and file benefited from a sub-scription 'for the Encouragement and Relief of the troops employed on the most important service in North America'. Soldiers and their de-pendants received shoes, stockings, warm caps and 500lb of 'Donation tobacco' per battalion, enough to last the ensuing campaign. Such philanthropy contrasts with the neglect of basic necessities forty years earlier, and predates Victorian public generosity. The main problems at Halifax were boredom and cold. Mrs Collins sent green tea and cheese, 'But my dear Mother,' wailed her son, 'where are the Magazines and News-papers you tantalised me with. I would really give you back the Cheese for the thirteen Critical Reviews.'[88] The men found paid employment, 'provided they do their own duty. . . and give up part or the whole of what they earn to the Captains to pay off their debts.' Colonel Collins took a progressive attitude to discipline. He preferred ridicule to brutality, confining unsoldierlike Marines to barracks with their coats turned inside out. He encouraged regimental feeling, marking the anniversary of 17 June, 'where the Marines behaved in a brave and gallant manner at the attack of the rebel redoubt on the heights of Charlestown', by a general pardon of defaulters. Dress reflected local conditions, Marines mounting guard in trousers, round hats and greatcoats slung over the back. However, 'any Man who presumes to cut his hair short will be severely punished.'[89]

The only action followed a night march by Royal American Fencibles and Marine light companies to surprise would-be revolutionaries, suggesting fieldcraft was not a rebel monopoly:

> When there was sufficient daylight to enable us clearly to distinguish objects, we began to ascend the hill, in a short time the advanced guard heard the Indians talking in their wigwams, and finding we were wholly undiscovered, I detached Captain Branson's company [Marines] to fall upon their right flank, and Captain Pitcairn's [Marines] on their left, whilst

I pressed forward in the centre with our detachment, but as we reached the top of the hill I heard them beat to arms, on which the men gave a loud huzza and ran like lions.[90]

Only one Marine was wounded, 'and when the Doctor applied the bandage the ball fell out.' The enemy body count remained unknown, 'the thickness of the cover rendering it exceedingly difficult to find them.'

General Massey, Commanding Officer at Halifax recalled wood fighting during the Seven Years War, for the benefit of Marine patrols:

if attacked by the enemy on the scout we had a good command "Down all Packs", the pack was one blanket and so many days' provisions dressed in it. . . It is therefore MGen Massey's orders that the D.A.Qm.Gen. orders good provisions to be dressed this day for Lieut Bourne's scout and that he fills their canteens with rum and that Lieut Needham give their scout two quarts of rice a man with a quart of treacle to improve their grog.[91]

French intervention in 1778 transformed a colonial police action into a world war, of which the Royal Navy bore the brunt. Scraping the barrel to man the Channel Fleet Admiral Keppel thought it 'absolutely necessary that the Marines serving as part of the Army in North America should be directly sent home.'[92] General Massey was sorry to see them leave on 30 August 1778:

The C-in-C cannot part with the Marine Corps without telling them he was pleased with their soldier like appearance at the review yesterday. . . he has had the honour to command that Corps for above two years without ever hearing of a Court Martial in it, or ever rebuking an officer or soldier. He will therefore make such a report of that respectable body of men as they merit; and now wishes officers and soldiers plenty of prize money, and makes not a doubt but they will always contribute to the glory of his Majesty King George's arms.[93]

The Marines' first commitment to a field army since Queen Anne had ended in anti-climax. A more imaginative commander than Howe might have made more use of their amphibious capability. Admiral Rodney, bound for the West Indies in 1782, thought his supernumerary Marine Field Officers: 'the greatest advantage to His Majesty's service, as frequent opportunities may offer of landing that Corps, and distressing the public enemy'.[94] A third of a century later the Three Marine Battalions of the War of 1812 would fulfil Rodney's hopes.

CHAPTER FIVE

Sea Service and Barrack Life

EARLY Marines spent only a small proportion of their time at sea in action. Sea service for most Marines consisted of interminable cruises, enlivened by the occasional chase, battle or shipwreck. HMS *Defiance* had been at sea 'in the whole upward of five years', when her Marines petitioned the Admiralty for relief in 1798, but this was not untypical. In 1807 HMS *Cleopatra* had been in the West Indies for two years, 'and from the condition she is now in may remain three years more upon this station at the expiration of that time perhaps I may come home.'[1] During these long periods at sea Marine detachments shared the daily routine of their ship, to which they added their own specifically military tasks.

Conditions afloat often fell short of the orderliness associated with a military existence. Major Edye, considering the Stuart Navy from the calm of the Middle Temple, wondered how 'In view. . . of the utter want of organization and comfort that then prevailed afloat. . . discipline was maintained and contentment secured.'[2] Life at sea in Queen Anne's reign resembled the apocalypse: 'continual destruction in the foretop, the pox above board, the plague between decks, hell in the forecastle, and the devil at the helm. . . having only the bare Deck to lye upon, which hardship caused abundance of our men to bid adieu to the world.'[3] A newly embarked subaltern of the 1780s was shocked to find:

The "pomp, pride, and circumstance of glorious war" compressed within the humiliating limitations of a m–of w–; where unguided tumult and undisciplined confusion involved all arrangements in one universal chaos.[4]

Sea service in a sailing warship was hard and dirty work, exposed to salt water and the pitch used as a universal waterproofing agent. Major Pitcairn expressed himself with customary vigour on the impractical white facings of Marines in the 1770s: 'I cannot keep my people in decent order. I wish his Lordship would give us Blue Green or Black, those fools that oppose it never had the good of the Service at heart.'[5] Officers were spared mind-numbing labour at the capstan or hauling on tarry ropes, but nobody escaped the sea's intrusions. Approaching the Cape of Good Hope, HMS *Minden*'s officers found their 'Wardroom afloat from a heavy sea, having crushed in the glass ports.'[6] Lieutenant John Fernyhough found the Bay of Biscay equally unpleasant: 'Our ship for two days was continually flooded; the sea stove in the larboard quarter gallery, and the wardroom had three windows stove in.'[7] Fernyhough was lucky: a brig disappeared with all hands during the storm.

Marine diaries sometimes present an image of sailors tumbling out of the rigging like rotten fruit: 'Brian AB fell from the fore rigging on the chest of Marine —— who was lying on his back on the forecastle. The only injury Brian sustained was the left arm broken in two places. —— out of bed in three days.'[8] Thomas Houle suffered a succession of accidents that left him incapable of work:

> being Cast Away Lousing all y^t I had but God bee praised Escaped with life but got great damage ye ship being lost & in 1704 in distress of Wether having A falle from ye mane yard of ye ship Boyne broake both my hand Wrists & att ye same time I received A great damage in my head & the Wharle Boane of my right Knee Cloven putt out of Joint & a small shott in my bodey on my left side by the Enemie severall splinters taken out of my lift legg by the graysing of A shott Across my shinn.[9]

John Howe was shipwrecked off the Savannah River in 1780:

> We Stuck at half Past nine in the morning Clued up the Sails and went all hands to the Pumps the Ship having Sprung a Leak and the Water Came in very fast three Days and nights we keept Continually Pumping. . . and on the fourth Day we left the Ship to [take] her Chance.[10]

In bad weather, men might go for weeks without rest or dry clothing. Howe's new ship and her consort nearly succumbed to winter gales:

> Six men Died at their Pumps with hard work and we had one Died. 16 Days and nights we were Constantly at it and not a Man could go to bed all this time every other 4 howers [at the pumps] when it was his watch belowe and the other 4 howers twas his watch on Deck and we must be there to werk the Ship.[11]

Everyday wear and tear must have contributed as much to the ragged condition of early Marine detachments as administrative neglect. The working dress for Queen Anne's Marines consisted of a white kersey frock, blue shirt, and a 'Mill'd Cap' of thick red cloth, but not all Marines had this. The Lieutenant of HMS *Berwick* provoked a mutiny in 1712 by ordering her detachment to unload the ship's cables into a hulk, in their regimental uniform. He confined three Marines who said they, 'had no clothes for that employment, and would not perform that office', and when their mates came aft in a body, crying 'one for all' in the time-honoured manner of mutineers, clapped them into irons as well.[12]

The incident suggests early Marines had either sea or land service clothes, but not both. In 1747 the Admiralty ordered Pursers to supply Marines, 'at their first coming on board from Quarters, with such bedding and slop clothes as they shall be in want of, for their Sea use (*in addition to their Regimentals*)'. They also required a store room, 'to be built on board each of His Majesty's Ships, abaft on the oarlop, to contain their clothing, accoutrements, and all other necessaries for the use of the Marines'.[13] The wise Marine officer intercepted his men as they came aboard, and locked up their new coats and hats in his store cupboard, along with their white shirts and a pair of shoes and stockings:

> By this Management the Men's Cloaths will be saved and the Marine Officer will be qualified to turn out a clean well-dressed Guard for the Reception of a superior Officer. . . and when disembarked to do Duty with Land Forces on Shore, they will be able to make a Soldier-like Appearance; besides it prevents their selling their Necessaries for Spirits or Tobacco. . . Soldiers should always wear Sea Caps, Jackets, and cheque Shirts on board a Ship.[14]

Marines had few possessions beyond their clothes. Out of nine who died in HMS *Invincible* on passage to North America in 1756, only one had a few items worth listing: two snuff boxes and a pen knife.

Officers, by contrast, possessed elaborate outfits. Second Lieutenant Lewis Roteley awaiting Lord Nelson's arrival aboard HMS *Victory* in August 1805, wrote home for a supply of white shirts in a trunk, besides 'my Yellow Leathers Boot Hooks Blacking Brushes a few Towels my Fiddle Music book case etc the little Blue Box-Powder Bag & put a small fowl Cloaths bag & anything else you think will be proper for a long Voyage'.[15] Prolonged absence wrecked the most extensive wardrobes. The Governor of Madeira muttered that officers returning from St Helena looked like Desperadoes: 'Certainly our Rigg was not very prepossessing being equipped in Surtout Coat and large studs of the Penang kind. Appendages truly unbecoming an assembly room.'[16]

Duties at Sea

Ships' Marine detachments carried out general naval tasks, and specific tasks for which their military training suited them. The Captain of HMS *Indefatigable* in 1812 recognized the twofold division, dividing his Marines into a working party and a guard. Marines were not natural topmen, although early historians of the Corps claimed its original purpose had been as a 'nursery for seamen'. Major Edye found no authority for this 'singular idea of raising and training men as soldiers, and then suddenly transferring them to the totally distinct duties of foremast men', and mocked the suggestion as 'perfectly ludicrous'.[17] A regiment of 1,200 men, who rarely went to sea for more than a few weeks at a time, can hardly have satisfied the Royal Navy's appetite for skilled manpower. The 1690 Memorandum hoped 'these regiments may prove "nurseries" whence the several necessities of their Majesties' service may be abundantly supplied', but the proposed draft of 300 able seamen a year does not seem very generous. Thomas Houle claimed to have followed both careers: 'Eighteen years in ye Nations service & not an Houer out of itt as first A Marine Souldger & Ever since A seaman before the Mast', but he did not state whether one led to the other.[18] Queen Anne's Marine Regiments were 'put on a different Foot', from those of the Nine Years War, 'without any regard to their being a Nursery for Seamen'.[19]

The manning crisis of the 1740s brought renewed requests for Marines to enter as seamen. The Admiralty allowed any Marine whose First Lieutenant, Master and Boatswain thought qualified as an able seaman to serve as such, authorizing the Captain of his old Company to deduct £4 from the man's pay to raise a new recruit.[20] The Board took a permissive attitude towards the work expected of Marines:

> They are to be employed as Centinels, and upon all other Duty and Service on board the ship which they shall be capable of, and therein to be subject to the Directions of the Officers of the ship: but they are not to be obliged to go aloft, or to be beat or punished for not showing an inclination to do so. . . On the other hand the Marine Officers are not to hinder nor discourage their men from applying themselves to do or learn the duty of a seaman.[21]

Regulations recognized contemporary practice, as reported in HMS *Leopard*:

> the marines on board the said ship were employed upon deck; but that no orders were given to them to furl the sails, though they did it voluntarily

at the Witness's desire; the reason of which was that the Men might be of use after they are discharged from this service.[22]

Detachments were sub-divided into squads of 12–16 men each under a Lieutenant or Sergeant, working the same 'relieves and tours of duty' as the seamen, while at sea, when they were divided evenly between the two standard watches. Their places in Muster Bills reflect their relatively unskilled status, alongside less active seamen as waisters, or with the afterguard on the quarterdeck. They assisted with labour-intensive tasks such as pumping ship or unmooring, when they appeared 'at the Swifter, Two between each bar' of the Capstan.[23] Marine Officers took station with the men to ensure they worked with spirit, and to 'suppress the absurd custom of huzzaing'.[24]

One area where Marines took the lead was in fitting out their ship for sea: rigging, cleaning, provisioning and getting the guns and other stores on board. A newly commissioned ship often had no personnel beyond her officers, and a detachment of Marines, whose first job was to make her habitable:

> As our party boarded the frigate fresh from the hands of the carpenters and caulkers, who, ever prodigal of their pitchy liquid, had left the deck in a sad mess of rubbish of all descriptions, all hands were immediately ordered to rig in fatigue-clothing, and scrape and swab the cabins and garrison out. This was a filthy and disagreeable job to many; but to me and some few others, who knew it was imperative and soon over it was an employment that was readily gone about.[25]

Naval Chronicle thought Marines well suited to the work, 'as they are from long habit in the late wars, good seamen, and very fit for rigging and getting ready for sea ships put into commission'.[26] A veteran naval officer remembered in the 1870s how:

> when a ship is put in commission marines are always at hand, and are taken on board before the bluejackets. In one or two ships that I have joined, before the bluejackets were on board, the Marine Artillery were hard at work turning in the lower rigging, and doing a great deal of the seaman's duty.[27]

Marines' ingrained discipline made them natural candidates for tasks that required regularity, rather than gymnastics: hauling in the log reel, or turning the sandglass, and proclaiming the passage of time, a chronological responsibility that survived into the twentieth-century. The most important military function of Marines, when not in action, was as sentries, to ensure the security of their ship, 'the greatest trust that can be reposed in a private soldier'. In 1712 the Captain of HMS *Oxford* requested 'a sergeant and twelve Mareens to make up my complement which number will man the Poop and do duty as Sentenalls'.[28] A Third Rate enjoying the enhanced discipline of St Vincent's day required a guard of fifty, posting fifteen sentries: two each at the quarter deck, pump, gangway and forecastle; one each at the ward room, gun room, fore and after cockpit, galley, bits and prisoners. To emphasize their status sentries in harbour wore full uniform, 'with their Hair well powdered, and everything in the compleatest order', including live ammunition and filled canteens in case they had to go ashore suddenly. Sentries were allowed twenty-four hours to clean their clothes and accoutrements before mounting guard, and might not be called for other duties. At sea, they had to:

> make the best appearance they possibly can in their second clothing or jackets, but such men as are sentinels at the cabin door are to appear in their best clothing, if their others should be too much worn to make a proper military appearance.[29]

Naval vessels faced a variety of internal and external threats: sabotage, fire, desertion, alcohol and sex. Marine sentries controlled access to the ship, ensuring no boats ran alongside without permission, or any unauthorized persons or packages entered or left the ship, being 'particularly circumspect in regard to Women, and People who are suspected to conceal Liquor'.[30] At night the sentries on the upper decks were to call out 'All's Well' every quarter hour, raising the alarm if the word was not punctually repeated around the ship. They also hailed any boat lurking about the ship or passing within the buoys. During the invasion scare of 1745 Admiral Vernon ordered ships at the Downs to mount extra guards, their arms ready for use in the coach-house: 'As we lay in an open Road, liable to Surprizals in the Night'.[31] Sentries were to fire on anyone jumping overboard or into a boat after dark, but had little time to distinguish between deserters and somebody fallen overboard by accident. Firing into boats was a risky business within the jurisdiction of British courts. A Marine sentry who shot a deserter from a hospital ship at the instigation of a surgeon's mate and boatswain's mate, was tried for murder at the Old Bailey. The jury found all three guilty of manslaughter: 'for which they received sentence to be branded in the hand, which was immediately executed in court.'[32] A Marine in HMS *Lynn* at Portsmouth:

> had orders to keep off the shore boats which were filled with people improperly crowding to get on board. Having in vain called for them to

keep off, he thereupon fired his musket in order to frighten them, whereby one woman was unfortunately killed.[33]

The Admiralty took the precautionary step, in that case, of seeking royal protection for their sentry, against his being found guilty of the capital charge of murder.

Within the ship, Marine sentries maintained domestic discipline. They prevented access to the officers' quarters, except by recognized servants, controlled issue of water from the scuttlebutt, and prevented anyone else using the galley grate while the officers' dinners were cooking. They were not to allow anyone to throw rubbish out of the ports, or lounge about the booms, hammocks or gangways, nor permit any noise or lights near their posts, beyond those required for the ship's business. When the Boatswain piped 'All Hands to Dance', and the ship was overrun with 'the merry-faced daughters of levity and dance. . . cheeks rouged to roses and rigged out in their most captivating dresses', Marine discipline remained 'more tensely screwed up and severely enforced than ever. . . ready, when called on, to repress with a strong hand the earliest attempts at insubordination or riot'.[34] Marines were also responsible for guarding prisoners of war, ensuring they remained quiet and sober, 'by no Means to abuse them, but to make Use of fair Words'. More severe measures might be needed to prevent prisoners rising against their captors. Fifteen Marines escorting 170 French soldiers across the Bay of Biscay had little choice but to batten them below hatches. Every man slept with a cutlass and loaded pistol, as did the crew of HMS *Sceptre* (64) when they:

> Discovered a Plott the Dutch Prisoners in our hold had Layd to Murder one half of our Men take possession of the Ship and Carry her into France Our Capt[n] finding this had all the Prisoners brought on Deck and their officers put in Irons and Manacled the rest and Put them Down in the same Place again and told them they were welcom now to Proceed on their Scheem as fast as they Could as he and his men should be well Prepard to meet and Put every man to Death who attempted it.[35]

When moving prisoners by boat, it was advisable to tow them separately, followed by Marines in a third boat, ready to fire among them if they cut the tow-rope. On a happier note, a French officer who rescued a Marine sentry blown off the gangway of a prison hulk into the River Tamar in 1800 received a free passport to return home without exchange.

Not everyone treated sentries with proper respect. A carpenter from Harwich dockyard:

being refused by the centinell admittance into the steerage where he had no business. . . knocked down the said centinell and took away his sword which mutiny the Lieutenant endeavouring to suppress was attacked by the same person with a large maul.[36]

Lieutenant John MacIntire gave extensive directions for clapping into irons anyone 'offering to insult a Centry on his Post which should never be suffered'.[37] In MacIntire's day sentries were often trifled with, but Earl St Vincent would not tolerate any nonsense, ordering the boats of the Mediterranean Fleet manned and armed to witness a seaman receive 100 lashes for knocking down a sentry: 'that no man can plead ignorance of the sacredness of the person and character of a sentinel, who is perfectly justifiable in putting any man to death who insults him at his post.'[38]

The only reason a sentry might leave his post was to give the alarm in case of fire. Fire prevention had been a military responsibility at sea since 1617, when Sir Walter Raleigh had ordered two soldiers 'to search between the decks that no fire or candlelight be carried about the ship after the watch be set.'[39] Marine NCOs assisted the Master-at-arms 'in his duty of putting out lights and fires', and patrolled the ship 'against the dreadful calamity of fire'. The Lieutenant of Marines himself looked into the Carpenter's, Gunner's and Boatswain's stores every evening, 'to be satisfied no light has been accidentally left in those places', before locking them up for the night.[40] Nothing could be more horrible than the destruction of a warship by fire. A Lieutenant of Marines in Nelson's flagship at the Nile described the burning of *L'Orient*, in words equally appropriate to the accidental loss of the *Queen Charlotte* the following year, when only four of her 200 Marines escaped, none except the officers being able to swim:

> Etna in flames may resemble her burning; the fire rushing from her ports, and flying up her sides, giving its own red colour to the water. . . then dashing like a thunder bolt along the rigging, primed as it was by pitch and tar, the dry sails in that hot climate catching like tinder and burning like blue lights. . . But the last explosion, the bursting of the magazine, the blowing into the air of a three decker of a hundred guns with all her crew; this can have no adequate parallel.[41]

The prospect of being blown to eternity in an instant could precipitate panic as observed when HMS *Minden's* Marines accidentally set her alight during musketry practice: 'All hands in a mass out on deck and notwith-standing the drum was beaten to Quarters, not one obeyed. Such a scene of bustle and confusion I never before witnessed.'[42] Captains looked to the Marines to maintain order, in such emergencies:

> On an alarm of fire being made, the Marines are to repair to their respective quarters, and those on the poop to fall in under arms, and be ready to move in any direction they may be ordered, and to suppress that confusion which generally happens on such occasions and tends to defeat the execution of those [measures] appointed to put it out.[43]

In the same way, Marines attended punishment, their loaded muskets and fixed bayonets emphasizing the difference between them and other members of the crew.

Inter-Service Relations

Marines enlisted for life, or at least many years, and were subject to constant military discipline. Seamen on the other hand were turned adrift as soon as their ship was paid off, and soon lost any discipline they might have acquired. The behaviour of the two classes was as different as their physical appearance: the red-coated Marine looking as if he had swallowed a poker, the blue-jacket rolling along as if constructed of springs and universal joints.[44] The relationship between such disparate elements, artificially confined within the cramped spaces of a warship, contained much potential for conflict. Naval officers exploited the Corps to support their authority, but were slow to accept it as an equal branch of the service. Inter-service relations were never straightforward, whether between officers, or on the lower deck. The Admiralty did its best, instructing Captains, 'to use the Marine officers on board them civilly, and that they do give the same countenance to the soldiers as to the seamen of their ships.'[45] John MacIntire urged his fellows to avoid friction with their naval colleagues, for, 'When the Sea and Marine Officers don't agree, a Detachment can never be properly regulated.' He encouraged Marine NCOs: 'to make the Soldiers live in good Friendship with the Seamen and never be partial to your own Men'. Terence O'Loghlen advised every Marine Officer, 'to make the Marines exert themselves upon every Occasion for the Good of His Majesty's Service, and to endeavour to promote Harmony and Unanimity between them and the Seamen'.[46]

Inter-service friendship was difficult to achieve. Parliament's use of the New Model Army to suppress seamen's demands for extra pay in the 1650s led to inter-service brawls, and in 1665 the Fleet put to sea to frustrate, 'the soldiers inciting to mutiny and falling upon the seamen'.[47]

The Admiral's Regiment threatened to fire on impudent seamen at Harwich in 1672, and trained Fort Landguard's guns on a ship whose boatswain had kidnapped one of their number. Queen Anne's Navy resented the Marines' allegedly better conditions of service:

> it is very hard on the poor seamen, that must do all the slavery without any refreshment, but ordered from ship to ship although come from a foreign voyage of three or more year, and at the same time the Marines must be ordered to Quarters for Refreshment. . . but now it's the *Spanish* proverb the seamen slaves and the Marines *Gentlemen,* by which reason all the world knows how theare Navy is governed.[48]

A less impassioned Captain applied for his seamen's Short Allowance money:

> they not having received any money this three years, and the Marines having received theirs makes them murmur very much, believing they are treated worse than they are.[49]

The Admiralty's assumption of financial responsibility for the Marines removed one cause of friction, as seamen and Marines were then paid together, but the old antipathy surfaced in the cry of a ringleader in a nineteenth-century brawl: 'Now, my lads. . . out with your handkerchiefs, and belt the sogers. Bang the empty bottles, they're only Marines.'[50] Such affrays cannot have been entirely one-sided. A bluejacket in HMS *Inconstant* was found guilty of manslaughter of a Marine in 1847, but under extenuating circumstances, which suggests provocation. As against that, Sergeant William Turner's heroes in the Crimean War included his old commanding officers ashore and afloat, the first Royal Marine VC, 'and last but not least, the captain of the main-top of HMS *Albion*'.[51]

A Marine Lieutenant of the 1780s thought it impossible, 'to reconcile the long established repugnance between the r— and the b—. . . Prejudice which springs from a dissonance of sentiment and education, when nourished by the imbittering consequences of situation are not easily vanquished.'[52] He was not the only disillusioned Marine officer:

> A captain of Marines, though of the highest quality, may be confined by the cook of the ship, the lowest of their Officers having the command on board over one of ours. He's allowed no other Provision than the meanest Sailor, and is often lodged less comfortably than a dog in a kennel; was I to say a hog in a sty, it would be a nearer resemblance. This year he's sent to be scorched under the Line, the next he's starved under the Pole; nothing certain but a variety of woes.[53]

The contrast between the Captain's elegant cabin and their own accommodation shocked newly commissioned Marine Officers:

> a place between two guns, about seven foot long and four foot wide, and divided only from some hundred hammocks, by a little old canvas or an old sail, where there is no light but for a candle, nor no air but what is unavoidably very foul, and as unwholesome as it is unpleasant.[54]

Junior Sea Officers were housed no better, and must have had difficulty imposing their theoretical authority. Richard Swale was arrested for pulling the Master's nose, but soon released:

> Next day he [the Master] was turned out of the Mess and no officer in the ship would speak to him. . . . he had before refused to let me go on shore and strove by every means to annoy me, but thank Gad we got clear of him two days later.[55]

The Admiralty had asserted its own authority over all personnel in HM Ships from the 1670s. Prince George of Denmark referred to a well-established precedent when he ordered the court martial of a Sergeant of Marines for striking the Master of HMS *Salisbury*:

> it being the pleasure of HRH that you do let the Marine officers know, that so long as they and their men shall be in service on board Her Majesty's ships, they must be subject to the Maritime Laws, settled by Act of Parliament in the reign of King Charles the Second.[56]

These subjected Marines at sea to the same capricious system of discipline as the seamen. HMS *Prosperine*'s seamen and Marines jointly suffered the brutality of a Captain who forced defaulters to drink salt water, stopped wine and other comforts for the sick, and beat men with his speaking trumpet. Naval discipline lacked even the imperfect checks and balances of a military court martial, where the Commanding Officer reviewed proceedings independently, and could apply a measure of clemency. John Howe was victim of a typical example of arbitrary naval proceedings. A single uncorroborated witness picked him out at random:

> the Lieu' would not allow me or any other person to Speak in my be half one Man was Confind and sent on board our Ship with me for [to] tell the truth to Clear me. And next day we were brought to the Gangway but wasnot allowd to speak in our own behalf and was punished with a Dozen Lashes each.[57]

Summary justice provoked resentment and genuine acts of indiscipline.

Private Thomas Bustle snapped his musket at a Midshipman while on sentry duty,

> but by providence it only flashed in ye pan. . . . twas a grudge the said marine had, he being some small time before negligent and deneying of his duty, ye s^d midshipman gave him a box or two on the ear, at which he was heard to threaten that he would be up with him e're long.[58]

The power of ships' captains was absolute, and had predictably corrupting effects, despite a few exceptions:

> that will not punish Marines legally, with a dozen Lashes, without the Knowledge and Concurrence of their own Officers; but those are Gentlemen who know the Decorum necessary to be observed between Gentleman and Gentleman, notwithstanding any local Superiority of Command.[59]

Lieutenant Tatton Brown thought his Captain in the *Royal George* in 1811: 'one who cannot respect any person, overbearing to his inferiors in rank and a sycophant before his Superiors and is seldom respected by either of them.'[60] Captain Edward Codrington, reputed a humane man, sentenced 188 men to be flogged in HMS *Blake* from 1811 to 1813. Thirty-seven were Marines: eleven of whom were forgiven, while twenty received the standard dozen. Only five suffered more, including one sentence of three dozen lashes for striking an officer. Drink provoked over half the offences including one of, 'Skulking and throwing his trousers overboard'.[61]

Some Captains seem to have gone quite mad. Maximilian Jacobs of HMS *Defiance* ran amok when the ship's people objected to the immediate flogging of two men, contrary to custom:

> This So exasperated him that he rund to the Sentinel at his Cabbin door and demanded his Cutlash. but he refuseing to give it. he runs to one of the Guns and takes out one of the handspikes and was Going to the Gangway where the People was assembled. and most probably would have beat out Some of their brains had not the officers interposed.[62]

Long cruises provided plenty of scope for mutual irritation, even between officers of unquestioned mental stability. HMS *Swiftsure's* Captain of Marines described his commanding officer as, 'the man with the bellyache. . . . as thoroughpaced a disagreeable as can well be met in the various changes and vicissitudes of the service'.[63] A contemporary found the Captain of HMS *Illustrious* 'a very unpleasant man. . . . but it is a

Soldier of the Lord High Admiral's Regiment wearing the original 'tawny' coat with red cuffs.

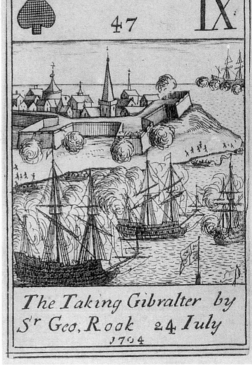

The capture of Gibraltar celebrated on a contemporary playing card.

Destruction of the *Royal James* at Sole Bay 1672, English Marines' earliest documented naval action.

Marine of the 1740s in
characteristic sugar-loaf
hat, as worn at Cartagena.

Marine detachment at action stations on the poop
of Liverpool privateer 1778.

Marine Officer, Grenadier, Drummer and Private Marine of 1776,
at the outbreak of the American Revolution.

Royal Marine sentinel
of the Napoleonic Wars.

Night attack on French invasion flotilla at Boulogne 15–16 August 1801:
Marines standing to fire from ships' boats.

An Exceedingly Comfortable
Corps: Marine walking out 1830.

The technological revolution in midstream: paddle gunboats and
wooden walls bombard Sidon 27 Sept 1840.

Officer and Gunners of the expanding Royal Marine
Artillery of the 1850s.

Marines and Riflemen rough it on Balaklava Heights.

The Blue Devils at Tel-el-Kebir, by a participant.

melancholy fact that the whole of the Marine Officers Service afloat is one constant struggle to maintain the character of a soldier with the dignity of a gentleman.'[64] An early Victorian handbook for young officers warned its purchasers that 'everything relating to soldiering is done by sufferance in a Man of War.'[65] Some Captains might have preferred to dispense with Marine officers altogether. When a newly wedded Lieutenant of Marines accidentally drowned, hurrying aboard his ship at the last minute, his unsympathetic Captain asked the Admiralty not to send another Lieutenant, 'but a good Sergeant that will always be under command'.[66] Marine officers rarely kept watch, and attracted charges of absenteeism, idleness and intrigue, 'disturbing the lieutenants who have the watch of the deck, with the rattling of backgammon, or the scraping upon a violin'.[67]

The coin had two sides, however. Sir Charles Littleton lamented the great slaughter among his officers at Schooneveldt in 1673:

> I think they lose their lives very unusefully, and certainly, if there be service intended for them ashore, they might have been better husbanded, for no land officer above a corporal does or can signify anything a shipboard above the rate of a private soldier.[68]

The mischievous Marine who lurked behind the nom de plume A Quondam Sub grumbled at how, 'the naval trumpeters [i.e. Lieutenants RN] labor'd hard to ease me from the burdensome drudgery of command.'[69] Boredom might give way to depression. A surgeon wrote of his ship's Lieutenant of Marines, that despite being a sportsman and staunch bottle companion, 'the confines of a ship gave him an over proportion of general disease and melancholy, and his not having any taste for letters prevented him from using one of the most efficacious remedies on board ship for ennui.' Letters from home brought welcome but erratic relief from the isolation of sea service. John Fernyhough complained on the eve of Trafalgar, 'Sometimes I fancy myself deserted by all the world, every ship brings letters to everyone but myself.'[70] Transatlantic postal delays drove Lewis Roteley to despair:

> I am quite tired of writing letters its now 6 or 8 months since I received any letters from you or my wife I have written by all conveyances by ships we fell in with at sea by way of America & by Post I begin to think you are all dead.[71]

Wardrooms were boisterous places and demanded a robust style. Quondam Sub thought it essential never to give way on service matters, right or wrong: 'This will procure you the character of a d—d obstinate fellow, who sticks to his point like a rusty weathercock; and will enable you to carry many essentials to your own ease.' To resolve debates at the dinner table he recommended brandishing a joint of mutton: 'This wielded with tolerable dexterity and prowess, will bring many converts to your side of the question. . . [and] make your antagonist particularly cautious, at least with respect to the time of his venturing to oppose you in future.'[72] Small ships, commanded by a junior Lieutenant with only a Sergeant of Marines, offered most opportunity for inexperience and class distinction to lead to a catastrophic breakdown in relations. The commanding officer of HM Sloop *Griffon* was hanged in 1813, amidst universal lamentations, after stabbing his Sergeant, who had refused to walk the quarterdeck like a common sentinel, as punishment for foul-mouthed insolence.[73] Violence between officers was common. Lewis Roteley conducted two affairs of honour with HMS *Cleopatra*'s Second Lieutenant, who subsequently committed suicide:

> I was under the necessity of calling the deceased out or to have forfited all pretentions to the Character of a Gentleman after Firing I received the most soothing apology for which I am under the greatest obligation to Mr Masterman. . . had it not been for him either Longfields Body or mine must have been left on the Field as it was the second time of going out with him.[74]

Luckily for himself, Roteley could show he was elsewhere at the moment of the subsequent tragedy, as 'the set of Illiterate Fellows that composed the Jury was very inquisitive concerning me.' The Admiralty banned duels in 1844, but as late as 1845 a Captain in the East Indies put a Marine and a naval officer ashore to settle their differences, the Marine shooting the other, 'right through his Sunday seat as he stood sideways'.[75] The same year saw one of the last duels in England between Lieutenant Hawkey RM, who shot a Hussar officer at Gosport, and escaped hanging when the inquest attributed the subsequent fatality to medical incompetence, rather than the bullet.

Wardrooms were not universally unhappy, or Captains tyrannical. Lewis Roteley reported on joining HMS *Victory* at Spithead: 'I like the ship very well, they are a fine set of fellows. . . . We have Capital Dinners on board', although Lord Nelson's imminent arrival threatened domestic calamity: 'in case of sailing without receiving my trunk, I shall be in a pretty state for a two year voyage with half a dozen shirts.'[76] Richard Swale spent his first few months 'at sea' in a receiving ship twenty yards from Portsmouth Hard, 'here we carried on the War in very handsome

Stile. . . Suffice it to say no young men could have enjoyed themselves more.' A subsequent trip to Cork occasioned further jollity:

> We all dined in the Wardroom, drunk coffee and supped in the Captain's Cabbin he made one of the party, Several of the ladies sung very well indeed. . . after 12 we began to dance and kept it up until the daylight. We all went to bed for about 4 hours and after Breakfast began again to Dance and kept it up until 3 and the same evening sailed with a fair wind for Spithead.[77]

Personal relations varied, as might have been expected. A young Marine officer's thumbnail sketches of his messmates in 1812 ranged from 'A good officer, a most honourable messmate, and a gentleman in all his dealings', through a variety of good fellows, fools and drunkards to 'B-g-r'.[78]

Marine Officers' poor career prospects provided an enduring institutional basis for wardroom friction. Quondam Sub wrote of the 'particularly distressing and singular' predicament of the Corps, being subject to 'the depreciating jealousy' of the Army, but systematically excluded from honour and promotion by the Royal Navy:

> I well know what portion of glory the engrossing grasp of n—l despotism can allow to others, where it holds the situation of supremacy. In short, THE LAURELS WHICH YOU WIN, OTHERS WEAR.[79]

When Paul Harris Nicholas compiled *Historical Record of the Royal Marine Forces* in the 1840s, he lamented the failure of naval despatches to name Marine Officers. The First Lieutenant of every ship of the line present at a Napoleonic fleet action was invariably promoted, but Marine promotions in the same circumstances were limited to the most senior officer in the fleet:

> if the Captain of Marines has more pay, the Sea Lieutenant has more authority. In the event of an action, the latter was morally certain of promotion upon the death of his Captain, while the former could gain nothing but the honour and gratification of having done his duty.[80]

The paradoxical result of this amphibious neglect was to encourage Marines to surpass more favoured units, on the parade ground, and in action:

> Thus situated, your conduct must continue to be such as will defy the breath of defamation. . . so that when other corps with reluctance shew

the colour of their facings to an entrenched enemy, you may never leave off dusting pipe clay, and dashing THROUGH THICK AND THIN.[81]

The Private Marine could expect little personal advancement, but all ranks shared one great inducement: prize money. The Admiralty first allowed soldiers in HM Ships to win prize money in 1696. Captains shared with the naval lieutenants, lieutenants with warrant officers, and NCOs with petty officers. Queen Anne's Declaration of Council at the outbreak of war in 1702 omitted Marines, forcing a company of Villiers' Regiment to petition for their share, after their ship took a valuable French prize. The authorities, having no personal interest in the proceeds, reasserted established practice: 'Petitioners were borne on the ship's books and at all times took equal risks with the seamen. . . Her Majesty is inclined to grant the request.'[82] No privilege could have had so satisfactory an effect on recruitment into the service, or to exertion once within it.

Private Marines at the capture of the Spanish treasure ship *Hermione* in 1762 received £484 each, echoes of which may have decided John Howe to enlist. His own winnings were more modest, ranging from 'a Skeyn of thread and needle each man', to £14 for an American ship, 'Loaden with flowr'.[83] Howe was doubly unfortunate when he helped take a convoy of Dutch East Indiamen off South Africa. As an acting Sergeant he appeared in the ship's books as a Corporal, so only received a private's share. Two of the prizes were lost at sea and others plundered at Limerick: 'Where Some of the Princeple officers Robd the Ships they had Charge of and made off Deal of the Goods was Stol here and Caried on Shore and Sold by the Ships Crews.'[84]

Prospects of a successful cruise encouraged a business-like approach. Ships made formal agreements to share the profits of a given station. Lewis Roteley traded places on the sea service roster to join HMS *Milan*, rather than a less profitable two-decker:

> It cost me Ten Pounds to get into this Frigate for a Handsome Present to a Person High in Office and a Trifle to the officer who Exchanged Sea duties with me who by the by had no Idea at the time that this Ship would fall to his lott he has since offerd me Twenty Guineas to Cancle the Exchange.

Subsequent letters evoke the thrills and frustrations of the chase: 'Rig out Studding sails – a prize a prize was the cry a Spanish Frigate full of Dollars by God all was expectation I thought I should be Thousand Pounds richer before night.' That chase ended in disappointment, but even a successful interception began a protracted and uncertain process: 'I have not heard of our Tortola prizes yet as that place is a den of Rogues. I am afraid some Foul Play is going on there but we seldom get money for Neutrals under two years.' A year later Roteley was still waiting. He had bought the Master's rights to an American prize for £10 down, but the Prize Court let her go: 'the first time I ever speculated and I think it will be the last.'[85]

Single Men in Barracks

While their character as soldiers set Marines apart from their shipmates, the occupation of permanent quarters ashore distinguished them from their military comrades in arms. Marines were the first complete British corps to possess fixed headquarters, and to live in barracks. Regiments of Foot led a nomadic existence, marching from one billeting area to another and would not have fixed depots until the late nineteenth century. The institutional stability that followed from the Marines' co-location with other parts of the Royal Navy's infrastructure had profound consequences for the character of the Corps, compensating for the dispersal and unpredictability of sea service.

Marines had been associated with naval dockyards from Stuart times. A company of the Admiral's Regiment occupied a 'Blocus' at Chatham as early as 1665, while three companies were at Plymouth in 1667, and another three at Portsmouth in 1672. Marines wintered near Deptford in the 1690s to work in the overstretched dockyard there, 'with the encouragement of sixpence a day'.[86] The headquarters of Queen Anne's Marine Regiments were near rather than in the already crowded ports, but the Order in Council definitively established the Marines at Chatham, Portsmouth and Plymouth, where they would remain for 200 years. It also made provision for them to work in the dockyards, when not required at sea, 'and have such allowance for the same as shall appear reasonable'.[87] This was pure profit as the Clerk of the Cheque paid the men their sixpences without any deduction on account of their military pay. Marines received no extra pay for guarding dockyards, for example during the strike of Portsmouth shipwrights in January 1743, when they had the Commissioner's orders to fire if the rioters threatened the Dockyard. Marines nearly came to blows with shipwrights again in 1768, when they took the maties' timber off-cuts for firewood:

> Both sides drew up in a line of battle, the Shipwrights armed with adzes
> and axes, and the Marines with their muskets and bayonets fixed, but

happily the superior officer having notice of this fray, arrived just time enough, and prevented the consequences by ordering the Marines to restore the chips.[88]

Marines were too valuable in wartime to leave ashore as watchmen. The Admiralty rebuked Admiral Vernon for misusing Marines during the Jacobite scare of 1745, as they could be 'employed much more usefully to His Majesty's service in serving on board his men of war for which immediate purpose they were raised, and not to garrison untenable old castles.'[89] In the crisis of 1778, Admiral Keppel stripped 150 Marine sentries from Haslar Hospital and Forton Jail, for the Channel Fleet.

The establishment of the Grand Divisions did not change the nature of Marine accommodation immediately. Like other soldiers in Georgian England they lived in little groups of eight, six or even two in the only quarters permitted under the Mutiny Act: 'Inns, Livery Stables, Ale-Houses, Victualling Houses and all houses of persons selling Brandy, Strong Waters, Cyder or Metheglin'. Garrison communities had to endure the consequent drunkenness and indiscipline, not only from the rank and file. Lieutenant la Boulay of Mordaunt's short-lived Marine Regiment at Peter Port, Guernsey faced cashiering: 'having on 25 June at night come with the guard to the door of Jean Martin, who was ill, and called him by foul and abusive names, called on him to come down and that he would kill him and all his generation.' Boulay was beyond financial penalties, having 'nothing but his sword to depend on', and could not be confined, 'as there was only one other officer fit for duty [and] the French swarm on the coast.'[90]

Dockyard expansion during the Seven Years War combined with the formation of the Marines to put unbearable pressure on the home ports. Chatham Division spilled into Rochester, 'to the great distress of the inhabitants'.[91] Portsmouth had a hellish reputation until the first Marine Barracks opened there on 20 May 1765, in a converted naval cooperage. Chatham and Plymouth acquired new buildings, opening in 1780 and 1781 respectively. The Marines' settled existence allowed a succession of progressive commandants like Mackenzie at Chatham (1771–83) and Collins at Plymouth (1784–93) to stamp their love of order upon the Corps:

> for the Good of the National Service, the Welfare happiness and Regularity of Individuals as well as to preserve a true Military Subordination. . . without which there can be no regular Discipline.[92]

The social implications of concentrating soldiers in barracks were as significant as the aggregation of factory hands in mills and foundries. Thousands of individuals became accustomed to the regulated group behaviour that would form the basis of industrial society. Officers in barracks had to wear uniform at all times, one bold subaltern refusing a blue-coated Colonel Mackenzie entry. Printed Instructions in every barrack room reminded every Marine of his duty. Colonels Commandant issued streams of orders dealing with the novel circumstances of barrack life: the issue of pewter chamber pots 'to prevent a nuisance in the Barracks', window cleaning, unauthorised 'Scaling or going over the Walls', and sentries who defaced their sentry boxes 'by carving Names, and making holes with their Bayonets'.

Divisions employed barrack women to wash clothes and scour bedsteads with hot water, soap and sand, 'to destroy as much as possible Bugs and other Vermin, breeding in the Crevices or Joints'. Hygiene was as essential in barracks as on board ship:

> Particular care to be taken, that on no pretence whatsoever, are any old Cloathes, Rags, Living or Dead Dogs or Cats, or any other Animal or thing whatsoever, thrown into the Boghouses, which may prevent the Drains in performing their so necessary office.[93]

Ancient military pastimes such as poaching came under attack, as did the sexual licence that must have been commonplace in billets:

> The Commanding Officer is sorry to find it necessary in this public manner, strictly to forbid any officer bringing or suffering to be brought into the Barracks or Guard Room, any Woman of loose or suspected bad Character or to lodge a night in the Barrack.

Officers doing the rounds at night were 'particularly to enquire that no other women lye in the Men's Rooms, except those who are publickly appointed to that Business', although the exact nature of the business was not specified.[94]

Discipline in barracks allowed less arbitrary brutality than at sea. The Commandant at Chatham complained in the 1750s: 'the Men are struck and beat notwithstanding former orders to the contrary, he repeats that no Man be struck with Hand or Stick on any account whatsoever.'[95] Terence O'Loghlen argued that 'Soldiers of a Patriot King who fight the Battles of their country, ought not to be treated like Slaves at the Option of hot-headed Individuals.'[96] Marines were encouraged to regulate their own behaviour by such devices as excusing able and steady men from drill, except for the twice-weekly field days, and allowing leave of absence to those who met the complex uniform regulations, wearing their hat properly cocked, and their queue exactly eighteen inches long. Formal procedures replaced disorderly naval practices of petitions and coming aft onto the quarterdeck: 'whenever any complaint is made, it may be stated by one man accompanied by a non-commissioned officer – if the grounds are just, redress shall be given.'[97] Efforts were made to mitigate the rigours of the disciplinary process. John Howe fell asleep on sentry duty, after ten days in the Corps, when he 'knew very Little the nature of a Sentinal'. Sentenced to 300 lashes, he was pardoned by the Commanding Officer, his Sergeant and Sergeant-Major giving him a good character as 'a remarkable Clean Tractable Lad that gave no trouble to any Person', who 'Learnd his exercise faster than any he had observed a long time for he had been five days in the first Squad, tho only a fortnight in the Division.'[98] Unluckily for himself, Howe was not a quick learner in other respects. Later he suffered 300 and 400 lashes for selling his own and other people's clothing, and drinking the proceeds. Another young Marine had a narrow escape from the cat and from drowning. Treated to a drink by a smuggling acquaintance while standing guard on Southsea beach, William Dew was rescued next day from the middle of Spithead, still in his sentry box, 'unable to give any coherent account of how he got on the Mother Bank', while the shingle revealed the passage of heavy barrels. Unwilling to flog a recruit, and hardly able to stop laughing, the Colonel suggested he volunteer for the First Fleet, bound for Australia, to escape the triangle.[99]

Lesser crimes than taking a cruise in a sentry box attracted less terrible punishments. Men who failed to shave and shift their clothing on Sunday and Thursday had their grog stopped. One slovenly Marine in Bermuda was sent on board ship, and kept hard at work for 'being a disgrace to the Battalion'. Excessive drinking lay behind most misbehaviour. The Captain of *Queen Charlotte* complained in 1797 of 'The incorrigible drunkenness and irregularity of several of the Marines of this ship. . . the Centinels get drunk on their posts and the guard are equally criminal'. He wondered whether their removal might not be preferable 'to such incessant punishment as must follow unless I suffer the discipline of the ship to be entirely subverted'.[100] Major George Lewis RM fulminated against the 'disgusting scenes of drunkenness which took place' following his Battalion's arrival in Bermuda. He expected NCOs to set an example of sobriety, 'without which a Body of men becomes a rabble, a disgrace to themselves and to the Country which gave them birth'. The frequency with which NCOs lost their stripes for drunkenness, and as often had them restored, suggests they were as susceptible as anyone. Suitable candidates must have been scarce. Lewis also reduced a Corporal, 'being subject to fits and therefore unqualified for a NCO'.[101]

Concentration of personnel at three Grand Divisions offered unparalleled opportunities for training. Line regiments scattered in billets or pursuing smugglers could rarely bring together more than a company or two, and were often unfit for service. Marine Divisions, in peacetime, could form a full battalion of ten parade companies, including Grenadiers and Light Infantry. Two drills a day and twice weekly field days soon brought new arrivals up to scratch. On joining his Division in 1799 Richard Swale waited on a Captain to whom he had been introduced in London, and:

> With the greatest hospitality and attention he took the trouble to go with me to all the Field and other officers of our Corps in consequence of which they took great pains to instruct me in the methods I was to pursue and the rules to observe... in a short time had the satisfaction of being taken notice of as an attentive good officer Recommended and Qualified to take charge of a party.[102]

Thorough training at headquarters was essential as Marine officers depended on their own resources once at sea, with no one else in smaller vessels to turn to for advice. Wartime expansion in the 1780s inspired fears that 'those who stand first on the Roster for Sea Duty, and Service, may not be so well qualified for separate commands, as others lower down.' Two majors were appointed to 'examine into the military abilities of those officers and report their opinion to the Commanding Officer'. Demand for drafts varied wildly even in peacetime, for example from 3 at Chatham in April 1783 (103 all ranks) to 15 the following month (383 all ranks). Standing Orders ensured such requests were met promptly: 'The two Captains and three Subalterns first for Sea Duty, not to be Detached from Headquarters for more than 48 hours till ordered for embarkation'. Drafting policy was benign in principle, selecting Marines with least sea time, or most debts, and specifying that they were properly trained and equipped:

> The Adjutant to be very attentive that when any Marines are ordered for Foreign or actual immediate service, that they be forwardest in their Discipline, and Military Knowledge and the Quartermaster is to be very carefull, that every Marine is furnished with proper Arms and Accoutrements and every other thing necessary.[103]

The Corps had made substantial progress since 1711, when Admiral Sir Hovenden Walker had to check for himself that 'every man at his coming on board is provided with arms and all necessary accoutrements', and Colonel Bor's men pursued HMS *Devonshire* down the Solent in a small boat.[104]

CHAPTER SIX

The Marines and the Emperor

THE Marine Corps came of age during the twenty-two year conflict with Revolutionary and Napoleonic France. Marines took their full part in the sea battles that settled the century old Anglo-French struggle for maritime supremacy, and worked alongside bluejackets in countless raids and expeditions as part of an integrated amphibious team. The Corps acquired new disciplinary and gunnery roles so significant that they have sometimes been mistaken for its primary purpose. These new functions enhanced the military character of the Corps and its status within the Navy, recognized in 1802 by the title 'Royal Marines'.

The Breeze at Spithead

The single greatest threat to British victory over a French Marine crippled by revolution was the poor state of the Royal Navy's industrial relations. In 1797 mutinies at Spithead and the Nore paralysed the Channel Fleet, although the extent of Marine involvement remains controversial. In the long run the mutinies benefited Marines with better pay and provisions, and greater autonomy on board ship.

The real surprise about the disturbances of the 1790s is that they did not happen sooner. Admiral Vernon had prophesied large-scale mutinies, unless Government reformed a fleet 'defrauded by injustice. . . manned by violence, and maintained by cruelty.'[1] Arbitrary recruiting, poor food and accommodation, irregular pay and harsh treatment provoked disorders throughout the eighteenth-century. The Captain of a desperately overcrowded ship in 1707 reported his men 'so extreme mutinous that we do not know what to do with them, my officers cannot go between decks without being abused or knockt down.' He had thirty-seven Marines, but they could do no more than 'keep Centrys at the Cables for fear they should cutt 'em and run the ships ashore.'[2] In 1779 HMS *Defiance*'s people refused to sail with Maximilian Jacobs, claiming he had flogged fifty of them 'for meer trifles':

> On which they all Calld out togeather. Another Captain. No Jacobs. No Jacobs. and immediately got the foremost Gun on each side run in and Pointed aft these were brought as far as the fore hatchway where they Layd a bulwark of hammocks a Cross the ship to defend them from Small Shot that might be fired on them from aft.[3]

The Marines stood by with loaded muskets, but on this occasion the Admiral and ship's officers pacified the crew, without violence.

Early Corps historians believed Marines remained similarly loyal throughout the mutinies of 1797. Gillespie wrote of 'The steady faithfulness of all those Marine soldiers who had served during the American War', and their 'unshaken resolve to stand or fall with their officers'. Field suggested that, handled with resolution, the Corps could have 'reduced the mutinies at Spithead and the Nore to a mere flash in the pan', citing the refusal of HMS *Agamemnon*'s Captain to commit his Marines, 'because some of the men would be shot, and he could not endure seeing them lying suffering on the deck.'[4] As good regimental officers Field and Nicholas played down Marine complicity in the mutinies, blaming the whole unsavoury episode upon agents provocateurs: Corresponding Societies, United Irishmen, Sunday Schools and foreigners impressed into the Service.

The reality was more complex. Marines shared the seamen's economic grievances – the wages of neither had increased since the 1660s. The Spithead mutineers associated the Marines in their demands, referring to 'our brethren the Marines', and insisted they receive the same pay rise as Ordinary Seamen.[5] The great mutinies followed a tradition of lower-deck protest that Field himself traced back to Stuart times. They were in no way revolutionary, despite an anti-Jacobin Captain characterizing the outbreak as 'perfectly French'.[6] The seamen did not murder their officers and made it plain they would fight if the enemy put to sea. Lieutenant Mortimer Timpson remained on board HMS *Montague* throughout the mutiny at the Nore, as did her Captain: 'allowed our liberty and permitted to walk the quarter deck without any insult or molestation'. The only officer he saw mistreated was the Doctor, tarred and covered with handfuls of feathers from a pillow, 'as you would flour a piece of roasting beef with the flour dredge. . . even to the clocks of his stockings'.[7] HMS

Montague's detachment had repressed an initial outbreak with great steadiness. When cheering seamen loaded and pointed guns aft in the traditional manner, the Marines lined both sides of the lower deck: 'The seamen were then ordered to restore the Guns to their places & told, that if they did not, we should fire on them: they obeyed and we were dismissed'. The Marines' messmates must have suborned them overnight, for next day, 'Captain Knight found the whole of the Ship's crew, together with the Marines, forward on the Lower Deck in a state of mutiny and could get none of them to come aft to their duty.'[8]

Marine establishments had been cut to 4,495 after the American War of Independence, but quadrupled after the outbreak of war with France, so in 1797 most Marines were young soldiers. A Captain at Portsmouth explained the problem to Earl Spencer, the First Lord:

> No reliance can be placed on the Marines, who are recruits, and never had any habits of military life or discipline from the seamen, [who] are one class with them. This is one of the evils of keeping the establishment of that corps so low in peace.[9]

Isolated resistance to the mutineers came from NCOs. A Corporal of Marines was ducked twice at Spithead for refusing to take the delegates' oath, but was put ashore unharmed. Sergeant Jenkins of HMS *Monmouth* at the Nore received three dozen lashes and had his head shaved, for continued attention to duty. Against him stood Sergeants Dunn, one of the Nore delegates, 'whom they now call Captain of Marines', and Dickinson at Plymouth, who made one of HMS *Saturn*'s more literate Marines copy out a mutinous oath.[10]

Contemporary Marine officers were unsympathetic to the mutiny. Fitting out at Spithead, Lieutenant Robyns suffered 'the mortification of witnessing the state of anarchy and confusion of the fleet', and 'the disgraceful mutiny which has now happily subsided'.[11] The men generally displayed solidarity with the seamen. Admiral Duncan at the Nore reported, 'the Marines in most ships have joined the seamen', as they had at Spithead. In *Pompee*, 'The Marines mixed with the Ships Company, and were equally forward in the business.' In *Mars* they joined the mutineers when brought to the point of opposing their shipmates: 'ordered under arms and on the word being given to prime and load they immediately laid down their arms and came forward to join the ship's company.'[12] Naval officers usually avoided such confrontations, with one instructive exception. When the Spithead delegates attempted to board the *London* on Sunday, 7 May, Admiral Colpoys secured the ship against them, sent the seamen below, and posted Marines around the upper decks. When the men below grew restless, Colpoys had the officers fire down the gangways, until infuriated seamen broke into the magazine and unlashed the middle deck guns, when the Marines threw down their arms and allowed their shipmates on deck. Lieutenant Simms of Marines and one of his men were wounded, along with two more of the Admiral's party. Four or five seamen died, but the good sense of their leaders prevented further bloodshed. Colpoys had deceived himself as to the strength of feeling among the seamen, and the solidarity between them and the Marines. He claimed the Marines 'had given all reason to suppose they meant to stand by us', but the 'premeditated murder' of their unarmed shipmates had tried them too sorely.[13]

The 1797 mutiny at Spithead achieved substantial pay rises for seamen and Marines, and eliminated the abuse whereby pursers issued fourteen ounces of provisions for every sixteen allowed by the ration scales. Even the First Lord admitted, 'The wages were undoubtedly too low in proportion to the times', and expressed surprise 'that the purser's deductions, and the system of short weights and measures depending on it, should have been so long tolerated.'[14] In addition, none of the Marines' allowances ashore were to be stopped while at sea. The Nore mutineers were left with a variety of competing objectives: 'a different distribution of Prize Money – an alteration in their Provisions – That the ship should be docked &c &c: in short they hardly knew what they wanted.' The Grand Committee fell out with the Petty Committees in the individual ships, inspiring a gradual return to duty. HMS *Montague* was ordered round to Portsmouth, where thirteen 'ringleaders' were court-martialled, and her Marines exchanged for a fresh detachment. Timpson's confidence in his men was unshaken:

> I must say that the Marines, in the first instance, behaved as well as men could do, and, I am sure, that it was not without great difficulty and much persuasion, that they were at last induced to join the Mutiny: had they been kept to themselves, after the *first* outbreak, the result might very probably have been different.[15]

The separation of Marines from seamen is usually associated with Earl St Vincent, but the idea predated the mutinies. Admiral Knowles recommended in 1796 that Marines were 'birthed Aft next the Gun room on both sides'.[16] A Captain urged Spencer at the height of the Spithead mutiny:

> The Marines have ever been a separate body from the seamen. I have never known an instance of their having been concurred in a mutiny. . .

and they are men which we look to in general for protection in such disagreeable situations; therefore the fear of separating the Marines and seamen, is rather to be courted than dreaded.[17]

Earl St Vincent, Commander-in-Chief in the Mediterranean had both opportunity and will to implement the measure. He assembled his captains of Marines, 'under pretext of informing them about uniformity in dress, in exercise, and in economy: but really to give them some sense about keeping a watchful eye, not only upon their own men, but upon the seamen.' He laid down a deliberate policy of bringing the Marines forward and separating them physically from the seamen:

> to this effect I directed that in the ships of three decks, they should be berthed in the after part of the middle deck; and in those of two decks, close to the bulkhead of the gun rooms, or to the officers' cabins before it, giving them the two after berths on each side, from one side of the ship to the other, that they might not be burst in on.[18]

St Vincent implemented various measures to improve his Marines' status, and emphasise their distinct military identity, directing their officers to visit them at their meals, and keep up the pride and spirit of their detach-ments. A Quondam Sub had complained that lieutenants RN undermined Marine discipline by 'imposing on them such tasks, as sunk them in their own estimation, by insulting their military pride'.[19] St Vincent freed his Marines from ordinary ships' duties, to spend their whole time under the supervision of their own officers, except when shifting anchors or getting under sail. He recognized the importance of NCOs, and argued their numbers should be doubled to four sergeants and four corporals in a 74-gun ship: 'that they may be relied on in case of any further attempt being made by the seditious to wrest the command of His Majesty's ships from the officers.'[20] St Vincent stressed formal discipline to overawe the im-pressionable. He enforced uniformity of dress among the fleet's Marine detachments, each ship sending 'an intelligent Sergeant and their Master Tailor to look at the pattern winter and summer regimentals, working jacket, hat, etc', on board the flagship. Every morning, in full dress uniform, St Vincent watched the guard mounted, 'with all the form and order practised on the best regulated parades', while the band played 'God Save the King', and the Guard presented arms, 'with the respect and decorum due to the occasion'.[21]

An unlikely alliance of united Irishmen and conservative captains resisted the differentiation of Marines and seamen. St Vincent retaliated by forbidding use of Irish among the Marines, and appointing an Inspector of Marines to enforce the new regime. A retired Admiral accused St Vincent of 'completely overturning the natural order of things'. A military force could not enforce obedience at sea, as Marines would never challenge the seamen, upon whom the ship's safety depended. Their only qualification was their ability to load and fire a musket, and many never acquired 'what is called sea-legs and are therefore in great measure useless in bad weather at sea'.[22] As Marines spent years at sea, this was clearly nonsense. On the contrary, ships full of pressed men but lacking Marines would soon have been immobilized by desertion, or fallen victim to fire and disorder.

St Vincent put new vigour into existing practice. Many naval officers were happy to enhance the standing of their Marines, although few went as far as the Captain who appealed to his detachment to stand by King and Country with the words, 'Then, loyal and Royal Marines, we don't care a damn for the bluejackets!'[23] Captain's Orders for HMS *Mars* in 1795 had already addressed the 'general complaint that the marine officers do not possess sufficient authority and command over their own men when embarked', giving them exclusive responsibility for 'their interior economy as well as their prompt obedience and dispatch in coming upon deck and performing the public duty of the ship'. The author forbade,

> improper interference on the part of the naval officers of the ship. . . as they have only to acquaint the officers of marines upon duty what neglect he discovers and what is necessary to be done and he will order his sergeant etc to see it executed.[24]

Marine officers and NCOs became the main channel for issuing orders to the men, 'by which means the interference of the Boatswain and his mates may be less necessary'.[25] Marine officers learned to resent appeals against their authority. Objections to measures, 'to prevent Drunkenness and Rioting', among Marines in North America, drew a furious response: 'The Commanding Officer cannot avoid expressing his astonishment and displeasure at the conduct of those men of the Battalion who presumed to appeal from his decision to that of a Naval Officer.'[26]

Naval opinion regarded Marines more warmly now than in the 1690s when a 'Splenetick Gentleman' at the Admiralty had allegedly referred to them as 'Water Rats'.[27] Commenting favourably on the augmentation in 1801, the *Naval Chronicle* wrote of 'the admitted importance of this corps, than whom there are no better soldiers'.[28] At the Peace of Amiens in 1802 the Marine establishment was held at 12,119, preserving experienced cadres for resumed hostilities with Napoleonic France. Officers in the Channel Fleet suggested Marines provide a quarter of ship's complements, replacing landsmen for most duties, and forming 'the strongest possible barrier against internal irregularity'.[29] By 1810 a first-rate's detachment had risen from 100 Private Marines sanctioned in 1747 to 166. The 1808 regulations reserved the Admiralty's veto upon Marines transferring into the Navy, implying that they were now equal in value to seamen.[30]

St Vincent always admitted his partiality to the Corps, and looked forward to the day 'when there is not another foot soldier in the kingdom, in Ireland, or the Colonies, except the King's Guards and Artillery'.[31] As First Lord of the Admiralty he was instrumental in obtaining the Marines their Royal distinction, an honour borne only by the oldest and most distinguished infantry regiments. Communicated on 29 April 1802, the award occasioned grand festivities at the three Headquarters. Dark blue facings, as worn by all Royal regiments, replaced impractical white. New uniforms, modelled at His Majesty's express command on those of 1st Foot Guards, first appeared at the King's birthday parade on 4 June 1802. The beauty and fashion of Stonehouse filled the windows of the officers' barracks to watch the Plymouth battalion fire volleys in the air, while the band played 'God Save the King', the ladies fluttering their handkerchiefs in response to three hearty cheers for His Majesty: 'a most animating scene, as the Royal Corps of Marines, both in peace and war, have ever been considered by the nation at large as a family and constitutional corps.'[32] The Marines had travelled a long way since Tory publicists had denounced them as a danger to English liberty. At the end of his life St Vincent paid the Corps a last tribute:

> in obtaining for them the distinction of 'Royal' I but inefficiently did my duty. *I never knew an appeal made to them for honour, courage, or loyalty that they did not more than realize my highest expectations. If ever the hour of real danger should come to England they will be found the country's sheet anchor.*[33]

The Royal Marine Artillery

The Royal Marines' reliability and absolute dependence upon the Admiralty gained them a new function. Marines at sea had traditionally provided small-arms fire, an essential adjunct to great guns, but subordinate to them. In 1804 inter-service squabbles inspired formation of the Royal Marine Artillery, who soon became something of an élite within the Corps.

The Navy's makeshift recruitment policies prevented development of a body of seaman gunners similar to the French companies of Marine Artillery. In 1761 a cavalry officer had proposed demobilised Royal Artillery-men should replace naval quarter gunners, 'who having no education or instruction until they are pressed and carried aboard the Ships of War, are by no means equal to these men, regularly trained to the use of great guns'. A far-sighted scheme of the 1770s proposed Marine barracks should include a battery with gunports and sea service guns: 'The people to be constantly exercised with their guns in firing shot at a Target.' The author was ahead of his time, as was Admiral Kempenfeldt who argued, 'it would be great service to the Navy by rendering the Corps of Marines more useful, if they were trained to the management of artillery ashore, as in action it is generally necessary to quarter a part of them to the guns.' In 1796 Sir James Saumarez proposed training Marines as gunners, but deepening financial crisis allowed Earl Spencer to brush off the idea as 'well worthy of attention. . . which at a less pressing moment it might be worthwhile to renew'.[34]

Bureaucratic politics would speak louder than technical merit. The great advantage of Marines, for the Navy, had always been their unqualified submission to naval discipline. Straining every nerve to meet the French fleet in July 1778, Admiral Augustus Keppel preferred untrained Marines to soldiers: 'indeed they would have been raw and undisciplined. . . but yet as men really belonging to the fleet they must be more desirable.'[35] The employment of soldiers as Marines during the 1790s caused much friction. When government law officers supported military appeals against naval courts martial, Lord Cornwallis hauled down his flag in protest, post captains drafted mutinous petitions in Portsmouth coffee houses, and the Admiralty sent its infantrymen ashore. The only soldiers left on board HM ships were Royal Artillery-men in bomb vessels, whose mortars were technically beyond seamen gunners. Trouble continued as naval officers made Royal Artillery-men wash decks and stand sentinel, while the Army objected to their summary punishment. Nelson wrote intemperately of a military plot to subvert naval discipline:

> Let them once gain the step of being independent of the Navy on board a Ship, and they will soon have the other and command us. . . . it would embitter my future days and expiring moments, to hear of our Navy being sacrificed to the Army.[36]

Nelson's diatribe coincided with an undistinguished bombardment of Le Havre, when artillerymen refused to do more than serve the mortars. On 18 August 1804 an Order in Council established a company of Royal Marine Artillery at each divisional headquarters, selected from the most intelligent and experienced officers and men of the respective divisions, and paid at the same rate as their equivalents in the Royal Artillery. Each company consisted of 9 officers, 21 NCOs and drummers, and 62 gunners, the high proportion of cadres justified by the technical nature of their duties. The Admiralty established the RMA in a fit of pique, accidentally creating the Royal Navy's first gunnery specialists. Earlier Marines had manned guns on an ad hoc basis, first appearing as regular members of naval gun crews in the 1790s. In HMS *Indefatigable* in 1812 2 Marines joined 2 able and three ordinary seamen, 3 landsmen and a boy at each gun. The lowly position in the quarter bill of these extemporized Marine gunners differentiates them from the RMA, who in the coming century would make a key contribution to gunnery reform in the Royal Navy.

A period of neglect intervened, with much confusion over the remit of the new branch. The Board of Ordnance considered no part of the Field Train applicable to naval service, and refused to supply more than a single field gun, 'with which it being impossible to perform any evolution, they are neither able to perfect themselves in their profession, nor even to preserve that state of improvement to which they had arrived.'[37] When the Admiralty extracted guns from the Ordnance authorities, the Chatham gunners had to build their own storage shed in a disused chalk pit in their own time, with timber begged from the Dockyard. Naval officers objected for years to blue uniforms, despite the ruinous effects of powder smoke on red and white. Commanders of bomb vessels played the old game of climbing on the shoulders of the Marines who fought her. Lt Robert Steele RMA was twice passed over for promotion after directing the fire of HM Bomb *Etna* at the Basque Roads and Flushing, although,

> the commander of the vessel as compared with the commander of the artillery, in a bomb, stands in the relative position of the fly upon the coach wheel, when he says to his companion in rotary motion, 'what a devil of a dust you and I kick up'.[38]

Official neglect bred disciplined self-sufficiency. General Sir Charles Napier never forgot the Marines' refusal to join in the sack of Hampton during the War of 1812. While other British units ran amok, the RMA protested they were picked men, and refused to disgrace themselves by turning robbers and murderers: 'Never in my life have I met soldiers like the

Marine Artillery. We suffered much fatigue and hardship, but never was seen anything not admirable in these glorious soldiers.'[39] In Europe the RMA saw action from Sicily to Riga. A small detachment even served in the Battle of the Nations at Leipzig in 1813. In 1804 the RMA brought strange new weapons like Fulton's torpedoes and Congreve's rockets into action against French invasion flotillas, foreshadowing later Marine exploits with rocket-firing landing craft. At Cadiz, the last refuge of the Spanish Government, General Graham requested mortars and rockets, urging 'the expediency of sending these with some officers and men of the Royal Marine Artillery trained to the use of these weapons'.[40] The relative comfort of their depot ship contrasted sharply with the dangers of shelling French batteries from open boats, where a single round decapitated two RMA lieutenants, as they directed operations, somehow missing the Midshipman sat between them at the tiller. A red-hot shot burst through the filling room bulkhead of the bomb vessel *Hound*, glowing like a full moon amidst the loose powder, until Gunner John Collard RMA calmly emptied a fire bucket over both. Besides their primary function in bomb vessels, the RMA provided Marine battalions with close-support weapons. Field guns were more mobile than the ship's guns that usually accompanied landings, so could be deployed with less risk of capture. An RMA field battery formed part of a Marine battalion hurried off to Holland in 1813 with their old practice guns: six 6-pounders and two $5^1/_2$-inch howitzers. One of the 6-pounders saved the day at Krabbendyke in South Beveland, during a French sortie, alternately firing grape and changing position, its wounded commander perched on the limber.

The Nelson Touch

The RMA's widespread service reflected that of the Corps. The Marines' Royal title recognized not only their role as guarantors of the Royal Navy's internal security, but also their combat record, on every front of the naval war with Revolutionary and Napoleonic France. The decisive point of the war came at Trafalgar in October 1805. Twenty-seven British ships of the line defeated a Franco-Spanish fleet of thirty-three, to end a century of maritime conflict beginning with the first action of Torrington's and Pembroke's Marines off Beachy Head.

Marines still went into action closed up on poop and forecastle, as in *Le Juste* (80) where Second Lieutenant John Fernyhough RM 'was stationed with a party of Marines on the quarter deck, at the carronades. . .

to take up small arms, when occasion required, to annoy the enemy with volleys of musketry'.[41] The capture of the French frigate *Thetis* (40) by HMS *Amethyst* (36) in 1808, when both ships lost their mizenmasts, conformed to the traditional pattern of close-range mayhem:

> She had about thirty soldiers in her fore and main tops, and they kept up a constant fire, with their heaving their stinkpots on board; we sustained a heavy loss about this time, our ship being twice on fire, but was soon put out, and not time to clear the wreck on the quarter-deck. We lay muzzle to muzzle about an hour and ten minutes; our men often stealing their sponges, and the others serving us in the same way; and after an action of full three hours and twenty minutes, she struck after a most obstinate battle, leaving her deck entirely covered with dead and wounded.[42]

Minor details of Nelson's battles would have been familiar to Marines of earlier wars; only the results varied. Major Thomas Oldfield fought at the Nile, where Nelson destroyed or took eleven out of thirteen French ships of the line anchored in Aboukir Bay:

> At forty-five minutes past six, we were alongside the *Guerrier*, within seven yards of her. Our first broadside carried away her main and mizzenmasts; her deck was completely cleared; there was only one Frenchman to be seen. . . . We passed on to the *Spartiate* and anchored abreast of her; ten minutes afterwards the Admiral anchored on the other side; about half past eight we perceived the *Orient* to be on fire; at ten o'clock she blew up, and nearly 800 of her crew were destroyed by the explosion.[43]

Nelson achieved decisive results by taking risks against French squadrons debilitated by the Revolution that would not have paid off against the highly trained crews of the *Ancien Régime*. He could rely implicitly on his subordinates, as shown by an exchange recorded by Oldfield, as the British fleet closed on Aboukir Bay: 'at half past four the Admiral hailed us, and desired we would go ahead of him; this order was instantly and cheerfully obeyed. The Admiral bowed to me as we passed him; I never saw him looking so well.' It is hard to imagine a sharper contrast with the wretched squabbles that had disfigured the professional relationships of Admiral Vernon and his Marine officers.

The Royal Navy enjoyed a substantial moral advantage over its opponents throughout the Napoleonic Wars. Oldfield's description of the joy, 'instantly seen to illuminate every countenance' on discovery of the French fleet before the Battle of the Nile recurs throughout the growing number of accounts left by Marines of the period. John Fernyhough wrote of high excitement and 'joy inexpressible', when the French briefly emerged from Toulon in 1804: 'Now for the glorious conflict, for the honour of old England and her wooden walls!'[44] This confidence was not restricted to officers. Sergeant Packwood wrote how the Captain of *Thetis* 'was determined not to strike to a single decked ship, but she found Englishmen aboard the *Amethyst*.'[45] HMS *Orion*'s detachment yelled enthusiastically in response to their CO's laconic address, as they bore down on Aboukir Bay:

> "My lads, do you see these ships, and do you see that land there?"
> "Aye, aye, Sir."
> "Well, those are the enemy ships, and that's the Land of Egypt, and if you don't give those Frenchmen a damned good licking, you'll soon be in the House of Bondage!"[46]

Nelson became a talisman of victory, John Fernyhough reporting how his arrival off Cadiz on the eve of Trafalgar, 'dispelled all gloomy thoughts':

> Although the affair at Ferrol [Sir Robert Calder's indecisive action of 22 July 1805] has rather discomposed the public mind, I have no hesitation in declaring, that the result of a second attack will be both glorious and honourable for my country and the service; my confidence is founded upon the ardour and eagerness evinced by every individual under his lordship's command, so much is he respected and loved. [47]

Trafalgar is the first major naval action where sufficient detailed accounts survive to provide more than a generalized impression of the part played in it by Marines. This reflects public interest in a battle that ended a century of French invasion scares, and also the expansion of the Corps. The shortage of genuine Marines at the Glorious First of June in 1794 was such that half the British ships carried detachments of line regiments.[48] Cyril Field's only anecdote of the battle concerns a dead Marine's jacket, hoisted on a pike to replace HMS *Marlborough*'s colours. At Cape St Vincent it was a soldier of the 69th who smashed the *San Nicolas'* stern windows for Nelson's boarding party. By the time of Trafalgar, the Marine establishment had grown to 30,000, releasing line regiments for work ashore. A fourth Grand Division at Woolwich helped accommodate the additional numbers, which in 1807 peaked at 31,400. Some 2,600 Marines fought at Trafalgar, almost 10 per cent of the Corps.

Among them was Lewis Roteley of HMS *Victory*, who recorded his experiences in letters, a mutilated journal and notes for a speech. Sixteen-year old Paul Nicholas, the future historian of the Corps, also saw action there, in HMS *Belleisle* (74), an inspiring ship for any historically conscious Marine. Roteley and Nicholas were in the thick of the fight, sailing in the first and second ships respectively of the weather and lee divisions of the British fleet, among the first to break through the Franco-Spanish line. Further down the lee division in HMS *Revenge* (74) was Private David Newton, who many years later summed up the outstanding features of the battle for his village Rector:

> You see, sir, the enemy was drawn up in a kind of half-moon shape, two deep, and close together; so we went spank into them. . . and broke their line. But just as we had done so, and were getting into position, our tiller rope was shot away, and four ships at once set upon us, two taking us fore and aft. It was very hot work, Sir, while it lasted, and our second lieutenant Mr Little, came down between decks and ordered all the men to lie down flat on the decks. Fortunately the 'Billyruffian'. . . and another ship came to our aid, and it ended in two or three. . . of the Captains that had attacked us having to deliver up their swords on our deck to Captain Moresom.[49]

Roteley was more precise: 'At 9 beat to Quarters and finished clearing for action at 10 beat to Retreat and all hands went to dinner Made signal to form the order of battle in two columns'. After making the famous 'England expects' signal at 10.30, Nelson hailed his second, HMS *Temeraire* (98), to emphasise his intention to pierce the enemy line between the ninth and tenth ships, telling her to keep more open order, 'you will drop astern and follow my motions.' The British ships came on slowly, exposed to end-on fire for thirty minutes, with no chance of replying:

> Previous to breaking the Enemys line their fire was terrific the Victory was steering for the Four decker when four ships ahead and four astern together with the huge Leviathan brought all their broadsides to bear upon the Bows of the Victory, it was like a hail storm of shot passing over our heads.[50]

Nicholas and Roteley were on their respective poop decks. 'Horrorstruck at the bloody corpses. . . the shrieks of the wounded and the moans of the dying', Nicholas resisted the temptation to join everyone else, prone on the deck. He took comfort from his senior, Lieutenant J. Owen RM, who calmly paced the deck, 'an instance of how much depends on the example of those in command when exposed to the fire of the enemy.'[51] *Victory*'s Marines stood fast, 'no Man went down until knocked down. . . not a Man was hit below the waist'. Nelson, 'whose eye was every where', had seen nothing to surpass their steadiness in any of his previous battles, but they suffered accordingly: 'The Poop became a slaughter house and soon after the commencement the two senior Lieutenants of Marines and half the original forty were placed Hor de Combat.' Adair, *Victory*'s Captain of Marines, sent Roteley below for reinforcements:

> I need not inform a Seaman the difficulty of separating a Man from his Gun in the excitement of action the Marines had thrown off their Red Jackets and appeared in their check shirts and blue trowsers there was no distinguishing Marine from Seaman all were working like horses. . . we were engaging on both sides every gun was going off – and as Roderick would say "Oh what a Row".[52]

Belleisle broke into rather than through the line of Allied ships:

> It was just twelve o'clock when we reached their line. Our energies became roused, and the mind diverted from its appalling condition, by the order of 'Stand to your guns!' which as they successively came to bear were discharged into our opponents on either side. . . Although until that moment we had not fired a shot, our sails and rigging bore evident proofs of the manner in which we had been treated: our mizzenmast was shot away and the ensign had been three times rehoisted; numbers lay dead upon the decks, and eleven wounded were already in the surgeon's care.

Until supporting vessels came up, the leading British ships were out-numbered. *Bellisle* exchanged broadsides with *Fougueux* (74), losing mizzen and maintopmast, before becoming wedged between two more French ships: 'At half-past two our foremast was shot away close to the deck. In this unmanageable state we were but seldom capable of annoying our antagonists, while they had the power of choosing their distance, and every shot from them did considerable execution'. *Bellisle*'s surviving Marines fought the quarterdeck guns until 3.30, when an unidentified ship loomed through the smoke,

> which would either relieve us from our unwelcome neighbours or render our situation desperate. We had scarcely seen the British colours since one o'clock, and it is impossible to express our emotion as the alteration of the stranger's course displayed the white ensign.[53]

When Roteley returned to the quarterdeck, with twenty-five Marines separated forcibly from their guns, he found the French *Redoutable* (74) so close on the starboard quarter that the gun's muzzle flashes set both ships' timbers on fire. Sharpshooters in *Redoutable*'s fighting tops swept *Victory*'s deck with a deadly fire, reducing Adair's party to ten:

> himself wounded in the forehead by splinters yet still using his musket with effect – one of his last orders to me were Roteley fire away as fast as you can when a Ball struck him on the Back of the neck and he was a Corpse in a moment.

Nelson fell about the same time, the double loss exasperating Roteley's Marines: 'the first order I gave was to clear the mizzentop when every musket was levelled. . . and in five minutes not a man was left alive in it.' Beyond *Redoutable* HMS *Temeraire* engaged another French ship to starboard, the four vessels rubbing sides as if in harbour:

> it consequently became a great nicety in directing the fire of the Musketry lest we should shoot our own friends over the deck of the *Redoutable* I therefore directed the fire of the Marines to the main and foretops of that devoted ship – and but few of their Topmen escaped.

Redoutable struck perhaps half an hour after Sergeant Secker with two other Marines had carried Nelson below. *Victory* now engaged the Spanish flagship, the *Santissima Trinidad* (140). Already hard pressed, she could not avoid the fire of *Victory*'s larboard guns through her stern windows, and at 2.30 Roteley had 'the satisfaction of seeing the largest ship in the world haul down her colours'. More Allied ships surrendered about 3, allowing the smoke to clear a little:

> never did I behold anything so awfully grand stragelling ships engaging ship to ship, one of the enemy ships on fire and expecting to see her ascend every moment a number of ships laying like hulks upon the surface of the water totally dismasted.

Shortly after Nelson's death at 4.30 the Allied van 'tacked and stood along our line to windward firing indiscriminately upon friend and foe', but they were soon driven off, 'leaving us compleat masters of the field and twenty sail of the line in our hands.'[54]

In the heat of action many humble deeds of heroism escaped attention. Isolated exceptions included a corporal in *Victory* who bound up the stump of his arm with Adair's sash to lead a boarding party, and the private Marine who lost his arm to a cannonball, but with the good soldier's aversion to leaving his weapon carried his firelock down to the surgeon's quarters in the cockpit. There was keen competition to avenge Nelson. Captain Hardy gave credit to Midshipman Pollard, but an officer in *Euryalus* (36) thought the mysterious marksman 'was immediately shot by a Corporal of Marines from the quarter-deck of *Victory* – a poor satisfaction'.[55] A hilarious French bulletin claimed Admiral Villeneuve, the French commander-in-chief, had personally shot Nelson, but admitted their man was also missing, after boarding HMS *Victory*. Villeneuve was indeed in *Victory*, where a Marine guard of honour in full dress had presented arms as he came aboard a prisoner. Captain Atcherley RM had taken Villeneuve's surrender aboard *Bucentaure* (80), amidst carnage eclipsing that in *Victory* and *Belleisle*: the dead in heaps, mangled by repeated hits from raking shots, a single one of which had killed or disabled forty men. Lieutenant Owen of *Belleisle* found similar scenes in *Argonauta* (74), a confusion of wreckage and corpses across her deserted quarterdeck. Marines played a key role in securing the prizes. Atcherley had taken the magazine key and left just two sentries in *Bucentaure* as symbolic representatives of her captors. Many of the little prize parties must have perished in the storm that followed the battle. Among them was John Fernyhough, drowned in the surf, when *El Rayo* (100) was dismasted and lost in Cadiz Bay.

Those who escaped drowning found the battle's immediate aftermath an exhausting anti-climax. *Victory* had 'a very bad passage home with heavy Gales [in] a Leaky disabled Ship short of Water and Provisions', as most of the officers' stock had been thrown overboard before the action, and not replaced at Gibraltar, 'an uncommon dear place'.[56] Roteley was 'not a little Proud of having had the Honour of Commanding the Marines on board Lord Nelson's ship the Junior Lieutenant', but honour was the only immediate reward for many. Captain Tummins' brevet majority was the only Marine promotion for Trafalgar, a miserable reward for a Corps which supplied an eighth of the manpower, but suffered a quarter of the casualties.[57] Eighteen months after the battle Roteley found his Trafalgar prize money 'falls far short of my expectations'. He asked his father to invest it, 'that money was too dearly earned ever to be spent. In the Navy there is but little Prize Money to be made when there is much fighting for it.'[58] Noticed in his obituary as 'one of the last of the heroes of Trafalgar', Roteley gained his own majority as a mercenary in Venezuela. David Newton became an object of public charity, until a Marine General advised Newton's parish clergyman how to apply for a Greenwich Hospital pension of 1/6d a day.

Strangling the Eagle

Trafalgar shifted the focus of the naval war away from a struggle for command of the sea, to its exploitation. Until 1805 the Royal Navy had fought with one hand behind its back, striving to achieve naval supremacy, while supporting all the other naval tasks essential to the war effort. Trafalgar did not end the war with France: Napoleon's victory at Austerlitz, six weeks later, ensured French domination of Europe for a decade, but victory at sea freed British naval forces to pursue wider tasks that would eventually secure a favourable outcome to the war. These activities ranged from traditional naval operations, such as blockade or convoy, to participation in major military campaigns ashore.

A relentless blockade was both prelude and sequel to Trafalgar. John Robyns served off Brest throughout the winter of 1807–08 in HMS *Neptune* (90), except when south-westerly gales drove her into Torbay, or rumours of a breakout inspired a dash across the Atlantic to the West Indies. Enemy and weather demanded constant vigilance. One day *Neptune* 'Stood well into Brest Harbour and reconnoitred the French Fleet'; the next she clawed out to sea, as 'Coming on to blow hard we were all obliged to weigh and carry a heavy press of sail to gain an Offing.' At least there were 'regular communications to and from England by Cutter three times a week, which compensates in some measure for the tedious service we are employed on'.[59] Hopes of action were usually disappointed, although as late as November 1813, a fluky offshore wind nearly delivered the Toulon fleet to their jailers: 'the Fleet formed the line and prepared for action But from HMS *Scipion* going to leeward of the Enemy Ships instead of to windward the enemy escaped.'[60]

Nelson had understood the potential of properly constituted amphibious forces, promising that when he was First Lord every fleet should have 'perfect battalions of Marines, with their artillery; and commanded by experienced Field Officers. . . prepared to make a serious impression on the enemy coast.[61] Amphibious descents on a French shoreline extending from Denmark to Montenegro were a logical extension of the blockade. The French constantly sought to replace the ships lost at Trafalgar, provoking pre-emptive strikes on anchorages, such as the Basque Roads or Walcheren. At the bombardment of Flushing in August 1809 HMS *Statira*'s Marines took charge of her 32-pounder quarterdeck carronades, which became so heated that several dismounted. Lieutenant Robert Fernyhough RM lent a hand:

> If you had seen me during the action, you would have taken me for anything but an officer, for I was black as a sweep. In the middle of the conflict it became so hot that I threw off my uniform and neckcloth, and unbuttoned my shirt collar, consequently the powder had so completely blackened my

shirt and face, that had a soot bag been shaken over me, I could not have been worse. I have scarcely been able to use my right hand since, the skin having been taken off four of my fingers, by the friction of the ropes, in working the guns, for I pulled and hauled as well as my men, not choosing to remain inactive, when the shot were flying about.[62]

The British took Flushing, but the French warships withdrew behind Antwerp's formidable defences. Polder fever made dreadful ravages among the baffled invaders, as it had amongst Sir Charles Littleton's men in the 1670s, forcing them to withdraw after a fortnight.

Blockade ensured amphibious forces were on hand to fan the flames of local resistance to Napoleonic tyranny. Marines of HMS *Amazon* (38) and *Defiance* (74) provided early British support for Spanish patriots in 1808. Lieutenant William Pridham RM led them into the recently hostile naval base at Ferrol:

> where they were received with the joyful acclamations of the people whose enthusiasm in the cause of their country exceeded description – thus the almost extinguished flame of patriotism has again burst forth in this part of Spain so long oppressed by the French. . . returned to the ship in the evening accorded the thanks and caresses of thousands.[63]

The Spanish made difficult allies. Sergeant Thomas Rees RM must have wondered why the British had bothered, after his experiences at Fort Matagorda near Cadiz:

> we went on till nearly all our powder and shot were expended, and we had nothing to make signal with; for the staff had been shot through five times in one day. But the Captain sent a boat off to Cadiz for some more shot, when the Spaniards returned for answer, that they did not choose to supply us with any more; for as the French had got so much of their country, they might as well have that also. And oh! What a passion on hearing this did Captain MacLean get into! throwing his hat on the ground and stamping on it for very madness, to think that we had been day and night fighting for them, and this was all the thanks we got for it.[64]

The blockade served economic as well as strategic purposes, cutting France off from overseas markets, and strangling the coastal trade that compensated for poor land communications. Commercial warfare assisted the British war effort, and filled the pockets of practitioners. Its least profitable aspect was convoying merchant ships. John Robyns visited the 'ancient and opulent Empire of China' in 1799 to rendezvous with eleven

East Indiamen, 'computed to be worth Three million Sterling'. He spent the summer of 1806 ranging the North Atlantic, as reports of French frigates 'annoying our Greenland trade', drew HMS *Dryad* (38) from the Azores with their fresh produce and, 'Convents filled with charming and interesting young girls', to the snow-capped mountains of Cape Farewell. After blockade duty off Brest, Robyns sailed from Spithead with 220 sail bound for West Africa, the Mediterranean, and West Indies, as part of an escort squadron of just two ships of the line and three frigates. Privateers usually had the legs of men-of-war, so Marines on commerce protection suffered more inconvenience than danger. HMS *Swiftsure*'s abrupt departure after a threatened convoy, 'sans wine, sans tea, sans onions, sans everything', inspired anything but professional interest in her Captain of Marines:

> Our going on without replenishing at Madeira will sadly derange all our system in the mess, and economy must be adopted in the expenditure of port wine to make it last until we get to Barbados. Had I not fortunately laid in a pretty good stock we should have been in a famous scrape.[65]

Trade denial, as opposed to trade protection, could be highly profitable, although Robyn's experience in *Dryad* in 1805 was 'most unfortunate having cruised six weeks between the Western Isles and Cape St Vincent. . . at the commencement of a Spanish War without making a single capture'. He did better during the War of 1812, assisting in a single week at the capture of two US whaling ships, laden with oil and 'a beautiful Packet Sloop of about 60 tons from Charlestown. . . having passengers, and a cargo of Cotton and Rice'.[66] Such operations gave Marine officers a rare chance of independent command. Lieutenant Bland RM took charge of HMS *Seine*'s barge off Porto Rico:

> in which he destroyed a Spanish sloop, and captured the *Conception*, a large Spanish Felucca, cargo cocoa and cochineal for Cadiz, of two long 4prs and 14 men, after an Action of three quarters of an hour.. . . This is the second very gallant dash of Mr Bland since our arrival here; in both he has acquired much credit.[67]

The men were keen to take part in such expeditions. When HMS *Cleopatra* manned boats to board a suspected privateer, Lewis Roteley found: 'all the Marines wished to accompany me but was not able to take more than 12', although after 'pulling with our oars for 6 hours during one of the Hottest days I ever experienced', the quarry turned out an innocent American.[68] All rates worked together, regardless of rank or branch of service. HMS *Arab*'s Lieutenant of Marines spent a whole day on a capsized schooner, under the Caribbean sun:

> unrigged her, and got as much as we could out of her, principally silks. . .
> Self and party on her all day naked, the ship having gone in chase, without
> refreshment of any kind; the skin so scalded as to confine me to my bed
> for several days and at length the cuticle came off in large strips.[69]

When French merchant ships took refuge from the Royal Navy's ubiquitous cruisers under shore batteries, Marines won fresh laurels cutting them out. Richard Swale took part in a typical attempt on a 20-gun corvette at Morbihan, in cooperation with 250 men of 2nd Queens:

> a Black cloud overshadowed the Moon which brought us right in under
> their guns Unperceived or heard until the Soldiers were all landed, then
> the enemy began to fire at us without effect their shot passing over our
> heads, the Batteries were taken without any opposition, but the Brig opened
> upon the Boats and Fired away until She was boarded on all sides and
> carried with the loss of only one Man on our side and ten or eleven of the
> Enemy.[70]

Marines made such operations their particular métier. Nelsonian seamen lacked the military training that made Victorian naval brigades formidable, while soldiers lacked amphibious experience:

> The loading of boats with soldiers unaccustomed to the sea, very often at
> night, and their disembarkation and re-embarkation on a hostile shore
> would have been operations so fraught with difficulty and danger as to
> have been almost impracticable. On the other hand to have opposed the
> seamen of the period. . . to regularly trained troops fighting on their own
> element – the land – would have been to court disaster.[71]

Terse reports in the *Naval Chronicle* leave no doubt about the effective division of labour between seamen and Marines. Captain Brace of HMS *Berwick* gave credit for a successful cutting out near Toulon, to the 'seamen and marines. . . whose united exertions so fully accomplished my wishes'. Each played the part that best suited them, the Marines storming the enemy's positions at bayonet point, to cover the no less efficient cutting out and demolition work of the seamen. HMS *Eagle* (74) landed seamen and Marines at Farasina in 1813, under cover of her guns: 'A position was then taken by the royal marines, to secure the men while destroying the battery and its out-works.'[72] HMS *Curacao* (36) snatched two feluccas from the beach at Mesca, in the Gulf of Spezia, despite their being tied to the houses: 'shewing the broadsides of the two ships to the town, while the Marines took up a commanding position, we were enabled to get them off without the slightest misfortune'. More coasters, 'of considerable tonnage, deeply laden', were scuttled at Campo del Porto in Elba:

> the Marines and boats of the two ships [HMS *Curacao* and *L'Aigle*] having first paved the way by routing a considerable body of militia, taking a battery of two 12prs, a square tower on the Martello principle, armed with a 6pr, (all of which were thrown into the sea), killing several of the enemy, and making prisoners of two artillery men.[73]

Such raids were not left to the unsupported initiative of individual captains. Viscount Melville, First Lord from March 1812, sent additional Marines to the Mediterranean Fleet, and placed 3–400 more at Lord Keith's disposal in the Channel: 'if you think they can be usefully employed on the coasts of France in destroying signal communications and other petty harassing modes of warfare.'[74]

The Imperial government in Paris responded by constructing shore batteries, but coastal fortifications acted as lightning conductors, rather than deterrents. More than one naval officer justified attacks on batteries as 'affording considerable protection to the trade of the coast'. Conventional ground forces rarely caught a will o' the wisp enemy, who struck from the sea, and was gone before reinforcements could arrive. Thirty Marines from HMS *Apollo* (38) pursued twice their own number of French troops ashore from a felucca at San Cataldo, taking twenty-six, while the rest threw away their muskets and ran: 'As we came away, some cavalry, and about one hundred and fifty soldiers came from Leece to assist their friends', but they were too late. When reinforcements did arrive in time, naval gunfire kept them at bay. Four coasters were destroyed at Vernazza:

> by anchoring the ships close to it, and landing the royal marines, who driving the enemy's troops out, occupied it, whilst a considerable body hastening from the neighbourhood to its relief, were kept back by the fire of the ships, until the vessels were burnt.

The iron ore, sulphur, and timber destroyed that day suggest the strategic significance of such raids, which in this case earned a specific mention in despatches for 'The royal marines', who, 'behaved in their customary gallant manner'.[75]

Such praise was not mere formality. British amphibious forces developed such moral superiority by the end of the Napoleonic Wars that opponents might offer no resistance, as at Porto Ré, where 'Captains Hoste and

Markland landed with the marines, and found the forts abandoned by the enemy, who had spiked the guns, and thrown the ammunition into the sea.' Numerical odds and physical difficulties hardly seemed to matter. Hearing of a convoy 'only guarded by a captain's party of about 60 men', Commander Harper of HM Sloop *Saracen* attacked it with forty, taking half the defenders prisoner, without a single fatal casualty. At Cassis in August 1813: 'The citadel battery could only be carried by escalade, but nothing could withstand the boldness of the gallant marines, led on by Captain Coghlan, who surmounted every obstacle opposed to them.'[76]

Perhaps the last such affair took place at Corigeou in Brittany a month after Waterloo. Two Marine officers left accounts, one written in red ink with a pin, a reminder of the problems correspondents faced on active service. They recorded features typical of amphibious raids. Major warships kept below the horizon, to ensure surprise, while small craft reconnoitred the coast, and took compass bearings from the proposed landing beach to a high building on the skyline as a point of direction. The assault force sheltered behind rocks, a quarter of a mile offshore, until moon set, when they landed without incident, despite a row of stumps that resembled cannon in the darkness:

> To add to the effect a figure was now seen creeping toward the supposed battery – this I guessed was the French sentinel. I, first taking aim at him, demanded who he was. It proved to be an English officer from another boat, under the same mistake as myself.

The 165 Marines, with 80 seamen in support, set off on the known bearing, a little knot of frigate captains carrying a spy-glass, a Union Jack, and a compass. As they crossed the hill in grey daylight, the convoy opened fire, and the Marines ran down the slope under a shower of grape to storm the batteries. With masterly timing British gun-brigs swept into the harbour as they pushed across the cornfields:

> This was the most bustling part of the business – the musketry from the rocks and guard-house on our left, the grape and canister from the vessels in our front, made noise enough. . . our escape is attributable to the rapidity of our advance down the declivity, since the enemy could not depress their guns quick enough.

Concluding the assault by turning a captured gun onto the hostile ships, the Marines established an outpost line on high ground beyond the port, until the ebb-tide allowed the captured vessels to negotiate the harbour entrance.[77]

Per Terram

Maritime pressure alone could not defeat a major land power like Imperial France. British armies saw action in Egypt, the Iberian Peninsula and North America supported by Marines along their seaward flanks. A contemporary analyst thought lack of training in larger units than detachments sometimes left Marines:

> at a loss in forming a brigade. . . as well as in marching, which is one of the springs of military mechanism. But they have on all such occasions organised themselves with such celerity as to gain the approbation of the Line, and even the praise of some of the square toes of the old school.[78]

For a while the regular Army's losses in the West Indies gave Marines the edge over line regiments filled out with militia. Sir Edward Pellew commented of his Marines at Belle Isle in 1800: 'They won their laurel here, and I verily believe will wear it well; they are 600 strong and full of spirits. I wish I could say as much of certain Regiments.' St Vincent called a military witness to the same effect:

> Be assured the troops you have at home are not up to a difficult enterprise. Brigadier Maitland is so sensible of this that he wishes me to take them [the Line infantry], and to give him the marines, in which he shows a great deal of penetration.

Admiral Keith landed a Marine battalion to help Sir Ralph Abercrombie evict the French from Egypt in 1801, after a succession of fiascos had moved St Vincent to pray, 'Good Lord deliver us from all conjunct expeditions.' Keith was no more enthusiastic, but realized the Marines' symbolic value: 'I am convinced were I to refuse or withdraw a man the troops would re-embark and charge the failure to me.'[79]

The Egyptian battalion earned themselves the soubriquet of 'The Bulldogs of the Army', but not for their fitness:

> We marched about Ten miles over sand which often came over our ankles. . . [and] arrived at the Army after the most Fatiguing march I ever experienced, great numbers of our men were not able to march more than half way being entirely exhausted.[80]

Nevertheless the whole army was in close action at daylight, the Marines suffering heavy losses in their eagerness to close with the enemy.[81] In his thanks after the battle General Abercrombie associated the battalion with hard-hitting corps like the 92nd Highlanders, but left them filling sandbags at Aboukir Castle, in case Keith needed them at short notice. The Marines' essential shipboard functions clearly conflicted with their use ashore, the Admiral expressing his relief when they re-embarked, the fleet being 'in a wretched state for want of men'.[82]

Not all amphibious commanders were as careful as Keith and Abercrombie. Commodore Sir Home Popham and Colonel William Beresford improvised a descent on Buenos Aires in 1807, with 1,630 Highlanders, Marines and sailors, dressed in red for moral effect. Avoiding shipwreck among the foggy shoals of the Rio Plata, the British infantry won a neat little battle described by Richard Swale, present with HMS *Diadem*'s Marines. The attackers advanced within artillery range, in two battalion columns of companies, and formed line, pairs of guns on the flanks, and two howitzers in the centre:

> We advanced in slow time the enemy all this while remaining perfectly quiet and steady until two of our guns stuck fast in a swamp that caused a pause when the enemy immediately opened fire. . . luckily most of it went over our heads, our advance at that moment became more rapid and in a few minutes the General with his hat off ordered the charge through a most infernal swamp in which several men stuck fast and all our artillery. It was not however broad and soon we got over it close to them on which the enemy fled in all directions.[83]

The city surrendered on 2 July, handing over 30 tons of silver as ransom, but instead of withdrawing with their plunder, the British waited for reinforcements, exposing the weakness of a small amphibious force amongst a hostile population. Assassinations multiplied as Argentine militia surrounded the captured city. On 11 August they opened fire from the surrounding houses, 'the top of each being flat, with a kind of breastwork, with loopholes, so that a person might fire without being observed'. Heavy casualties made the defenders' situation impossible, forcing the British to surrender:

> We hung down our heads sorrowfully, and instead of carrying our swords erect, we dropped them by our sides. . . the most distressing scene I ever beheld, there was scarcely a dry eye amongst us: some of the men, when they came to deliver up their muskets, broke them against the ground, cursing the day they ever took them in their hands.

The Argentinians broke the surrender terms, marching their prisoners into the interior: 'a dreary prospect to the captive; its flatness resembling the ocean; not a tree to relieve the eye of the wanderer; cheerless as the wide expanse of waters; an interminable world. . . bounded only by the sky'. Captive Marines dressed in ponchos, wide hats and long beards wandered among the llamas and condors of the Andes, a thousand miles from Buenos Aires: 'We now began to despair, and to give up all thoughts of seeing England again. . . expected our destination was to the coast of Chile, where we would be lost to the world.'[84] Not until July 1808, a year after their capture, did orders come for the survivors' repatriation.

The Peninsular War of 1808–14 was the most significant British contribution to the land war against Napoleon. Once again Spain's long coastline and poor communications provided opportunities for amphibious support of land operations. When an overwhelming French force drove Britain's last army within the fortified lines of Torres Vedras in October 1810, Marines occupied the innermost defences as a long stop. A Marine battalion remained at Lisbon until 1812, when it was withdrawn to Portsmouth, refitted as a mixed force of infantry and artillery, and sent back with a flying squadron operating off northern Spain. Lord Melville thought, 'much good might be done in the way of annoyance to the enemy by keeping them engaged on that coast.' He had two aims:

> The first, to alarm the enemy by frequent attacks in different quarters and thereby keep in sufficient employment as large a portion as possible of the enemy's force. . . The other. . . to endeavour to seize upon some strong position. . . which might be useful as a point of communication with the guerrillas in that quarter.

As so often with amphibious operations the political aim exceeded operational capability. Spanish support was erratic, and army officers overestimated the ability of sailing ships to loiter off a lee shore. Lord Keith, now Commander-in-Chief of the Channel Fleet, recommended caution in committing the Marines: 'They are calculated to distract the enemy upon the coast, but not to undertake any too forward movement into the interior, and I recommend that you do not engage in any operations of too tedious and extensive a nature.'[85]

The Battalion sailed in HMS *Diadem*, stripped of her guns, and equipped with flatboats to act as a Landing Ship Infantry, their departure timed to coincide with Wellington's opening moves in Central Spain. The Marines fell upon French garrisons scattered along the Biscay coast, between Santander, Bilbao and San Sebastian, threatening hostile lines of communication through the Pyrenees. Early successes at Lequitio and Bermeo ensured the French Army of the North missed the Battle of

Salamanca on 22 July. A second Marine battalion arrived soon afterwards, Santander falling to a combined force of British seamen and marines, and Spanish regulars, while the French evacuated Bilbao, the capital of Vizcaya. When the fortress of Burgos defied Wellington's inadequate siege train, Marine artillery-men set off across the Cantabrian Mountains with two naval 24-pounders, dragged along steep and broken roads, by whatever oxen and peasants they could enlist. They had reached Bazconcillas, 30 miles from Burgos, when word came that Wellington had abandoned the siege. The Marines jettisoned their ammunition, but got the guns safely back to Santander. The rest of the year was spent blockading Santona, 'the Gibraltar of the north coast', until bad weather led to the Marines' withdrawal in December 1812. They had contributed materially to the success of Wellington's main campaign and secured an advanced base for the following year's operations, within easier reach from England than the inconveniently distant Lisbon.

The Three Battalions

The two Marine battalions remained in being, but hostilities with the United States prevented their return to the Peninsula. In 1813 Wellington had to call on ships' detachments, such as RMA mortar crews landed from HM Bomb *Strombolo,* to take the Fort of San Felipe, between Tortosa and Tarragona, 'absolutely the key of the only road for cannon into this province'. The precision of the brief bombardment that blew up an expense magazine and persuaded the defenders to surrender was only half the story. Parties of seamen and marines had worked three days and nights to drag heavy ordnance up inaccessible heights, under incessant shellfire by day, and torrential rain at night, accompanied by violent thunderstorms, more terrifying for the piles of ammunition exposed to the lightning.[86] Meanwhile the 1st and 2nd Battalions had crossed the Atlantic, to take part in amphibious operations in Chesapeake Bay, and help repulse American attempts to invade Canada. At Fort Oswego Lieutenant Hewett climbed the flagpole through a hail of rifle bullets to tear down the Stars and Stripes, but offered the chance of taking flag and despatch home to certain promotion, he refused, as long as fighting continued.

Most of the two Battalions transferred to gunboats on the Great Lakes, the remainder joining a 3rd Battalion sent out early in 1814, and confusingly renumbered the 2nd. Organizational fluidity defies chronology, but a surviving order book shows the working of a Marine battalion on active service. Before taking the field the officers 'disciplined their men', training skirmishers and making them sleep inside their tents, instead of sprawling drunkenly outside to catch chills. Equipment was modified:

> Commanding officers of companies will see their Men's pouches filled and be particular that the Cartridges are all perfectly serviceable – each man is to take ten rounds in addition to the sixty in his pouch and two spare flints. . . every man is to put on his Flannel and blue trowsers and have his Blanket rolled up on his Pack.

Gaiter straps required attention: 'that they are strong and good and such as will support a Shoe in heavy ground'. March discipline was strict: no man to fall out to ease himself without leaving his pack and musket with his section, nor sick men to be left without a ticket. A field officer and surgeon followed to discourage stragglers, and 'explain to them they will certainly be murdered if they do'.[87]

Among the Marines who took part in the British counter-offensive that culminated in the burning of Washington in August 1814 was Captain John Robyns. He spent early summer spreading destruction along the waterways of Chesapeake Bay, and joined the raid on Washington with 350 Marines from ships' detachments. Their advance along the narrow River Patuxent more than justified the Corps' motto, as they frequently landed to scour the country, wading up to their necks to prevent Americans firing into the boats from the banks. The British advance guard brushed Washington's defenders aside at Bladensburg, to the annoyance of 2nd Battalion:

> Though they pressed on with the greatest anxiety to be in time for some of the fun, the Marines could not get up 'till it was all over, & there was nothing left for them, but to give vent, which they did pretty loudly, to their feelings of disappointment.[88]

The British destroyed Washington's public buildings, and came away well pleased with, 'a most dashing and daring Enterprise', which had 'succeeded beyond our most sanguine expectations'. Operations against Baltimore were less successful, although the Marines showed they were as fit and well trained as any infantry regiment: 'It was one of the hottest Days I ever remember, and although the Men had only Blankets several dropped on the road side, particularly the 4th who must have left 100 behind. Not one of mine was left behind.'[89] Along the way the Marines provided covering parties against marksmen in the woods. Marines were often chosen as 'light bobs', being particularly adept in the 'advances, retreats, and manoeuvres which constitute what is called carrying on the "petite guerre"', perhaps because their informal training was not, 'confined to the mere acquirement of a proficiency in the use of arms'.[90] When their shabby appearance excited comment, the naval Commander-in-Chief replied that with 3,000 such fellows he would march from one end of America to the other.

The 2nd Battalion had to show different qualities at Tangier Island, in Chesapeake Bay, where they spent the rest of 1814 constructing a fort and barracks with a single saw and one bucket of nails. Robyns was unimpressed by this, 'Depot for runaway Negroes. . . it being all sand and swamp and covered in myriads of Mosquitoes'.[91] Colonial Marines, as the black recruits were known, took part in operations from May 1814, when Admiral Cockburn presented them with a captured American field gun, for their steady behaviour before the enemy. There were enough of them by September to reconstitute the 3rd Battalion with three companies of regular Royal Marines and three of Colonials, trained by Sergeant Hammond RM, who received a local commission for his efforts. Tangier Island's Commanding Officer 'particularly remarked the steadiness of the 1st, 2nd, and 3rd Companies' on parade, but encouraged the Colonials who 'only require a little instruction, when he is sure they will equal their brother soldiers in the performance of every part of their duty'.[92] Both got an extra half ration of rum to drink the King's health, but life at Tangier Island was usually less jolly, 'the tents at first being scarcely habitable from excess heat', and later 'so completely covered with ice as to render it almost impossible to pack them'.[93] In November 1814 British forces in the Chesapeake were placed on half rations of bread and rum, which is of less interest to the well-fed historian than the care taken to explain the situation, and assure the troops that 'everything will be purchased that can add to the men's comfort and the short allowance money promptly paid.' Sweet potatoes replaced bread, while American civilians willingly traded with the enemy, selling fish, eggs, fowls and even cattle.

The 2nd Battalion's last action was at Cumberland Island, Georgia, after which Royal Marines returned home and Colonials received land grants in Trinidad. Marines from the fleet stayed on until news of the Peace of Ghent crossed the Atlantic. Six hundred of them served before New Orleans, drinking ditch water and sleeping in reed huts, proof against neither weather nor bullet. Men died of cold. The American defences were immensely strong, an attempt to storm them on 8 January failing with heavy loss. The Marines and 85th were the only British units to achieve their objectives. 'Having with much labour cut a communicating

Canal from the Landing place to the Mississipi', they brought up boats and crossed the river, to capture artillery positions that enfiladed the main British attack, an anticipation of Second World War commando activity on the flanks of assault landings. Another precursor of later Special Forces practice was support given to the Creek Indians. With a few hundred Indians supplied with British muskets, Major Edward Nicholls RM pinned down 5,000 Americans on the Mobile and Alabama Rivers, preventing them from reinforcing either Canada or the Mississipi.

Peace came slowly to the Corps. Lt William Pridham RM saw official confirmation of peace between England and America when boarding an American brig on 12 March 1815. He disembarked in November 'with hopes that she is the last man of war I am ever to belong to.'[94] The arrangements for Napoleon's detention detained Lieutenant Edward Wilson at St Helena for eighteen months:

> Great consternation among the Corps from an order to disembark a portion of them. . . . The party seemed much affected and on leaving I discovered many of them in tears. Nor could I scarce refrain from indulging my feelings in the same. . . . Endeavoured to raise my spirits with an extra glass of port.[95]

A high point of Wilson's exile was an exercise with blank cartridges to test security arrangements for the Corsican ogre. The Marines accomplished a dangerous landing from ship's boats, but were pinned down on the beach until they opted for honourable surrender and breakfast with the victors.

The Royal Marines' share in Napoleon's incarceration was entirely appropriate. Until Waterloo they were the only British infantry to face the Emperor on the battlefield. A Sergeant of Marines is even said to have marked the young Napoleon with his bayonet during the Siege of Toulon in 1793. General Bonaparte himself admitted that he had missed his destiny at Acre where Marines from HMS *Theseus* and *Tigre* (74s) helped a Turkish garrison administer the first check to his career in 1798. Major Thomas Oldfield had found a soldier's grave there, leading a sortie, of which the French Chief of Staff wrote: 'They attacked like heroes and were received by heroes – death only checked their bold career.' Major Douglas acted as Chief Engineer, and accompanied the Ottoman pursuit, swarming up the ramparts of El Arish on a rope to take the French commander's sword, a display of agility that must have astonished friend and foe alike. The Captain of Marines in the ship that carried Napoleon into exile at St Helena was himself wounded at Acre, a discovery the

Emperor took with good humour, pulling the Captain's ear like one of his own *grognards*. He had taken other liberties when HMS *Bellerophon*'s detachment turned out in his honour: speaking to the oldest Marine through an interpreter, thrusting himself among the bayonets to demonstrate some difference between French and British drill, and observing to Count Bertrand, forgetful of the brave men whose lives he had squandered: 'How much might be done with a hundred thousand soldiers such as these.'[96]

CHAPTER SEVEN

Pax Britannica

GREAT Britain emerged from the Napoleonic Wars as the predominant world power. Napoleon's pursuit of empire had consumed the navies of Europe, while alternative centres of naval power in America and Japan had yet to arise. Except for Navarino in 1827 the Royal Navy fought no fleet actions for a century. The long Victorian afternoon contrasts sharply with the invasion scares of the preceding century, or the world wars of the next, but the image of sleepy complacency is misleading. The Corps' motto was more than ever justified, as the Royal Navy exploited the maritime supremacy that men like Rotely, Swale and Robyns had helped win. Capital ships may have swung idly around their buoys, but sloops and gunboats were active, chasing slaving schooners and pirate junks, and spreading the benefits of Free Trade wherever there was sufficient water beneath their keels to do so.

Flexible training and organization made Royal Marines an essential element in the exercise of naval command, as detachments landing from a gunboat, independent battalions conducting regular campaigns ashore, or garrisons of remote coaling stations and diplomatic missions. A Marine officer thought Wei-hai-wei, where ponies shied at the mere sight of Europeans, 'the uttermost ends of the earth', but a Maxim detachment from HMS *Sphinx* might have disagreed as they climbed bandit-infested Iranian passes 6,000 feet above sea level, en route to the British Consulate at Shiraz. Marines were ideal for imperial defence as they did not need 'that array of cocked hats which under the army system seems to be inevitable'. They could move ten or a thousand miles, at twelve hours notice, 'without all the necessary departmental arrangements which are involved in moving a regiment of the line. . . knowing that their organisation is of such a character that wherever they may go they can take care of themselves.'[1] When sailors despaired of winning glory on their natural element, Marines formed the backbone of naval brigades that policed an Empire denuded of regular troops by economy minded governments. Wherever the Royal Navy went, Marines went too, coaling ship at 112 degrees in the Gulf, double awnings rigged against the Arabian sun, or standing guard in sealskin helmets at Balaklava, with icicles in their beards.

Nelson's Legacy

The end of the Napoleonic Wars brought inevitable reductions. The Admiralty marked the Emperor's abdication in 1814 by demobilizing all Marines of foreign origin, over forty years old, or under 5 foot 3 inches tall. The Corps fell from 31,400 and 3,000 supernumeraries, to a peace establishment of 6,222. This was half as many again as had survived the reductions of 1763 and 1783, implying official recognition of the value of Marines in peacetime. Recognition of those discharged was less overwhelming. Rank and file were 'on no consideration to trouble the Lords of the Admiralty respecting pensions unless absolutely worn out in the service, so as to be rendered incapable of labour.'[2] Lucky officers received a pension. Captain Mortimer Timpson had been blown up in the Washington arsenal, shooting up in the air like a rocket, but had to soldier on until 1826. William Pridham had merely suffered 'a contraction of the muscles of the right leg caused by a check of perspiration', but possessed sufficient influence to retire on full pay: 'thus I am at once liberated from a service I [have always disliked]. . . the happiest day of my life – God be praised!'[3] For those who stayed, peacetime brought a promotion block of comic proportions. Lt-Colonel William McKinnon remained a subaltern for twenty-eight years and ten months, from 1809 to 1838. 'Slow March RM' spoke for many in 'The Marine's Lament':

> When age-oppressed and gout possessed,
> Our companies we get, Sir,
> Some scarce can stand, much less command –
> We are a luckless set, Sir![4]

New divisional colours presented in 1827 were a more positive peace dividend. The old set dated from 1810: the King's Colour or Union Flag, decorated with a fouled anchor encircled by roses, and a similarly emblazoned divisional colour in the dark blue of a Royal Corps. When George IV received a list of 106 possible battle honours to decorate the Royal Marines' new colours, he baulked at 'The greatness of their number and the difficulty of selecting amidst so many glorious deeds'. Instead His Majesty set his distinctive stamp upon the Corps' standards, replacing the customary badges with those still borne: the single battle honour 'Gibraltar', the motto 'Per Mare Per Terram', and, for the first time, the Great Globe encircled by a laurel wreath: 'the most appropriate emblem of a Corps, whose duties carried them to all parts of the globe, in every quarter of which they had earned laurels by their valour and good conduct'. As a reminder of the source of these honours the King directed, 'that whatever King or Queen they might serve under hereafter, though the cipher of the reigning sovereign must of course appear on their standard, still on those of the Royal Marines the cipher GR IV was for ever to remain.'[5]

The Corps' participation in 'little wars far and wide' justified royal imprecision. Royal Marines were ideal for interventions in areas of instability left by the Napoleonic Wars, winning such ironic titles as 'Lord Palmerston's Own' and 'The Old Tagus Rangers': 'the pressure of the service has been occasionally so great. . . as to leave less than 500 Marines disposable on shore in England. . . only sufficient for three ships of the line.'[6] Marines represented a less serious commitment than regular troops, who in any case were themselves fully committed:

> ambassadors often are told
> When two foreign factions compete,
> "Should you want either faction controuled
> Just land the Marines of the Fleet"[7]

The home government could disavow naval action, as it did when returning Argentinian cannon captured by Royal Marines at Obligado in 1846, opening the River Parana. Many of these operations 'in the great cause of non-intervention' have a post-Cold War ring to them: rescue of hostages at Algiers in 1816, or international efforts to prevent genocide in Greece culminating in destruction of the Ottoman fleet at Navarino. Both actions were essentially bombardments, despite plans for Marines to storm the mole at Algiers and throw rockets into the casemates in a preview of the 1918 Zeebrugge raid. Interventions in Spain and Syria provided more extensive evidence of the Corps' amphibious capabilities.

When Don Carlos, wicked uncle of the infant Queen of Spain, disputed the Spanish throne in 1834 the British Government supported Isabella, the constitutional claimant. Parliament permitted recruitment of an auxiliary legion of British mercenaries, the Royal Navy imposed an arms embargo on northern Spain and Marines secured the Basque ports. In

May 1836 a full RM battalion arrived at San Sebastian, a self-sufficient expeditionary force with seven infantry companies and one of artillery, with 6-pounder field guns, 12-pounder howitzers and rockets. They occupied strong points along the northern Spanish coast, notably an old convent near Bilbao, where they found: 'How very necessary it is for soldiers to be supplied with two bars of yellow washing. I need not say the convent was in a disgustingly filthy state, or it had not been a Spanish lately inhabited convent.'[8] Accommodation was scarce. Major Owen, last seen pacing the quarterdeck of HMS *Belleisle*, could get nowhere to imprison a delinquent Marine as 'there were many Spanish soldiers sleeping in the streets who would jump at a black hole.' The Royalists, or Christinos, only controlled areas within range of the Royal Navy's cannon, while Don Carlos had 'such a flying army that no-one knows where they are'. Marines thought little of their allies, remarking: 'Well for my part I'd as soon shoot some Spaniard, I don't care whether he's a "Christiner" or "Carlew", but I should not like to go home without shooting some fellow!'

They thought even less of the British mercenaries, blaming the failure of Christino offensives on the 'Isle of Dogs Legion'. At Hernani (16 March 1837) everything went well until Carlist columns materialised on both flanks. The Christinos gave a volley at 300 or 400 yards, twice the maximum range of their weapons, and fled, leaving 400 Marines to get away the guns, watched by an appreciative Royal Engineer:

> it would have done your heart good to have seen the manner in which they did their work. You must know the system of fighting here is regular guerrilla – every man for himself – firing as often as you can behind walls, etc., in contrast to this it was beautiful to see the battalion throw in a regular fire, as steady as on parade, and Colonel Owen just as cool as in the barrack yard: it was the admiration of all who saw it, and soon quieted the Carlists. What a fine example of discipline the Marines gave! Had they not acted as they did, our right would have been forced, and the army would have been cut to pieces. They certainly have added another laurel to their many.[9]

However gratifying, the episode showed the risks of operating with irregulars, who may take to the hillsides at any moment, leaving their less agile auxiliaries to get out as best they can. The rest of the campaign was less dramatic, the RM Battalion remaining in garrison until September 1840, when Don Carlos fled to France.

The Marines' deployment to Syria in autumn 1840 followed a similar pattern of amphibious intervention against a narrow coastal strip. The

British regarded the Levant as a short cut to India, even before construction of the Suez Canal, and opposed destabilization of the Ottoman Empire. An invasion of Syria by Mehemet Ali of Egypt precipitated British naval action. Two battalions of Marines, an Austrian rocket battery and 5,000 Turks mounted the first steam-powered assault landing near Beirut on 9 September 1840, at Jounie. Steamers with Turkish soldiers perched on their paddle boxes drew the Egyptian defenders to one end of the bay then chugged off to land 10 miles away, before the enemy could react. Here the invaders dug in with thousands of sandbags, to encourage Lebanese resistance to the Egyptians, rather as twentieth century Special Forces provided a focus for indigenous opposition to Communist subversion. Inter-allied relations in Syria were better than in Spain. Companies of Marines accompanied Turkish battalions on patrol, although, unaccustomed to marching under a fiery sun, they were hard pressed to keep up. Lieutenant Simon Fraser RM shared boiled beef and sherry with his Turkish opposite number:

> before taking it he rose slowly to his feet and cautiously looked all round, then taking his Turkish sentry by the collar, he turned him round with his face from us, at the same time saying something sharp to him; he then returned to his old position – not seeming to mind *my* sentry – took the cup and drained it to the bottom.[10]

Assault landings on the Syrian coast were less agreeable. Mehemet Ali's Albanian mercenaries repulsed poorly reconnoitred efforts against Tartus and the medieval castle of Jbail, but had no effective response to broadsides from line of battle ships, or paddle steamers' shell guns. Fraser's detachment had charge of HMS *Princess Charlotte*'s wardroom guns at Acre (3–4 Nov). One of their shots struck an Egyptian gun on the muzzle, splitting it open and wiping out the crew, at which the Flag Captain ran down calling out, 'Well done Marines! Well done!' The honours of the day belonged to the paddle-wheel frigate *Gorgon*, whose RMA detachment dropped a shell into the principal magazine of the fortress, instantly 'illumined with an intense blaze of light. . . as suddenly succeeded by a dense cloud of smoke, dust, bursting shells, and large fragments of stone'. Two Egyptian regiments were annihilated and the survivors evacuated Mehemet Ali's last Syrian foothold overnight: 'never was a place more completely torn to pieces.'[11] The carnage at Acre haunted Fraser long afterwards; the swollen bodies of men and animals, covered with dust from the ruins, were so close together, 'there was scarcely room to place one's feet when passing over them.' He diverted himself with thoughts of the Marines' defence of 1798–99, but was brutally interrupted, as smouldering rubbish set off unexploded shells from the bombardment, killing the prisoners employed in clearing wreckage.

The Russian War

Russia's attack on Turkey in 1854 provoked the first major European war since Waterloo, while inspiring a novel rapprochement between Britain and France. The war at sea was disappointing, although an RMA Gunner at Odessa claimed the first British shots of the war as the Russian Fleet remained firmly in port. HMS *Castor* (36) chased imaginary Russians in the South Atlantic, officers loading pistols, and the watch below sleeping by their cutlasses, but the 'enemy' turned out to be French: 'So all our visions of Russian frigates and glory vanished, though certainly, if they had been two Russian frigates we should have been thrashed.'[12] Three Royal Marines would win the newly instituted Victoria Cross, despite the poor prospects for amphibious action offered by Russia's limited coastline.

The conflict's modern name comes from the main theatre of war in the Crimea. Allied operations there are often dismissed as a futile shambles, but they had the merit of directly supporting Turkey and striking at the only accessible target: the Russian naval base at Sebastopol. General mobilization of the fleet left no Marines for independent RM battalions, so ships' detachments carried the burden of the war. The Black Sea Fleet's steamers needed all their Marines, but sailing warships landed 1,200 in the Crimea, forming two battalions to protect the army's base at Balaklava. Like the Torres Vedras Battalion in 1811 they had an unglamorous but essential job. Sir Colin Campbell, tasked with defending Balaklava, assured Major Simon Fraser at No. 3 Battery on Marine Heights, that he 'would not guarantee the safety of the ships in harbour for 48 hours were it not for my friends the Marines'.[13] The index of Kinglake's *History of the Crimean War*, however, makes no mention of them. Their Commanding Officer thought them 'the only Corps serving in the Crimea excluded from any service that confers on them honour or credit.'[14] Sergeant William Turner, a Crimean veteran, wrote, 'Historians have passed the poor Joeys over, and put some crammers in instead. That yarn about the old Scotch woman stopping the runaway Turks at the Balaklava fight is a cracker. Don't tell such tales to the Marines, ye Historians.'[15]

This neglect is especially odd as Marines played a crucial part in the most over-blown incident of British military history: the Russian attack on Balaklava of 25 October, the stand of the Thin Red Line, and the charges of the Heavy and Light Cavalry. Turner's eyewitness account challenges accepted views of the battle and shows the essential part the Marines played. The action opened with the loss of some advanced redoubts, whose Turkish troops are usually supposed to have run away, but, 'No, Sir, the Turks were annihilated, or taken prisoners':

> About 9 a.m. the Cossacks galloped out and extended across the plain, closing in as they neared Nos. 1 and 2 redoubt at full gallop. The two redoubts opened fire upon the advancing Cossacks and brought them to a halt; then the Heavy Cavalry rode out, wheeled round on their right, and charged the Cossacks, who were close up to the Marines' ditch. The earthworks had to cease firing to allow the Dragoons to charge.

As soon as the British cavalry were clear, the Marines sent the remaining Russians on their way with a series of well-aimed shells: 'Thus the Marines and Heavy Cavalry not only repulsed the Russians, but regained the position lost by the Turks.' The battle was won, when the Light Brigade's inexplicable disaster intervened:

> The main body were hid by the hills, but there was a roar of guns and one could see horses without riders, and in a very short time small groups returning back to the ground. The first news was that all had been killed or taken prisoners.[16]

Just over a week later Turner was in action again at the Battle of Inkerman, where 7,000 British infantry defeated three times their own number of Russians. The presence of 312 Marines 'has been a puzzle to all writers of the Crimean War who have avoided mentioning them',[17] but one of them won the Corps' first VC. An isolated group of Marines were attacked at close quarters, allowing Corporal John Prettyjohn to demonstrate his unarmed combat skills:

> As soon as the first man stood on the level, Prittyjohns [*sic*] gripped him and gave him a west country buttock, threw him over upon the men following, and a shower of stones from the others knocked the leaders over. Away they went tumbling one over the other, down the incline; we gave them a parting volley, and retired out of sight to load; they made off and left us, although there was sufficient to have eaten us up.[18]

The abiding image of the Crimea is of appalling hardships. The storm of 14 November mocked individual preparations for winter, whirling up tents like balloons, and sending water bottles, haversacks and blankets flying through the air:

> After a hard scramble in an Enemy's Country we had got together a few Comforts, such as a bottle or two of brandy and rum – part of a Cheese – two small basins to drink out of, supplemented by two jam pots, and one or two other invaluables – not forgetting a lump of Cocoa and some biscuit. . . all was lost – one basin was saved, the Cheese deluged in mud.[19]

Turner slept in a barrel, his legs sticking out in the cold, until his mates burnt it to brew up. He was then pitchforked in as Quartermaster Sergeant: 'fighting the commissariat, transport, the weather, and in some instances my own folk, who tried to bounce me on the road, and tap my barrels for me.'[20] His vigilance earned the nickname of Old Gimlet Hole, but someone still ran an underground iron pipe into a buried rum puncheon, draining all but 4 of its 74 gallons. Marines at Balaklava may have suffered fewer privations than infantry in the front line, but like everyone else they met 'constant delays and humbugging' from civilian Commissariat officials, who rebuffed Marine ration parties: 'as we belonged to the fleet we must apply to the Admiral for help.'[21]

These penny-pinching antics took place during weather that nearly achieved what the Russian Army could not:

> The barrels of our guns froze our fingers, and it was painful to hold them; the wind drove the snow into our eyes, ears, and down our backs into the folds of our clothing. Icicles hung from our nostrils and down our beards. . . Our coats were frozen stiff; our boots wet inside and out. Our coffee was green. We could not get any fire; the scanty scrub and roots were covered with snow. Many suffered from cramp and vomiting and dysentery followed. The commissariat broke down, and we were in a tight fix for food. I wonder often how we lived it through.[22]

Sebastopol fell after a series of prodigious bombardments, during one of which Gunner Thomas Wilkinson RMA repaired a sandbag parapet under heavy fire to gain the Corps' second VC. Turner and other survivors of the 'Old Brigade' regained their ships in September 1855, almost a year after landing at Balaklava.

Meanwhile blows had been struck in the Baltic suggesting what might have been achieved at Sebastopol. Nearly 700 Marines joined an Allied attack on the Russian fortress of Bomarsund in August 1854: 'On all sides the greatest disgust was expressed for the modern system of naval warfare; the principle of which seemed to be, to keep out of gun-shot –

"None of that d—d nonsense now we're ashore" said a Marine officer.'
Three naval 32-pounders ineffectively battered Fort Nottich, one of a
circle of iron-roofed gun-towers around the fortress, until an RMA detail
brought up fresh ammunition at midday. As a favour they were allowed
to give the seamen a spell, and promptly demonstrated the superiority of
military gunnery by concentrating all three guns on a single point, instead
of firing independently. Three or four shots set the great stones 'chattering';
one block fell out, then another, until 'an avalanche of loose rubbish, just
as you see macadamising stones pour out from the back of a cart when
the tail-board is removed'. Marine infantry occupied the shattered fort
that evening and next day watched more than 2,000 Russians march out
of Fort Bomarsund: 'A more horrid looking set of men can scarcely be
imagined, nearly half of them, including the Greek priest, were drunk.'[23]

One Marine officer realised the potential of an amphibious raiding
strategy, suggesting 2,000 Royal Marines in steamers at Bomarsund

> might effect a great deal in the way of destroying telegraph stations, cutting
> up roads, and surprises, that would have the effect of harassing the enemy's
> troops, and keeping the whole of his exposed coast in constant alarm; but
> this force should never be allowed to remain ten hours in one place, or a
> strong force of the enemy would be concentrated to crush them.[24]

Instead the 1855 Baltic campaign was spent reconnoitring the defences
of Kronstadt:

> built of solid blocks of granite, and rising like an island from the water, or
> standing on the edge of it, with their three or four tiers of guns frowning from
> the embrasures there seems little chance of a ship being able to cope with them.[25]

An unsuccessful attack on Viborg in July justified caution, a British cutter
crew owing their lives to Lieutenant George Dowell RMA, who towed
her out to win the Corps' third VC.

The naval success of the war was at Sveaborg, the Gibraltar of the
North, where the RMA revived an obsolete weapon to destroy Russia's
second naval base in the Baltic. Fifteen mortar vessels were available,
each equipped with a 13-inch mortar, operated by the RMA. More
Marines went aboard the steam gunboats of the 'Mosquito Squadron',
their 10-inch shell guns augmented by 32-pounders borrowed from the
line of battleships. Unusually the Admiral entrusted the attack to an RMA
officer, Captain Wemyss, requiring naval officers in command of gunboats
'to comply with the requisitions of the Artillery Officer or Non-Commissioned
Officer in charge'.[26] The mortar vessels anchored just over 3,000 yards

from the target, while divisions of five gunboats closed to 2,500 yards, where they steamed round in circles, firing their bow guns as they approached the enemy, and the 32-pounder on their starboard quarter, on turning away. For the first time the Royal Navy used camouflage, painting the boats lead grey, while gun crews fortified their ears with cotton wool against the anticipated din.

Lieutenant Francis Lean was in HM Gunboat *Biter*, her 10-inch shell gun cocked up to maximum elevation, by removing the quoin. The Russians were quick to return fire:

> sending the splinters in a shower all round, while the red hot shot buzzed close past, or fell with a hiss in the water alongside. . . Had it been 1,000 yards nearer there would have been a different <u>bill</u> at the end of the fight, but the constant motion and indistinct colour of the gunboats, with the long range baffled the precision of their fire.

Lean's own gun stretched its breechings, jamming the recoil mechanism, and snapped off the bolts hooking it up to the ship's side, but mortars and gunboats were too much for the defenders. A terrible explosion tore the heart out of the fortress, momentarily paralysing both sides:

> It seemed as if part of the island was blown into the air, or as though a volcano had broken forth with increased fury. Volumes of smoke filled with shot, shell, stones, and rafters ascended to an immense height. . . guns tumbled down in every direction into the water, which for some distance around was greatly agitated, boiling, and foaming.

When darkness made the gunboats' manoeuvres unsafe Lean had a pipe and cup of tea, before hunting about for ammunition, by light of the blazing fortress. He experienced 'a little of the Balaklava humbug', most of the fleet being armed with 32-pounders, and unable to supply the larger cartridges used by the gunboats' shell guns. Meanwhile engineers from the appropriately named *Volcano* rowed around soldering cracks in poorly manufactured mortars.

After three hours sleep, Lean had rearmed *Biter*, breakfasted off chocolate paste in hot water and returned to the gun line, where the Russians had found new life:

> Their shot fell with a hissing sound in the water around us and their shells were continually bursting overhead, scattering the pieces in a shower around, but a charm seemed to hang over the jolly little gunboats, and they appeared to dodge the shot, and pass on uninjured.

Both sides were exhausted. Lean catnapped, despite the noise, while mortars fired reduced charges, as molten solder ran from their cracks. *Havoc*'s mortar split in two, one piece clearing the bulwarks, despite weighing two or three tons. Rocket boats ended the bombardment next morning after forty-five hours, 'leaving the fortress of Sveaborg with its dockyards, stores, arsenal, and public buildings in flames and ashes. The defences had not been much injured, but most of the property they were built to defend had been destroyed.'[27] Not a single allied serviceman died. Wemyss proclaimed it 'a great week for the Marine Artillery', and attributed wider significance to an action proving 'vertical fire is irresistible, and that we can do the same with most other seaports of the enemy.'[28] It was a lesson in naval firepower that helped bring peace the following year.

The Crimea was the last major British conflict until the Boer War over forty years later and the last to employ warships recognizable as such to earlier generations of Marines. The disappearance of wooden walls fundamentally changed the service. Major W.H. Poyntz served seventeen years, but apart from a twelve-month tour at sea in the 1850s, he was employed exclusively on staff duties or with RM battalions ashore. Imperial expansion brought major deployments outside Europe: in China, West Africa, Egypt and the Sudan. Royal Marine infantrymen were known as Light Infantry (RMLI) from 1855, in recognition of Crimean battle honours. It was a curious title for men of above-average physique, but reflected their role as light forces committed independently of the main line of battle. Victorian Marines enjoyed significant advantages over their predecessors, travelling in steamships, improved food and hygiene ensuring timely deployment in good fighting condition. At the end of the century Marines sailed in scheduled P&O steamers and played quoits or deck cricket with 2nd class saloon passengers, a far cry from the horrors of the voyage to Cartagena in 1741. Then Marines had possessed no technical advantages over their Franco-Spanish opponents – now their weapons and organization outclassed any non-European enemy they might meet.

The Celestial Empire 1839–60

Nowhere was this more apparent than during the China Wars of the 1840s and 1850s. The Chinese objected to opium imports from India, while the British would not tolerate interference with free trade, however discreditable. Royal Marines took a prominent part in forcibly opening up Chinese ports. Private Henry Derry of HMS *Fox* (50) was known as 'resurrection man', after a mine blew a tree on top of him:

> Rather risky work I can tell you. Many's the time I've had to put up the barrel of my Brown Bess to ward off the down cut of a sword or the thrust of a spear. . . What I didn't like was when they bolted out of their war junks, and blew them up just as we used to pull alongside. By Jove, it was look out, I can tell you. Splinters, fire balls, stink pots, smoke and mud in all directions, and it used to stick to one for weeks after. As for the boat work, we would be away from the ship sometimes for three weeks, creeping up rivers and creeks that no one knew anything about, and we had it hot, and got some ugly knocks I can tell you.[29]

Operations centred round the ports and great rivers. The first landing at Canton in May 1841 was under 'the great disadvantage of having to form the Marine battalion as the men landed, many of them meeting for the first time'. Logistical preparations were no better. By the following winter many had wooden-soled Chinese shoes, and a variety of nether garments:

> To the eye of the nice martinet our *assemblée* at parade would be too motley; to the serviceman, however, though wanting uniformity in appearance, it is neither offensive nor discouraging. Light hearts and thin trousers carry brave hearts through the world.[30]

Arrangements for operations in November 1857 were more elaborate. Two battalions from England, over 1,500 Marines, arrived at Hong Kong with lavish equipment: 300 new tents; a hospital marquee with waterproof flooring; 3,000 calico bandages with lint pads; rugs and waterproof capes, even files for the cross-cut saws. The artillery had 4.4-inch howitzers and rocket tubes with lanyards, portfires, marline skeins, thumb stalls, spirit levels and plumblines.[31] Marines stationed at Calcutta brought the Brigade to over 3,000: 'a noble body of men acknowledged to be the finest Corps in the world. . . all in excellent health and spirits.'[32]

The China Wars were the first to demonstrate the benefits of improved weapon technology. In the 1840s Royal Marines had percussion muskets, still smoothbore but more reliable than flintlocks, while the 1857 battalions carried Enfield rifles. The advantages of percussion became clear when a company of Marines rescued some Indian infantry unable to fire their water-logged flintlocks during a downpour. The Enfield was a very superior weapon, sighted to 1,100 yards compared with the 200 of Brown Bess. Desperate Chinese counter-attacks at Canton in 1857 were 'all in vain for their matchlocks was not equal to our enfeilds (*sic*) rifles for they was enough of them in numbers'.[33] Chinese weapons at Amoy were derisory:

> The shot passed over us and between us harmlessly; the spears, though long, never reached us; the arrows seemed arrested in their flight, and did not fly with deadly aim, as two wounds only were inflicted in this brilliant campaign.[34]

RM battalions in China acted as spearheads for joint operations against coastal cities, then as garrisons, while sailors went back to their ships and diplomats haggled with evasive mandarins. Marine sharpshooters at Canton were 'so far in advance shells from the ships burst amongst us, and shot from our own guns on the ridge behind passed through the wall we were firing from'. Noticing bluejackets on the walls, the Marines 'joined them in a general rush along the Ramparts. . . No other Corps was in our front.'[35] Military success no more guaranteed political settlement in the nineteenth-century than it does now. Nightly pyrotechnics put 'the City all of an uproar and nothing but the sound of guns and wistling of their shot and the sissing of their rockets'. Off-duty Marines 'had to keep our eyes open for. . . every day their (*sic*) was someone or other beheaded'.[36] Chasing 'braves' proved unrewarding. Paddy fields at White Cloud Mountain in June 1858 restricted the British to single file, making it impossible to catch the enemy before the sun halted operations. Many dropped out from the maddening heat, lunch baskets went astray and the doctor was ambushed, his head cut off, and two fingers for their rings. Only one Marine was killed, but the sun accounted for three.

Continued denial of diplomatic representation at Peking led to the Royal Navy's heaviest defeat of the century on 25 June 1859, before the forts at the mouth of the Peiho River. Three gunboats were lost out of eleven and almost half the Marine landing force. Over 100 fell in as many yards, struggling across mudflats knee-deep in water. Ammunition was soaked and rifles jammed with mud, leaving only cold steel to fight with. The ladder parties were all killed and their ladders smashed. After standing half an hour before the walls, picked off by Chinese archers, the survivors fell back from ditch to ditch, sending their wounded before them and not quitting the beach until early next morning.

Next year an Anglo-French force imposed peace at the gates of Peking. Royal Marines 'were engaged in every battle and encounter with the enemy. . . no other Corps doing the same'. They repulsed Tartar cavalry at Sinho, stormed the Taku Forts, despite grenades and vases of quick lime, and helped scatter the immense army of 'Sam Collinson', a Chinese General alleged to be a renegade Marine.

Two more RM battalions left home during the 1860s: for Mexico in 1862 and Japan in 1863. Neither saw much action, except for the assault on the Straits of Simonoseki in September 1864, the last occasion an RM battalion carried a pair of colours in combat. The battalion at Vera Cruz is significant partly for the choice of Marines out of deference to American sensibilities, and partly as a manifestation of the Horse Marine, a troop of 'Naval Cavalry' making a 500-mile diplomatic cruise to Mexico City dressed in sombreros and red Marine tunics, armed with cutlass, revolver and boarding pike. Light relief must have been welcome as fifty Marines died in two months on Mexico's fever-haunted shore.

Ashanti 1873–4

Disease was the major threat to Royal Marines deployed during the Second Ashanti War of 1873–74, when disagreement over Asante access to civilized amenities like soap and gunpowder resulted in their attacking the Fante of the British Gold Coast protectorate. With a sublime mixture of confidence and myopia, the British government despatched 110 Marines aboard the paddle gunboat *Barracouta* to deal with upwards of 12,000 Asante warriors: 'a people as clever, and as brave as the Maoris – as warlike as the Caffres – and far better armed; in a country as difficult as Abyssinia'.[37] Within 6 weeks of landing, 2 of *Barracouta*'s Marines were dead, and 67 too sick for duty; 10 more died on the way home. Lt-Col F.W. Festing RMA, the Commanding Officer, was baffled: 'the best of everything that could be obtained was got for them, but as you know this destitute country has no resources.'[38] *Barracouta*'s Captain blamed War Office 'geese' for stopping the Marines' usual rations, 'while we have the Colonial Office sending out preserved chocolate, and even ice-making machines for the Fantees who are accustomed to live on rice and fish'.[39] Others blamed overcrowding in *Barracouta*, or lack of sun helmets. Nobody suspected the mosquito.

Fortunately Festing fought 'the most important battle of the campaign in a strategic point of view'[40] less than a week after landing. Marines, bluejackets and local Hausa police cut off the Asante arms supply at Elmina on 12 June 1873, and bloodily repulsed attempts to interfere. The Asante had never seen so many men killed in so short a time and withdrew. Festing hoped to attack them again 'if the weather keeps fine, whether it will result in anything much it is impossible to say for these beggars can move so quickly in the bush and we have only about 140 dependable men (Haussas) who can equal them.' The weather proved atrocious, mud huts at Cape Coast Castle 'almost literally washed away', and Festing's room 'like a sluice – I was turned out of bed by it'.[41]

The troopship *Simoom* brought 150 more Marines, prompting the colonial governor, 'a man whose temperament ran to extremes', to urge an advance on the Asante capital Kumasi. Luckily Festing quashed the idea, the new arrivals taking part in local offensives contributing to the Asante withdrawal in October. Fifty Marines helped garrison Abrakrampa, on the Asante road home. They cleared fields of fire, loop-holed houses and stripped the Mission Church roof, to mount rockets and an old brass gun, christened Nelly, on the ceiling or 'upper deck'. For two days 10,000 Asante attacked the post to a wild accompaniment of horns and tom-toms, the occasional crackle of Marine sniders piercing the yellow powder-smoke that wreathed the trees. Local levies, organized by a handful of Special Service officers, followed the Asante respectfully, bringing in abandoned slaves, 'half starved. . . almost literally walking skeletons'. Lieutenant Parkins Hearle RMLI was reminded that he was not dealing with 'educated or civilised beings, and that consequently the utmost good temper, affability, and patience mingled with firmness of purpose and determination are of the greatest importance'.[42] He needed all these when his levies bolted at the first shot: 'stopped them as they were rushing past and by dint of thrashing and hard work managed to get them on, although at first they were huddled together like a flock of sheep'.[43]

A punitive expedition to Kumasi in January 1874 bore little resemblance to the previous year's alarms, when a handful of Marines and bluejackets had borne the heat and burden of the day. Sir Garnet Wolseley, 'our only soldier', was given sufficient white troops, including a Naval Brigade, to overwhelm the Asante in five days. Hearle went as far as Adansi, where white calico squares nailed to trees as peace tokens were belied by 'an immense pit. . . full of human bones or skulls, and. . . a complete skeleton fixed to a bamboo stake'.[44] A few Marines accompanied the Naval Brigade, commanded by a Lieutenant RN for lack of their own officers. Absence from the final push was paralleled in the honours lists. Wolseley begrudged Festing's KCB and promotion to full Colonel and ignored him in his final despatch. The *Army & Navy Gazette* found Wolseley's attitude symptomatic: 'The Marines are not a generally favoured body of men (though we should be much puzzled to find a reason)', and condemned the injustice: 'If the men who have distinguished themselves survive to return to England, a step to brevet rank is surely but poor compensation for the ruin of their constitutions.'[45] A parcel of helmets finally turned up, causing much excitement on the coast: 'every native being determined to get one if possible, whether he owned any other costume or not'. The joke, such as it was, had cost the Corps dearly, for little return.

Egypt 1882

When unrest in Egypt threatened the Suez Canal in 1882, the Royal Marines played a key role in resolving the emergency, at last earning the recognition they deserved. Marines from the fleet combined with divisional contingents as an amphibious striking force, modulated into standard leg infantry and ad hoc gun crews to consolidate their bridgehead, and shared in the decisive engagement at Tel-el-Kebir. The Royal Marines fielded the equivalent of three battalions, a significant contribution after the anticlimax of their 1879 Zulu War deployment. Military bands had played them off to South Africa, sprigs of evergreen in their rifles, but they arrived too late to see action and returned without giving a shot almost before their wives had spent their quota of two months' embarkation pay. Egypt was another story.

The first RM battalion (300 RMA and 500 RMLI) left Plymouth on 30 June, a fortnight before the Mediterranean Fleet's bombardment of Alexandria brought the crisis to a head. Unfortunately the Admiral had not appreciated the need for a floating reserve. While Alexandria's inhabitants looted their burning city, the RM battalion cruised round the Mediterranean, arriving after parties from the fleet had restored order, and secured the city's perimeter. Unlike the Asante the Egyptians had plenty of modern weapons and could have disputed a direct advance on Cairo indefinitely. Sir Garnet Wolseley, the British Army's effective Chief of Staff, preferred to exploit his sea-borne expedition's strategic mobility to turn the enemy flank, seizing the Suez Canal while Egyptian attention was focussed on Alexandria. A second RM battalion (120 RMA and 450 RMLI) arrived on 8 August, but were disappointed not to join their comrades ashore.

Both RM battalions soon found themselves off Port Said, ready for the boldest amphibious coup of the century. Captain Tulloch, of the intelligence department, and six Marines rowed quietly ashore on the night of 19/20 August to secure the sentries, while more Marines captured the barracks without a shot fired. Gunboats loaded with Marines steamed down the canal, to reinforce bluejackets landed at Ismailia from warships quietly pre-positioned in the Bitter Lakes. First troops through, the Marines were ready for trouble with machine guns in the fighting tops to pepper anyone who shot at them from the canal banks. The day after landing the two contingents formed separate RMA and RMLI Battalions. Marines from the fleet, enough for a third battalion, helped garrison Alexandria. The 1,100 RMLI were the strongest battalion present, an American observer believing it 'second to no other body of troops in the field in organisation, discipline, and performance'. With their high average age and experience afloat the men combined steadiness and handiness, 'the characteristic of the sailor, and a most desirable habit on the part of the soldier.'[46] The Army's introduction of short service had left Marines the only long-service infantry in Her Majesty's forces, comparable in physique to the Brigade of Guards. Measuring at least 5 feet $8^1/_2$ inches, and an inch more in the RMA, the 1879 RM Battalion had 'presented a striking contrast to the mere striplings who formed a large proportion of the line regiments previously despatched to the Cape.'[47] Even before the change some Marines in China had found army boots too small.

They needed to be fit as Wolseley hurried them forward to secure Ismailia's fresh water supply, the misnamed Sweetwater Canal. Only the Marines kept up with the cavalry through knee-deep sand, while the RMA surprised brass hats by relieving exhausted horse artillery detachments. Cooking pots littered Egyptian camps, but the promise of hot food was illusory, British troops eating biscuit and potted meat, known as Fanny Adams after a celebrated murder victim. Helmets or water bottles served as pillows, exhausted men lying down wet with perspiration and awaking wet with dew. The RMA took the brunt of the Egyptians' first serious counter-move at Kassassin, suffering thirty-one out of the sixty-nine British casualties. Much of the day the only British gun in action was a Krupp 8cm gun the RMA had assembled from abandoned weapons. Pushed up and down on a railway truck it bore a charmed life, shells and shrapnel bullets falling all around without hitting anyone.

The Marines spent the next twelve days unloading supplies from railway trucks in preparation for the decisive battle. An Egyptian sortie from their lines at Tel-el-Kebir allowed the RMLI to capture two more guns, but a more memorable incident was the rush for the water camel. Captured by Lieutenant Cyril Field for the *Graphic*, his sketch caught the attention of Queen Victoria herself. By 12 September Wolseley was ready. Facing well-entrenched troops with modern weapons he planned a night march and dawn assault, leaving all day for cavalry to exploit the anticipated victory. Cyril Field remembered the dreamlike quality of the advance:

We halted more than once, but there was nothing to differentiate one halt from the other, always the same shadowy battalions to our right and left, the gravely ground underfoot, and the enclosing night. . . at last, just as the stars were beginning to pale, the whole of the leading battalions were formed into line and then everyone woke up, and pulled himself together.[48]

The RMLI were towards the British centre, massed artillery on their left and then the Highland Brigade. As dawn streaked the sky the Egyptians opened a hail of fire:

but thick as it was, the order was given "Advance" and thick as they were dropping in front of us, every man advanced without the least thought of being shot. We advanced within 100 yards, or so, when the order was given to "fix Bayonets" & the next order was "Charge" as soon as they gave us that order, we all seemed to have the devil in us. . . we all shouted with all our might & on we swept, down into the embankment, climbing over the earthworks & God knows it was a terrible sight, the Arabs took to their heels & we after them, cutting and shooting them down like a flock of sheep.[49]

The RMLI advanced four miles, while the cavalry swept on to Cairo, ending the war at a stroke. Marine casualties were higher than any other corps – eighty killed, wounded or missing – and there was some debate whether they or the Highland Brigade were first into the enemy lines.

The RMA missed the fighting, having transferred to the Artillery Reserve. They loaded captured guns onto railway trucks for evacuation, 'not as a task, but as a lark, as a race almost', while Staff officers debated how long the job might take. The RMLI had to bury the dead, a job 'so awful, totally unfit for human beings, that we simply threw men and animals, arms and ammunition in all together and covered them up with sand.'[50] The enemy had referred indiscriminately to Marines as Blue Devils, as both Artillery and Light Infantry wore dark blue, their helmets and equipment dyed brown with coffee, an early example of camouflage. At the Cairo victory parade, by contrast, the RMLI marched past in 'new red tunics and brilliantly white helmets. . . quite eclipsing in appearance all who had passed before'.[51]

The Marines had 'as usual received all the hard knocks', but for once their efforts were not unrecognized. An ecstatic crowd at Plymouth jammed the streets and surged uncontrollably across the hallowed divisional parade ground. The *Hampshire Telegraph* devoted almost a page to the return of Portsmouth's RMLI. The Division occupied new quarters in 1848, across the harbour at Forton where, 'Gaily bedecked and brilliant Gosport seemed waiting like a Venus to welcome her Mars.' After a drill-shed banquet, accompanied by 'an immeasurable supply of beer', Captain Frampton assured its municipal providers of the Battalion's gratitude: 'It was worth going to Egypt for (Laughter). Personally he would not mind going out again to get a reception like that (Renewed laughter and cheers)'. The paper drew a more serious conclusion. Reviewing the annoyances which beset an amphibious corps, it suggested right had at last asserted itself: 'The Marines have at last had justice done to them, and have displayed qualities in the field which it is as impossible to surpass as it would be ungracious not to extol.'[52]

The Devil's Hole – Sudan 1884–85

Tel-el-Kebir shook Egypt's hold over its empire in the Sudan, provoking a jihad led by the chosen deliverer from foreign misrule, the Mahdi. Revolt spread to the shores of the Red Sea, which to the British was an extension of the Suez Canal. The Royal Navy moved swiftly to relieve the Egyptian garrison of the old slaving port at Sawakin, and secure the route to India. Royal Marines were among the first troops landed in February 1884: 360 from the Mediterranean Fleet and 140 from drafts returning home from China.

The enemy they faced was unlike any Royal Marines had faced before. The shock-headed Hadendoa tribesmen of the Sudan became known as 'fuzzies', with more respect than derision: 'The beastly mixture they put on their heads and body being enough to upset the machinery of one's stomach for the rest of one's natural existence.'[53] In battle they combined death-defying courage with an unnerving ability to appear out of nowhere. The *Army & Navy Gazette* wrote of 'naked barbarians armed with primitive spears and javelins', but their charge spelled death for any who flinched. The Hadendoa broke more than one British square, demanding all the steadiness of the long-service Marine. At El Teb and Tamai, fought outside Sawakin in early 1884, the Marines occupied an unenviable position behind the square:

> plodding in heavy marching order through clouds of dust in tight fitting blue clothing attracting the full heat of the sun. . . obstructed by the tail ends of mules, constantly straggling from the mass inside the square.[54]

On both occasions they prevented Hadendoa irruptions turning into disaster. At El Teb the RMLI closed the gap when the weight of attack pushed their neighbours back, while the RMA 'showed they had something more in them than the usual display, for they went up the slope like Devils let loose', turning two captured Krupp guns onto the enemy, 'fetching them down like rabbits'.[55] A fortnight later the British went into action at Tamai in two squares, for mutual support. The Hadendoa broke the leading square, driving it back half a mile, the men jammed too closely together to use their weapons, dazed and incapable of anything but walking steadily towards the rear. The Marines began the rally, showing the value of esprit de corps and the old discipline instilled on the barrack square, as Major Colwell, 'the fortunate possessor of a voice like a bull', roared out an appeal to the Portsmouth men to rally around him.[56]

A shocked Cabinet dithered. It withdrew the Army, but sent another RM battalion: 'Really this place Suakin is an awful hole & it is generally asserted that for the 3 worst months of the year no white man stays here but yet they kept the Marines here.' They occupied corrugated-iron forts, equipped with machine guns and searchlights: 'an electric machine for searching the country is placed on top but does not act well. Nearly every night the rebels come down & fire at us but so bad is their fire that no one is hit.' Marines endured 'the fearfully dull monotony of Sudan life', and temperatures of 98 degrees at breakfast. The sick list contradicted official claims that their health was satisfactory, 'when in reality it is just about as bad as it can be'. Survivors saw replacements from England as 'candidates for the fever battalion', and joked they might 'go on from here to China and then finish up in Zululand'. The divisional system kept the battalion a constant 600, an administrative feat beyond infantry regiments of the day. Officers diverted themselves with butterfly collecting, impromptu concerts of the comb and paper variety, provoking showers of stones from the next tent, and native funerals: 'The women are beautifully ugly and when a funeral goes on have a fine set to, to see who can scream longest, loudest, and shrillest.'[57] Rebels killed in nightly skirmishes were disposed of with less ceremony: dumped out on the main approach as a warning to their friends.

The government had sent General Charles Gordon to evacuate the Sudan, but the Mahdi trapped him at Khartoum, forcing the British to mount a rescue mission. Four officers and 102 Marines from Sawakin joined the Guards Camel Corps, adding a new twist to the concept of Horse Marines. After four days training on government camels marked with a broad arrow they took part in the dash from Kurti to al Matamma in January 1885, hoping to link up with Gordon's 'penny steamers' on the Nile. When the Naval Brigade's Gardner gun jammed at Abu Klea, and Mahdist spearmen broke into the square, the infantry training of

Guards and Marines saved the day, as they faced about to fire volleys over the heads of their comrades. Gordon's death had been rumoured since November, but the approach of a relieving force finally precipitated the fall of Khartoum on 26 January 1885. The Camel Corps was left hanging, withdrawal the only option. A quarter of the Marine company had become casualties, including Major Poë, whose red tunic amongst the universal grey had attracted an Arab sniper.

Fresh troops were despatched to 'the devil's hole', putting the garrison 'in a state of great excitement as it is promised the Marines will go. . . This looks like business.'[58] They were preparing a desert supply depot at Tofrek, when the shout went up, 'They are on us', and a wave of spearmen swept down on the unformed square. Thomas Holbrow, an old Fusilier re-enlisted as a Royal Marine, was the type of unimaginative professional indispensable in such an emergency:

> I should say there [were] between 7 or 8 thousand of the Arabs to our three. The devils came on – saw no fear whatever. . . the officers had no chance whatever to give words of command. If they did they could not have been heard. It only lasted twenty minutes. There were hundreds of camels, horses and mules lying besides hundreds of Arabs. There were a good few killed and wounded on our side. I myself had a narrow escape. I had a bullet through the breech of my rifle – grazed right side of my face – mentioned in the papers. I did not mind it a bit, it was good sport while it lasted.[59]

The Hadendoa carried away an Indian infantry battalion and wiped out the crew of a naval Gardner gun: 'It was a most awful scene of confusion for about a quarter of an hour. The enemy got well inside the zareba, but not one got out again.'[60] The battle's aftermath was grisly, even by Sudanese standards, but Holbrow was blasé: 'in that twenty minutes everyone of us got hardened enough to face the devil.' He and his mates had turned imminent disaster into crushing victory. The next two months were spent guarding navvies on the derided Sawakin-Berber railway, until a Russian war scare allowed the Government to cut its losses. Holbrow took the train back to Sawakin, sailing home in May 1885 to the now obligatory dinner, 'quite a treat after living on sand for so long'.[61]

Naval Brigades

RM battalions operated against a background of continuous low-intensity conflicts, whose frequency and geographical spread defy chronological narrative. Small groups of Marines provided the hard core of the naval brigades that were an essential part of Pax Britannica: ad hoc formations put together to meet imperial emergencies that rarely gave time for despatch of larger military forces from home. Historians preoccupied with eighteenth and twentieth-century struggles for maritime supremacy have mocked naval brigades as a distraction from the Royal Navy's primary functions, but they were a rational response to the nineteenth-century strategic situation, when the Royal Navy's main function was to exploit command of the sea, not fight for it. Communications were slow, outside the European and North American network of telegraph and railway lines, and ships still the most efficient means of moving guns and men to trouble spots. In the absence of any recognized framework for peaceful resolution of international disputes, such as the United Nations, the Royal Navy's gunboats provided a cost-effective means of imposing minimal standards of commercial or diplomatic behaviour in a disorderly world. Their inability to fight or run away from real cruisers was irrelevant, as long as a handful of powerful warships held the Channel and Straits of Gibraltar against possible predators.

Naval brigades were not the improvizations of amateurs playing at soldiers. The Royal Navy displayed increasing military expertise from the 1850s, on the parade ground and in the field. Ships devoted a day every week to training for service ashore, just as they did for action at sea, with landing equipment kept ready for use. A typical naval brigade might field two small companies of bluejacket riflemen and one of Marines, besides gun crews, demolition parties and stretcher-bearers. Numbers varied with the size of the ship. HMS *Boadicea* landed 56 Marines and 90 naval small arms men at Witu in 1890, compared with 8 and 15 respectively from HMS *Swallow*, a gunboat. Marines represented 22 per cent of the total numbers at Witu, but 38 per cent of the rifle strength.[62] A naval brigade's lack of Marines in 1881 attracted adverse comment:

> Seeing how well our Blue-jackets and Marines have always worked together. . . the idea of a portion of a ship's crew being landed without Marines, who are as much land forces as sea forces, strikes the most casual observer as being peculiar.[63]

The 1897 Benin expedition was more typical. Some bluejackets were sent back to conserve supplies, but all available Marines were retained for the flying column. Responding to a toast to the Royal Navy's work in the Boer War, Lord Charles Beresford: 'did not forget his old friend the Royal Marine. While expressing his pride in the Navy being able to work on land as at sea, he was sure they could not do it without the help of the Marines.'[64]

Naval brigades took two main forms: artillery batteries with a Marine escort, or flying columns of infantry with integral support weapons – light field pieces or machine guns. The former organization usually provided fire support for a larger military force, while the latter might operate on its own. Naval brigades from HMS *Shannon* and *Pearl* during the Indian Mutiny of 1857–59 illustrate both operational styles. *Shannon*'s bluejackets manned a siege train of 8-inch shell guns at Lucknow and Cawnpore, in a complex series of operations that forty years on defied Henry Derry's powers of recollection: 'At times there is a feeling of the sun on my head and at the back of my neck even now, but it seems to me we must have been months about the river and the place'. The seamen tackled hostile positions at point-blank range, while Marines provided covering fire:

> The marines were detailed for outpost duty and rifle pits picking off the [enemy] gunners from the battery to save Captain Peel's men, who were within close range and who suffered very much. "It's no use unless we are close up", he said, "We must bring the whole place about our ears and then get to close quarters".

Between fights the Marines helped move the guns, the heaviest British forces had ever used ashore:

> By Jove, they were stubborn customers over soft ground. We had to be our own horses and bullocks and face the fiddle and enemy too, I can tell you in a blazing sun. There was no galloping away with our guns, like the soldiers did. We had to stick to them under all conditions.[65]

HMS *Pearl*'s Royal Marines were for many months the only professional British infantry in northern Uttar Pradesh. It was savage counter-guerrilla warfare, chasing elusive sepoy rearguards, portable gallows at the ready, or hurrying to rescue friendly Rajahs, along roads knee-deep in mud:

> guns and provisions were carried on elephants, it being impossible to drag them through the water and mud. Often someone would slip off the muddy road into deep water and have to be pulled up again, and Jack often remarked that we wanted our boats with us.

Columns outran their supplies, living on green corn, washed down with river water, or chupattis made by their Sikh allies: 'a sort of thin cake baked on a hot iron plate, they eat something like sawdust'. When they met the enemy, 'the cavalry was sent to the front, guns got off the elephants, mounted and hurried forward, and the Seamen and Marines doubled up to support their guns', but the rebels always slipped away.[66] *Pearl*'s Brigade set something of a record, being ashore for almost seventeen months, and fighting twenty-six actions.

The great playground for Naval Brigades was Africa. Military weakness invited intervention, but the deadly miasma of the coast precluded more than the briefest stay ashore. A few hundred white men might have occupied the whole Sultanate of Witu, but Admiral Fremantle 'was glad to embark our men so as to avoid sickness and to keep the ships efficient'.[67] The ability of amphibious forces to insert and extract striking forces before fever took hold became particularly valuable as the scramble for Africa reached its climax, with significant naval brigades at Witu (October 1890), in the Gambia (February–March 1894) and Benin (February 1897). Most of the Royal Marines involved came from ship's detachments, although 100 reinforcements sailed for Benin from the Albert Dock, played off by the Grenadier Guards in a blinding snowstorm.

Enemy numbers and fighting qualities were usually obscure. Only 800 of the Sultan of Witu's men turned out, although total estimates ran to 8,000. Like the Asante they carried long-barrelled trade guns, 'their usual charge a handful of coarse powder, two or three spherical bullets, and a dozen or two jagged bits of iron for use at close quarters.'[68] These were more noisy than dangerous, thanks to 'the enemy's aiming high, most of them firing from the hip'. The Sultan's men were not afraid to come to close quarters:

> and with savage fearlessness advanced to within a few yards of the square several times, but the steady and well directed fire of the machine guns and rifles was too much for them, and they had reluctantly to retire to the jungle.[69]

West African fights usually consisted of a furious fusillade:

> Lying down, we fired volleys by sections, into the bushes wherever the flashes of their guns appeared thickest. For more than half an hour the fire was very heavy, slugs were flying about too thick to be quite pleasant, and the unmistakeable whiz of Martini bullets was to be heard just overhead.[70]

Even when a section of Marines simulated panic, 'not a man showed himself in the open'. Any casualty was 'at once seized by his comrades and bumped over the ground to the rear', leaving only a few bloodstained guns as evidence of a battle. Stockades, a common feature of African warfare, were elaborate structures: gates 4 inches thick, a bamboo screen concealing an inner ring of 15-foot-high tree trunks embedded in the ground, and a shelter trench within. They were rarely defended to the death:

> the Mandingo, in common with most savage or semi-savage tribes, has a wholesome fear of being surrounded and caught in a trap. . . Threaten his flank or rear, and he feels it is time to be off.

Marines suited tactics to terrain. East African savannah permitted open squares, with flanking parties to search the jungle, but dense West African bush forced columns into single file, 'while the advance guard fired volleys at frequent intervals as a precautionary measure into the bush in front and on either flank'. Heavy weapons were dragged along, sometimes decorated with bunches of fowls, presenting 'the appearance of a poulterer's shop at Christmas'.[71] Maxim guns were useful against snipers in trees, ammunition boxes being placed under the front tripod legs for extra elevation and lime-juice in the water jacket for lack of the usual coolant. At night columns occupied positions for all-round defence, while standing patrols outside the perimeter were ordered not to disturb the camp unnecessarily, or 'Don't fire until you are hit.'[72]

The greatest problem in bush warfare was transport, that is human porters: 'a nondescript lot of all shapes and sizes, but wonderful hands at carrying loads of up to eighty pounds'.[73] In an ambush they were a liability:

> Everything was stopped, as before, by the carriers, guns, tripods, and belt boxes being anywhere, and the carriers burying their heads in the earth. The respective Nos 1 shouldered the guns, another picked up the tripods, and the rest of the guns' crews brought up the belt boxes, but it was with difficulty that any advance was made as the coolies laid down on, and hid, the ammunition.[74]

Clausewitz's concept of the Culminating Point of the Offensive had real significance in Benin, where the flying column entered the city with just the water in their bottles. For several days they 'lived on "wind". . . a helmet of biscuit served out daily for forty Marines'.[75] They must have felt very near Conrad's Heart of Darkness: 'Horrible sights were to be seen; city reeking with blood; human sacrifices everywhere; place like a slaughter house.'[76] No one can have been sorry to leave the Hausa police in charge and hurry back to the coast. Malaria broke out, despite prophylactic quinine and bottles of stout, and the march was completed in darkness to pre-empt its effects: 'Luckily we had a box of candles, so formed an illuminated procession, but it was horrible, tree stumps and holes innumerable.'[77]

The retreat from Witu was less dreadful, Marines amused by the distress of less fit stretcher-bearers, 'comprised as they were of idlers from the ships, and armed to the teeth'.[78] Gambia's geographical configuration gave full play to Marines' amphibious capabilities. After defeating an incursion into the British part of the peninsula, they re-embarked to deal with an enemy stronghold on the Atlantic coast. While 300 black soldiers of the West India Regiment approached from the north, warships softened it up from seawards: 'the bush in the rear of the landing place being occasionally shelled and swept by volleys of musketry from a picked party of Marines, all marksmen, stationed on the *Alecto*'s hurricane deck.'[79] When the Naval Brigade stormed through the surf with fixed bayonets, they found the birds flown and some very pleased West Indians in possession. There were no moral scruples about imperialist aggression, and not much ceremony:

> Corporal Hunt then produced a Union Jack from the breast of his serge tunic, lashed it onto a bamboo pole, stuck it into the roof of the Headman's hut, the troops saluted, and the British Empire was so much the bigger.[80]

Men who had seen the valley of skulls at Benin had a workmanlike sense of a job well done: 'We had been on shore eighteen days, completed the job we were landed for, and I think all hands were pleased to be once more on board Transport No. 7.'[81]

Imperial Coastguard

Timely intervention by Naval Brigades depended on the ships' ability to remain on station, tirelessly patrolling sea lanes and coastlines. Seven months into a commission on the Cape HMS *Goshawk* had already crossed the line twice: 'As a small gunboat I think we have done a fair amount of running about. I believe up to the present we have covered over ten thousand miles.'[82] Most of the ships maintaining Pax Britannica were small, slow and uncomfortable. *Goshawk*'s top speed under steam was eight knots, slower than the frigate taking Lieutenant Henry Woodruff RM to the Cape, obliged at thirteen knots 'to take the top gallant sails in and double reef topsails, as we were afraid of carrying something away'. Transferring into a brig, HMS *Dart*, Woodruff 'did not much like the look of the Gun Room, it seemed so very small', and his cabin was alive:

'I heard the Cockroaches running about and making a rustling noise on the shelves. . . but I did not feel any of them crawl over me.' HMS *Sphinx* began her career at El Teb in 1882 by bracketing the RM battalion with three shells, but she was still serving in the Gulf in 1905. Her complement of 108 included a sergeant and just 7 Marines.

Such detachments retained ceremonial and security roles, providing guards of honour for consuls and such dignitaries as the Turkish commodore at Basra, or the King of Calabar. Woodruff changed into blanket frock and trousers to preserve his finery from the surf and to look his best for the Portuguese authorities at Quelimane: 'I put on my red shell jacket and my forage cap with a white cover and the Ornament on the outside. I also put on my red silk sash round my waist and my sword on; we were all in white trousers.'[83] Marines still maintained shipboard security. Sentries on HMS *Goshawk*'s bridge had ten rounds and orders to fire, 'if they [the natives] persisted in coming on board',[84] but a diplomatic touch must have been necessary when HMS *Sphinx*'s paymaster 'broke into the Captain's wine cupboard, and stole three bottles of whiskey, which he drank, he then had delirium tremens. . . a hard task to keep him in his cabin'. Marines joined in routine shipboard evolutions: Out stream anchor; Arm ship and repel boarders; Clean and paint ship; Cutlass and heavy gun drill; Coal ship: 'We got in 115 tons from 6 a.m. to 1 p.m. in 112° in the shade, we were nearly naked and did not stop for any food. Our Captain was warned by the Admiral not to let it happen again.' Training ashore could be equally tough:

> At 6 a.m. the whole ship's company landed in full marching order with the two 7pr field guns and carriages and carried out skirmishing, pistol firing, and field gun drill, firing blank and shell, retiring back to the ship at 11.30 a.m., having had a good morning's work as it was very sandy soil and the gun wheels sank well into it. Away portable fire engine at 4 p.m.[85]

Long cruises in harsh conditions tried physical and mental health. HMS *Goshawk*'s Sergeant of Marines thought his detachment 'a very discontented lot', but was himself 'Very despondent. . . a feeling very often felt on the West Coast of Africa'. Riverine operations were worst:

> I shall be glad when we have done with this river work and then perhaps we shall be able to feel ourselves and have a little hope. I feel done up. Sometimes when up these rivers, we scarcely know what to do with ourselves.[86]

Off Mozambique Woodruff was 'in an awful sweat all day and all night', and could scarcely sleep for the heat. Thunderstorms offered the only relief: 'I took off everything but my shirt and trousers, and went on deck and enjoyed it, it being as good as a bath.' Half a tub of fresh water between every ten men was a Christmas treat in *Goshawk*, after two days washing with salt water. Tempers flared. *Goshawk*'s Sergeant applied to buy himself out after a reprimand 'for standing in a slovenly position when drilling the detachment'. HMS *Dart*'s officers fell out comprehensively, Woodruff and the Captain eating in their cabins alone, after exchanging 'disgusting and ungentlemanly language'.[87]

The Gulf ran tropical Africa close for unpleasantness. Only thirteen out of seventy-three men sent to Bombay to commission *Sphinx* in 1902 lasted the full three years 'in one of the hottest and worst places for a white man in the world'. Her first visit to Basra coincided with a three-day sandstorm, sand lying half an inch thick on the decks. Fresh bread rotted overnight in heat, which once reached 150 degrees. Once there was no mail for seven weeks and no potatoes for sixteen. A stay in the Sailor's Home in Bombay or action against gun-runners might relieve the tension: 'suddenly aroused by the pipe "Hands Man and Arm boats" we all knew then, that there was sport of a stern nature in the air.' Gun-running dhows drew less water than a warship and had to be pursued in ship's boats. *Sphinx*'s Marines took the whaler. When revolver shots drove the Arabs ashore, 'we had to jump out of the boat up to our waists in water which wet all our ammunition, we knew then it would be hand to hand':

> Our Serjeant hit one a terrible blow over the head with his rifle which soon put him "Hors de Combat", then we were in the thick of it, they had horrible looking knives which they attacked us with. We clubbed our rifles and slashed out at them, I caught one a hit on the shoulder as he was going to knife one of our chaps and down he went like a log, it was horrible.

The bluejackets' cutter ended the fight, with a haul of 7 prisoners, 130 rifles and 12,000 rounds, 'not at all a bad capture'.[88]

Sea Change

The flow of modern weapons through the Gulf to fuel trouble on India's North West Frontier was a sign of changing times. The British no longer monopolized naval power or modern weapons; new navies had appeared. Sixty US Marines helped restore order at Alexandria, beginning a tradition of cooperation between the Corps, continued by HMS *Intrepid* and USS *Marietta* at Bluefields, Nicaragua in 1899:

> Two watches, each composed of British and American Marines mixed, were arranged, the command being given alternately to an American and British Lieutenant. It is said to be the first instance on record of an American officer commanding mixed British and American troops. The men declared blood brotherhood and exchanged the buttons on their uniforms. At the Consulate the United States and British flags were displayed crossed, and the men cheered them every time they passed on patrol duty.[89]

The Boxer Rebellion, next year in China, took Anglo-American cooperation a stage further, and suggested the capabilities of a reorganized Chinese Army:

> having the latest Mauser pattern rifle and Mannlicher carbines. . . I have been in action every day for the last fortnight and have had three hair breadth escapes, 1 bullet across the throat, graze across the arm, and watch worn on the wrist broken by bullet.[90]

Marines of both nationalities defended the diplomatic Legations in Peking, where: 'A splendid feeling of affection existed between our men and the Americans. . . quite in contrast to the feeling shewn by two other nationalities, alongside whom we have to fight.'[91] One joint sortie against Chinese positions overlooking their barricade, was led by Captain Myers USMC: 'a night never to be forgotten... It rained torrents (As it can only rain in China) there was no shelter and we were already soaked through.' Myers was speared in the foot, but the enemy 'were taught a lesson that night and they never forgot it for we could never catch them napping again'.[92] All Royal Marine officers present during the siege became casualties, among them Captain L.S.T. Halliday RMLI, who left a self-deprecating account of how he won the Corps' fourth VC:

> Went down a narrow alley and came upon five men with rifles round the corner of a house. One immediately plugged me in the shoulder cutting the left brace of my Sam Browne in half. I then began to empty my revolver into them, as they were only a yard away there was no question of missing. I finished four and the fifth bolted. . . That finished my active share in the siege which was rather hard luck.[93]

Captain Myers received a unique honour, appearing on the Royal Marines memorial by Admiralty Arch in London in his campaign hat, a reminder of the inter-corps friendship the siege had sealed.

As new competitors emerged, old enemies recovered their nerve. HMS *Sphinx* responded to a telegram, 'expecting to see some fun, fighting with the natives by way of a change', only to discover a French and a Russian cruiser at Kuwait, 'flashing their searchlights on the town, much to the natives dismay'. Shadowed to Muscat, like suspected burglars, the two left for quieter waters on the appearance of three more RN cruisers.[94]

Great power rivalry prevented despatch of an RM battalion to South Africa during the Boer War. Officers grumbled at the neglect of 18,000 of the finest troops in the world, but *Army & Navy Gazette* thought it 'bad policy to denude the fleet of its proper proportion of the force', faced with general hostility towards Britain's dealings with the Boers.[95]

The only Royal Marines to fight in South Africa came from the Cape Squadron. They began by escorting naval field guns, then mutated into gunners, regardless of cap badge: RMLI or RMA. They trekked from Simonstown to Mozambique and witnessed a military revolution. For the first time the British Army faced magazine rifles, whose flat trajectory bullets and smokeless cartridges swept battlefields with an invisible rain of death, preventing reconnaissance and mocking traditional tactics. Attached to the Kimberley relief column under Lord Methuen, the Royal Marines had their introduction to twentieth-century warfare at Graspan on 25 November 1899. Captain A.E. Marchant RMLI, a veteran of the Sawakin fever battalion, was appalled:

Ye Gods! Where was the Intelligence?

The marines and a small number of bluejackets were given the post of honour, were committed to the attack and carried it through, but at a frightful sacrifice. I have never realized what war is until now. The hail of bullets was awful. Officers and men dropped on all sides. How I got through, I cannot tell. . . Four of our officers were killed, two wounded, and 99 men killed and wounded, a total of over 40 percent.[96]

Many of those hit had practised open order tactics during weekly training sessions outside Simonstown. Extended in single line at four paces per man, the Marines brought up their left shoulders and advanced obliquely upon the line of rocky hills that made up the Boer position. Supporting artillery fell silent 700 yards from the objective, 'and almost immediately the kopjes, which a moment before had seemed quite clear of the enemy, opened a regular storm of fire.' Noise and extension made controlled volleys impossible, so men ran forward in short rushes, and threw themselves down to return fire. So perfectly did they carry out the drill that lines of cartridge cases still litter the uncultivated battlefield, revealing successive fire positions a century after the action:

> There was something fine about the men, they did not want leading in the rushes, but only wanted someone to give them the tip as to whether it was time to get up. . . all seemed to follow you like clockwork, there was no hesitation with them.

At the crest the Marines found three dead Boers, their wagons 'a wonderful but tantalizing sight. . . trekking away northwards as hard as they could go'.[97] It was poor exchange for the casualties and contrasted sharply with Marine attacks in earlier colonial conflicts. It was not immediately apparent that runaway developments in weapons technology had revolutionized warfare. Marchant expressed general fury after two more frontal attacks on Boer positions: 'we were sold by our Cavalry and intelligence. . . someone deserves a hanging over the business. The Infantry and Artillery have done everything that was asked of them at those 3 hard fights, and the fruits of all have been lost.'

In the New Year Marchant welcomed Lord Roberts, the new Commander-in-Chief, who emphasized manoeuvre: 'everyone expects good results. We are all glad that our tactics have been altered.'[98] Roberts turned Kimberley's besiegers out of their trenches, took the Boer capitals at Bloemfontein and Pretoria and drove Boer forces eastwards towards neutral Portuguese territory. Battles lasted for days, as Private F.W. Phillips found at Belfast, 24–27 August 1900:

> We started the fight on Friday evening and we found the Boers had taken up a very strong position which covered a front of sixteen miles. We did not do much on the Saturday, but on the Sunday morning we took our two 4.7 guns into position on a high hill and no sooner did the Boers sight our guns with their long teams of oxen than they started in real earnest and I need hardly add "so did we".
>
> On the Monday morning we shifted our position to another hill and the fighting began again. . . banging away until about 4 o/c in the afternoon and then the Boers again did what they have always done "Ran Away".

Marine casualties were slight, despite the time under fire: Lieutenant Wilson RMLI shot through the thigh and a sergeant's puttee torn by a bullet. The action was the Brigade's last, as the Army pressed on without them, to the relief of footsore Marines:

> Our skipper Captain Bearcroft was very much cut up about it but we

weren't for I think 700 miles marching in ten months is quite sufficient and I haven't the least desire to do any more trekking in South Africa.

As felt bush hats replaced helmets and sennet hats the distinction between Marine and bluejacket became blurred. The operational integration of the Navy's two types of manpower obscured the Marines' contribution 'through the war correspondents classing a Marine as a sailor'. Royal Marines bore the brunt at Graspan, but 'some of the papers had the audacity to call that action a Sailor's Battle.'[99] Tasteless correspondence in *The Times* revealed differences between the senior Marine officer killed at Graspan and his naval alter ego, whom Marchant remembered as 'a friend of mine ever since I joined at Greenwich'. As senior surviving officer of either service Marchant brought the Naval Brigade out of action at Graspan, Admiral Harris at Simonstown promoting him Major by telegram, and confirming him in command, 'an honour which no Marine officer in my time or as far as I know, had ever had given to him'.[100] Captain Bruce of HMS *Monarch*, guardship at Simonstown paid tribute to the contribution of Captain Guy Senior, killed during the battle, to the efficiency of the Naval Brigade: 'Marines loss of 90 out of 200 speaks for itself, they have seldom done anything better, and all fleet are proud of them'.[101]

The press was not wholly to blame for inter-service confusion. Even veterans were muddled: 'You see, chum,' said Henry Derry of an earlier conflict, 'I can't separate we Joeys from the Jacks, nor the Jacks from we Joeys, so we get lost in the Naval Brigade.'[102] The Corps was victim of an illogical chain of command that denied Royal Marine officers authority over naval personnel and hence over the Naval Brigades they were best fitted to command:

> So that Officers carefully and specially trained by the State for military operations on the land are placed under the guidance and direction of Officers carefully and specially trained for naval operations on the water.[103]

At Sawakin 'square pegging of round holes' inspired complaints of Marine officers 'kept on board ship, while Naval officers from the same ship have been landed to take part in operations ashore'.[104] Dark rumours circulated that the Mediterranean Fleet's Marines nearly went to the Sudan without any officers of their own Corps at all. It is hard not to agree with a contemporary claim that 'The present use and application of marine forces present a picture of confusion, anomalies and inconsistencies.'[105] This was nothing new, but the nineteenth-century revolution in naval technology sharpened contradictions in the situation of the sea soldier, which forms the subject of the next chapter.

CHAPTER EIGHT

The Advent of Steam

THE introduction of steam propulsion during the 1830s, followed by dramatic changes in construction and armament, revolutionized the way in which ships were manned and employed. Two centuries of steady evolution gave way to a period of breakneck innovation that baffled strategists and administrators with new ships and new weapons. Some ideas, like the torpedo, were replete with sinister possibilities; others, such as the circular Russian ironclads known as *Popoffkas*, were not. Fitful debates smouldered over the future of the Royal Marines as they adapted to the changed circumstances of 'an ancient sailing organisation. . . endeavouring to squeeze itself into the modern steam fleet'.[1]

The total number of HM ships fitted with steam engines increased from three to sixty between 1830 and 1844, as the new technology spread from auxiliary vessels to ships of the line. Steam eliminated many of the uncertainties of naval warfare, converted liners like the *Duke of Wellington* 'slashing through the Kattegat and Belts under steam, at the rate of 9 or 10 knots'. It became possible to write of 'the usual grind under steam', or to compare gunboats to 'railway trains rushing over the water'.[2] A veteran of the 1850s looked back with nostalgia upon the spectacle of a fleet under sail:

> a sight, which in these ironclad days, one likes to think of, for it was grand to see such a vessel as the *Duke of Wellington* ploughing gallantly along with the noble spread of canvas, the yards manned by swarms of blue jackets, and the port holes bristling with one hundred cannon.[3]

Within fifty years Sir John Colomb, late RMA, could speak of 'mastless ships resembling great floating fortresses, and entirely worked by labour saving machinery'.[4] Sailing evolutions were replaced by steam tactics, complex permutations of line and column, which 'to the uninitiated seem to consist for the most part in running around each other and generally getting in each other's way'.[5]

Lack of dockyards justified retention of masts for ships on distant deployments. HMS *Satellite* made a 44-day passage under sail to dry dock at Esquimault, after her propeller shaft bearings gave way off Mexico in 1895, the Captain postponing Christmas until she arrived. HMS *Sphinx* was conducting 'heat trials' in the Gulf in 1904 when 'a loud noise was heard in the engine room and suddenly the ship stopped', forcing her to limp home to Bombay under sail.[6] A ship's machinery became the basis of her mobility and safety. HMS *Duke of Wellington* delayed her departure for the Baltic in 1855 'as they could not trust her to sea without her engines'.[7] HMS *Calliope* survived a cyclone at Samoa in 1889, thanks to the first-class state of her engines, when every other ship in Apia harbour was wrecked. Enormous seas washed the upper deck, flooding cabins, sickbay and lower deck, the wardroom piano playing a different tune at every roll:

> a regular Bedlam. . . but owing to the great strength of construction, and the solidity of the engines, and not omitting the way in which the stokers and Engine room staff stuck to their work. . . everything held out, though the strain brought on the screw shaft as the ship pitched was immense, and shook her from head to stern.[8]

The price of independent motion was coaling ship, a back-breaking task which Gunner Craig of HMS *New Zealand* felt 'affords more amusement to the looker on than to the worker':

> The dust penetrates everywhere and anything. You swallow enough of it to keep an ordinary kitchen fire going for a week: there is a bag of it in each eye and your hearing is impaired by the few tons which have found an abode in your ears.[9]

The process was fraught for 'the winch man did not hesitate to whip it in. It was a case of keeping your eyes open every time a hoist came inboard, for you never knew where it was going to fall.'[10] Casualties were common: 'At 9.30 a Petty Officer had three fingers severed: at 1 o'clock a man's leg was broken and a little later another of the crew was badly hurt in the region of his right eye.' The same day a bluejacket was caught between the collier and another pre-dreadnought 'with a result that is better left to the imagination'.[11] Diarists recalled particular feats of coaling with pride. The battle-cruiser *Princess Royal* took in 2,260 tons in 15 hours at

Jamaica in 1914, with 23-minute breaks, some men being too exhausted to go below for their cocoa. At Halifax, Nova Scotia, ice jammed the barrow wheels, while water used to scrub the coal-encrusted decks froze solid.

In other respects steam reduced the hardships of life at sea. Steam from the engines heated washing machines and tumble driers, like those to be seen in HMS *Warrior*. Steamships' independence of the vagaries of the wind made the Royal Marines 'an exceedingly comfortable corps':

> long voyages are few to what they used to be, consequently men of war pass most of their commissions in port. If in a happy ship, a Marine officer's life is very pleasant, considering the opportunities of seeing foreign countries are abundant. Private individuals often spend thousands of pounds for that object without the same social position and advantage.[12]

In 1905 it was not unthinkable for the Atlantic Fleet to return home from Gibraltar for Christmas leave, steaming 1,058 miles in four days. Short voyages and refrigeration reduced dependence on salt provisions: 'Salt pork is quite eatable if well soaked beforehand but it has a flavour to itself. . . Salt beef has however a deep-rooted antipathy to His Majesty's Navy. . . it is hardly safe to approach it single-handed or unarmed.' Unreliable stories circulated of 'Marines having to mount guard over it with fixed bayonets'.[13] Steamships could usually condense sufficient drinking water, but on tropical stations the water tank might still need Marine sentries with strict orders 'not to allow water to go without a written chit signed by the commanding officer'.[14] Condensed water remained unpleasantly warm producing the curious complaint in 1914 that 'We have to put ice in the lime juice and rum.'[15] Larger vessels became self-sufficient for bread thanks to 'the Bakehouse, by means of which we were enabled to have fresh bread every day and look on ship's biscuit in the light of a luxury rather than a necessity'.[16]

Marines retained their original function of supplementing naval manpower throughout the nineteenth-century. The post-Napoleonic Royal Navy no longer pressed men, but 'cautiously cajoled in grog shops in the back slums'. Newly commissioned ships, with a careful assortment of naval officers and full complement of Marines, waited for weeks without tempting sufficient bluejackets to walk in.[17] 'Incapables of all kinds' volunteered for the Baltic Fleet of 1854, including butchers' boys, navvies, and cabmen: 'one night 350 fellows were marched on board who had never seen a ship, excepting from Tower Bridge.'[18] Even a crack frigate like HMS *Shannon* might find her complement among 'the refuse that had been hanging about the "Hard"', many refusing to go aloft. Marines made good the deficiencies of such reluctant bluejackets. Ninety percent of the bounty men mobilized during the 1859 war scare had never seen the sea: 'the whole of the gun gear was fitted and the lower rigging turned in principally by the Marine Artillery.'[19] The Admiralty justified improved Marine allowances in 1854 by the 'great care and pains . . . bestowed in training the Royal Marines when ashore, not merely in the exercise of the ship's gun batteries, but also to some of the duties of the seamen'.[20] The RM Office in London had to resist embarkation of Marines as substitute seamen during the 1840s, while insisting 'the Marine Corps is at all times ready for any service that may be required of them.'[21] Separated from their weapons and equipment such working detachments lost their military edge and threatened the ability of the Corps to respond to emergencies.

The 1853 Continuous Service Act, 'the first touch of broad true statesmanship to the Royal Navy in 188 years',[22] addressed the naval manning problems that had inspired the original experiments with Marines in the 1740s. Seamen now remained in the service between commissions, 'no longer birds of passage, emigrating from the Royal to the Merchant Navy. . . but a carefully picked and expertly reared body of men'.[23] The system 'equalised the opportunities for discipline and training in gunnery and other drills for bluejackets and marines'. They messed separately and wore different uniforms, but were increasingly indistinguishable, as steam and machinery reduced the need for traditional seamanship. Sir John Colomb argued in 1902 that the bluejacket was 'really the Marine of the past, brought up to date and dressed in modern seaman's clothes'.[24] The old style of sailor, 'powerful in physique, most capable in handling sails and ships in stormy weather; disliking gunnery, machinery, and musketry drill', had vanished along with sails and masts.[25] The disappearance of the rough old tar called into question the Royal Marines' disciplinary function. Continuous service seamen, 'originally from a better class than the Marine recruit, and. . . carefully trained and moulded in whatever form the Navy chooses', were more respectable than the men supposed to keep them in order,[26] leaving the Marines' police role 'a dream of the past'. Colomb concluded that progress had rendered the Corps superfluous: 'cradled in the most gloomy period of naval history. . . the necessity for its independent existence ceases with the birth of a new order of things in the Navy.'[27]

Smaller complements, and improved weapons handling by seamen supported his case. As steam power replaced 'handraulics', work parties of big Marines were less necessary than in the days of scratch crews and heavy manual labour: 'Formerly warships were floating beehives, into which men were swarmed by the nation. Engines and machinery have turned out the men, and the chief difficulty as to cost and time is ships – not men.'[28] Fresh from gunnery training ships young seamen were quite capable of standing sentry, or skirmishing with 'savages', although not all Marines appreciated the sailors' efforts. A very junior Lieutenant RM patronised HMS *Castor*'s guard mounting in 1856, 'of course they made a mess of presenting arms', while *Goshawk*'s Sergeant of Marines thought the bluejackets' exercises 'gone through in a very shuffling manner'.[29] As late as the 1920s a recruit's gunnery notebook would claim, 'The marine is the only dependable man on board, as he is sworn in while the sailor is not.'[30] Nevertheless Marines stood aside from the Invergordon Mutiny of 1931 and its bloodless resolution, although HMS *Malaya*'s RM turret crew did suggest putting a shell into the Prime Minister's house, which lay in range of the gunnery practice area. As Colomb had recognized, 'the day has gone by for the necessity of upholding discipline by "physical force". . . . if a ship requires Marine bayonets to support authority, there must be something wrong in the system.'[31]

Senior naval officers in the 1870s took a different view. They had grown up before continuous service 'under conditions which forced them to regard the Marines of a ship as a necessary security for discipline'.[32] They thought them 'the backbone of organisation and order in the Royal Navy', as they still might, for example when HMS *Warspite* ran aground near Vancouver in the 1890s, and her stokers were persuaded at gunpoint not to abandon ship.[33] Veterans of naval brigades did not believe sailors could replace Marines ashore: 'their efficiency and steadiness in actual service would always be, from the very nature and character of sailors, far inferior to that of a regular trained military force like the Royal Marine Corps.'[34] Then as now, successful active service justified the Corps' continuing existence:

> The history of the Royal Marines has been so distinguished, and their services to the state in war and peace have been so valuable, that it would be highly impolitic to disarm them, or even to permanently reduce their numbers.[35]

The Royal Marines may have been anomalous and illogical, but they were 'a popular force, easily recruited and raised to any required standard'. Recruits were plentiful in agricultural and manufacturing districts, which contributed little to the Navy. The Corps

> tapped a different stratum of the population from that which supplied boys destined to become seamen for the Royal Navy. Many a young fellow

desirous of seeing a little of the world, who had not had opportunity of entering the Navy as a boy, or who had become too old, or had missed his chance, could gratify his wishes by enlisting in the Marines.[36]

Recruits chose the Corps even before the Guards: 'Because in the Marines, they go to sea for three years, and return home with a pocketful of money, and they go down into their country village, and swagger away.'[37]

Such debates went largely unheard outside the service. The *Army and Navy Gazette* thought defence issues featured in parliamentary debates 'very much as stuffed fishes in a pantomime scene, to be hurled at the heads of all comers'.[38] There was little coherent discussion of service matters, particularly the Marines: 'There is no fighting force under the Crown less understood than the Marines. Few trouble themselves to know more than that they are useful. Why they exist or why they are useful are not questions which attract attention.' The 1858 Royal Commission on Manning observed, 'The Marines are a body of men second to none in the service of the State', but otherwise ignored them:

> A pay sergeant was asked some questions about pay and clothes, and that was all the direct evidence given on behalf of [Marine] infantry and artillery forces. . . numerically stronger than the total force which marched under Roberts from Cabul to Candahar. . . Thus were the Marine forces launched blindfold into the future.[39]

Fortunately their well-being did not depend entirely upon the interest of politicians.

An Exceedingly Comfortable Corps

In the services, as in civil life, the Victorians transformed the rough manners of the Regency, making life more tolerable for the many, and developing modern standards of professional conduct. In no area of military life was this so apparent as in the methods used to impose discipline. Flogging continued with unrelieved severity throughout the 1830s, subject to a maximum of 300 lashes in the Royal Marines, compared with the 4–500 inflicted 50 years earlier. Marines were obviously regarded as particularly hard cases, as the Army's maximum was 200. Officers doubted whether discipline could be maintained without the cat, as the alternatives of solitary confinement or hard labour were 'looked on very slightly', as the duty avoided outweighed the punishment.[40] The large sums paid to

Marines returning from sea service, as much as £40 or £80, encouraged wild behaviour:

> Two privates of the Royal Marines, just paid off from Her Majesty's steam-vessel *Pluto*. . . for a trifling wager commenced eating several £5 notes 'with bread, cheese and onions,' but were stopped by some of their more sensible comrades. . . Fortunately the numbers of the notes remained unmutilated.[41]

Against the thrifty sergeant who saved £100 at Ascension Island had to be set Her Majesty's bad bargains:

> The man who is picked up drunk from the kennel, kicked out of a bagnio, bleeding from wounds in the head and face, and brought almost insensible into the barracks and hospital; or has been *one of five*, three of his own comrades and two prostitutes, wallowing in the same bed together for a night, cannot surely suffer moral degradation from the lash. Yet such men and such practices require that, or some other mode of discipline, *if it can be found*, to restrain them.

Some men deliberately courted punishment 'to get rid of the service on any terms'. Private James Ramsey, of Woolwich Division, played that game, but died of tetanus after 134 lashes in November 1835 before he could be discharged in disgrace. Ramsey had been 'Twenty-three months in the service and five times a patient in the hospital, four of which were the result of his irregularities. He drank hard and he lived hard.'[42]

Despite the presence of such men, physical correction was already in decline. When an NCO struck a man with his pace-stick in 1816, the Marine 'came to the charge, and would have chased the Sergeant-Major to stick him', had not the Adjutant restrained him and ordered the NCO never to strike a man in the ranks again.[43] During the 1840s maximum punishment was reduced to forty-eight lashes, which the Admiralty sought to limit to persistent offenders.[44] The Defaulter's Book for HMS *Hastings'* RM detachment for 1849–53 suggests Admiralty pressure was not ineffective. Two men suffered four dozen, but only after repeated leave breaking, insubordination and drunkenness. One had concealed spirits in an officer's chest, made water on the port gangway while on sentry duty and knowingly received two bottles of wine, stolen from the wardroom. Lesser crimes invited lighter penalties: facing the ship's side, loss of smoking time or watered down grog. Both services had suspended flogging by 1871, never to be reintroduced.

The Surgeon in James Ramsey's case had thought the comforts of religion the best prevention for such cases, but the Sergeant-Major called in evidence noted that what Marines most disliked was stoppage of their pay. The introduction of Good Conduct Badges in 1833 stood this observation on its head, introducing financial incentives for good behaviour: 1d a day after three years trouble-free service, rising to 6d after eighteen years. Officers and other ranks were equally unwilling to see the loss of hard-earned stripes. Gunner Edward Taber was put under the sentry's charge as unfit for duty at Capetown in 1888, but the Captain let him off with a good talking to:

> seeing that I had got a clear defaulter sheet and 4 GCB Badges and not wishing to spoil my character he let me off with a courtion [*sic*] telling me at the same time that if I came before him again for a like offence he should take my badges from me.[45]

Standing Orders encouraged formality and restraint, reminding officers that 'Violent and irritating language is never to be used towards any soldier.' NCOs were 'to be treated with due consideration and are not to be reproved in the presence of the men'. NCOs in their turn 'must never make use of coarse, violent, or intemperate language to the men', but 'give their orders plainly and decidedly'. They were cautioned 'to avoid placing themselves within reach of men in a state of drunkenness', who were to be confined by the nearest Gunners, preferably 'without alter-cation'.[46]

Alcohol was no longer the only distraction for bored Marines, who began playing soccer and rugby in the 1880s. Chatham's Drill Shed functioned as a roller-skating rink after working hours, while Eastney had a skittle alley and recreation room that lent books and served tea and coffee. A run ashore in the 1880s might take in a temperance public house for orange cordial and mineral water, or tea at the Soldier's Institute. Many Marines were family men, encouraged to marry by their settled stations, short tours of duty overseas and opportunities for paid work within barracks. They were 'never idle but always usefully employed',[47] as were their wives who became laundrywomen or seamstresses, making shirts for the Corps. Couples lived outside barracks or in married quarters, where Standing Orders banned dogs, smoking or spitting in the corridors, and cleaning boots in the lavatories. Prospective wives required references showing them to be 'a most fit person to be admitted to the full privileges of a married woman of the Royal Marines'. Children over four years slept in dormitories, put to bed by their parents under a watchful NCO, and attended school within the barracks. The Royal Marines became a family affair, inspiring the claim that 'they don't recruit marines, they breed 'em'. The shared experience of successive generations eased passage into the ranks. Boy Bugler Smith followed his father and uncle into the Corps, at the turn of the century. He quickly recovered from homesickness, got on well with the Corporal and left a glowing account of contemporary military cuisine:

> I have just finished such a lovely dinner. . . Roast beef thick batter pudding fine greens and excellent new potatoes, one of my favourite dinners, but how about Sunday, boiled pork, broad beans, potatoes, and gippa. . . afterwards we had a huge cherry pie about 2 foot 6 inches long and 2 foot wide and 6 inches deep. . . the only fault was that when you had finished your mouth and teeth were as black as ink.[48]

From 1861 recruits received initial training at Walmer Depot, away from the temptations of a garrison town. 'Beware of the ladies,' said one First Drill, 'we have none down here.' The variety of training reflected the increased physical and mental demands of warfare, with boat pulling, swimming, tests in semaphore and forced marches, ten miles in two hours in full marching order. Standards and wastage were high, perhaps thirty dropping out of a squad of seventy. One recruit, who first saw the sea at Deal, had a terrifying time at first, 'our brains were turned inside out', while 'muscles were trained. . . until we felt like elastic. . . day after day until movements became automatic and words of command began to make sense and you began to feel you were part of a machine.' Nevertheless he remembered his Depot training as:

> the best any youth could get, our Instructors the best you could find, with the patience of Job and a wonderful command of words. The officers were very watchful and as far as I can remember there was very little severe punishment.[49]

Recruits went to their Divisions after eight months, for Field Training, Naval and Land Service Gunnery. Only then did they join the sea duty roster, not being considered fully trained Marines until embarked for at least twelve months. Officers were proud of a system that 'enables us to take a man from the plough's tail, and with two year's training, to send him on board ship, fit to compete with a gunner of the "Excellent"; no mean feat of instruction and training'. The process bred a discipline that a Victorian naval officer thought 'distinguishes the two parts of the Queen's sea service, and makes naval officers so long for the presence of the marine on shipboard.'[50] HMS *Caernarvon*'s overbearing Gunnery Lieutenant on the other hand met his match in her Royal Marine Corporal:

[He] rattled off some orders I did not understand and told him so. . . He told me I was just as big a b. . . f. . . as the man I had relieved. I did not like this. . . and requested to see the RM Officer to make a complaint. But it was soon settled. We had some ups and downs after that but nothing serious.[51]

Edwardian Marines with their robust self-sufficiency, building society accounts and ability to resolve vulgar fractions were very different from the improvident creatures who had laughed at the treadmill or devoured their banknotes with bread and cheese. 'For esprit de corps in all ranks,' wrote an officer in the 1890s, 'I most certainly believe no service can beat it.'[52]

Their officers followed a similar pattern of professional improvement. At the end of the Napoleonic Wars Lieutenant Tatton Brown of the *Royal George* could write that one Captain of Marines was of 'no education', while another 'likes to see his men in good order yett does not know how to do it.'[53] Graduates of the RMA's 3$\frac{1}{2}$-year training programme of the 1880s, however, could claim a higher standard of education than any combatant officer of the Royal Navy. Marine officers studied gunnery at HMS *Excellent*, musketry at Hythe and the new sciences of gymnastics and signalling at Aldershot. Royal Marines were at once the most scientific and the most under-utilized officers in the service.

Queen's Regulations still denied Marine officers the chance 'to assume any Naval Command or authority whatever, unless ordered to do so by their superior Naval Officers.'[54] Naval officers incapable of delegation reduced RMA captains to irresponsible spectators of their ship's artillery work, while RMLI officers, carefully trained as weapons instructors, looked on as the naval gunnery lieutenant trained bluejacket riflemen. One officer euphemistically described sea service as 'a long trial of patient well-disciplined inaction'.[55] Cynics joked that a Captain of Marines had even less to do than the Chaplain, as the Marine had a subaltern to help him do it. Lack of meaningful occupation at sea persuaded many Marine officers that their time for serving on board ship was passed, although as one of them reportedly said, 'Where can I get so much money for doing so little?'[56] The Deputy Adjutant General, who had commanded a division of mortar boats at Sveaborg, made a plea for equal professional opportunities in 1871: 'If we be not useful let us go; we are unwilling to exist as a sham. If we are useful, keep us.'[57] Adventurous officers transferred to the Indian Army, built railways alongside the Nile or worked in the Naval Intelligence Department. Lieutenant R.A. Marriott RMA combined both options, reconnoitring the forts at Alexandria in 1882, 'dressed as a low-class Italian', before joining the Egyptian Camel Corps. The wardroom sofa continued to feature largely in the life of those Marine officers who remained within the Corps. In 1915 Major F.J. Harvey RMLI of HMS *Lion* deprecated his situation in terms little different from those employed by Sir Charles Littleton almost 250 years earlier: 'truly there seems no use for a Major RM. My job on board here can be done by an RM Gunner.'[58]

The only systematic attempt to recast the relationship between the two branches of the Navy's officer corps was the Selborne Scheme of 1902, a revolutionary attempt to introduce common entry for all naval officers, including Engineers and Royal Marines. Its instigator, Sir John Fisher, was one of those naval officers who appreciated the Marines' military example, but distrusted the military system that produced them:

> *The Marine officer can't be loyal!* Just look at that statue outside the Admiralty in honour of the Marines, recently put up by them! It has its back turned on the Admiralty, and *it's looking at the War Office!* The Marine officers (not the Marines) are always hankering after the Army! *D—n the Army!*[59]

The Selborne Report expressed regret at the 'comparative non-utilization of the services of the marine officer on board ship', but the historians of the RMA thought this was a joke.[60] The true reason for such enforced idleness was the professional jealousy of the Royal Navy's fighting branch, whose continued grip upon senior posts Selborne assured. Few were prepared to specialize as Lieutenants (M) on that basis, and in 1911 the Royal Marines returned to the old direct entry system for officers. As so often the Corps would work out its own salvation, following lines laid down before the new scheme, in response to another aspect of nineteenth-century technological change, the revolution in naval gunnery.

Monster Guns

The RMA's original remit had been 10- and 13-inch mortars, but they soon became acknowledged experts in other aspects of naval gunnery. Lack of continuous service inhibited development of such skills in the Royal Navy, where 'In Nelson's glorious system of "close quarters" the science of gunnery was perhaps purposely neglected.'[61] The RMA by contrast pursued a rigorous course in scientific gunnery. When the Admiralty established a gunnery school in HMS *Excellent*, it turned to the RMA for its first instructors, appointing Lt Dover Farrant with five NCOs and gunners, 'to superintend when seamen are sent to exercise, and to keep the guns, etc, in perfect order.'[62] The Royal Marines can therefore claim to have been the fathers of modern naval gunnery. In 1835 Farrant published *Questions and Answers in Naval Gunnery*, while Marine NCOs continued as instructors at HMS *Excellent* until 1868. Francis Lean found their practical training helpful when his 10-inch shell gun snapped its breeching bolt at Sveaborg, and required a jury rig:

> my gun's crew consisted chiefly of sleepy headed recruits, not accustomed to ropes and anything but smart seamen, so that I found my "Excellent" knowledge came in most useful, and in all these disasters had to put my own hand, as well as head, to work.[63]

Captains in the 1850s freely used RMA officers and NCOs 'to fit gun gear and to teach the seamen gunnery, just as corresponding grades in the infantry companies taught seamen the use of small arms and to drill'.[64] RMA sergeants instructed *Shannon*'s bluejackets in gunnery on the voyage to India, to such good effect that they subsequently 'established a naval reputation by their advance upon Lucknow'.[65]

In an astonishing attack of bureaucratic myopia, the RMA were savagely cut, just as the Fourth Sea Lord was issuing the new gunnery school's prospectus. Only two companies survived 'to prevent the total extinction of the Artillery Service and skill which they have acquired. . . and as a nucleus whereon to form any greater body which may hereafter be judged desirable'.[66] Gunnery would soon assume new prominence, as technological change affected ships' armament, as well as propulsion. Hydraulic turrets replaced trucks and tackles, while broadsides of thirty to fifty cannon measured in hundredweight made way for handfuls of monster guns weighed in tons, their massive shells propelled by nitro-cellulose instead of gunpowder. The post-Napoleonic Royal Navy had standardized its armament around the 32-pounder smooth-bore gun, a simple weapon firing solid iron projectiles that was well suited to prevailing standards of naval gunnery. French experiments with explosive shells during the 1820s forced the Admiralty to introduce shell guns, particularly useful in paddle steamers whose limited broadsides prevented them mounting large numbers of less powerful weapons. The increasing number of war steamers from 1839, 'on board each of which a proportion of Marine Artillery are required to fight the long pivot guns with which they are armed', began the RMA's recovery, which 'kept pace with the introduction of heavier and less simple armaments'.[67] Sidney Herbert, First Secretary at the

Admiralty, found additional gunners by redistributing infantrymen among re-established artillery companies. By 1860 there were over 3,000 Marine artillerymen, enough for an independent division with its own head-quarters at Eastney, on the eastern edge of Portsmouth.

The threat of explosive shells inspired naval architects to protect ships with wrought iron armour plating, whose increasing thickness was matched by greater gun calibres, culminating in the $16^{1}/_{4}$-inch 110-ton guns deployed in HMS *Inflexible* at Alexandria. Naval tacticians of the 1890s assumed ships would open fire at 4,000 yards, and clear their opponents' decks with machine-gun fire at 1,500 yards. The Royal Marines' traditional small-arms role had become an irrelevance.

The Royal Navy's only action against an armoured ship during the ironclad period took place in 1877 between HMS *Shah*, an unarmoured steam frigate, and the Peruvian turret-ship *Huascar*, which had been preying upon British shipping after a failed coup d'etat. *Shah*'s Marine subaltern observed the changed conditions of naval warfare. Independent of the wind, *Huascar* manoeuvred freely in shallow coastal waters, while the deeper draught *Shah* circled around further out, at ranges of 1,500 to 3,000 yards. Only her two 9-inch guns could penetrate *Huascar*'s armoured turret at that range and judging the distance by eye proved uncertain. After ineffectually potting at long range, the *Huascar* tried to run past her opponent, which laid her guns for a simultaneous electric broadside at 300 yards:

> Swiftly the "Shah" bounded after her formidable little antagonist and soon commenced to gain on her – all was silent between decks, the guns being laid and the men standing clear of the recoil. Presently we heard the rattle of the Gatling Guns in our fore-top pouring a stream of bullets onto the enemy's deck, and through the ports we can just see her, but she is not flying now, on the contrary she is trying to ram us. We hear the roar of our steam steering gear as the helm is put up, and feel the good ship heel over as she swerves away from that death dealing ram.

Huascar retired 'under a shower of iron, her upper deck being literally swept from stem to bow, and the funnel riddled with shot', only to escape overnight and surrender to loyal Peruvian ships. *Shah*'s officers went aboard to inspect the results of their shooting, and won over their hosts by praising *Huascar*'s handling in broken French. Their observations showed the fine balance between offensive and defensive that made ramming attractive:

> The upper deck of the "Huascar" was awfully knocked about, there wasn't a single whole thing left on it except for the turret and conning tower. All

the boats were smashed, bridge cut in two, ventilators knocked to pieces, Funnel riddled, Forecastle and poop both pierced, four bulwark plates blown away, side dented in several places and pierced in two and covered with marks where the 64pr shell had hit and exploded without doing any damage. The turret was very fortunate having only been hit once by 7″ shot which penetrated to a depth of three inches then broke up. *Down below the damage was trifling.*[68]

The *Huascar* action also saw the Royal Navy's first use of a locomotive torpedo, although 'as she was going 11 knots and the torpedo only 9 knots the infernal machine did not reach its prey'. The Royal Marines had first experienced 'infernal machines' off Kronstadt in 1855, where the term signified fixed mines, which shook their victim: 'as if she had struck upon a sunken pile – it made the ship quiver from stem to stern and the masts shake as if they were coming down by the run.' HMS *Firefly* got off lightly with the destruction of her domestic crockery, but *Merlin*'s copper sheathing was torn off, and a 13 cwt water tank propelled 4 feet across the ship. Pairs of boats went fishing for mines with weighted lines suspended between them 'and got a pretty good whack of them'. Admiral Seymour chose the hard way of proving the devices were not buoys: 'he incautiously tapped a little bit of iron which projected from its side saying "this must be the way they are exploded" and bang! the thing went off.'[69] Often the Russians failed to set the fuses, obscuring the potential of a weapon, which with the locomotive torpedo would transform naval warfare.

Meanwhile the heavy gun would provide Marines with their main combat role at sea. Some naval officers were slow to appreciate the RMA's potential, prompting Admiralty instructions that Marine gunners were 'not to be employed as stokers'. A forward-looking order of 1867 sought to have them 'quartered at some of the more important numbers at the guns', suggesting that 'when it is practicable, one or two guns [are] to be manned entirely by Marine Artillery, under their own officers.'[70] Some captains took note. At Alexandria in 1882 Marines manned a turret and the central battery in HMS *Inflexible* and *Sultan* respectively. Regulations remained elastic allowing captains to subordinate their carefully trained Marine gunners to inexperienced bluejackets. Admiral Sir Thomas Maitland thought Marine artillerymen 'totally thrown away on board ship; for if we get a seaman capable of being captain of a gun, we put him to it, because we do not like the guns of the Navy taken out of our hands.'[71] This dog in the manger attitude was overtaken in the 1870s by a shortage of gunners. RMLI other ranks were offered extra pay to qualify in gunnery and practice batteries appeared at Chatham and Forton. The RMA had possessed such a battery on Southsea Common in the 1820s, rigged as a ship's gun deck. Relocated eastwards to the less populated area of Fort Cumberland, the new facility offered such amenities as mortars on turn-tables, and a 6-pounder on a moveable platform that simulated the motion of a ship. A local volunteer battalion complained Fort Cumberland's practice had 'disarranged' their drill, but the Corps retorted that it treated its own recruits just the same: 'it steadied the men under fire, and accustomed them to the dodging of shells.'[72]

The increased size of the fleet after the Naval Defence Act of 1889 made it impossible to man the guns of the fleet from naval resources alone. Positive instructions compelled ship's captains to employ Marines at the guns and ensure their regular training. The RMA alone were insufficient. Only first-class battleships carried RMA detachments from 1892, their place elsewhere taken by RMLI who became eligible for key positions as turret layers and sight setters, all at extra pay. By the eve of the First World War it was customary for Marines to man a main armament turret and a group of secondary guns in all battleships and cruisers. Gunnery qualifications had become so widespread that 'trained in gunnery' was discontinued as a rate, as all Marines were expected to reach that standard. Recruits worked at the double, learning every part of each gun and its function, how to strip down and then replace them all:

> if at any time a class became slack there was a little extra round the Dummy Loader humping 100lb shells into it as fast as one can with the Instructor's tongue lashing you all the time. After a few doses you were like a limp rag.[73]

Ships also carried dummy loaders, a record-breaking Marine crew putting twenty rounds through in fifty-six seconds, over a ton of shells in a minute. Preparations for gunlaying tests were frantic: '"General Quarters" for breakfast, "Deflection teacher" for dinner, and "Dotter" for tea, with loading drill thrown in as a tonic'.[74] In 1906 HMS *New Zealand* hit her battle practice target, one-sixth her own area, 97 times out of 115 at 5,000 yards. At the other end of the scale came the Nile river gunboats that accompanied Kitchener's advance into the Sudan in 1897. Each carried a pair of Marine NCOs to work the guns and keep order among the assorted crews: Egyptian soldiers, Sudanese stokers and Arab river pilots. An RMA Captain in charge of river transport was incensed by honours awarded to 'birds of passage' at the expense of men who had proved themselves 'not only useful, but absolutely indispensable. . . the broken down embrasures of every Fort along the shores of Omdurman and Khartoum point to the fact that what our RMA Sergeants didn't know about shooting wasn't worth knowing.'[75]

Marines rarely served in such small vessels, although Colour Sergeant Nathaniel Hiscock doubled as Master-at-Arms and wardroom steward in HMS *Gossamer* in 1910: 'We had no proper separate quarters, and she was a horrible little tin can – pitch and roll – dreadful! I was sick very often'. A two-year commission in HMS *Argyll* was more typical:

> Shaking down exercise and gunnery; then RM landings to get to know your men for shore work. Captain Trew was a stickler for physical fitness and kept us very much on our toes with paper schemes in our own time which wasn't much. Then the Gunnery Officer was always wanting greater efficiency around the guns so life was one continuous round of "Do this or that".[76]

For the first time in almost a century, the Royal Navy was preparing for war against a first-class opponent.

CHAPTER NINE

Action Under Steam

THE Royal Navy that went to war on 4 August 1914 had altered in almost every respect since 1815, technically, socially and strategically. The end of 'splendid isolation' and the Entente Cordiale had transformed Britain's strategic position. French sailors had entertained Corporal Albert Saunders RMA and his shipmates from HMS *Princess Royal* aboard the *Danton*, while only weeks before the declaration of war, the Imperial Russian Navy gave them the reception of their lives at St Petersburg. Germany was a different matter, however:

> Many I think would have been disappointed had things blown over. . . one and all were wishing to pit their strength against a country that somehow or other, quite naturally it seemed, we had come to look upon as our natural enemy.[1]

Nobody had any clear idea of how the struggle would turn out. The fleet that left Portland on 29 July was on an errand, 'the like of which had never been seen since the entry of steam into the navy'. As men lay at their action stations, on bare decks black with coal dust:

> The whole topic. . . was a Naval Battle, and what it would be like. It was difficult to try and imagine such a thing. One thing we knew, it would be awful while it lasted, but one and all were ready for anything.

Reality failed to match expectation, for there was no climactic naval victory. The Grand Fleet fought a single inconclusive action at Jutland (31 May 1916), although battle-cruisers clashed at Heligoland Bight and Dogger Bank (28 Aug 1914 and 26 Jan 1915). The stark certainties of sea warfare under steam left the probable result too clear to tempt the Germans out, to the frustration of Saunders and his messmates:

another night of excitement, waiting for a scrap that didn't come off. . .
They weren't having any. Their glorious high seas fleet don't relish the
idea of trying conclusions with our Grand Fleet.[2]

Excluding operations directly in support of the Army, the Great
War at sea resolved itself into three separate struggles: the Grand Fleet's
vigil in the North Sea; a distant blockade that diverted German trade
to the Allies' benefit; and the protection of British commerce against
surface raiders and new underwater weapons, the mine and submarine.
Notwithstanding the debates of the previous fifty years Royal Marines
contributed to all three, as they resumed the role they had performed
in every war since their formation, 'the reinforcement of the personnel
of the Royal Navy'. Despite heavy losses and many unexpected calls
the Corps never failed to meet the Navy's needs, the number of Marines
at sea rising from 10,047 at the start of the war to 16,494 at its end.[3]
Not only did they man new ships, additional Marines joined existing
ships, whose complements had been cut too finely for war service,
proving correct those who had argued that 'Marines are still the first
reserve of the Navy, the readiest, the best disciplined, and the cheapest.'[4]
Better educated than previous generations, Marines of the Great War
left a mass of personal diaries and letters. These do not form a detailed
narrative of the First World War at sea, but they faithfully record
Marine perceptions of the war. After all, 'the business of the Marines
was to fight their guns and keep them in action.'[5] not provide a detailed
strategic commentary: 'As regards the actual progress of the battle we
know no more than the outsider who reads the facts in the news-
papers.'[6]

Stalemate at Sea

Naval actions under sail had been up close and personal. Under steam
they became remote and inhuman. Men hidden behind slabs of armour
hurled tons of steel and lyddite at unseen targets beyond the horizon.
HMS *Agincourt*'s company crowded her upper deck before Jutland, to
watch the battle-cruisers' gun flashes, but went below to Action Stations
long before the enemy came into sight. Marines in *Iron Duke*'s shell room
'had no earthly idea we were going into action at last'.[7] Machine power
supplanted individual strength and gallantry, reducing men to cogs in a
mechanical process, where they needed a new type of undemonstrative
courage. Marine bandsmen had most need of stoicism, battened down

below in the Transmitting Station (T/S), the nerve centre of the ship's gunnery control system:

> In this very cramped compartment was a "horseshoe" shaped table with a gunnery officer standing in its centre space. Everywhere was a clinical mass of dials, pointers, telephones, switches, plots, a firing gong and gun-ready "tell-tale" clocks which would illuminate when the guns had loaded and were ready to fire.[8]

The T/S lay between the bunkers at the foot of innumerable ladders, hatches and watertight doors, making it virtually impossible to escape in an emergency. In the Second World War the Band Service lost a quarter of its strength, a higher percentage than any other branch of the armed forces: 'we not only lived together and played music together, but we died together all in tragic circumstances. . . an elite, the "Gentlemen of the lower deck".'[9]

British battlecruisers outclassed the opposition at Heligoland, reducing the shoot to an exercise:

> At first the firing was controlled. That meant a certain turret would be detailed to fire a round or two to get the range. Then came the order "Rapid Independent" and for a few moments fury was let loose. Crash upon crash rent the air and right and left swung those great turrets and guns as those 13.5″s spoke for the first time in angry tones. Then came a long continuous ringing, the Captain's cease fire bell calling upon the guns to stop. . . The first naval engagement for over a century had been fought and won.[10]

Queen Mary's detachment had a rare view of the effects of their fire:

> one German cruiser sank about 200 yards off our ship, it was a very fine sight to watch she went down stern first, we could hear shells flying over our ship expecting every minute to get one burst by our gun but we went through without a hit.[11]

At ranges of 20,000 yards automation replaced the eyesight of individual gunlayers, as Captain Alan Bourne RMA of HMS *Tiger* recognized at Dogger Bank:

> From my turret (X) the enemy were over the curve of the earth out of sight except for some smoke so that individual [fire] would have been out of the question. . . we all swear by the director now – no noise no hurry no excitement, no worry about glasses or object.

Major Harvey, Bourne's counterpart in HMS *Lion*'s 'Q' Turret, was similarly relaxed:

> As to fighting in a turret one doesn't suffer discomfort and my chief feeling has been that of "curiosity" mixed with the idea that whoever else is coming to grief, oneself will be alright![12]

Increased weapon power accompanied unwillingness to give or take quarter. In *Princess Royal*, 'a White Ensign was nailed to the mast, a silent but very significant factor... No hauling down therefore no surrender.' At Dogger Bank the doomed German cruiser *Blücher* was 'in an awful state flames shooting up from her decks great gaping holes in her side and her mast down, but still her flag flew', so HMS *Indomitable* poured in another salvo. German atrocities in Belgium fuelled bitterness not seen since the early days of the French Revolution:

> why should we show pity? We read of the barbarities they carry out on shore, so we take our share in the dealing out of the punishment with no feeling except gladness that we had sent them to the bottom.[13]

Jutland was harder to grasp than most battles, as innumerable coal-fired ships moved rapidly over a vast area, thickening the usual North Sea haze. Captain Chandos Hill RMLI enjoyed unrivalled observation from the bridge of HMS *Colossus*, but found the quick succession of fleeting targets baffling:

> The thing that impressed me most was the rapidity at which events took place, passed, and gave place to others. I lost all sense of time, and it is only by comparing notes with others that I have been able to form a correct sequence of events.

It reminded him of pigeon shooting, 'You never knew when one was going to butt':

> The mist and smoke was so thick that we had constantly to be on the lookout for enemy craft appearing ahead, and we could not remain long on one object. Often though we could not see the enemy ships we could see the angry red glow of their guns through the mist.[14]

After nearly two years of waiting the battle came as a surprise: 'when we closed up at our action stations we did not imagine for one moment that we should meet them', but the first shot 'was like the letting off steam. All the bottled up anxiety of the past months was let loose then.'

Only the Battle-Cruiser Fleet were in action at first, running south then north again, with the catastrophic loss of *Queen Mary* and *Indefatigable*:

many a heart beat a little faster when they thought of chums gone for good, and it made one more than ever determined to fight on. Of the ultimate result we had no doubt. We knew we should have to lose ships, that is part of the game.[15]

This confidence was not misplaced. Just after 6 p.m. the battle-cruisers linked up with the heavily armoured battleships of the Grand Fleet, HMS *Tiger*, 'a fine sight with flame and smoke pouring from large rents in her funnels, and large columns of water springing up on each side of her.'[16] With almost magical skill Sir John Jellicoe deployed his twenty-four dreadnoughts to port, crossing the 'T' of the High Seas Fleet, as yet unseen in the mist:

> Soon after six we had our first taste of the Huns as a large projectile hit the water on our starboard bow, ricocheted into the air and passed over. We could plainly see it turning over and over. . . By this time we had deployed into line and the Fleet presented a beautiful sight. Miles of ships all with their guns pointed to where we knew the invisible enemy were. Every ship was flying three or four huge new White Ensigns, and strings of flags were continually going up.[17]

The crisis of the battle was over too quickly to ensure the destruction of a well-protected enemy. HMS *Agincourt* was in action for perhaps eleven minutes:

> 18.24 opened fire at 10,000 yards, increased, because the mist lifted a bit, we could now see the enemy plainly so we took advantage of it, and gave them a few quick broadsides. A German battle-cruiser, believed to be the *Seydlitz*, had been badly knocked about, and was on fire, when the enemy's small craft came down between the lines and made a screen of smoke under which the German battleships turned and steamed away from us, but apparently our admirals knew what they were up to, so we altered course and steamed in their direction. When we got through their smoke screen we could see the battleships scurrying away.

About 6.35 the enemy disappeared in the mist, reappearing at 7.05 as the Germans tried to escape Jellicoe's net: 'we at once engaged them but the small craft that were with them made a smoke screen and blotted them from our sight.' German destroyers launched torpedoes at *Agincourt*, 'but the ship was manoeuvred splendidly therefore both missed'.[18] The experience of smaller ships was altogether more fraught. Their torpedoes made them a fair target for heavy ships, which in Nelson's day would rarely have fired on a frigate, as one of HMS *Yarmouth*'s Marines saw for himself:

> We were in about as hot a position as was possible to be about that time. There was on our port beam our own Battle Cruiser Fleet line sailing at about 28 knots whilst on our starboard beam were all the enemy Battle Cruisers. Shells were falling all around and very close to us; too close for comfort. . . Two of our destroyers were being made a target of by the heavy enemy ships: one went up in smoke and the other came up on our port beam and sunk just as the Invincible blew up on our port quarter. . . When everything had cleared away all that was to be seen was two riblike parts, sticking up out of the water like pieces of rock.[19]

Dusk ended the big ship action, the Germans escaping under cover of darkness. Jutland was less decisive than Trafalgar, but British casualties in ships and men were far higher. A tenth of the Royal Marines engaged became casualties, 589 out of 5,832. Over 90 per cent of these were killed, compared with 1 in 3 at Trafalgar. This reflected increased weapon power. Fourteen British ships went to the bottom, including 3 battle-cruisers carrying over 1,000 men each. Only one Marine survived from HMS *Invincible*'s detachment of 106.

The story of HMS *Lion*'s 'Q' turret sheds some light on the disasters that befell her sisters. An 11-inch shell struck the junction of the thick front armour and the roof plates, peeling them back like the top of a sardine tin. Major Harvey, who had been under no delusion 'that if a proj [sic] does hit one's turret it will in all probability come right in and send one to glory',[20] was mortally wounded. Before he died he ordered 'Q' magazine to be flooded, but the impact of the hit had dislodged a previously loaded charge from the breech of the left gun. Falling into the gun well it blazed up, killing everyone in the main trunk. Had the handing party not closed the magazine doors at once Admiral Beatty's flagship must have blown up, 'with who knows what result to the British Empire'.[21] The only survivors from 'Q' were the turret sergeant sent to report to the bridge, one wounded Marine who reached the forward Medical Station and a sick-berth attendant found unconscious beneath two dead Marines. Harvey's devoted action earned him the sixth and perhaps the hardest won of the Corps' ten VCs. As if the circumstances of his death were not dreadful enough, the myth has spread that he lost his legs in the initial blast and that his orders drowned the magazine party. Captain F.R. Jones RMLI, Harvey's second-in-command, denied both stories. Jones spent the night after Jutland in 'Q' turret, identifying the dead with a torch, and helped carry out Major Harvey's body:

> His legs were **not** blown off; had they been he could not have reached the mouthpiece of the voice pipe, which would have been essential, as the noise was terrific, with enemy shells exploding, our own guns firing, and the ship steaming full ahead with front and roof plates clear of the turret.[22]

As for the magazine party, the cordite fire killed them all in the main trunk.

An obsession with rapid shooting had led to dangerous accumulations of ammunition near the guns throughout the Grand Fleet. HMS *Tiger*'s 'X' turret narrowly escaped destruction, thanks to a recently arrived Private Lambert RMLI. Noticing the extra charges slipping back out of the receiving trays, he suggested lowering the main and gun loading cages, until their contents were imminently needed. This was done minutes before 'Open Fire', when a German shell entered the turret with a shower of sparks like a rocket: 'Burning material fell all over the two empty Receiving Trays, and the fact of these being empty. . . probably saved the ship from blowing up.'[23] Cut off from the director and without electric power the turret crew reopened fire in seven minutes, working around the dead body of the centre-sight setter, the ship's only RM casualty. Their coolness earned Beatty's special congratulations: 'It is my belief the Corps of Improvisors is never really happy unless it is compelling adverse circumstances to do obeisance to its will.'[24]

The Royal Navy's disproportionate losses at Jutland have provoked acrimony ever since, despite the strategic appreciation of an RMLI Corporal in *Iron Duke*: 'Our Battle Fleet is still intact and we still hold command of the sea. . . it is disgusting to read the reports in some of the ½d "rags" I should think half the nation is "all-is-lost".' The High Seas Fleet never came out again, while the Grand Fleet returned to Scapa Flow: 'one of the worst places there is for weather round the British coast':[25]

Its the same old deadly programme
The same old lack of news
The same old daily spreading
And close up Turret crews
The third day's tribulation
The same old coaling feat
And still there's nothing known
Of the German High Seas Fleet

Marine messes entertained themselves with cinema shows, mandolins, and wind-up gramophones all playing different patriotic tunes: 'Someone in his hammock "serving out a drop of Acid" because he can't go to sleep and he had got the middle watch... there is a limit to patriotism'. Many were embarrassed at their safe if uncomfortable lives, and missed the strategic importance of the waiting game they had to play:

> The chief thought that was before us was that our sister service was at grips with the enemy, and it was felt we were getting rusty. Stopping merchantmen and ruining her trade and all those sorts of things that may be so vital and important to the country don't seem to strike the average lower deck man as being enough.[26]

The Grand Fleet, however, was the keystone of the British strategic system. Without its deterrent presence, the humdrum business of securing the home base and maintaining expeditionary forces around the world would soon have been rudely interrupted. The Grand Fleet's Royal Marine detachments may not have been confronting the enemy's main force on the Western Front, but the seas around the British Isles must always be the Royal Navy's first theatre of war. The peacetime training of the 5,000 Marines at Scapa Flow made them an irreplaceable component of the Grand Fleet's firepower. An insignificant handful compared with the million-man armies on the Western Front, they were too valuable to be thrown into the cauldron of the land war.[27]

Protection of Trade

While the Grand Fleet's Marine detachments awaited an indefinitely postponed day of reckoning, other Marines served in ships that were anything but grand. The Royal Navy had the same economic responsibilities as in previous wars, seeking to disrupt enemy trade, while protecting British commerce. Technological change had altered these activities, as it had the clash of battle fleets. Mines and torpedoes made it impossible to impose the traditional close blockade of the enemy coast, although this was not immediately obvious. HMS *Queen Mary* spent the opening weeks of the war 'steaming about the North Sea looking for submarines'.[28] Anti-submarine measures added to the labour of active service, as detachments swung out torpedo nets of interlocking steel rings, on booms 20-feet from the ship's sides. Men tried not to think about mines and torpedoes: 'We might get morbid if we did, and grey-headed before our time', but false alarms were common. HMS *Lion* and *Queen Mary* engaged an imaginary

Royal Marine Artillerymen in the variety of uniform required for service overseas in the 1890s.

Nile gunboats in action at al Matamma 1898: 'what our RMA Sergeants didn't know about shooting wasn't worth knowing'.

Betsy the international gun at the Peking Legations 1900: RM detachment and US Navy Gunner.

CITBDĀL. GUARD.
"SCUTARI." ALBANIA. MAY. 1913.

An early Balkan entanglement: Royal Marine peacekeepers in Albania 1913.

The Transmitting Station:
a Bandsman's view of
the Battle of Jutland.

THE BATTLE OF JUTLAND BANK:
BANDSMAN'S VERSION.

Engaging the main force of the enemy: RND Christmas Card 1917.

HMS *Lion* after Jutland: a shell-torn 'Q' Turret
under examination amidships.

Landing craft trials in Langstone Harbour 1929,
with Morris–Martel tankette.

Buffaloes and Weasels disembark from an LCT at Walcheren: Marines forming up under cover of the dyke.

By Sea, Land and Air: HMS *Theseus* off Suez preparing
to land 45 Cdo by helicopter.

Jungle Greens: 1960s Marines in Borneo with Armalite automatic rifles.

The battle-scarred streets of Stanley: Marines of 42 Cdo ready for trouble after the Argentine surrender.

The banner says it all: Marine foot patrol in Ulster 1987.

periscope in Cromarty Forth in October 1914: 'a proper bombardment for several minutes. The shells were ricocheting onto the beach and set several trees on fire. . . The village people must have thought the Germans had arrived.'[29]

The loss of HMS *Aboukir, Hogue* and *Cressy* with 1,400 casualties including 200 Royal Marines persuaded the Royal Navy to institute a distant blockade, with less valuable vessels:

> we wallowed about in the North Sea between Norway and the Faroes, a most miserable time – stopping and searching. One of our ships was torpedoed with great loss of life. . . During this time we were allowed to let our beards grow. We were a sorry looking lot for Royals, and one day our RMO had a little chat with us, so we scraped it off and felt a lot better.[30]

The aim was to prevent 'contraband' war material reaching Germany directly or via Dutch and Scandinavian intermediaries. North Sea patrols required constant vigilance, and a readiness to board neutral merchant ships in all weathers, with the off-chance of their being an armed raider in disguise. Bona fide intercepts were allowed through, but others were clearly blockade-runners, carrying false papers, flying obsolete clearance flags and painting themselves grey to escape observation:

> At 5.15 we saw a steamer and gave chase and she would not stop in answer to signals we let go with a full charge from the 6-inch gun and still she hopped it then bang went a live shell from the 6pr the shot striking just alongside of her then she pulled up being as she was a curious looking craft we took no risks and fired again to see if she would answer and after a time we lowered the boat with a prize crew. . . the same time all our guns trained on her.[31]

A major difference from earlier wars was radio communication. HMS *Vernon*, the Royal Navy's technical training centre, had an RMO wireless telegraphy instructor from 1903, the rank and file finding 'Wireless Marine' an attractive billet, which excused them from coaling ship. Radio provided economy of force, making sea control a matter of organization and technique rather than numbers:

> 18 June: received orders from the Admiralty to stop a certain vessel found out where she was by wireless and went after her steaming $17^1/_2$ knots,
>
> 19 June: picked up the ship we were after stopped and searched her and brought back a very important German official said to be a spy from America.[32]

Marine detachments in the elderly cruisers and armed merchantmen that patrolled the sea lanes were usually reservists. One in *King Alfred* had twenty-four years service, while HMS *Donegal* boasted a sixty year old, 'as lively as a cricket'. They were inveterate grumblers:

> what about us poor devils who has completed our 21 years and still serving our country even men in this ship 50 years of age and still ploughing the briny in all weathers and we have done so for the past 18 months and remaining 50 days at sea at a stretch who is worse off of the two in the trenches or at sea never know how your luck is going to turn enough said.

They were not immune to patriotism, but had a proper sense of their own value:

> it is such ships as these who is doing their bit and always at sea keeping the commerce open and the grub coming across the seven seas of which the man in the street knows very little about only those who have the chance to read the diaries of those who keep them.[33]

HMS *Bellona* belonged to the Grand Fleet, but contributed directly to sea control by minelaying. She carried eighty, in four lines on the quarter deck:

> it was a ticklish job when you reached your area. The ship steamed slowly and a mine had to go every seven seconds, first port then starboard. . . one of the mines got stuck in the slipway so they had to push the next one over. At the same time the first one cleared so they both entered the water together. Fortunately when they came to their depth we were fifty yards away; they touched and the explosion was terrific. I was knocked off the gun platform and several others were grovelling about, but luckily nobody was hurt.[34]

Trade protection was handicapped by the Royal Navy's refusal to institute convoy, preferring offensive patrols and defensively armed merchant ships. RM pensioners and reservists made a key contribution to the original 'DAM ships' or DEMS, and their offshoot, the Q-ship. Two thousand Marines signed ship's articles, providing gunnery training for six times their own number of merchant seamen. They used all manner of unlikely guns, from 4.7-inch quick-firers to Japanese field guns, and bomb throwers improvized from drainpipes. Temporary mountings were usual, as gun crews worked double tides in port to transfer their weapons to a fresh ship. A Marine ordered to take a gun from London to Dundee noted laconically: 'Spasm getting gun to station (King's Cross)', but did not state whether it travelled in the guard's van.

DEMS had twice the chance of surviving surface attack, as few U-boats would risk a gun battle, while a few hard-bitten Marines might help in other ways:

> Submarine appeared off our Port Quarter about 400 yards away. Dark. Fired three rounds at her. Bad light for shooting; she submerged as soon as I opened fire, Chinese stokers refused to stoke at first. Got their bags ready for leaving. . . Persuaded Chinks in seaman fashion to go below.[35]

Unrestricted U-boat warfare reduced the proportion of surface attacks and the value of DEMS, but they still limited the submarines' scope by forcing them to rely exclusively on their limited supply of torpedoes.

Q-ships resembled DEMS, except that they carried a naval crew and concealed their guns. Their sole business was to hunt U-boats. The most notorious was the *Baralong*, armed with three 12-pounder quick-firers, a large quantity of empty barrels for flotation, and 'special boards to slip into slots on the ship's sides the boards being painted to represent some American and some Dutch [ships]'. She flew neutral colours, while the crew continually altered her appearance by repainting funnels, masts and cowls. For three months *Baralong* trailed her coat between Falmouth and Berehaven, but saw no more sign of U-boat activity than wreckage and upturned lifeboats. Then, on 19 August 1915, she responded to a distress signal from SS *Nicosian*, an American mule transport:

> 3 pm sighted Nicosian and were ordered to our Action Stations. . . all fighting crew under cover, Hoisted signal asking permission to save life, got to 700 yards and cleared for battle hoisting the White Ensign at the same time The American Ensign dropped over the Stern. Rifles opened fire and cleared the Germans from the Guns, our second shell hit the Conning Tower and blew it into scrap iron everything sunk in $4^1/_2$ Mts. We then picked [up] the "Nicosian's" lifeboats, meanwhile the Huns were doing their best to get aboard the liner by climbing the lifeboats' falls, we fired two shells and hit a few of them. We then ran up to "Nicosian" and shot all of them in the water and the sea turned red. Next the 10 Marines were ordered to fix bayonets and search the liner for any Huns that were aboard her so we got aboard and found 5 and shot them but it was a pitiful sight to see the mules who had got wounded by the shell fire.[36]

Nobody thought much of the affair at the time: 'No one injured on our side so we had some sport for nothing.' Admiral Bayly came aboard at Queenstown and described the massacre with some exaggeration as the 'Finest action in the war'. Doubts set in when ungrateful American sailors claimed to have overheard orders to 'Get them all and take no prisoners', and to have seen bodies with bullet holes in their foreheads. By modern standards the boarding party's action was a war crime, but in the circumstances it was entirely understandable. A First Sea Lord had denounced submarine crews as pirates fit for hanging, while earlier on the 19th, *Baralong* overheard SOS calls from the torpedoed liner *Arabica*, in which thirty-nine civilians died. Q-ships operated under continual threat of sudden death, surrounded by evidence of submarine attacks, but rarely able to strike back. It is, perhaps, surprising there were not more reprisals against U-boat crews who routinely drowned women and children without warning.

The main significance of *Baralong*'s commission, however, was its futility. She steamed 44,734 miles in 466 days, but only saw action twice. U-boat sightings usually resulted in such unsatisfactory diary entries as: 'a lot of wreckage one piece marked SS WOLF LONDON a raft and a boat bottom up. . . no men or lifeboats'. Only when Britain faced starvation did the Royal Navy grudgingly adopt convoy. Few Marines saw escort duty, which usually fell upon smaller vessels without RM detachments. HMS *Bellona*, however, discovered that with all the changes in naval technology some risks remained the same. Returning for refit after storm damage in Norwegian waters, 'we had a Royal Marine washed overboard and no trace could be seen of him. . . a great loss to us and everyone felt it very much.'[37] In a Second World War such experiences would become commonplace as the operational focus of sea warfare shifted away from formal clashes between fleets, to direct naval support for specific strategic tasks: convoy, evacuation and invasion.

Total War

Throughout the inter-war years the Royal Marine's primary role remained naval gunnery, despite amalgamation of the RMA and RMLI in 1923. Elderly officers grumbled that the forced union of the two Portsmouth divisions amounted to abolition of the RMA, but the measure was the logical end of a process going back to the 1880s when the RMLI first acquired gunnery skills. The change gave the Corps a single identity and clarified its function, making it easier to defend against further cuts. Little else appeared to change between the wars. Boy buglers still relayed orders from the bridge, while: 'It was a point of pride that a marine could do anything an experienced able seaman could do, whether boat handling, splicing, hoisting stores with derrick, whip and inhaul, or whatever.'[38] The war at sea of 1939–45 could not have been more different from that of 1914–18, however. The expulsion of British land forces from continental Europe put the Royal Navy, and hence the Royal Marines, in the front line of national defence. British capital ships abandoned their deterrent role in home waters to engage in costly battles for sea control. The Royal Marines' last battleship actions, like the first battles of the Admiral's Regiment, took place in a context of invasion scares, convoy actions and heavy casualties.

In some respects the experience of Marines embarked in 1939 resembled that of 1914–18, except that oil fuel saved the tribulation of coaling. RM stores still held greatcoats and the kit of sick Marines, but also found space for Bren guns, PIATs, and 2-inch mortars. Detachments adapted their traditional functions to modern conditions. The Corporal of the Gangway, Keyboard Sentry and Wardroom Attendants were lineal descendants of the sentinels who assured ships' security under St Vincent, while the working party now included butchers, lamp trimmers and the ship's postman. HMS *Venerable*'s Standing Orders for 1944 attributed paranormal responsibilities to the Mess Corporal, who had to ensure before closing up to Action Stations: 'that all moveable fear in his mess is secured'.[39] Occasionally the concerns of senior officers resembled those of two centuries earlier. Dockside sentries were to load after a second unanswered challenge and fire after a third, always remembering that a dockyard was a populated area. In 1944 the FRMO in the Mediterranean drew attention to the fatal consequences of Marine sentries 'in un-authorised possession of S.A.A. firing their rifles promiscuously'.[40]

Marines still provided a quarter of a ship's firepower, typically manning one of three or four main turrets, and a pair of secondary mountings: one port and one starboard. Action Stations were integrated vertically. A senior NCO acted as Captain of the Turret in the gun house with a number of men at each gun and a small group of specialists, such as the turret trainer, while a Second Captain took charge of ammunition supply in the lower quarters. HMS *Ceylon*, a 6-inch gun cruiser, had twenty-six Royal Marines in 'B' turret and ten more below, under overall command of the ship's Lieutenant RM as Officer of Quarters.[41] In the Battle of the River Plate, the first significant gunnery action of the Second World War on 13 December 1939, HMS *Exeter*'s RM detachment also manned 'B' turret. An 11-inch shell from the German pocket-battleship *Graf Spee* struck the gun house, silencing both 8-inch guns:

> All lights were extinguished and the pump and all machinery stopped as No's 1 were about to ram for the next broadside. . . The G.H. was filled

with dense acrid smoke fumes which made breathing very difficult, burning nostrils and throats.[42]

Exeter did not explode catastrophically, however, suggesting something had been learned about ammunition handling since Jutland. Survivors put out the fires in the gun house, and manhandled unexpended charges over the side, while the handing room's crew calmly placed all remaining cordite in flameproof Clarkson's cases before leaving. When another 11-inch hit set the CPOs' messdeck on fire, immediately above 'B' magazine, Sergeant Puddifoot, Second Captain of the Turret, decided to flood:

> The lights were out but ERA Bond equipped with a torch followed me down and together we inshipped the Hopper guards, battened down the doors, flung what cordite we could find through the escape door [i.e. into the magazine], battened that, and then opened up the Flood and Seacock.

Both turret captains' reports leave an impression of calm efficiency amid terrifying circumstances, men spontaneously implementing safety measures and caring for wounded comrades. In the emergency there was no nonsense about inter-service demarcation, Puddifoot leaving the Petty Officer in charge of the Fire and Repair party 'to use my people as he liked'.

Usually the musicians remained battened down in their 'tomb', with half a dozen Horlicks tablets as an 'action ration'. When the battleship *King George V* engaged *Bismarck* (27 May 1941) the bandsmen in her T/S had no way of judging the accuracy of their plots:

> There was no break in the firing. In the inferno of shouting, the crashing of our guns, external explosions, and the irregular movement of the ship as she changed course in the heavy seas, there was no way of telling whether or not we had been hit. . . We must wait and hope that our ship will not suddenly disintegrate and follow the Hood into oblivion.[43]

The mechanical nature of the system helped men carry on despite imminent disaster, as in HMS *Exeter*'s last action in the Java Sea (27 February–1 March 1942):

> from the point of view of those of us who worked the guns and supply routes it was just an endurance test which was accompanied from time to time by bumps and a shudder which told us we were in range of the Japs too.

At last *Exeter*'s guns and machinery faltered, and the lights finally dimmed:

> It had not seriously occurred to us that we were at last to become just a "Sitting Target" for the Japs, as right up to now everything had been

going so smoothly, just a very prolonged drill in the Royal Marines turret as it had in [other] parts of the ship also.[44]

The great change from 1914–18 was the Royal Navy's tactical flexibility, integrating different classes of ship, which at Jutland had fought separate battles. In the Royal Navy's last big gun action off the North Cape on Boxing Day 1943 an ad hoc task force consisting of the KGV class battle-ship *Duke of York*, cruisers and destroyers combined to ensnare and destroy the German battle-cruiser *Scharnhorst*. Cruisers shielded the convoy that had baited the trap then shepherded their more powerful opponent towards the *Duke of York*, whose Marines manned 'X' turret (four 14-inch guns), and two out of eight 5.25-inch secondary mountings. Her broadsides reduced *Scharnhorst* to a blazing shambles, leaving cruisers and destroyers to sink her with torpedoes. The electronic age had taken the automation of naval combat a step further, both sides using radar to direct their fire in darkness made more impenetrable by blinding snowstorms. All eyes in HMS *Norfolk*'s T/S turned to the small screen, when her bugler sounded the alarm over the tannoy, to see the legendary *Scharnhorst* turned into a pulsating blob.

Norfolk was hit early on, the seamen in 'Y' turret informing the T/S, 'X Turret is afire and abandoned, and their magazine has been flooded! The marines down there must have had it!' Disregarding smoke creeping through the air ducts, the bandsmen continued relaying corrections from the ship's Gunnery Officer aloft in the Director to the remaining turrets. A high rate of accurate fire, broadsides every ten seconds, might pre-empt the enemy's killer shot:

Our Commissioned Gunner's eyes were always roving over the panel in which lights glowed immediately when guns had been reloaded and were in readiness for firing. He might well order the fire gong to be pressed if even five of the lamps glowed. A wait for the remaining three guns could mean the vital difference between death and survival.[45]

Scharnhorst turned away, pursued by her weaker opponents. *Norfolk* fell behind, leaving HMS *Belfast* to illuminate the target for *Duke of York*. As in the First World War the doomed ship fought to the death:

on fire from bow to stern, magazines all blowing up. . . a perfect target, but she is still firing with every gun possible. One destroyer has just gone in and raked the *Scharnhorst*'s decks with pom-pom and Oerlikons.

Private Ralph Thomas RM, aged only nineteen, had escaped from *Norfolk*'s

'X' turret as burning debris fell among the ammunition. Miraculously unscathed when a second 11-inch shell hit his compartment amidships, he was on deck when *Scharnhorst* keeled over: 'Survivors were jumping into the sea and the whole scene was brilliantly lit by searchlights and star shell. It was the most thrilling moment of my life.'[46] Searchlights swept the sea, finding nothing except a large patch of burning oil and thirty-six survivors. A 300-year tradition of ship-to-ship gunnery action had ended.

Air Power

Long before *Scharnhorst* met her end in the Barents Sea new airborne weapons had become the greatest threat to surface ships. In the First World War, Marines had seen aircraft fleetingly and Zeppelins: 'miles away just above the horizon like some huge sausage'. Warships acquired token high-angle guns, but air raids on civilian targets suggested 'That's about all they are fit for, Places that can't hit back.'[47] Nevertheless the first four naval officers trained as pilots had included a Royal Marine. Lieutenant E.L. Gerrard RMLI received his certificate on 2 May 1911. Lieutenant C.H. Collet RMA struck one of the first blows in the struggle for air superiority, dropping two 20lb bombs on Zeppelin sheds at Dusseldorf. He also shared in the seaplane raid on Cuxhaven on Christmas Day 1914, the first offensive use of ship-borne aircraft. Royal Marine pilots continued the tradition on 10 April 1940, when Fleet Air Arm Skuas sank the German cruiser *Konigsberg*, the first large warship destroyed in active air operations. Thirty-one RM pilots and two observers flew in action during the Second World War, while nine NCOs transferred to the Fleet Air Arm as rating pilots.

Most Royal Marines of the period were on the receiving end of air power. While the abiding image of the Napoleonic War at sea is the careless pursuit of glory, cutlass in hand, and the First World War is remembered for its chilly but rarely lethal vigil at Scapa, the overwhelming impression left by the 1940s is of frantic attempts to repel waves of dive-bombers, ending too often with clusters of oil-soaked survivors, awaiting rescue from a cruel sea. Lieutenant Philip Beeman could not recall HMS *Calcutta* 'ever going to sea without suffering air attack of one kind or another.'[48] A survivor from HMS *Devonshire*, sunk on 5 April 1942 in the Indian Ocean, had no time for post-traumatic stress, however:

> in the war at sea there was war today, tomorrow, the day after, and for a
> long time to come. There was not a post battle period which did not turn

into a pre-battle period. If anyone suffered nightmares from a violent battle, these would soon give way to nightmares of the next battle.[49]

Humour distracted minds from the horror. Sinister bubbling after a near miss reminded Bandsman Joffre Swales of vulgar bath-time noises. HMS *Calcutta*'s Marines dubbed the Fleet Air Arm 'men on bicycles', after watching German bombers fly away from Fairey Fulmars, sold by propaganda as the 'Spitfire of the sea'.

The loss of *Prince of Wales* and *Repulse* to the Japanese in December 1941 was a rare example of British capital ships sunk by aircraft. More common victims were the cruisers and destroyers in the front line of the air/sea battle. HMS *Calcutta* was an old 'C' class cruiser converted for anti-aircraft duties, with a crude high angle control system and four twin 4-inch mountings, two manned by her sixteen-strong RM detachment. Unfortunately the system was ineffective against dive-bombers, which suddenly dropped from a great height. Until the adoption of radar proximity fuzes late in the war, ships fired a barrage of shells, set to explode at the likely range of bomb release, but 'with the attacker coming through this curtain in a fast dive, the chances were not high.'[50]

HMS *Calcutta* took part in four opposed evacuations without a scratch. She brought off 800 soldiers from Norway, despite the Stukas, 'Cavorting around fiords at top speed trying to avoid their bombs'. Returning to Scapa Flow her detachment 'looked more like pirates than Marines after all the days at sea, with hardly an item of uniform to be seen'. One smote HMS *Rodney* with a fuze hammer, to express his opinion of the battleship's quiet life, and as a metallic tone came forth shouted, 'Cor, I thought it was only made of wood.'[51] With fresh gun barrels *Calcutta* headed for Dunkirk, OCRM ordered to leave behind all confidential papers except the 'Dangerous Waters Set':

> The smell of gunfire and smoke was all-pervading. The soldiers must have found it most uncomfortable, climbing up over our sides with the 4-inch guns, pom-poms, and .5″ machine guns banging away over their heads – perhaps they found it comforting.

The ship saved 1,600 men, but appearances belied the 'Miracle of Dunkirk': 'smoke everywhere and the floating bodies of drowned soldiers and sailors increasing in number the nearer we patrolled towards the shore.'[52] The evacuation of Greece in April 1941 was no better, 'Flares and guns going off all round the harbour and aerial mines on parachutes floating down'. *Calcutta* escaped once more with 900 troops, her grey paint blistered and blackened after firing 1,200 4-inch rounds. Her luck ran out off Crete, when two Ju88s blew out her bottom. Beeman was last man out of the ship, the sea coming up to meet him as he left the Director.

Two more cruisers were lost off Crete, with six destroyers, casualties of an over-ambitious offensive strategy that left the Royal Navy 'exposed to very heavy air attacks from shore bases very close by without the benefit of any fighter cover. A situation according to the rules of naval warfare in which one should never find oneself.'[53] HMS *Gloucester* and *Fiji* had been under intense air attack for days. The crews were exhausted, and high-angle ammunition running short:

> we had no shells for the six inch, or four inch guns left at all, and were firing C.P.B.C (common pointed ballistic cap) at the bombers, which meant that to knock a plane out of the sky, one had to have a direct hit, an impossibility.[54]

Bandmaster MacDonald was the only survivor from *Gloucester*'s band, his escape from her T/S the stuff of nightmares:

> The heavy explosion on the starboard side, the failure of all lighting and the sound of water pouring into the compartment – The Control Officer giving the order to abandon the TS – The disciplined evacuation in the dark, ascending the straight ladder one at a time, degenerating into panic when water came flooding down through the manhole overhead – Climbing up through the cascading water into the Low Power Room to become embroiled with the crews of both HACPs (High Angle Calculating Position) and repair parties, all struggling in the gloom and fast rising water to reach the only avenue of escape, the manhole in the Armoured hatch above.[55]

MacDonald had attracted peculiar looks by inflating his Mae West in the T/S, but it saved his life, floating him out of the rapidly filling Low Power Room. Once over the ship's side he avoided the Luftwaffe's machine-gun bullets as they strafed survivors, only to be picked up by a German patrol boat next day. Many uninjured men from both cruisers died in the water 'as if seeking death willingly':

> a lot of men gave up. They had been under such impossible conditions for weeks now, culminating in the last three or four days, under constant bombardment. . . They just didn't believe that the destroyers would come back.

A third of *Fiji*'s crew were lost, 243 out of 766, including Boy Bugler

P.J.M. Avant, at 15$^{1}/_{2}$ the youngest British serviceman killed during the war. Dressed in scratch uniforms back in Alexandria, the survivors heard of the destruction of HMS *Hood* with all her 151 Marines: 'I think at that point, most of us thought the war was lost.'[56]

Convoy

Shocking as the loss of HMS *Hood* seemed at the time, it was neither decisive nor typical. Few British warships during World War Two were sunk in such stand alone battles. The decisive actions in European waters and the main cause of naval losses were convoy battles. The escort craft that fought the Battle of the Atlantic were too small to carry RM detachments, but some armed merchant vessels did, as they had in the previous war. Colour Sergeant Harry Wright, a veteran of the 1918 Zeebrugge raid, spent a week in an open boat after his ship was torpedoed, with never a chance to fire his 12-pounder gun. B. Knapton had arranged space in SS *Natia*'s refrigerator for various dainties obtainable at her destination, 'A pleasant surprise for the Wife', when a German commerce raider put a shell through the ship's rudder beneath his feet: 'Fortunately it did not penetrate the next compartment which was the magazine. . . "How near I was of making a date with the Angels".' Taken aboard the raider, Knapton had the unusual experience of serving in a German ship, as steward to captured merchant skippers, until transfer to a prison camp in Germany. He waited another four years for liberation, diary entries as thin as the midday soup, 'a basin of hot water with two or three scarlet runner beans from a tin floating on the top with perhaps a potato'.[57]

Early in the war ships like *Natia* took their chance outside home waters, but convoy was essential through the Mediterranean or on the Murmansk run. HMS *Fiji* ran the gauntlet with reinforcements for the British Army in Egypt:

> It was literally hell on earth. We all aboard swear that it was only the skill of our skipper that brought us through. Our only respite was a few hours of darkness but – even then one had to sleep at action stations, not in a comfortable hammock, but on the hard floor. Food too was hard rations, mostly 'corned dog' as we called the tins of corned beef, and tinned soya sausages. Even I thought they were horrible.[58]

Malta, blocking Axis supply routes to North Africa, needed constant resupply. HMS *Calcutta* entered Valetta her guns still 'firing over the heads of the crowd lining the harbour. They were all clapping us as if it were the Royal Tournament.'[59] HMS *Penelope*'s RM bandsmen played for Maltese stevedores working through an air raid, and were no doubt excused if they missed the odd beat. Malta's desperate situation inspired one of the greatest convoy battles. Operation Pedestal, in August 1942, involved two battleships, four aircraft carriers, seven cruisers and numerous destroyers, to cover just fourteen MVs.

Philip Beeman had returned to Chatham after the loss of HMS *Calcutta*, to find it 'degenerated into little more than a transit hotel full of guests quite alien to me and their predecessors'.[60] Appalled at the atmosphere he volunteered for sea service to the amazement of unblooded Hostilities Only captains, busily scheming for promotion. A Lieutenant despite three years very active service, Beeman took part in Pedestal as OCRM in HMS *Charybdis*, another AA cruiser. Different types of aircraft and ships cooperated for tactical advantage. *Charybdis* provided close defence for the carrier HMS *Eagle*, whose fighters broke up incoming air attacks. Hostile aircraft dropped self-propelled circling mines ahead of the convoy to disrupt its mutually supporting formation, while low-level torpedo attacks distracted AA gunners from dive-bombers waiting to pounce. E-boats and submarines took over at night, as Italian cruisers manoeuvred threateningly off-stage. A U-boat sank HMS *Eagle* on 11 August. Next day a synchronized attack by Stukas and Italian torpedo bombers wrecked HMS *Indomitable*'s hangar lifts, reducing the vital fighter cover. E-boats sank or crippled four cruisers including HMS *Nigeria* with her fighter direction equipment, preventing the convoy calling up Spitfires from Malta.

By morning of 13 August only six out of fourteen MVs were left. *Charybdis* was close behind when three JU88s shallow dived one of them:

> the whole ship just disappeared before my eyes as did the plane which attacked her. We steamed on through the blazing debris, oil and smoke. . .
> One moment a large ship steaming along at 14 knots, a few seconds later just small pieces of debris floating on the surface.[61]

She was the last casualty, as the covering force handed over to escorts from Malta, and turned for home. Despite a last brush with E-boats, 'Complete chaos with all sides firing with tremendous gusto', there were no further warship losses. Notwithstanding the casualties, Pedestal had a decisive effect in the Western Desert, as aircraft and submarines based on Malta cut off the supplies that had fuelled Rommel's drive into Egypt.

The most arduous convoys were those carrying war material to the Soviet Union under the nose of German forces in occupied Norway.

Regardless of human opposition, the atrocious weather made life practically impossible. One monster wave tore the roof off HMS *Norfolk*'s 'A' Turret, flinging it down on top of 'B' Turret, and flooding the 'A' magazines. Tons of ice collected on ships' upperworks, up to a foot thick, turrets had to be chipped free to train, and bugles were kept warm in the quarterdeck lobby to prevent them stripping the RM buglers' lips. Condensation froze onto deckheads below. Swill buckets of 'gash' food that could not be thrown overboard lest it attract U-boats, added greasy decks to the hazards of movement about a violently pitching ship. Food was dreadful, cooked hours beforehand, then liquidized into a sloppy mess by the ship's motion. Reconstituted potato resembled wallpaper paste, but was better than fresh ones, alternately frozen and thawed on the upper deck, 'until they emitted the stench of a super sewer'. The natural consequences of eating brought special problems. Located well forward the heads pitched violently and had steel handholds either side to prevent users tumbling across the deck, 'trousers down and all'. When the ship plunged into a trough, the 'G' force of a thirty-foot drop clamped unwilling buttocks against the seat, while the failure of a non-returning valve might convert a WC to a bidet, filling ankled trousers with icy water, or worse. When weather permitted there were the usual U-boats and JU88s, sometimes backed up by *Kriegsmarine* surface units.

HMS *Trinidad*'s RM detachment was particularly unlucky. In March 1942 one of her own torpedoes malfunctioned in the cold and circled round to blow a hole 42 feet by 24 in her side. It flooded the T/S, killing most of her fifteen bandsmen. The forward turrets lost all power, the Marines in 'B' taking half an hour to traverse 90 degrees by hand. Towed into Murmansk the crew shivered in corners of an unheated ship, while they pumped her out, posting sentries to watch out for the OCRM's waterlogged confidential books. The Russians were unfriendly, arresting the padre and shooting at sailors who sledged down a snow-covered tip. They were good at camouflage, however, spreading ashes on the snow to move the dockside 800 yards inland, and keep German bombs away from the crippled cruiser. She sailed home in May, the worst time of year, in bright weather and continual daylight. While a torpedo attack distracted the AA gunners, two JU88s dropped from the sky to knock out 'B' turret. The magazine numbers were killed and the remaining Marines forced to evacuate. The forecastle blazed like a furnace, but there was no water for the fire hoses, so destroyers rescued survivors and torpedoed the wreck. Twenty Marines died out of ninety, but their sacrifice symbolized allied solidarity at a time when the British could provide little direct help for their Soviet allies.[62]

Invasion

While convoys brought material to continue the war, sea-borne invasions finished it. The German inability to launch such operations ultimately lost them the war. HMS *Dido*'s interception of their attempt to land troops in Crete from requisitioned craft suggests what might have happened, had they forced the Channel in August 1940:

> Wholesale murder. Italian destroyer and two transports sunk. Many schooners were shot to pieces and German troops could be seen waving white flags swimming in the water. Those that were spared the machine gunning probably died of drowning or exposure.[63]

Less than three months after Pedestal, in November 1942, the Allies began the series of assault landings in North Africa, Sicily, Italy and Normandy that would take them to the borders of Germany. Historians usually focus on the landward side of these operations, but Naval Gunfire Support (NGS) was essential to get the troops ashore and maintain their precarious bridgeheads. Sea service Marines made a vital contribution to this task, which was not always as comfortable or safe as it may have looked from the beach.

The speed and rapidly deployed firepower of warships makes them ideal for artillery raids to soften up or distract opposition, for example HMS *Dido*'s attack on Marsala during the Sicily landings: 'at long range approximately 500 rounds. Searchlights on shore fixed ship and batteries open fire later, but ships are out of range, speeding westwards. Damage unknown but several fires observed on shore.'[64] Seeking the illusory advantage of surprise the Allies landed at Salerno (9 Sept 1943) without a preparatory bombardment and met a ferocious German reaction. NGS was perhaps the single greatest factor in preventing them driving the Allies back into the sea. HMS *Dido* joined the naval effort on 17 September, with a ringside view of the battle area, close enough to hear the machine guns, while near misses from surrounding hills inspired suspicions the ship had been used to draw German fire. A radio-controlled glider bomb hit HMS *Warspite*: 'actually seen circling the ship then hit it below the water mark with such force that it blasted a huge hole in the stern of the ship, killing many of the crew'.[65] At night the heavy detonations of depth charges could be heard out at sea. *Dido* fired 1,500 rounds at German infantry, tanks, and transport, going close inshore to reach targets further inland: 'about 500 yards from the shore, where the mountains rise to about 1,000 feet, very picturesque scenery here'.[66]

The Royal Marines' single greatest effort of the war was D-Day, when 17,500 Marines were deployed, almost twice their 1939 strength. Veteran warships like *Warspite*, two of her three operational turrets manned by Marines, acted as mobile heavy artillery as long as the Army remained in range of the beaches. The first ship into firing position was the 6-inch cruiser HMS *Arethusa*, which opened fire at 05.50 on a sea front hotel overlooking Sword Beach. Two RM bandsmen on opposite watches contrived to keep a twenty-four diary of her eighteen days off the beaches. It was a near thing whether the continual broadsides would put her out of action before the Germans did. Concussion split the upper decks, opening cracks in deckheads below, through which the fireproof lining fell onto mess tables. Flying light bulbs may have seemed a more immediate hazard than asbestosis: 'A and B turrets fired a full broadside. . . there was a flash above my head and the lamp fell out of the holder and hit my head in a shower of glass. We had at least half a dozen fresh lamps in up to dinner time.'[67]

Fire control equipment was unreliable, the radar screen 'a mass of lines going all ways', and a control table breakdown on D+1 forced the T/S to fall back on a mechanical dumaresq, familiar to RM gunners before 1914. Nevertheless, fire had to be accurate, preferably within 100 yards of the target, to avoid hitting friendly troops in close combat. Forward Bombardment Officers walked shells up and down the target area:

14.00 Target. Village containing enemy troops. . . 16 rounds by broadsides. Change target to 400 yards right. More jerries in the same village, four rounds fired. Change target to 200 yards left and 100 yards up. First broadside hits. Up 100 yards and then up 50 again, two broadsides each time. Left, 100 yards another broadside, hits again. Shoot ends 14.30.[68]

Arethusa's main armament dealt effectively with armoured counter-attacks, for which the lightly armed infantry of 6 Airborne Division sent their thanks:

19.55 Opened fire on a concentration of enemy tanks and guns T.162x [16,200 yards]. While firing in rapid groups we had at least 1 hit. FBO reports that 2 tanks have moved off out of the way. I don't blame them either.[69]

The diarists had expected plenty of opposition, but 'surveying D-day from our own point of view we find it wasn't as bad as we had thought.' Early air raids were as ineffective as the fire they provoked: 'Its six of one and half a dozen of the other. The Jerry bombers hit nothing and we don't hit them.' *Arethusa*'s first two tours, during which she fired 1,300 HE rounds, fell into a regular pattern, where the main danger appeared to be the tiddy-oggies dished up as action rations:

> It has been the same this time as it was just after D-day. The days taken up by bombarding and the nights with air raids. We don't get much sleep, only in the afternoons when we are off watch. The smoke we put up as a screen makes it very uncomfortable. The food is awful, but we are still alive so why worry?[70]

By D+18 the Germans were making the landing area 'too hot to be healthy'. In the small hours of 24 June as a doodle-bug's exhaust flames lit up the anchorage, an old-fashioned 500kg bomb off the port side lifted everyone six inches off the deck, broke the cathode ray tubes in the radar screens, disabled the director training gear and split various pipes and storage tanks: 'All of us. . . were as white as this paper for a while.' A destroyer cracked in half against a mine and sank, while artillery hidden in the woods beyond the Orne set a tanker ablaze. Vessels shifted billet to confuse enemy gunners, at the risk of hitting unswept mines. That evening the Luftwaffe returned, dropping parachute mines lit by 'chandeliers' of flares. Going astern to avoid a mine by the forward anchor cable *Arethusa* set off two others, and bounced a foot out of the water, throwing furniture about cabins, smashing radar sets, control table motors and the last gyroscopic compass, and jamming 'Y' turret. One of the diarists scalded his foot with a mess tin full of cocoa. Front-line soldiers ashore may have envied ships' crews the chance of a hot drink, but laying offshore, a sitting target for mines, shells and glider bombs, was not always a soft option.

The invasion of Okinawa (March–June 1945) was the last act of the war at sea and it rang down the curtain for soldiers at sea. Battles in the Pacific were decided well beyond gun range. Two battleships accompanied the British Pacific Fleet, with tropicalized machinery but not messdecks. They acted mainly as anti-aircraft escorts for carriers whose aircraft struck at targets hundreds of miles away, compared with the hundreds of feet typical of sea battles under sail. The gulf between Marines of the 1940s and their red-coated predecessors must have been less, however, than that between them and the Japanese kamikaze pilots. Anti-aircraft action during suicide attacks was short and violent. Gun crews engaged targets under local control, as waiting for orders would have left it too late. Boy

Bugler Rowe had a grandstand view from HMS *Howe*'s after bridge. He gave his messmates a nightly commentary on the latest attacks, like some macabre spectator sport. Often the younger Marines' hands trembled as they ate. Hardened to the daily spectacle of planes crashing in flames or bouncing off the carriers' armoured decks, Rowe thought it was 'harder for them while they worked the guns in the turret at an unseen enemy, not knowing whether death was coming straight at them or passing by a thousand yards away'. One day a doomed plane headed straight for Rowe's exposed station on the catwalk, flashing past him, so close he could see the pilot slumped at the controls. That night his own hands shook, 'as if the Divine Wind had blown for me personally'.[71]

One aspect of the Pacific War reminiscent of earlier times was the duration of cruises. Fleet trains and replenishment at sea allowed ships to stay at sea longer than any fleet since Nelson's time. The food was arguably better, but weevils still infested bread and macaroni, the fastidious blowing them out of each little pasta tube. The influx of Hostilities Only recruits had caused some tension with regular 'barrack stanchions', but by 1945 there was little difference between the two in soldiering or seamanship. HO recruits 'brought a breath of fresh air onto the messdeck with their questioning of all manner of long standing and sometimes useless tradition. . . The services were never to be quite the same again.'[72] For the Royal Marines the most pressing concern would be the gap between sea-going and land-orientated elements of the Corps, a division that originated in the unusual strategic conditions of the First World War.

CHAPTER TEN

Poor Bloody Infantry

THE Royal Marines' experience of war at sea in the early twentieth-century followed a familiar pattern of blockade, convoy and bombardment. On land the Corps was engaged in operations of a quite unprecedented character. The continental commitment that drew the British into the First World War compelled them to engage a powerful European enemy in battles of attrition they usually left to their allies, while the Royal Navy pursued more profitable fringe activities. In 1914 most of the European coastline remained in friendly hands, affording few opportunities for amphibious operations like those around Spain or the Mediterranean in the days of Rooke and Keith. German colonies were few, and the Fatherland's European shoreline was short and heavily defended. Despite these strategic constraints, a cartoon in *Globe and Laurel* suggested that, like plum and apple jam, Royal Marines appeared on every front of the First World War. They formed naval striking forces in Belgium and Siberia, and secured naval bases at Scapa Flow, Ascension Island and Petrovsk on the Caspian. Marines in armoured cars chased Uhlans and aeroplanes in Flanders, while others laid mines for Austrian gunboats on the Danube, or hauled naval guns through African swamps. The RMA's 15-inch howitzers, transportable in nine separate tractor loads, provided the ultimate symbol of an immobile artillery war. Specialist units included submarine miners, a motor transport company of London bus drivers and the RM Labour Corps that handled military stores at the Base Ports of the British Expeditionary Force in France. The Royal Marines' most significant contribution to the land war were infantry battalions that fought at Antwerp, Gallipoli and on the Western Front. Their progress from hopeful improvization, through terrible sacrifice to forgotten triumph epitomizes the general experience of the British Army during the First World War.

Flying Column

The Admiralty, under Winston Churchill, had foreseen the need for an amphibious striking force, issuing orders for a Flying Column Royal Marines on 2 August 1914, two days before war was declared. Each division contributed a battalion, but material preparation lagged behind political will. Divisions gave up their adjutants and quartermasters to staff the new RM Brigade, but lack of subalterns moved commanding officers to despair: 'I do not know how we can possibly do on the officers told off for us. The young officers are absolutely useless. . . They had far better be left behind.' Other ranks were old and unfit: 'The vague statement that the Battn is not to interfere with the requirements of the Fleet leaves too much latitude for palming off of all the old crocks on the Battn.' Khaki uniforms only arrived during the RMB's second excursion to the Continent, requiring a quick change on Dunkirk's quayside: 'I have clothed many Royal Marines,' said the Quartermaster, 'but never a whole battalion in ten minutes.'[1]

The opening gambit of the war was a wheeling German advance through Belgium into France, providing a short-lived opportunity for an amphibious force to menace their open right flank. On 27 August 1914 the RMB, under Major-General Aston, landed from obsolescent battleships at Ostend, but once ashore was immobile, except for bicycles hired from helpful but rapacious Belgians. Sand dunes obstructed ship-to-shore communication, precluding naval gunfire support for the Marines' overextended perimeter. Vice-Admiral Bethell saw little prospect of diverting German reserves from the decisive front, 150 miles away on the Marne, and fretted about torpedo attacks. Fortunately the RMB's re-embarkation on 31 August was unopposed. They had covered redeployment of 6,000 Belgian troops and cheered Ostend's nervous population, but the episode exposed the material and intellectual deficiencies of British preparations for joint operations. An ill-tempered exchange of telegrams between Bethell and the First Lord on 30 August included requests for information freely available in *Jane's Fighting Ships*. The Admiralty's inability to check elementary facts invited disaster, as would soon become apparent.

Aston reorganized his brigade after Ostend, weeding out the unfit and incompetent. The RMA departed to form howitzer and anti-aircraft brigades, the Deal depot raising a fourth RMLI battalion. As hostilities shifted north in October, with the misnamed Race to the Sea, the Admiralty ordered the RMB to the Belgian national redoubt at Antwerp, to encourage an ally in extremis, and gain time while British troops secured the Channel

Ports. The Belgians fed the Marines fruit and biscuits, but the military situation was unsatisfactory, despite a line of forts and barbed wire between the River Scheldt and defensive inundations along the neutral Dutch border. Major-General Archibald Paris RMA, the exhausted Aston's replacement, was scathing. The forts were ill armed and offered admirable artillery targets. The hastily fielded RMB had neither tools nor engineers to improve Belgian trenches, which were 'almost hopeless. Wide and shallow – no dugouts or head cover'.[2] The RMB munched black bread and dodged German artillery, whose accuracy they blamed on spies rather than poor concealment from aerial observation:

> shelled from one end to the other, in front and in the rear. It was too warm while we were there. The exact range must have been given to the enemy for they had us nicely. . . Later on, the order to retire came and we moved back along the road. Here we helped ourselves to some turnips. Only a few days previously, we had been laughing at lads in trains we passed eating turnips.[3]

Two scratch brigades of naval reservists arrived to form a notional Royal Naval Division, without staff, artillery or transport, but numbers alone were no answer to German howitzers. Paris 'decided the situation was hopeless, and if possible I must try and save the Naval Division.'[4] The British withdrew overnight (8–9 October) by the light of blazing oil tanks:

> the long column swerving from one side to the other to keep as far away as possible from the huge tottering and burning buildings. . . There was hardly a whole window left and broken glass crunched under one's feet. . . numerous obstacles such as fallen trees, dismantled tram wires, dead horses, etc. . . added to the hard cobbles, made marching difficult.[5]

Most of 1st RN Brigade wandered into Holland and was interned, inexperienced staff officers not realizing the need to hurry, or maintain touch. Portsmouth RMLI, the rearguard, were equally tired, but barged through a German ambush at Moerbeke, despite darkness and crowds of terrified refugees: 'A German officer called on us to surrender. The Major's reply, sharp and short, was, "Surrender be damned! Royal Marines never surrender".'[6] Another Marine Officer wandered into Holland, but returned cigar in hand after bluffing the border guard into showing him the road to Ostend. Antwerp may have 'showed the need for adequate forces at Admiralty disposal for Naval purposes', but there was nothing essentially naval about the intervention.[7] The RMB travelled to Antwerp in requisitioned omnibuses and returned by train. Their next operation would reveal similar confusion.

The Great Adventure

Turkey's entry into the war as a German ally in October 1914 seemed to expose Constantinople to a knockout blow from the sea. The Fleet's failure to force the Dardanelles, the waterway between the Mediterranean and Black Seas, escalated into an amphibious assault on the Gallipoli peninsula, to reduce the forts and minefields blocking the straits. Chatham and Plymouth Battalions joined the Mediterranean Fleet 'for special services' in February 1915, the rest of the RND soon following. Their experiences cruelly exposed the difficulties then facing combined operations.

Several Admiralty studies had advised against attacking the Dardanelles, while military opinion condemned assaults on beaches defended by magazine rifles and quick-firing artillery:

> any attempt to land troops in the face of an enemy thus armed must now be considered almost impossible, owing to the tremendous loss which must certainly be sustained. . . covering fire from ships and boats would be more powerful than formerly, but the high velocity guns of ships are not very formidable against entrenchments, and it may safely be said that Amherst's and Abercrombie's exploits are never likely again to be attempted.[8]

Fast troopships, carrying flat boats and stern-wheel steamers, might have achieved strategic surprise but none of these conditions for success applied at Gallipoli. Ineffectual bombardments betrayed Allied intentions and when two companies of Plymouth Marines went ashore on 4 March 1915 to finish the fleet's work, they 'tumbled into cutters and pulled for the shore' in the traditional manner. Several men were shot approaching the beach at Kum Kale and more after landing: 'All this time we had not seen anyone.' Pinned down by invisible enemies, Marines could no longer carry out their Napoleonic role of covering naval demolition parties:

> an awful job to get back, it was like running across a range while firing was going on. If it had not been for our destroyers coming up at the right moment and opening a terrific bombardment on the enemy I don't think any of us would have got back.[9]

Sergeant Edwin Kershaw in HMS *Albion* witnessed the definitive failure of the naval offensive on 18 March:

Bombarded the forts at Chanck [*sic*] and the forts on opposite bank about 2 P.M. there was a Frenchman sunk 40 secs after being hit few saved Irristable was torpedoed about [blank] The Ocean going to assist her also torpedoed large amount saved on "Irri" and practically all from "Ocean" during the evening Chanck caught fire, burning furiously also No 15 fort. . . the day's work was very good but disasterous [*sic*].

Kershaw also witnessed the consequences of assaulting beaches covered by machine guns at Cape Helles on 25 April 1915:

SS River Clyde with 2,000 troops D.F. Munsters and Liverpool Reg. Ran ashore and dropped her sides for troops to get out this was very bad for the troops that were in the boats coming under Maxim Fire between ship and shore. . . it was Hell upon earth for nearly 4 hours during the evening boat loads of wounded was removed from the beach. . . the sights that came aboard us were gastly [*sic*] in fact they won't bear describing.[10]

Only one RMLI Battalion was used, in contrast to the Royal Marines' spearhead role at Ismailia in 1882, landing at 'Y' Beach, three miles north of Helles. Plymouth Battalion was not even first ashore, Colonel Matthews reporting 'that more reliance could be placed on Regulars than on his own half-trained troops'. This was not just regular army prejudice against 'men specially enlisted for the war': a naval officer found 1st King's Own Scottish Borderers 'handier than the Marines in boatwork', a comment on amphibious unpreparedness.[11] Against all odds the landing at 'Y' Beach achieved surprise, the Turks evidently thinking it a ridiculous landing place:

"Y" Beach the Scottish Borderer cried
While panting up the steep hillside
"Y" Beach!
To call this thing a beach is stiff
Its nothing but a b— cliff
Why beach?[12]

Marines probed inland to locations out of reach for the whole campaign, but higher command, absorbed in the shambles further south, sent neither orders nor reinforcements:

We'd just got back to the top of the cliff (about 11 am) when the lid came off with a bump; shells and bullets came over in a sheet, in the midst of which we were trying to dig in.

Soon the British were pinned against the cliff, with dwindling ammunition and water, and a growing number of wounded:

> It wasn't till darkness came on that the show really started, and things got really mixed. . . hide and seek going on amongst the bushes on the cliff in the dark, our wounded who were there having a very unpleasant time. . . bullets appeared to be coming from every direction, and the Turks from any direction.[13]

Although ship-to-shore communication is an essential element of amphibious operations signallers had been ordered to leave lamps and flags behind. Sergeant Frederick Meatyard signalled for help with the Colonel's torch. When boats came for the wounded at dawn many unwounded men also left, prompting general withdrawal. They had been thirty hours ashore, instead of the planned six, and suffered over 300 casualties. Matthews and two companies of RMLI were last off the beach. Like other regimental officers placed by senior commanders in impossible positions during the First World War, he was made a scapegoat. The Official History selected Matthews alone for personal criticism, while admitting 'no other part of the operation was free from calamitous mistakes.'[14] Matthews may not have displayed a Commando's initiative, but neither he nor his men were trained as such. Nor did the official historian address the probable fate of an unsupported battalion, without signals or artillery, surrounded by Turkish reserves.

The precarious British situation after 25 April drew the RND into Gallipoli piecemeal, rather than as a single decisive reinforcement. Most RN battalions went to Helles, while three RMLI Battalions landed further north at ANZAC Cove.[15] Few were the seasoned Marines of Victorian campaigns, the Australians finding them 'strangely young and slender'. For the first time in its history the Corps had enlisted short service recruits, many younger than the Army minimum of nineteen years. The sheer cliffs around ANZAC were hard work after months at sea:

> Orders kept being passed: 'Gangway!' 'Get a move on!' 'Hurry up the ammunition!' 'Come on the machine guns!' 'Stand clear of the wounded!' 'Get your packs off!' 'Everybody up in the firing line!' 'Now, Australians, the RMLI are here!'

Led over the top into the worst sectors of the line, survivors had no false modesty: 'The Marines absolutely saved the situation for the Australians many times, and also consolidated the position as the Australians had no idea of trench making.'[16] For three days after their arrival, the RMLI held much of the ANZAC line, bearing the brunt of Turkish counter-attacks and launching their own counter-attacks:

> Everyone dropped the different jobs they were doing, and rushed up the hill, fixing their bayonets as they did so. What a sight it was! Just like a cinema show, men falling down the hillside, killed and wounded by dozens.

Lance-Corporal Walter Parker, Portsmouth Battalion, won the Royal Marines' first VC of the war, assisting wounded at Lone Pine, when every other member of his stretcher party had been killed or wounded: 'It was pitiful to see chums lying there on stretchers in a boiling sun, smothered in flies, and not able to help them. The days went, and life was a nightmare.'[17] Portsmouth and Chatham lost almost half their strength before the Australian Light Horse relieved them on 12 May.

The Allies could switch reserves between ANZAC and Helles by sea, but ashore they found the same stalemate as on the Western Front, under worse conditions:

> "Gallipoli" is a fearful place. No words can describe it. The conditions are horrible, lack of water, disease, stench, heat and most horrible of all – the flies and lice! The flies got in everything; when having a meal one almost ate as many flies as food, weight for weight.

Part of the trouble was lack of numbers: 'How enough of the men taking part in the assault managed to get ashore and hang on to their foothold is beyond comprehension.'[18] The attackers never had as many men as the Turks, who were fighting on their own doorstep. Turkish possession of the high ground made it impossible to move without attracting shellfire. Casualties were often higher while resting than in the line: 'shell from Asiatic Lizzie came over. . . the rush of air caused me to fall down flat on ground bruised my hip and then fell about four yards away thank God it did not burst.'[19]

General Paris feared a second débacle:

> hard luck that I should drop in for the two events which will be more criticised than any other. . . strategically this has been a grave error. . . The Turk couldn't have done us any harm and yet 100,000 Allied troops are employed in a sideshow. . . a barren strip of land subject to shell fire.

The RND had lost its striking force role, becoming just another infantry division, but without artillery, a particular disadvantage in trench warfare where 'with sufficient high explosive one can take a trench with a walking stick. The difficulty is to stay there.'[20] Attacks were appallingly costly to both sides:

> when we arrived and jumped into the trenches it was like jumping on a spring mattress, so thick were the bodies. . . In digging the communication trenches we had to wear respirators so awful was the stench. . . the sun very soon gets at the dead, and a corpse is black in an hour.[21]

Casualties reduced the RND to a trench holding force. It took no part in the offensives that accompanied the Suvla landings in August, a final attempt to restore momentum with an amphibious assault behind the Turkish right flank. Replacements proved insufficient, despite drafting 'War Babies', the four RMLI battalions reducing to two, to form 2nd Brigade RND with two bluejacket battalions.

Survivors adjusted to trench warfare and learned new skills. The RM Cyclist Company specialized in Tickler's artillery, named after the jam manufacturer whose empty tins were 'made into bombs by half filling them with high explosive and putting nails, old bullets, pieces of barbed wire etc, then a detonator and fuse, part of which comes through a hole in the lid, the remainder of the lid being soldered down.'[22] Machine-gunners learned to build invisible loopholes and fire Maxim guns across a sandbag without tripods: 'one gun suitably placed can break up a battalion in less time than it takes to write this.'[23] Expertise paid off in successful raids: 'Owing to the splendid work of the Chatham and Deal machine gunners and bombers they accomplished their task without a casualty. It was death to any Turk who looked over the parapet.'[24]

As in the Crimea winter's approach threatened a stalled expedition with extinction. On 'Black Friday', 27 November, hailstones as big as cricket balls flooded trenches, stove in ships' boats and wrecked piers. Sloshing round the line, 'gumboots full of icy cold water', Paris was the antithesis of a chateau general. He wondered how his men stood the cold and wet: 'I have a fairly dry place to crawl into and plenty of dry clothes. They poor devils, only one suit and a puddle.'[25] An outbreak of strategic realism in December saved the battered RMLI from reliving their fathers' experiences at Sebastopol. Evacuation of ANZAC and Suvla cleared the way for a last whisper of an amphibious role for the RND, as bluejackets and Marines returned to the sea. Thinning out at Helles began with an embargo on letters and a simulated withdrawal to discourage curious Turks: 'stood to at 5.10 hoping they would attack but only a few came out, and very few of them got back.'[26] Companies held the line at half strength: 'it got too rotten for words: Don't speak; don't make a noise;

don't walk about; don't smoke; breathe gently.'[27] The RND took over the French sector to their right, inheriting a live and let live agreement: 'it would have been a pity to disturb the truce at an inconvenient moment. So I borrowed French uniforms. . . and all was peace.'[28]

The RMLI were among the last to leave on 8/9 January 1916: 'There was only 12 of us. . . manning 300 yards of firing line. For the last 4 hours we were walking to and fro on Guard. It was a nerve-racking experience and had the enemy tumbled to our little game it would have been all U.P. with us.'[29] Embarkation proceeded smoothly, 'One couldn't realise it was war. Everything went so well.'[30] As 2nd RMLI incorporated remnants of Plymouth Battalion, which had raided Kum Kale the previous March, the Corps maintained its claim to be first into action and last out. Lieutenant Bastin of Deal machine-gun company tried to relax aboard the troopship *Olympic*: 'what a comfort to have a decent meal and bed, bath, etc dreamed an awful dream punched the side of bunk and skinned my knuckles.'[31] *Army and Navy Gazette* paid tribute to the RMLI's part in what was so far 'the most costly and arduous campaign in British history'. The 'largest homogenous unit from any one part of His Majesty's forces', Marine losses exceeded any other unit 'actually and relatively', over half the Brigade becoming casualties.[32] Gallipoli was the last major amphibious operation of the war. The RND's destiny now lay on the Western Front, where battles dwarfed anything in the peninsula.

The Bells of Hell

The RND's departure for France was by no means inevitable. The Admiralty was unsure what to do with their 'enfant terrible', as were some senior RM officers. Paris admitted 'it was the greatest mistake forming the Division, but it could be a worse one to break up now.' He mocked instructions that 'No more proper Marine Officers or men. . . drain away to the Army', and wondered 'What is an improper Marine?'[33] Despite the service chiefs Paris and his influential friends in London saved the Division from disbandment, or worse still Mesopotamia. It arrived at Marseilles on 19 May 1916 to fight on the Western Front, no place for a lightly equipped striking force. For the first time the RND received proper artillery and technical troops. Royal Marines manned the Machine-Gun Battalion, Engineer, Signals and Trench Mortar companies, and learned to handle the Divisional Train's horses and mules. Rechristened 63rd (Royal Naval) Division, the RND renumbered its brigades 188, 189, and

190, the RMLI serving in the first. After trench familiarization on a quiet sector near Vimy they marched south for the Somme battlefields.

The Somme was the first of the 'wearing out' battles that continued through 1917, and still dominate British attitudes to the First World War. The Marines took part in four major offensives between November 1916 and October 1917:

Battle	Date
Ancre (Beaumont Hamel)	13–14 Nov 1916
Miraumont	17–18 Feb 1917
Arleux: Gavrelle Windmill	28–29 Apr 1917
Second Passchendaele	26 Oct 1917

Casualties exceeded RM losses at Jutland on three occasions out of four, and were always a shocking percentage of battalions only 500 strong to begin with. 'Sepulchred Gavrelle' remains the worst single day for casualties in Corps history, with at least 885 casualties.

Marines arriving on the Western Front in October 1916 benefited from lessons of the unparalleled disaster of 1 July 1916, the first day of the Somme, when 60,000 men were lost for minimal gains. A rolling barrage ahead of attacking infantry had replaced the preliminary bombardment that failed so completely in July. Mimeographed notes issued to RND platoon commanders stressed the importance of following the barrage closely, and rushing the enemy trenches as soon as it lifted. Captain Lionel Montagu RMLI, of Hood Battalion, remembered his Colonel 'watching and waiting for our barrage to move. At the exact moment we moved on again about twenty to thirty yards behind our barrage, Freyberg in front.'[34] Assaulting troops infiltrated no-man's-land before zero hour to keep up with the barrage and escape German SOS fire. Companies still attacked in waves, but at Passchendaele supporting platoons advanced in 'worms', sections in file preceded by scouts, suggesting the more flexible tactics of the Second World War. Communications depended on fragile telephone lines, but the optimistic Montagu drew confidence from the contact aircraft, 'which went up and down the German lines peppering them with machine guns. It seemed to me master of the whole situation and a strong link with the high command.'[35]

Clausewitz's maxim that war is a resistant medium was never so true as on the Western Front. Artillery fire was an essential accompaniment of every attack, but it pulverized the soil and wrecked drainage systems. Passchendaele was 'a mass of shell holes, flooded to a depth of several feet, a path had to be picked over ground only less impassable'.[36] Landmarks vanished, baffling the advancing infantry:

> the concrete building shown on the map at VARLET FARM, proved to be a concrete pill-box some 200 yards further east. . . VARLET FARM did not exist in reality and, except for a few scattered bricks, all the farm buildings had completely disappeared.[37]

Troops could neither reconnoitre nor stay in the line while remaining fit to advance. Battalions preparing for the Ancre offensive fell from 700 to 500 bayonets in a month:

> Autumn had set in and we had a lot of rain and the trenches and land had become a quagmire. To make matters worse it had turned bitterly cold. . . we were invariably soaked to the skin, and often up to our waist in mud and water for hours on end. It's amazing that anyone could possibly survive in such conditions.[38]

Uncertain of support, troops staggered into action under the innumerable appliances of modern warfare: 'Calls us blooming light infantry they does,' soliloquized one old soldier, 'I feels more like a Christmas tree.'[39] Marines floundering in Passchendaele's mud lost the barrage, allowing the enemy to leave their concrete pill-boxes and open fire.[40] The morass then swallowed the casualties:

> Indeed it was only the fortunate ones who managed to get back after being wounded. It was said that 50% of the wounded lost their lives getting back to the dressing stations, as it was only possible to walk on the wooden tracks called duckboards. This was the reputation of Passchendaele and Ypres.[41]

The Somme had been no better. Two thirds of 1st RMLI's fatal casualties on the Ancre were 'missing'. Sometimes mud prevented fighting altogether. A thaw in the Flesquières salient in 1918 drove both sides above ground: 'two lines of troops, within hailing distance, walking about in the open, lighting fires to cook food and waiting till the trenches could be cleared.' One German approached 1st RMLI to trade tobacco, and 'arrange a fraternal party with us. It took some time to convince him that we had to decline the invitation.'[42]

The great obstacle besides mud was ferocious enemy resistance. Firmly entrenched in the richest corner of France, the Germans showed no sign of leaving. Half the Marines' casualties for the battle of the Ancre fell to German artillery crossing no-man's-land, including all four of 1st RMLI's company commanders killed. Neighbouring units were held up and the leading waves melted away under enfilading fire. Following in support, 2nd RMLI became entangled with remnants of 1st RMLI, instead of leap-frogging through to the next objective. Nevertheless bombing parties of 188 Brigade secured Hood Battalion's left flank, before the advance on Beaucourt next day that won Freyberg's VC, and has overshadowed the Marines' part in the battle. The Marines at Gavrelle were victims of a hopeless underestimate of the enemy. Their attack was unsupported, the wire uncut and the Germans ready. A strongpoint left over from a previous attack annihilated 1st RMLI, while casualties in 2nd RMLI were so high that their fate remains obscure. Three companies reached the enemy trenches, but were cut off by counter-attacks and all killed or captured. Anson Battalion watched helplessly as 'khaki figures crossed the ditch behind the enemy line – Marines with their hands up.'[43] Only 'B' Company held out around the Windmill as thirteen separate counter-attacks flowed around them. The Germans further refined their system of elastic defence at Passchendaele. Every shell hole was under fire from machine guns deployed in depth. The few Marines that reached their objectives found themselves out of touch with the barrage and one another. Elements of 2nd RMLI crossed the Paddebeek, urged on by the dying words of their four times wounded Company Commander, but could not hold their ground:

> The Marines' rifles were so choked with mud that practically none of them could be fired, but the [counter-]attack was beaten off by the machine guns and, when the machine guns had become clogged with mud, by the rifles of the machine gunners.[44]

Both flanks in the air, the detachment fell back with heavy losses including all their officers: 'what a remnant, just a handful of officers and two companies of ORs. . . An English paper we received sometime later had but half a dozen lines comment or official report of this stunt.'[45]

Not all attacks were so devoid of military or journalistic consequence. Hundreds of Germans surrendered at Beaucourt:

> It was an amazing sight, they came out of their holes, tearing off their equipment. I myself rounded up at least fifty, waving my revolver and shouting "schnell". They offered us food and souvenirs and were only too anxious to propitiate us.[46]

At Miraumont 188's Brigadier called down artillery fire on the inevitable counter-attack with a telephone to each ear, reducing the sector to a 'shambles of German dead'. 1st RMLI's CO reported 'Boches bolting like rabbits', and his indiscretion passed up the chain of command to earn a rare telegram of congratulations directly from Sir Douglas Haig.

The war exacted an emotional as well as a physical toll. Newly arrived with 2nd RMLI Private Walter Popham noticed the change in men he had known at the RND depot at Blandford, and the strange habits of trench veterans who 'stayed up the whole night playing cards by the light of a candle fixed on a steel helmet'. He was even more shaken by the contrast between the cheery bus-loads who rumbled up slushy roads to Passchendaele, waving their rifles and singing parodies of popular songs, and those who returned to 'Dirty Bucket' Camp: 'occasionally a stray man came in as from a wilderness to the fold, & told awful news brokenly. One I can remember was in a bad nervous state, and two men were told off to keep him continual company.'[47] The motivation that sustained men through such nightmares baffled 2nd RMLI's Naval Surgeon, who watched them shrieking with laughter in the divisional cinema, the night after facing almost certain death.

A few seemed born to war. Major F.W. Lumsden RMA left the relative safety of the Howitzer Brigade and General Staff to win the DSO and three bars for front-line reconnaissance work. Serving with 32nd Division at Francilly-Sélency in 1917 he was awarded the third Royal Marine VC of the war, for bringing off five captured guns through the barrage and blowing up a sixth. Lumsden was finally shot through the head in a night action while commanding a Brigade, but 'there was hardly a day when he did not expose himself to danger.'[48] Lumsden was clearly exceptional, but the loneliness of the modern battlefield demanded similar qualities from all: 'the unbelievable obstinacy, courage and endurance of the private soldier along the whole line of battle which turned the scale'.[49]

RMLI battalions enjoyed some moral advantages over other infantry-men. Walter Popham and his mates volunteered rather than wait to be conscripted, thinking the Royal Marines 'a better Corps than some'. They were introduced gradually to the rigours of military life. Universally admired drill sergeants at Deal made way for merciless instructors at 'wild and bleak' Blandford, physical training 'a "hardening of horror". . . feeling your blood freeze up in your hands, arms, ears, and feet'. Like the Guards and Dominion divisions the RND trained overseas drafts at its own Infantry Base Depot outside Calais and returned men to the familiar surroundings of their own battalions. Less-favoured formations took replacements where they could, regardless of cap badge or ignorance of divisional practice. Just in case, the RND distributed 'Tips on Trench

Warfare', a pocket-sized reference card full of useful advice: 'Don't push your rifle muzzle into the side of the trench; Don't stand behind loopholes; Don't forget to use earth after going to the latrine'.[50] Popham joined his battalion at misnamed Cushy-la-Tour, where route marches left older men staggering like 'vessels in a rough sea'.[51] Night exercises with real Very lights added realism to a programme nearer late twentieth-century Commando training, than the formal drill of earlier Marines.

Royal Marines on the Western Front possessed a solidarity based on defiance of military convention. The Corps suffered a double blow when a shell hit General Paris reconnoitring the Ancre trenches, Paris losing his leg and the RND its bulwark against the Army. Immortalized in verse as 'that shite Shute', his successor had no time for unconventional soldiers and told them so: 'After inspection we were formed up into a large square and he sat on his horse in the middle. He then tore us off an enormous strip, We were the roughest, raggedest, scruffiest bunch he had ever set eyes on, we didn't salute army officers and discipline was unknown. All this was going to be changed.'[52] Shute reported scathingly upon seamen and marines whose only experience of the sea was crossing the English Channel. The Fleet had taken the best men; NCOs were old and below pre-war RM standards; training and physique were poor. Without improved cadres Shute predicted: 'the two Marine battalions will be such a discredit to the Marines that they will cease to exist.'[53] The RND survived Shute's departure to become one of the BEF's 'Stormer divisions', while the RMLI continued to assert their unique identity. They grew beards in the trenches and went ashore to the estaminet, 'imbibing the various qualities of French wines, some of them doubtful, and all extortionately dear. . . egg and chips for F1.75. . . and strange coffee'. French farmers, however, treated their involuntary guests kindly, 'and tried to cheer us in the cause.'[54]

The individual Marine's devotion to his mates underpinned more exalted loyalties. Walter Popham was 'quite prepared for the progress of duty' on going overseas, 'having a good range of chums I did not wish to be separated from, and also imbued more or less with the spirit of bravado, and will to do my bit.'[55] A naval surgeon noted how this solidarity made any exertion acceptable: 'Call digging a "fatigue" and the "grouse" becomes pronounced; call it a "working party" and there is hardly a murmur. Tell them they are going over the top tomorrow, and no man, however ill he may feel, reports sick.'[56] This was not just officer's hyperbole. Walter Popham remained in the frozen Flesquières salient with trench fever, rather than abandon the other signallers. A veteran of Gallipoli regretted leaving it all behind after a 'Blighty one' at the Ancre: 'taking the rough with the smooth (and believe me some of it was rough) I had enjoyed life in the service and it was an experience I wouldn't have missed for the world.'[57]

Victory

Nineteen eighteen contrasted sharply with the RND's first year on the Western Front. The German March offensive drove great dents in the line, until the Allies recovered to chase the Germans back across occupied France. Like other British battalions, the RMLI, after a painful apprenticeship, showed themselves masters of the battlefield, but it was the Germans' turn first. 2nd RMLI were near Cambrai on the morning of 21 March:

> a terrific barrage opened around us, more terrible than we had ever dreamt of previously. . . At times even the candles in the deepest and most secure part of our dug-out were blown out. . . the world seemed to groan, howl, screech, and rock.[58]

Phosgene streamed into dugouts, where gas-helmeted figures sat like 'caged rats with fear upon us all and a sense of hideous impotence'. The Germans avoided attacking 188 Brigade frontally, breaking through the Division on the right, and forcing the Marines to retreat. Both battalions lost heavily in prisoners, as storm-troopers infiltrated around them, almost cutting off the Regimental Aid Post: '"Boche is in our front line – two companies have surrendered, run for your life". We dived for our packs and gear, and I leading the way, we ran like rabbits.'[59] Perhaps 120 from each battalion rallied beyond the box barrage, but failing to re-establish a continuous line continued to withdraw. Living on cigarettes from abandoned canteens, they left a trail of blazing dumps and ditched tanks. Casualties had to be carried or left: 'the struggles of wounded men for liberty beggar description. Some walked or stumbled, unsteady from loss of blood. . . Occasional motors carried men on the wings, & bonnet of the car, while others looked on, and read to themselves hopelessness.'[60] On 25th March 188 Brigade covered the withdrawal across the Ancre, of evil memory:

> the battle was absolute confusion. Our left and right were wildly in the air and no one knew anything. . . We slowly backed across the hideous old battlefield till we reached Thiepval Ridge. . . a terrible scene as long lines of straggling and demoralised troops were streaming in.[61]

Next day 2nd RMLI showed their 'ability to stand a hard knock as well as to give one',[62] signalling the end of the retreat. They were resting on cobbles at Martinsart, when 'a hooting and roaring aroused us to find the enemy had broken through and was swarming up the road. . . With wild yells officers and men rushed off to drive them back. . . as if devils had been put in them.'[63] After a week of frustration and retreat, 'a joint mob of RMLI and Ansons dashed off literally shouting with joy to drive back the Hun.' The recapture of Aveluy Wood, 'due entirely to the jaded ranks of the 2nd RMLI and Ansons. . . had the instant effect of giving a great "buck up" to the morale of the battalion.'[64] Renewed optimism possessed survivors of the retreat, although lack of replacements compelled the RMLI battalions to amalgamate on 29 April: 'it looked as though the enemy had exhausted his offensive, and we had held him. Things had quietened down – very little gun fire. His quick advance meant that his supplies and communications were difficult on account of the devastated country.'[65] Convincing Allied victories at Soissons and Amiens in August changed attitudes to the war. Instead of digging rear defences, the RMLI began training for open warfare. The rebuilt battalion went up the line at Les Essarts on 18 August to find 'a new pandemonium, for most deadly fighting commenced, with tanks and aircraft'. Operations assumed a modern aspect. Brigade signallers carried loop wireless sets, instead of Sergeant Meatyard's clumsy wires and panels. Aircraft dropped ammunition to Marine spearheads, progress measuring kilometres instead of yards: 'No definite sleep now, as things were quite uncertain, and trench warfare had ceased.' September opened with the fall of the redoubtable Hindenberg line, after a 10 mile night approach over shattered terrain: 'Marvellously built trenches, half as deep as some railway cuttings. . . and dug outs a perfect maze capable of holding thousands of men, undoubtedly the best on the Western Front'. Royal Marine machine-gunners avenged Passchendaele when 'the queer fellow actually hopelessly counter-attacked. . . our machine guns popped them down like rabbits.' At the end of the month the RND stormed the Canal du Nord, alongside the Canadians and Guards, in a complex three-stage operation unthinkable the previous year. The same night RM Divisional Engineers bridged the Canal de l'Escaut, 10 kilometres further on. Men returning from leave found the advance 'so swift that we felt we would never catch up our units'.[66]

The RMLI's last set-piece of the war was at Niergnies on 8–9 October 1918. Leapfrogging arrangements that bogged down by the Ancre and Paddebeek worked perfectly, demonstrating the proficiency of staffs and troops, and the decline in German fighting power. Supported by tanks, Marines encircled defending machine-gunners and drove off a counter-attack supported by German armour. A sergeant stopped a German tank at 100 yards with a Vickers machine gun, perhaps the Corps' first anti-tank kill: 'By this time the prisoners appeared to exceed our numbers. . . one old man who was long interrogated must have been nearly sixty years of age, and was in great fear of being murdered.'[67] After a short rest the RND rejoined the pursuit, along roads heavy with autumn mud, 'the Queer fellow seeming to move faster away than we could follow'. Wanton devastation, booby traps and a recently evacuated camp for French civilian hostages left no doubt about the nature of the enemy: 'far better that this part of the earth be forgotten entirely so complete was the destruction and ruin.'[68] The Germans fought to the end, inflicting unnecessary casualties, before fading away with a last display of coloured flares. The Armistice of 11 November found the RMLI once more on Belgian territory near Mons, 'on the starboard bow of the army'. A single officer from all those mobilized in August 1914 was still with the battalion, the original 4,000 rifles whittled away to 200. Most of them had fallen in a sustained struggle ashore, that some might think the province of the regular army. General Paris' joking question about the proper nature of a Marine remained unanswered.

Well done, Vindictive!

The amalgamation of April 1918 was not just the consequence of losses during the March retreat. A new 4th RM Battalion had absorbed all available replacements, to take part in a dramatic coup. Admiral Roger Keyes' daring and well-planned raid on the U-boat base at Zeebrugge on St George's Day 1918 fulfilled essential amphibious requirements: swift yet thorough preparation, secrecy and surprise. It was a portent of how future Royal Marines would come to operate.

The concept followed Napoleonic precedent. Marines were to land on the Zeebrugge Mole to cover demolition parties of seamen, while blockships and a submarine crammed with explosives substituted for fireships. The Battalion concentrated at Deal in February 1917, with the traditional three RMLI companies. Many were volunteers, tired of swinging round a buoy at Scapa Flow. Close-quarters fighting at Zeebrugge would make a decided change from battleship practice. Realistic training with ball ammunition, smoke floats, flares and torches went on day and night, 'as darkness was essential to accustom all ranks to the conditions of the operations ahead'.[69] Bomb-throwing on the beach drew complaints about damage to Deal's invasion defences. Every combination of circumstances was rehearsed over a taped layout of the Mole that 'for purposes of secrecy. . . was supposed to represent a canal bed in France that had been drained'. Nobody slept out, to the frustration of recently married Sergeant Harry Wright: 'We cannot find out what lay we are on, but some seem to think we are only down here to defend the coast against an invader.' There was much PT, snapshooting at close range, and 'commando type training such as disarming sentries'. Harry Wright was unimpressed:

> The NCOs have to drill with the men and are entirely turned over to the depot staff who have been skulking down here for ages and now using to the best of their ability all the sarcasm they can bring forth. This to men who have fought in France.[70]

Perhaps the bull was part of the cover. In March the Royal Marines' Colonel-in-Chief, King George V, visited Deal, directing that in future the best all-round recruit should be styled 'King's Badgeman', and wear the Royal Cypher. Only after embarkation on 6 April was the real operation explained, with a detailed model of Zeebrugge Mole. Secrecy was maintained, despite cancellation of the attack on 11 April:

> These disappointments and the strain were very trying, especially as the men had been trained to a pitch and then left to wait on board. . . Everything possible was done in the way of amusements and games but there could be no communication with the shore.[71]

Two RMLI companies sailed in the old cruiser HMS *Vindictive*, barricaded with splinter-proof mattresses, and armed with howitzers and Stokes mortars. Chatham Company sailed in *Iris*, a Mersey ferry. Her sister HMS *Daffodil* carried demolition parties, to land across *Vindictive*, via thirteen ramps or 'brows'. The men fought in light order with rubber-soled gym shoes, life belts and steel helmets, and carried Lewis guns, Mills bombs, flame-throwers and coshes.[72] Orders emphasized 'the idea of carrying the operation through with the Bayonet: Rifle Fire, Machine Gun Fire, and Bombthrowing are only to be resorted to when necessary to break down enemy opposition.' This can be seen as an outdated obsession with cold steel, or recognition of the need to maintain momentum along the bare concrete mole. *Vindictive* would provide covering fire, guided by red Verys from leading units.[73]

The assault ships were only a quarter of a mile from the Mole when the wind shifted, clearing the artificial smoke screening their approach: 'Then the searchlights got onto us properly; we were lit up like daylight. . .

I had cotton wool in my ears, and it sounded as if someone had pulled the props from under the sky and it fell down.'[74] Several shells hit the crowded decks, causing heavy losses, before *Vindictive* reached the quayside. Lacking intimate experience of shellfire the CO and Second-in-Command ignored the Adjutant's advice to keep down and were killed by the same shell standing together on the bridge. Much special equipment was smashed and the gun detachments killed, except for the after 11-inch howitzer crew and Sergeant Finch RMA, overlooking the sea wall in *Vindictive's* foretop. Finch poured in an encouraging fire from the pom-pom, as survivors of the run-in scrambled ashore over two remaining brows, climbing 20 feet down the sea wall on hook ropes. Some turned right to block the mole against German counter-attacks from the shore. Others tried to silence a troublesome German destroyer alongside the mole, or cleared No. 3 Shed opposite *Vindictive*:

> We had a grand chance of chucking bombs in the door of this dump-house, as we had splendid cover. Whilst amusing myself here, a portion of concrete was removed out of the Mole by the explosion of the submarine. . . I could not attempt to begin to describe what this operation sounded like. It was the very last word in noise.[75]

Further demolition seemed unnecessary as 'the defenders were doing more damage with their own shell-fire than we were likely to do.' *Vindictive* had overshot the battery at the seaward end of the mole, affording the grim prospect of 'attacking a prepared position across some two hundred yards of flat pavement devoid of any form of cover'.[76] Captain E. Bamford, awarded the DSO for Jutland, had set out on this forlorn hope with Portsmouth Company, when *Daffodil's* siren sounded the recall thirty minutes early. Calmly the Marines fell back over ladders placed against the sea wall, taking their wounded with them through a hail of shrapnel. Gangways heaved up and down as shells burst between *Vindictive* and the sea wall, 'not an encouraging prospect for our retirement'.[77] Private James Feeney threw his rifle on board, scrambled after it and went over to the starboard side, away from the sea wall:

> It was terrible here, and I was mad with myself. I was getting nervous and funky from looking at the dead and dying. I threw off my equipment and gas-mask, and sat down next to poor Tubby Smith; he had one leg clean knocked off, and was talking bravely. There were some deeds done that night that make words seem light, and not able to touch on the thought you wish to express.[78]

Vindictive pushed off without further damage, flames pouring from her funnels, but *Iris* suffered a direct hit and caught fire. Intended to moor ahead of *Vindictive*, she never landed her Marines, who still lost forty-eight dead, in a one-sided exchange of fire, terminated when the bridge was shot away.

Back at Dover the *Vindictives* found themselves the 'star turn', cheered by all vessels in port: 'I saw one old chap stop half-way through a spit he was letting go when his eyes rested on *Vindictive*'s funnels.' Other ships returning from the raid, 'all seemed to forget that they were there at all, and only looked at our battered old hulk, and cheered and waved frantically.'[79] The battalion was less euphoric, having suffered nearly 50 per cent casualties: 366 out of 740 embarked. In few engagements has a British ship lost so high a proportion, and in fewer still has she succeeded in face of such losses.[80] 'We felt that our part of the operation had been a complete failure. We had lost many good men with what seemed to us no result. We felt extremely despondent.'[81] Keyes cheered them up, claiming the Marines had created a splendid diversion for the blockships, which now lay diagonally across the canal mouth at Zeebrugge. Whatever the raid's strategic merits, it provided a much-needed boost to public morale just after the March retreat:

> the newspapers said it was very good, and asked us to repeat the dose often. Those blessed quill drivers, I should like to see them on a stunt like that, and to be told before they have got their wind to repeat the dose![82]

The King recognized the 4th Battalion's collective bravery with two VCs, chosen by secret ballot. Captain Bamford 'whose totally unperturbed manner had the most reassuring effect on all who came in contact with him that night',[83] was selected from the officers, while the RMLI majority remembered Sergeant Finch's steadfast support and chose him for the other ranks. Perversely, the Corps has commemorated Zeebrugge by never forming another 4th Battalion. Amphibious landings were another matter. Long before Sergeant Finch died of old age, a Yeoman Warder at the Tower of London, surprise assaults from the sea, in stranger craft than *Vindictive*, had become the métier of other Marine formations.

CHAPTER ELEVEN

Where Sea Meets Shore

THE Royal Marines' evolution from Sea Soldiers to Special Forces would have astonished most inter-war observers. Until 1939 the first priority of the Corps was naval gunnery, while planners mindful of the carnage on Gallipoli's 'V' Beach remained suspicious of amphibious operations. The Naval Staff College would only contemplate landing lightly armed raiding forces, never 'large masses of troops. . . encumbered with equipment necessary for a land campaign'.[1] No immediate change followed the collapse of the twenty-year truce with Germany. The Corps resisted conventional military commitments, while missing alternative opportunities 'per terram'. It took political intervention at the highest level to free Marine energy and expertise to make an essential contribution to victory, and to meeting the challenges of the post-war world.

Marking Time

The quarter century of uncertainty that preceded this happy sequel was not the fault of more thoughtful Marine officers. Hardly had ink dried on the 1919 peace treaties when a conscious pursuit of a distinctly Royal Marine identity began that would continue throughout the twentieth century. *Globe and Laurel* correspondents rightly argued '*a policy*' was essential for the Corps to survive post-war retrenchment. Rejecting recent experience of continental warfare, they also turned their backs on sea service. Naval actions appeared unlikely after the German Fleet's surrender and sailors were perfectly capable of what military duties were required afloat. Marines were urged instead to consider the 'unsettled state of the world', which offered 'innumerable opportunities for the employment of a specially trained force, such as the Royal Marines'. When training with the Army they should not be treated like 'mere infantry of the line' as they had on the Western Front, but 'given duties of the nature likely to be required of them, preferably in combined operations involving a descent or raid on a coast, and as advanced base troops'. Marine weapons should be rifle and Lewis gun, although 'rifle grenades might be effective against Savages'.[2]

Distrust of the Army cannot have been diminished by the Royal Marines' unfortunate share in the anti-Bolshevik intervention of 1918–19 in North Russia. An RM Field Force equipped with specially designed Arctic gear were so mishandled they petitioned their officers in terms reminiscent of Queen Anne's reign:

> If after tomorrow's parade we have no satisfaction as regards going home we will 'down tools' for forty-eight hours. If nothing happens then we will commandeer the first train in the direction of Murmansk. . . We have been nothing but a dung heap for the Army, and have only been wanted, when there was any work to be done, or something lost.[3]

A newly formed 6th Battalion RMLI replaced the Field Force. Its young soldiers, untrained except in ceremonial duties, bungled an attack that sea service officers lacking experience of fighting ashore failed to press. An artillery officer then told them to get the hell out of it and they misguidedly took him at his word. Unsympathetic and possibly illegal courts martial found two RM officers and eighty-nine other ranks guilty of various offences short of mutiny. None of the thirteen death sentences were carried out and all those imprisoned were released early. This heavy-handed treatment of a 'second rate but not cowardly or mutinous' battalion was symptomatic of poor inter-service relations, and naval protests against an undeclared war. The poor performance at Murmansk contrasts with HMS *Kent*'s detachment who volunteered to take a 6-inch gun 4,000 miles by train, to support White Russian forces in Siberia, 'a stirring example of good leadership, improvisation, and high morale under the most trying and unpredictable circumstances, in the highest traditions of the Corps'.[4]

The debate over the Corps' future resurfaced in the 1920s. Calls for an end to embarkation of Marines for naval gunnery urged the Royal Navy to recognize that 'the first use of the Royal Marines is as its striking force.'[5] Economic constraints frustrated this desirable step: 'the Army was reduced practically to a police force; the Royal Air Force was almost abolished; and the Royal Navy and Royal Marines were similarly and drastically cut. . . the average Marine spending more of his time at sea than the average seaman.'[6] The Madden Report of 1924 accepted the idea of an independent striking force, but was unwilling to drop naval gunnery and the Admiralty could not fund both.[7] As the Corps struggled to maintain 'per mare' commitments, training 'per terram' became almost impossible. While frustrated officers sought employment elsewhere, the Royal Marines were not even preparing for war, let alone amphibious operations: 'From a military point of view. . . the Corps was living on tradition.'[8] There were some gleams of light. The Mobile Naval Base Defence Organization conducted experimental landings over Eastney beach from 1923 onwards. It ran trials with the first purpose-built Motor Landing Craft or MLC, and practised defending anchorages with quaintly obsolescent ordnance and a naïve disregard of concealment. MNBDO did not represent an offensive amphibious capability, but it extended the Royal Navy's reach, allowing it to occupy advanced naval bases such as Alexandria during the Abyssinian crisis in 1936. Britain's evident amphibious weakness inspired calls for an Inter-Services Training and Development Centre, which opened in July 1938 with a Royal Marine adjutant. ISTDC observations of a much-derided exercise at Slapton Sands, using Crimean landing techniques, inspired two crucial pieces of equipment: the Landing Craft Assault designed to carry an infantry platoon, and the Landing Ship Infantry (Large) capable of launching a flotilla of LCAs. Prototypes of the smaller craft were available in August 1939, three weeks before the Second World War began.

At that point the British neither possessed nor needed a capability for offensive amphibious operations. Nevertheless amphibious formations absorbed many HO Royal Marines. Civilian tradesmen built up MNBDO, while an RM Brigade was formed 'to perform, if necessary, certain amphibious tasks which did not require the full supporting weapons or the "services" of an Army Division', typically 'the seizure of islands or bases necessary for naval control of sea communications'.[9] Neither formation achieved its potential. After Dunkirk, coastal batteries and home air defence fully occupied the MNBDO, while the RM Brigade was one of the few trained formations left in the UK for counter-invasion purposes. Expanded into a Division of two small brigades, the formation was earmarked for divers secret operations which never came off, against the Azores, Cape Verde or Canaries. Marines participated in an abortive attempt on Dakar in September 1940, but never fired a shot. Early morning tea onboard passenger liners not yet converted to a war footing, long menus and white-coated stewards underlined the lack of serious preparation:

> hardly anyone had any idea of what we were proposing to take on. We
> did not realise in those days either that landing in ship's lifeboats towed

by motor boats with inadequate engines was not a good way to carry out such operations!

Staff cars blocked Bren gun carriers and medical stores and one CO was retrieved from the bilges dead drunk: 'If it had not been for Churchill calling off the enterprise,' a participant surmised in the 1970s, 'I would not be writing this.'[10] MNBDO suffered similar frustration:

> picking mushrooms to help with our rations. We had lectures on what MNBDO's War Role was. When an enemy port was captured we were to move in and consolidate. This never happened. . . It is best to draw a veil over this two years.[11]

Back in Devon 101 RM Brigade's anti-tank gunners resented their obsolete 2-pounders, 'confounded pop guns. . . just not good enough and we all knew it.'[12] Hard trained to commando standards, bored infantry hunted rabbits with Bren guns or set fire to the bus returning from the fleshpots of Exmouth. The ultimate injustice was substitution of army units for MNBDO and 102 RM Brigade in landings in Madagascar in May 1942. Intended to pre-empt Japanese capture of the Vichy French naval base at Diego Suarez, Operation Ironclad was ironically placed under command of General Robert Sturges, GOC RM Division, who deplored the effect of his disappearance on active operations with another formation: '101 and 102 RM Brigades had been raised for just such an operation as "Ironclad". . . All ranks of these brigades were eager to see active service, and had suffered many disappointments.'[13]

HMS *Ramillies'* Marine detachment provided slight compensation. When the Army's advance stalled, Sturges asked the Royal Navy for a diversionary raid in the French rear. Within thirty-five minutes fifty Marines were ready in steel helmets, with 2-in mortar and anti-tank rifle, to go aboard HMS *Anthony*, the destroyer tasked with running the gauntlet of minefields and shore batteries into the darkened French naval base at Antsirane. As she backed stern first onto the quayside Marines scrambled over her depth-charges, and raced inland through naval workshops and the cooking pots of French native infantry, until they found the brass door plate that helpfully identified their objective: 'Direction d'Artillerie'. Equally helpful, the office switchboard had flashed news of the Marines' arrival to the front line, drawing off its defenders. Bursts of machine-gun fire made way for fervent declarations of loyalty to the Allied cause. Prisoners poured in, the detachment palming off 500 of them on the Army in exchange for something to eat. Next day Sturges rubbed it in, as a tired but immaculate detachment provided a guard of honour for the formal capitulation. Soldiers unaccustomed to the Corps on parade 'looked in astonishment at their red bands and white cap covers, their clean tropical rig and the officers with their archaic swords and wondered why these old-fashioned soldiers were marching in ceremonial fours.'[14]

Hit and Run

While dedicated amphibious formations missed the boat, smaller ad hoc forces of Royal Marines saw frequent employment on the maritime fringes of the war. They followed patterns set by earlier Marines: meeting short-lived emergencies, covering landings by regular military units and all too often their evacuation. Small Marine detachments displayed a talent for 'petite guerre', neglected by larger more formal organizations.

German invasions of Scandinavia and the Low Countries in early 1940 demanded prompt action to forestall them at potential naval bases in the North Atlantic, or rescue heads of government and their gold reserves. Royal Marines of Sandall Force occupied the Faroes in April, Sturges Force doing likewise at Iceland in May. Neither party saw action, which may have been fortunate as Sturges' 2nd RM Battalion had less than a month's training. Their most dramatic moment involved a fire extinguisher, when the German Consul's wife in Reykjavik, still in her nightdress, set light to his secret papers. Excursions to Boulogne and Holland were equally bloodless, 50-year-old pensioners despatched to the Hook in khaki and blue, like a rerun of Ostend in 1914. A covering party for naval demolition teams at Calais (25–27 May) were less fortunate, sixty casualties out of eighty portending worse things to follow.

The concurrent Norwegian campaign was as 'unhappy as a campaign could be, unplanned, unprepared, divergent instructions, non-tactical loading of ships, inadequate equipment and intelligence'.[15] Marines and bluejackets from capital ships in refit set off for Trondheim: 'a truly comic opera operation, except that it was nothing comic [for] the men engaged in it'. The codename for this superannuated naval brigade, scraped together 'with no more than the usual shortages and omissions', betrayed the ill-conceived nature of the whole affair: 'of all curious names given to this campaign some ambitious some allegorical none more inappropriate than this "Operation PRIMROSE"'.[16] MLCs based in the MNBDO depot ship *Mashobra* mounted some bold assault landings at Narvik with an unlikely mixture of Foreign Legionnaires and French tanks, 'discharging cannon and machine guns all over the landscape', but lost all their landing craft

in the evacuation that followed the German invasion of France.[17] A Force
Primrose officer wrote of 'ghastly failure' in central Norway:

> German bombing gets more accurate and intense. . . news trickling back
> down the line tells of battalions routed, of equipment abandoned, of
> scattered survivors straggling back to rear units in a condition of hysteria.
> Their story is always the same: countless machine guns, tanks, and bombs,
> bombs, bombs.

The Marines' bridgehead defence ensured stable rearguards for the
inevitable evacuation:

> the morale and spirit of the men was magnificent throughout. Nothing
> seemed to disconcert them. . . There was always great argument among
> the Lewis gunners as to whose turn it was. . . and many bad words when
> the planes didn't come low enough to make it worthwhile opening fire.[18]

Perhaps it was fortunate they were unaware of plans to abandon them to
surrender or be interned in Sweden. Ordered to hurry aboard the waiting
destroyers without his 3.7-inch pack howitzers, the battery commander
responded that they were naval guns, and he would never abandon them,
generalized memorably as: 'It is not the policy of the Corps to leave its
equipment in enemy hands.'[19]

The Corps did leave equipment in enemy hands in Crete in May and
June 1941 – perhaps the darkest point of the war for the British; over a
quarter of Royal Marine deaths for World War II occurred during 1941.
MNBDO I had sailed for the Middle East to create a second Scapa Flow
at Suda Bay, but only 2,000 men out of 5,000 had arrived before German
airborne attacks began on 20 May:

> there was a complete absence of our own air support, formations of
> German bombers and fighters kept up a continuous circuit and "blitztag"
> of the front and back areas. . . By day no movement of any sort was
> possible.

MNBDO anti-aircraft gunners fought until their guns were knocked out
then joined signallers and searchlight crews fighting as infantry, but 'the
Germans were armed with Tommy guns, hand grenades, and mortars,
and when once having taken up a defensive position were very difficult
to dislodge especially by troops armed only with a rifle.'[20] As British positions crumbled, a composite Marine unit covered the retreat, with automatic weapons taken from demoralized soldiers. 'S' Battalion were among
the last to retire from the hills overlooking the evacuation beaches at

Sphakia. Marines with loaded rifles prevented an ugly rush for the boats but were themselves sacrificed. Admiral Cunningham, C-in-C Mediterranean, found it 'particularly galling that a large part of the men left to surrender consisted of the Royal Marines, who fought so gallant a rearguard action.'[21] Two groups made their own arrangements, escaping in broken-down landing craft. Jury rigged with improvized masts, and steered by men swimming over the side, their week-long voyages from Sphakia to North Africa were a triumph of fortitude and luck, one famished party landing 'dead in the centre of an RASC camp, who started feeding us right away'.[22]

The fall of Singapore to the Japanese in February 1942 had no happy endings. Amidst circumstances as hopeless as those at Cartagena 200 years before, Royal Marine survivors from *Repulse* and *Prince of Wales* upheld the reputation of the Corps through the worst of trials: their ships sunk under them, their senior officers flown out as resistance collapsed, the only foreseeable outcome a Japanese prisoner of war camp. Their varied assignments were typical of the Marines' transitional role in the 1940s: dockyard sentries, Special Service troops i.e. Commandos, and finally reinforcements for 2nd Argyll and Sutherland Highlanders, collectively known as the Plymouth Argylls. The serio-comic title devalues the steadfastness with which the scratch unit faced disaster. The Marines had ten days to absorb the lessons of six months' jungle training and fighting before they were thrown into the battle for Singapore Island. Unimpressed by Australian stragglers who advised them to 'get back out of it before the Japs come', they held out against Japanese tanks and encirclement. At night they organized all-round defence, 'with orders to use bayonets only, for fear of shooting our own troops in the dark'.[23] In grim silence they ignored jitter parties who called on them to surrender: 'The Japs wore all sorts of rigs. Some were in shorts, some with equipment, others without; some wore only sarongs. You couldn't tell whether they were Japs, or Malays, or Chinese.'[24] Ignoring the example of 'numbers of troops, largely Australian, to force their way aboard merchant ships at the docks', the Marines did their duty to the last. On 15 February the battalion surrendered as part of the general shipwreck: 'There was no one left to put up a show, they were all squandered up.'[25]

A final tale of courage in adversity was that of Force Viper. MNBDO I had trickled out to the Far East, where eternal garrison duty persuaded 102 Marines to volunteer for 'special service of a hazardous nature'. In March 1942 they joined British forces retreating through Burma to India, with half a dozen river craft sporting Vickers guns, crates of beer and (by special permission) White Ensigns – a twentieth-century counterpart to the Irrawaddy flotilla that had opened up the country in the 1880s. Force Viper's activities combined traditional river work with pointers to the future: ferrying pack mules and bullock carts across the Irrawaddy on rafts, covered by a Royal Marine anti-aircraft guardship; sabotaging oil installations; and destroying powered river craft to delay the Japanese advance. The strategic value of their efforts can be gauged from the Japanese threat to cut any Royal Marine prisoners into pieces and roast them. Ten weeks after leaving Rangoon and 500 miles from the sea, the Marines destroyed their motorboats beside the Chindwin River, and began the 200-mile trek to the Indian border. Forty-eight of the original detachment made it, still carrying their rifles.

The Great Reformation

As the smoke of blazing oil tanks hung over Singapore and Rangoon, a new type of Royal Marine unit was taking shape. The birth of the Royal Marine Commandos, by happy chance, coincided with the end of the war's catastrophic opening, and the start of the Allied counter-offensive that would carry Marines across the beaches of Italy and Normandy, to the Baltic.

The expulsion of British forces from mainland Europe in 1940–41 caused a strategic revolution. Far from having no amphibious warfare requirement, British strategists became completely dependent on such operations. A fortnight after Dunkirk the Chiefs of Staff issued a secret directive on 17 June 1940, initiating raiding operations: 'to harass the enemy and cause him to disperse his forces, and to create material damage. . . on the coastline of Northern Norway to the western limit of German-occupied France'. They foresaw 'development and production of special landing craft and equipment', and envisaged three brigade groups preparing for combined operations 'as soon as they can be equipped'.[26] The first commander of the Combined Operations Organization was a Marine, Lieutenant-General A.G.B. Bourne, HMS *Tiger*'s OCRM at Jutland and now AGRM, but the effort was beyond Corps resources. The first independent raiding companies, christened Commandos after Boer guerrilla fighters of the South African War, were Army volunteers, while Mr Churchill decided Bourne lacked the high profile that Combined Operations required, replacing him, first with Admiral Keyes of Zeebrugge, and later with Lord Louis Mountbatten. Not until February 1942 was 'The RM Commando' formed at Deal under Lt-Col 'Tiger' Picton-

Phillipps, erstwhile adjutant at ISTDC. Most recruits were bored RM Division HO rates: 'it looked as though the war would be over without me – so with several others I volunteered for anything which came on the noticeboard.' Selection was rigorous:

> The platoon commander and his sergeant would be the judge on whom they wanted to keep as suitable men. If you were not fully confident about an individual or his attitude was not right – off he went back to his unit.

Marines already considered themselves 'something special', a suspicion confirmed by Commando training in the Scottish Highlands: 'At the end of three months I believed I was better than anything else and the training was such that you began to feel that you were one of the lucky ones to be a marine.' By summer the unit was in prime condition, with a desire to prove itself, 'as many felt frustrated at not seeing much of the war.'[27]

It was their misfortune that their first action was Operation Jubilee, a frontal attack on the German defences at Dieppe. Billed as a dress rehearsal for the Allied return to continental Europe, Dieppe was deliberately chosen as 'having the best and most complete defensive system that a landing force was likely to meet'.[28] Without Jubilee, the official history of the Combined Operations Organization claimed that 'the final invasion of the Continent could hardly have been so successful', but the lessons seem too fundamental to require teaching: avoidance of frontal assaults on obvious targets; effective preparation by fire in the absence of surprise; provision of comprehensive communications and a floating reserve. Either way the operation was a landmark, the largest and most ambitious raid of the war.[29]

Originally assigned a cutting-out mission in Dieppe harbour, the RM Commando was diverted to the main landing beach. They ran in under machine-gun fire and mortar bombs, mixed with low-trajectory rounds from anti-tank guns mounted within the cliffs, 'a sea parallel to the charge of the Light Brigade'. Casualties from earlier waves lay neatly on the beach, in reversed arrow formation: 'As the range shortened and the smoke cleared there was no doubt in any man's mind that an attempt to reach the town over that beach would mean certain death to the majority.' Not until he had personally proved the uselessness of the adventure did Picton-Phillipps call it off 'stood in the stern in full view of all, placing his white string gloves on his hands and waving to the boats astern to return to the cover of the smoke'.[30] Picton-Phillipps was killed almost immediately, but his self-sacrifice saved hundreds of lives, as few who landed got away unscathed. Sergeant Heffernan's LCA missed the signal to withdraw:

As we lowered the drawbridge my right hand section and part of the centre section was wiped out the rest we got away some getting clipped on the way up the beach. Their was bodies everywhere with a yard wide river of blood on the Edge of the Sea. Craft burning Planes Dive bombing and thousands of large stones flying Everywhere.

Half-blinded by grenade fragments Heffernan was taken prisoner.[31]

Sergeant Kruthoffer swam two and a half miles out to sea to escape. He bitterly resented the waste of the new Commando:

probably the best trained unit which went to Dieppe – and not given a chance to do a job. Split up and dumped on an impossible beach – and the humiliation of having done nothing much to contribute and having to swim out – run away to fight another day.[32]

The descendants of that first Royal Marine Commando still celebrate Dieppe Day as their Unit Memorable Day, for, disastrous as it was, it had shown the way forward. In three years of war, the RM Division and MNBDO had done little to justify tying up half the Corps. General Bourne, 'anxious to see the Marines properly used', resisted War Office efforts to absorb the RM Division, as they had the RND, but as in the First World War it was not always clear what constituted a 'proper' Marine. Hare-brained schemes circulated for landing the RM Division in the Channel Islands or Cotentin peninsula, while a chance of participation in Operation Torch in North Africa was missed. Meanwhile a second RM Commando was raised, the two units numbering 40 and 41 respectively. Internal organization reflected their light raiding role: a small headquarters with four troops of 100, lettered A, B, X, and Y as a reminder of the Marines' gunnery role at sea.

Mountbatten needed more Commandos and landing craft crew, as pinprick raids made way for major assault landings. His answer, sold to Mr Churchill in July 1943, was to break up the RM Division and MNBDO to create another six RM Commandos. The surplus would become landing craft crew, striking a nice balance between 'per terram' and 'per mare' aspects of the Corps. A new Adjutant-General, with the more combative title of GOCRM, replaced the irreconcilable Bourne, while an expanded Special Services Group came under Royal Marine command. In November 1943 General Sturges took over four brigades made up of eight Army Commandos, plus eight planned or actual RM Commandos. Royal Marine functions were redefined to authorize formation of units to conduct amphibious operations alongside other services, by implication outside naval control. The centralized direction of modern wars by a War Cabinet and Chiefs of Staff had left 'no place for private expeditions by Naval Commanders-in-Chief with private Royal Marine striking forces of their own'. Mountbatten's revolution from above not only solved his manpower problems, but made the Royal Marines 'the nucleus of the amphibious forces of the Crown', their true hunting ground 'the line where sea meets shore and where the Navy meets the Army'. Mountbatten had saved from imminent extinction a Corps paralyzed by conflicting priorities, a service recognized by his appointment as Life Colonel Commandant in 1965.[33]

The Army's volunteer Commandos resented the conscripts drafted into RM Commandos, but RM Battalions had years of similar training behind them, while the leaner Commando organization allowed units to choose only the best men. Landing craft crew faced different challenges. The Royal Navy's admission of Marine officers to command commissioned ships was a particularly striking departure from tradition. RM Division gunners were for the first time 'pointed towards the direction most of us had joined the Marines for: Sea Service'.[34] Landing craft had evolved to suit every amphibious requirement. The original LCA acquired a mortar and machine guns to become a Landing Craft Support or LCS(M). The need for tank support inspired the Landing Craft Tank (LCT), and ocean-going LST. For high-speed raids motor torpedo boats mutated into Landing Craft Infantry (LCI(S)), which bounced about on top of the water instead of floating in it like a proper boat. Dieppe left no doubt of the LCS(M)'s inadequacy, leading to LCS(L) mounting anti-tank guns, Landing Craft Gun (LCG) with 4-inch gun turrets, and the fearsome LCT(R) with over a thousand 5-inch rockets fired in salvoes to terrorize defenders and disrupt obstacles. Decked over and armed with 2-pounder pom-poms and 20mm Oerlikons, LCTs became Landing Craft Flak (LCF) for anti-aircraft defence.[35]

Fleet service was still the ultimate ambition of most Marines – 'the bigger the ship the more one had to be proud of.' Special Sea Service squads had a nasty shock when they saw their new homes: 'just about as ugly as and ungraceful as a ship or craft could be. . . the upper deck literally bristling with guns'. Little more than floating mobile magazines, LCGs and LCFs had little space for crew:

> Bulkheads were always dripping with condensation, men slept on tables, under tables, on the wash basins, on the lockers, and if you were lucky, there was just enough room, after a great deal of hard struggling to put up six hammocks.[36]

At sea these 'winkle barges' handled like 'high sided saucers with inadequate power', high freeboard sending them rapidly to leeward. Storms tossed them around 'like corks in a bath', and flooded the Oerlikon gun-pits, threatening to capsize the craft. Health was poor as the bilges tainted fresh food, forcing crews to live on canned rations or beg from larger ships. Marines with their naval affinities were better suited than most to adapt to discomforts reminiscent of the 1740s. Nine months after receiving their new mission, Royal Marines crewed two-thirds of minor British landing craft at D-Day, 'ample evidence of the adaptability of the Corps and of the excellence of the training organisation. . . set up to meet the commitment'.[37]

Justification by Fire

Changes in organization and doctrine were all very well on paper, but what mattered was their result in the field. It was the success of Commandos and landing craft flotillas in action, above all in Italy and North West Europe, that justified Mountbatten's policy and ensured post-war survival of the Corps.

The first sea-borne troops ashore in Sicily in July 1943 were 40 and 41 RM Commandos. As at Zeebrugge the plan was only revealed at sea, after extensive rehearsals ashore: 'Every Marine knew as nearly as possible what he had to face.' Operational success repaid careful preparation:

> touchdown had been made within 100 yards of the point originally planned. Well memorised land marks were picked up and the Troops moved off to their allotted tasks. . . green success signals going up from point to point as the Commando stormed its way westwards.[38]

In September Messina and Salerno saw the Royal Marines' first heavy Commando casualties, including 80 per cent of 41 Cdo's officers: 'The landing was without incident, but next day the Germans gave everyone a pasting.'[39] Intended as lightly armed shock troops Commandos were drawn into a pounding match against a skilful enemy. Panzer Grenadiers in camouflage suits, hands and faces painted green, exploited steep overgrown hillsides to infiltrate 41's positions, tactics the Commandos adopted themselves, as mortar fire knocked out wireless sets and heavy weapons.[40] In October an amphibious hook by 40 RM Cdo restored momentum to a flagging offensive, provoking a five-day battle behind German lines at Termoli before Eighth Army broke through, to the relief of an anonymous Marine of X Troop: 'Thank God for that because we are all cold and tired in fact I don't know how we done it'. In January 1944, 40 RM Cdo became storm troops, pushed ahead of the main battle line on the Garigliano: 'a new job for us because it is not at sea/land this time, but all the same we can do it. . . all the lads are for it because we shall show the 5 Army how it should be done.' One of the front-line diarist's last entries reveals the strain of continuous operations: 'Been fighting now for a hell of a time and we could all do with a good rest.'[41]

Sicily saw the début of RM landing craft flotillas. Beached among the unloading vessels, the LCFs had the 'most arduous overall task of all the RN small craft. . . [having] to undergo for weeks what the others had only to undergo for days'.[42] Continual vigilance in dazzling sunshine strained eyes protected by sunglasses, 'as sold by Messrs Woolworths at 3d a time to cheap beach belles and day tripper types'. Oerlikons were quicker to engage fighter-bombers sneaking in low over the hills, while pom-poms proved better in barrage areas: 'many bombs were aimed and fell close but not one ship was hit in the area covered by the LCFs'. Fire control was deadly:

> On one occasion four JU88s came in to attack the beached craft we were busy unloading. The LCFs held their fire until the aircraft were well within range. Suddenly we let them have everything. One crashed on shore. Two more turned from the attack losing height and pouring out smoke. . . only two bombs were dropped, which fell harmlessly.[43]

By coincidence, Sicily saw perhaps the only effective use of the specialist amphibious units in which the Corps had invested so much. At Augusta MNBDO II:

> provided signals, medical and security services, and malaria control. . . fifty percent of the ships unloading in the port was carried out by Marines. In the early days they handled the petrol for the whole of the Eighth Army. Their Detailed Issue Depot, designed for 7,000 handled rations for 35,000 men.

7th RM Battalion were only the second such unit to see action as a formation, but they made up for it by the number of jobs they did. Before the Middle Eastern invasion forces sailed for Sicily, instructors and demonstration teams from the 7th Battalion had provided them with a blueprint for beach maintenance and combined training. Immediately after the landings, 7th Battalion rifle companies formed the hard core for 4,600 specialist troops of 31 Beach Brick: engineer, signals, ordnance and medical units, including an Airfields Group. Besides handling 5,000 POWs and upgrading its Maintenance Area into XXX Corps' Field Maintenance Area, the Brick found an RM driver for a railway engine left in a village siding. The Battalion then fought with 51 Highland Division in 'complex and unsatisfactory operations' on the Dittaino River, where they had to withdraw 'through the smoke of burning hayricks' after taking their objectives with 150 prisoners. The third episode makes the most exciting story, but the first probably represents the Royal Marines' most significant contribution to the invasion of Hitler's Europe: 'spreading the gospel of Combined Training throughout the Middle East forces'.[44]

Their Finest Hour

The Normandy invasion of 6 June 1944 was the largest and most successful amphibious landing ever mounted. It saw the largest single commitment of Royal Marines in their history: reinforced ship's detachments, landing craft crews, underwater obstacle clearance units, an armoured support group of eighty Centaur tanks equivalent to two tank regiments, plus remnants of MNBDO – provosts, signallers, radar operators and port clearing parties. Royal Marines provided five out of eight Commandos, and one of two Special Service Brigade HQs:

> It was not a situation one would be in for pure pleasure, but it was not quite high drama either. The organisation was so comprehensive, the degree of preparation so impressive, that it was impossible to think of failure or defeat.[45]

The scale of the invasion precluded pessimism, 'There was no open sea to be seen. Landing craft seemed to occupy every inch of water in every direction.' Long before the beaches came in sight, the bombardment drowned out the roar of diesel engines: 'battleships and monitors some fifteen miles out, cruisers some ten miles, destroyers about five miles'.[46] As the moment of truth approached, the density of shipping increased: 'So many craft and ships about it looks like a Regatta Day, but hardly Henley'[47]:

> No longer an orderly formation moving in same direction at a steady pace. More and more craft pouring in. Numerous craft coming out, having discharged their cargoes of men and materials. Then the unlucky ones. Craft at crazy angles sunk in shallow water. Others out of control, often on fire. . . The whole picture was to a background of explosions and gunfire of every kind. . . It seemed incredible that any single shell could fail to hit something.[48]

But shells did miss as most landings were successful. The converted LSI *Clan Lamont* lowered her LCAs full of Canadian infantry into waves so high they had trouble finding the Navigating Leader's motor launch. Once found he led them in to St Aubin-sur-Mer, the flotilla increasing speed to 9 knots, to hit the beach flat out:

> Water piled high, through the very high winds, and instead of being to seaward of the obstacles, found ourselves slap in the middle of them. Much confusion at high water mark: AVREs and DD tanks not yet ashore. . . Hit the beach at 08:03. All craft appeared to be doing fine and nobody hit. Canadians left the craft in good order. LCA 609 between two posts, both with mines on but she seemed alright so left her and pulled out. A hell of a lot of confusion on the beach, but all craft appeared to leave safely.[49]

Other landing craft were less fortunate. A second flight from *Clan Lamont* lost five out of seven. West of St Aubin LCF 34's Sub watched an LCT explode, 'hurling men and machines into the air like rag dolls':

> LCAs loaded with troops under a storm of mortar and heavy machine-gun fire either caught fire or broached to in the surf presenting an easy target. . . but those 18-year old Cox's, mostly Royal Marines, beached their craft and off-loaded their troops.[50]

Sunk by mortar fire Corporal Charles Brumpton went to help another craft, not leaving until her engines were blown out, although shrapnel had carried away one of his anklets. Marine William Long:

> remained in a half flooded LCA engine room for three hours nursing his remaining engine. . . gassed by chlorine gas from his batteries caused by contact with salt water. . . On leaving his engine room he was in such a condition that he became unconscious and fell into the sea, from which he was rescued by a Canadian officer.[51]

The result of such devotion to duty was successful landing of the assault troops, among them 2,500 RM Commandos. Unlike Sicily where they had landed first, in Normandy the Commandos followed the leading waves, pushing through them, as they had done on the Garigliano, to carry out special missions ahead of the main infantry battle:

- 45 RM Cdo on the left to reinforce 6 Airborne Division beyond the Orne River;
- 41 and 48 RM Cdos in the centre between Lion-sur-Mer and St Aubin, to clear coastal defences;

- 47 RM Cdo on the British right to capture Port-en-Bessin, and link up with US forces at Omaha Beach;
- 46 RM Cdo held as a floating reserve.

Commandos crossed the Channel in LCI(S), their enclosed mess decks hot and smelly. Everyone was sick:

> what a rotten way it was to take troops to war, but how right it was that all our training had concentrated on trying to dent morale before demanding the impossible. There was nearly a sense of normality about it.

Landing down the LCIs' steep bow ramps, as waves drove the craft further ashore was not easy:

> I saw the great bows coming over me and the next thing I remember is finding myself walking up the beach, wet through of course, and with some of my equipment torn off, including my pistol, but still clutching my stout ash walking stick.[52]

The first assault wave had not always secured the beach, and German machine-gunners picked off Commandos struggling down exposed ramps with handcarts and folding bicycles – 48 RM Cdo lost over half its men coming ashore in front of an uncleared strongpoint. A signaller with the similarly depleted 41 reflected how 'Success is seldom witnessed by the ordinary soldier.'[53]

Marine Commandos had one advantage over the dazed infantry pinned down behind the sea-wall, trained since 1st RM days to clear beaches quickly, 'a long straggling line of green berets heading for the check point'.[54] Despite casualties and loss of equipment they pressed on to gain their objectives in gritty infantry actions that confounded the critics. Often out of wireless contact with supporting artillery, these attacks on heavily defended localities resemble First World War trench fighting, with ditched tanks hammering at concrete emplacements, while small parties of Marines blew gaps in wire with bangalore torpedoes and cleared rubble-blocked streets under a steady flow of stick grenades. German resistance varied. Prisoners included 'a mixture of Asiatic Russian types who had been recruited from POW camps, and young frightened german boys', but others 'had to be shot out ruthlessly, and didn't seem to give a thought to their own lives'.[55] 41 RM Cdo took Douvres radar station after a week's siege, breaking through its legendary defences with the help of flail tanks and an intense barrage. Two customs officials were among the prisoners, 'both feeling rather out of place since the Commando had omitted to carry either bottles of perfume or cigars.'[56]

The most daunting and strategically important Commando task of the invasion was 47 RM Cdo's march through enemy-held country to capture the fishing village of Port-en-Bessin, halfway between the British and American beaches. It was very much a Commando operation, against limited time, beyond reach of support. All weapons and supplies had to be carried, an average weight per man of 88lbs. Four out of fourteen LCAs blew up off the beach, survivors struggling ashore without their equipment. The rendezvous was still in German hands and had to be captured, allowing men who had lost gear in the water to re-equip at the enemy's expense. Confused by the telltale rattle of MG34s, 'a German officer sprang up and shouted "Stop shooting, you fools. We're your own troops". That was the end of the war for him.'[57] The 10-mile approach march left 47 RM Cdo in an uneasy situation next morning, unable to find the Americans, with one operational wireless and a single 3-inch mortar with no sights. Nevertheless, they organized naval and air bombardments, followed by smoke from 25-pounders at Arromanches, and stormed two out of three strongpoints around the harbour, despite flakships knocking out twenty-five of A Troop. The last strongpoint fell after dark, after Q Troop had captured the German commandant in his own dugout and persuaded him to summon the remainder of the garrison to surrender.

While Marine Commandos fought to expand the bridgehead, other Marines secured their rear, with anti-aircraft gunners atop the Mulberry harbour sections and in the support craft. LCFs saw little of the Luftwaffe, but their accurate close-range firepower kept enemy heads down during the assault landings, firing broadside at targets glimpsed through the smoke haze. The few German aircraft got a warm reception:

> out of the smoke screen. . . came two FW 190s. I don't think they knew where they were, because two seconds later both were blown to pieces by LCF 36's gun fire, it was impossible to see who was hitting them.[58]

After nightfall the support craft formed the innocuous-sounding Trout Line, a nerve-racking but largely unrecognized duty. Moored at two-cable intervals off the Orne estuary LCGs and LCFs faced a threat unimagined by their designers: radio-controlled motorboats or 'Weasels' packed with high explosives, and human torpedoes drifting in on the tide to get among the shipping off the beaches. Night after night was spent staring apprehensively into the darkness, snatching half an hour's rest on the steel deck of the gun-pits, pessimists supplementing their naval lifejackets with the flimsy belts left aboard by departed infantry. The LCGs'

medium guns had punched hard at pillboxes on D-Day, but they lacked
the close-range firepower to stop Weasels at night, a frenzied business
'only to be compared with the experience of riding a motor bike at nearly
a hundred miles per hour.'[59] Several craft were blown in half before look-
outs learned to lie prone on a mattress to get a better angle of sight. The
less deadly human torpedo was more difficult to spot. Only a perspex
dome showed above water, through which the pilot conned his way, sitting
astride the motorized shell of an old torpedo:

> I will always remember the look of sheer horror on one human torpedo
> man's face caught in the light of our Aldis lamp. Our strip Lewis opened
> up, shattering the dome and turned his face into a bloody pulp.[60]

As in Italy, Commandos stayed ashore much longer than expected: 41
RM Cdo spent over six weeks in the line, 'We were meant to come out
on D+4!!'[61] As units completed their D-Day tasks they moved over to
defend the extreme left flank of the British perimeter, east of the Orne.
The Commandos reverted to type, patrolling aggressively to maintain
the initiative, while Allied resources were devoted to breaking out
elsewhere:

> We always believed that the secret of a quiet life was to be thoroughly
> aggressive and dominate the area, but it was more than ever necessary
> here to disguise our weakness in numbers.[62]

Raids aimed at the elimination of whole German platoons were more
than ad hoc scrimmages with tommy gun and grenade. Fire plans involved
RA Field Regiments and destroyers, besides mortars and Vickers guns
from heavy weapons troops:

> the barrages were spectacular, the dust raised 75–100 feet in the air, when
> our Boys overran the enemy position it was terrible to see, older men who
> were not even Germans were brought out and we were totally amazed to
> see the standard of these German frontline soldiers.

Discouraged from leaving their own lines, the Germans limited themselves
to firing bombs full of incendiary liquid from multi-barrelled mortars:
'had a whooping sound that was not unlike that of a cow. . . I think our
own artillery at night was the worst, the crack of it going over head was
shattering.'[63] The Orne was the pivot of the Allies' left-wheeling advance.
Not until 18 August did the Germans there give way, allowing the
Commandos to join the advance. A final night attack killed so many that
a signaller looking for 48 RM Cdo was told: 'go to the foot of the hill and

follow the corpses.'[64] Crossing the Seine in a pontoon, Bill Andrews of 47 RM Cdo realized the scale of the victory:

> Kennebec (*sic*) was to be seen to be believed. . . the RAF had trapped a German Divisional HQ there and with rocket firing Typhoons destroyed it, there were track vehicles, motor transport, ambulances, admin trucks and field kitchens and buses. . . German dead all over the place, they had just got over the Seine and just left everything.[65]

Raiders and Storm Troops

Normandy was not the only theatre where RM Commandos saw action. They were distributed throughout the Special Service Brigades and visited all theatres of war:

Special Service Brigades – April 1944[66]

Brigade	Theatre	Commandos
1st	NW Europe	3, 4, 6 Army; 45 RM
2nd	Italy/Balkans	2, 9 Army; 40, 43 RM
3rd	India/Arakan	1, 5 Army; 42, 44 RM
4th	NW Europe	41, 46, 47, 48 RM

Often they trod paths familiar to earlier Marines. No. 2 SS Brigade helped Yugoslav partisans, as their ancestors had Spanish guerrillas, remaining cheerful and healthy in places possessing 'no electricity, no wood, no culture, no education, no sanitation, and little or no happiness'.[67] At Vis they found memorials to Royal Marines who died there in 1812. In the Far East, No. 3 Brigade languished in a defensive role, like Collins' Marines at Halifax, until the Japanese withdrawal from the Arakan in early 1945 provided an amphibious opportunity. Wearing 'Hats, slouch with special lining, magnificent in their grandeur and terrifying in aspect',[68] Commandos penetrated tidal chaungs to land behind the enemy at Akyab and Myebon, but the Japanese were not easily ensnared. The battle at Kangaw yielded 2 posthumous VCs to Army Commandos, but only 4 prisoners, and 340 dead Japanese in an area no more than 100 yards square. Paradoxically, this under-utilized brigade from the Forgotten Army would become trustees of the Commando spirit and the Royal Marines' main operational formation.

Once established on European soil, Allied planners neglected Commando potential for short-range tactical descents on the German coastal flank. Long slogging battles replaced the quick and silent landing. Special Service Brigades served as heavy infantry until the German surrender in May 1945, acquiring their own transport, and enjoying appropriate artillery and armoured support. No. 4 Brigade's defensive deployment masking German troops in Dunkirk from landward justified old fears of Army misuse of amphibious assets, for Commandos were urgently needed for a final assault landing. German batteries at Walcheren in the Scheldt estuary prevented ships reaching Antwerp with supplies for the Allied drive into Germany, and could only be stormed from the sea. Luckily specialist ships and men were available, the Support Squadron understanding the difficulties facing the troops: 'we had no doubt that if we could get the Commandos ashore without heavy losses, they would speedily wipe up any succession of strong points and batteries along the dunes.'[69] The attack on 1 November 1944 was the swansong of the support landing craft. With no room for manoeuvre and bombarding warships blinded by smoke, XXX Support Squadron tackled enemy batteries head on: 'One of the most gallant actions of the war pitting their small calibre guns and lightly armed vessels against some of the strongest defences in the world.'[70]

LCF and LCG crews were 'told quite bluntly this was to be no picnic', receiving the Nelsonian injunction that 'no commanding officer could do very wrong if he engaged the enemy more closely.'[71] Battle ensigns flying they ran for the beaches, bottoms scraping on the seabed. LCF 37 'went up in a ball of flame'; LCF 26 was 'swamped with water and clouded with spray from the shells falling around her'; LCF 32 took a shell 'through the gun platform, through the Skipper's cabin under the Bridge, through the Radio Room and Spud Locker, the Drying Room and into the Galley. . . before bursting and blowing up the deck by my starboard Pompom killing the PO Motor Mechanic'. Ready-use ammunition blazed, a Marine 'up to his elbows in the burning locker, grabbing the ammunition and tossing it over the side'. Others following time-honoured damage control principles, 'jammed hammocks in the hole and drove in wooden wedges to stem the flow as the sea rushed in'.[72] Two new LCG(M)s armed with 17-pounder anti-tank guns mounted in 5-inch thick armoured turrets had been designed to flood down on the beach to form a stable gun platform while engaging pillboxes at suicidally close range. LCG(M) 102's only survivor was recovered unconscious from the water; LCG(M) 101 kedged off and sank, after an epic fight in which 'B' Turret's periscopes were shot away and ricochets through vision slits knocked out two of the four Marines inside, their blood dripping through the wire mesh floor onto the magazine crew below. After three and a half hours, only five out of twenty-five landing craft support were still fit for action, but they had drawn the coastal batteries' fire away from the assaulting infantry.

For the first time Marines landed from armoured amphibians, or LVTs, launched from LCTs. LVTs were an 'excellent means of landing troops', enabling them to land dry-shod behind a comforting $^1/_4$ inch of armour. They also allowed 47 RM Cdo to redeploy after three LCTs hit the wrong beach. Once ashore the Commandos justified naval confidence, despite having to attack positions organized in depth, along the narrow space between the beach and the flooded polders to 'landward'. Soft, yielding sand jammed automatics and hampered efforts to keep up with supporting artillery fire, but German morale crumbled under persistent Commando attacks supported by fighter-bombers with 500lb bombs and rockets. Captured officers called upon their countrymen to surrender, which they did in embarrassing numbers, a process hastened by German-speaking Commandos. The last of the 29,000 defenders surrendered on 8 November and minesweeping began. Casualties had been high. Among the dead was Captain Peter Haydon, at nineteen the youngest Marine ever awarded the DSO. In three days fighting 47 RM Cdo lost 90 men out of not quite 400, a similar proportion to the Support Squadron.[73] Half the major landing craft participating were sunk or unfit for further use. In the grim balance sheet of war the cost of opening Antwerp was well justified, assuring 21 Army Group's supply lines. Royal Marine Commandos and landing craft crew had again demonstrated the strategic leverage that properly trained and equipped amphibious forces can exert. To the end of the war they remained on 21 Army Group's seaward flank, containing the enemy on a 100-mile front by a vigorous raiding policy, carrying out forty patrols in the five months to the end of the war. Meanwhile 5 RM AA Brigade, the only surviving MNBDO formation, defended Antwerp against flying bombs, suggesting an extended Corps motto: 'Per Mare Per Terram Per Astra'.[74]

Renamed in November 1944 to avoid confusion with less savoury SS formations, the Commando Brigades retained their character as shock troops, fulfilling 'important tasks in accordance with the Commando design – tasks of a spearhead or diversionary nature'.[75] Riding in LVTs, No. 1 Brigade preceded XVII Airborne Corps over the Rhine to clear Wesel in forty-five minutes, supported by Bomber Command and four Field Regiments. They continued their 'series of jumps over the rivers' with the Weser, Aller and Elbe, employing 'a technique of infiltrating behind the enemy's lines and attacking their objectives from an unexpected quarter which seems to have been largely responsible for the remarkable success they achieved.'[76]

No. 2 Commando Brigade's first operation as a formation was its last. Previously split up in support of Balkan partisans, the Brigade concentrated in 1945 for an attack on the seaward flank of the German line on the River Reno that still barred the way into the North Italian plain. Operation Roast, another inappropriate codename, was planned for 1 April 1945. It required Commandos, not so much for the watery location, a narrow spit of land between Lake Comacchio and the sea, but because only the toughest soldiers could maintain tactical momentum over unusually difficult terrain. 43 RM Cdo fought on their feet, infiltrating between enemy strongpoints, but Army Commandos in storm boats floundered through 'a nightmare mixture of Venice by Moonlight, and the end of the Henley Regatta transferred to a setting of mud, slime, and a few inches of stinking water'. The difficulty was making effective use of the Allies' material superiority over the enemy: massed Field and Medium Artillery Regiments, LVTs, Weasels, Kangaroos and DUKWs. The staff had 'little experience in dealing with such a considerable and varied collection of supporting arms and the Wireless Establishment of a Commando Brigade HQ was quite inadequate'. A Radar unit hinted at greater complexities to come.

Infantry no longer had to follow a pre-arranged barrage as they had in the First World War. The Comacchio fire plan allowed for attacks from three different directions, and incalculable delays crossing the lake: 'Timed programmes were therefore laid on from initial calls for support from the assault troops themselves.'[77] This was not universally perceived as a success:

> Commachio was our last operation of the war and I would say it was the worst and fiercest, except Dieppe. . . the support we expected did not materialise, and our casualties were heavy. The reinforcements to our troop were almost killed to a man – I didn't even know their names.[78]

Certainly mud inhibited the tracked vehicles, but 43 RM Cdo took their early objectives and numerous prisoners, with the help of very effective artillery concentrations and a diversion or 'Chinese attack' by 40 RM Cdo, who played Wagner over loudspeakers to conceal the attack's opening moves. The offensive continued with tank support on 2 April, but hit serious opposition south of the Valletta Canal, which blocked further progress. Despite the apparently hopeless situation, some of C Troop reached the canal bank, led by Corporal Tom Hunter, who charged three

MG34s firing his Bren gun from the hip. Having cleared several houses, he was killed drawing the fire of half a dozen more machine guns, to save the rest of his Troop crossing the open ground behind him. Tom Hunter was the only Royal Marine awarded the VC during the Second World War. A month after his death, German forces in Italy surrendered unconditionally. Hunter's sacrifice, so near the end of the war, seems particularly sad, but was indicative of the quality of soldiers whose commander claimed 'have done more to bring about the defeat of Germany than any other Formation of similar size'.[79]

CHAPTER TWELVE

Survival of the Fittest

THE end of hostilities soon had the services fighting for their own lives. Army Commandos, like early Marine regiments, were first in line for disbandment, 'condemned. . . of setting too high a standard' for a peacetime army. The totemic Green Beret faced the axe as 'a thing of war not peace'.[1] The CGRM, however, attached great importance to 'Royal Marines continuing to carry out the functions of Commandos'.[2] Admiralty committees instigated by the First Sea Lord, Sir Andrew Cunningham, reaffirmed the Royal Marines' traditional and wartime-acquired responsibilities. Administrative changes followed, the old RM Divisions becoming functional groups in 1947. Cunningham stands with those naval officers who have served the Corps well, although some were less supportive. In 1949 Chatham Group, with local connections going back to the Admiral's Regiment, was sacrificed to frustrate the Harwood Committee's proposal to disband the Marines wholesale. The decisions of the late 1940s have proved remarkably resilient, surviving strategic changes unequalled since the Marines' formation in 1755.

Blue and Green

Retention of 3 Commando Brigade, with 42, 44 and 45 RM Cdos, gave Marines their first permanent land role in peacetime since the 1680s – 44 Cdo was renumbered 40, so the Brigade now represents Commandos present in all three Second World War theatres. A small amphibious warfare squadron provided the Royal Navy, after centuries of improvization, with the basis of a trained landing force. Sir Thomas Hunton, CGRM, insisted, 'an amphibious force must be both per terram and per mare', appointing Continuous Service officers to Commandos as 'the one-track

Marine officer ceases to be of value as he reaches the higher ranks.'[3] Efforts were made to bridge the wartime gap between 'Sailor Marines and Soldier Marines'. Fifty blue beret Marines, for example, spent eleven weeks with 3 Commando Brigade during HMS *Belfast*'s 1946 refit at Hong Kong: 'On one side there was suspicion and a feeling of inferiority, on the other, something approaching contempt; on each side, ignorance of the way of life of the other. All this was swept away'. Commando troop leaders 'would gladly exchange such men for many with us now', while keenness replaced ship-bred apathy: 'the men had gained confidence. . . they were very fit and many of them were requesting transfer to Commandos.'[4] Ship's detachments were left in no doubt that they were 'soldiers especially trained for service afloat', expected to reach the standard 'of the best infantryman', even in fieldcraft, an unlikely area for quarter-deck training:

> Interest is gained if a Bren can be fixed up to fire on its own tripod out to sea, and the Section advances towards it as it fires over their heads whenever the section is visible.[5]

With landing craft work, canoeing, underwater swimming and cliff climbing, the Marine officer's naval colleagues could no longer accuse him of being 'the idlest man in the ship'.[6] Ashore there was no harking back to the pre-war 'stereotyped, sheltered, and barrack square variety of training'.[7] Royal Marines would become light infantry par excellence, the Green Beret recalling a title more appropriate than ever since its discontinuance in 1923.

Nuclear weapons and Britain's post-war decline ended the Royal Navy's requirement for large RM detachments. The battleships were all scrapped by 1960, while the 6-inch guns of the last cruisers remained silent at Suez in 1956. A few Marines served in aircraft carriers and large destroyers on a reduced scale. In 1959 HMS *Ark Royal* had an RM detachment of only thirty-seven. HMS *Ashanti* embarked twenty-one Marines in 1965, but only the Sergeant-Major had more than one previous commission at sea. Most of those with sea service had gained it in a Commando carrier. The following year a Colour Sergeant in HMS *Tiger* was the last Marine to fire a 6-inch gun under manual control. Sea service as understood by Rooke and St Vincent had become a memory. The post-war survival of the Corps owed much to the realization that while change was certain, its nature was unpredictable: 'Much that appears important today will appear trivial tomorrow. Equally problems with a comparatively low priority at the moment will suddenly become of major importance.'[8] The unlikely prospect of re-enacting the Normandy Landings had to be balanced against winning the peace. Commando soldiers' individual skills have proved well suited to low-intensity operations, while shifting strategic patterns have placed a premium on the speed and flexibility of amphibious forces and their ability to operate without an assured base in-country.

Britain's imperial decline took time to become apparent. Post-war conflicts, such as Korea, recapitulated Second World War themes. Marines engaged shore targets with 6-inch naval guns for the last time. HMS *Belfast* endured 23° of frost in the enemy's backyard at Chinampo, 'the sea covered with large slabs of ice which gave it the appearance of being shingled'.[9] Volunteers from ships' detachments blew up Korean railways and made the Royal Marines' first landing from a US Navy submarine. A reformed 41 (Independent) Commando joined 1st US Marine Division's breakout to the sea from Chosin (29 November–10 December 1950), when surrounded by the People's Liberation Army. In nineteen days 200 Commandos suffered 79 battle casualties and 19 from the weather, the American Divisional Commander commending their conduct as 'worthy of the highest traditions of Marines'.[10] Mutual admiration extended to USMC insistence that 41 Cdo share the Presidential Citation awarded for the breakout.

The first 100 per cent operational deployment of 3 Commando Brigade in 1948 was more indicative of late twentieth-century trends. The last days of the British mandate in Palestine saw an unsavoury mixture of ethnic cleansing with Jewish mortar attacks on Arab markets, and imperial pomp, Grenadier Guardsmen and Royal Marines providing the departing High Commissioner's guard of honour. The Commandos' controlled response to provocation changed perceptions of the suitability of Special Forces for internal security duties, although restraint was relative. Armoured cars and PIATs knocked out machine-gunners strafing Haifa's traffic: 'to the delight of the weapon's crew, three rounds were enough to blow the sniper to bits and his sheltering armour.' Vehicle checkpoints were another foretaste of things to come:

> "Haganah" said the Marine, "Who are they, what do they do?"
> The driver drew back in his seat. "We are soldiers of God", he replied.
> "Well" said the Marine, "You're a long way from your barracks, aren't you?"[11]

The residual amphibious capability proved as useful for leaving hostile shores as assaulting them. The last British troops to depart were 40 Cdo's 3-inch mortar section, their final base-plate position in the bows of the last LST.

By Sea, Land, and Air

Anglo-French intervention against Egyptian nationalists in 1956 demonstrated the impossibility of retracing the first steps backwards. Indian independence had undermined the strategic rationale for British control over the Suez Canal, but old habits died hard – 40 and 42 Cdos stormed ashore at Port Said on 6 November in the old style. Shot in by destroyers at point-blank range, they ran the gauntlet of sniper-covered streets in LVTs, finding their pin-on armour had been left at Malta as bullets came through the vehicles' sides. Meanwhile 45 Cdo made history by landing from helicopters in the first vertical envelopment mounted by British forces. The whole unit landed in 91 minutes from 2 fleet carriers, 10 miles out to sea. Neither ships nor helicopters were purpose built, but they provided a more practical approach to triphibious warfare than the glider-borne Marines proposed in 1945 as a means of avoiding submarines and flying bombs.[12] The Palestine emergency had seen 45 Cdo fly into Haifa by Dakota. Now helicopters added tactical and logistical air mobility to the amphibious repertoire, flying stores directly to forward troops, speeding build-up rates and reducing congestion on vulnerable beaches.

Despite the unsatisfactory political outcome of the crisis, Suez was an opportune demonstration of the continued potential of amphibious operations in the nuclear age. *Globe and Laurel* drew a direct parallel between the landing role of early Marines, before the British had acquired any shore bases, and the late twentieth-century situation as they handed them back: 'The Navy can take its own base to within striking distance – its aircraft carriers, some with jet aircraft and some with helicopters and Marines.'[13] In the short term 45 Cdo used helicopters in Cyprus, to chase EOKA gunmen. In the longer term helicopters became an integral feature of amphibious ships newly acquired to replace the worn-out material legacy of D-Day. The Suez fiasco prompted a wholesale review of British defence policy, in Duncan Sandys' White Paper of April 1957. His bi-focal view of war as total, i.e. nuclear or limited, requiring small professional forces, favoured the Royal Marines who had never depended heavily on conscripts.[14] Earl Mountbatten, now First Sea Lord, predicted a 'bright future' for a Navy able to keep 'a first rate mobile air power in the form of the Fleet Air Arm, and an equally first rate mobile land force in the shape of the Royal Marine Commandos'.[15] While ancient infantry regiments suffered painful amalgamations, two Commandos were reactivated: 41 in 1960 and 43 in 1961.

They were needed to back up two light fleet carriers converted into Commando ships: HMS *Bulwark* and *Albion*. Each carried a Commando, powerful enough to deal with 'brush fire' wars that the spread of cheap modern weapons had placed beyond the capability of a traditional ship's detachment. Commandos now carried a full inventory of support weapons: recoilless anti-tank guns, GPMGs and mortars, soon to be upgraded to NATO standard 81mm weapons. The conventional Army company structure replaced the old Troop organization, which was too light for units now expected to fight as infantry battalions. The term Troop transferred to platoons, although lettering of sub-units throughout the Brigade still continues – 45 Cdo for example consists of HQ, Support, X-ray, Yankee, and Zulu Companies. Besides Wessex helicopters, Commando carriers carried four LCAs from davits. Royal Marines of the ship's detachment crewed these, also supplying an Air Control Team and Assault Supply Staff, the whole organized as an additional infantry platoon, 'the skilled nucleus of the Bulwark Light Horse'.[16] Naval officers found the new dispensation refreshing, as Vehicle Mechanics replaced WRAs and Keyboard sentries:

> Gone are the days of a well trained but little practised landing party with a number of dull and monotonous routine tasks to fill the time. All the changes are for the better, and the detachment now clearly fulfils the proper duties of Royal Marines.[17]

Supported by two new Landing Ships (LPDs) and six supply ships (LSLs), the Commando carriers earned their keep during the imperial retreat of the 1960s. The senior naval officer at Singapore told her Captain: '*Albion* to me is the most useful ship on the station.'[18] Confrontation with Indonesia, however, hindered evaluation of Commando ships, as troops and helicopters had joined counter-insurgency operations ashore, while the LPHs acted as troopers. Only at Kuwait in 1961 were they used as intended, being on the wrong side of the Indian Ocean for typical brush-fire operations at Limbang in Brunei in 1962, or disarming mutinous East African soldiers in 1964. In both cases landing equipment was improvized: lighters with Vickers guns and ASW helicopters flown from HMS *Centaur*, a standard strike carrier. While some Marines felt amphibious ships were 'the medium for the continuance of our existence today', others felt they were 'rapidly becoming an expensive irrelevance'. Over-specialization might leave Commandos like the RM Division 'all dressed up and nowhere to go'. Conversely standard infantry might usurp their function, as there was 'no black magic in using helicopters and life-jackets'.[19]

The debate reflects the dilemma faced by any specialist force, whether to pursue whatever opportunities arise, or wait for something more appropriate. In a period of defence cuts 10,000 men could not sit about 'waiting hopefully for an amphibious commitment'.[20] Almost a century after Sir John Colomb suggested the idea, the Royal Marines became a colonial garrison force – 3 Commando Brigade did not return to the UK until 1971, twenty-eight years after sailing for the Far East. No longer were Commandos first in and last out: they stayed on until relieved by another Commando – 45 Cdo spent almost seven years in Aden in the 1960s, its personnel regularly replaced in a way conventional autonomous infantry battalions could not emulate. In the Radfan Mountains they discovered the settling effects of familiarity: 'You learn what is possible and what is not. You learn how to be reasonably comfortable and, above all, you become more and more philosophical about the involved military and political situation.' Marine picquets joked with camel drivers while running mine detectors over their load, 'Not that anyone wants to find anything suspicious. When you live close to nature for long you develop a sympathy for the natives who are living similar lives to your own.' Some criticized such deployments as cold-shouldering naval connections, 'merely to get in on the act', but counter-insurgency operations developed a 'flexible professional attitude at all levels of soldiering in its roughest and most basic forms. . . more amusing, more stimulating, and more satisfying than the press-button warfare we may shortly have upon us'.[21]

Imperial Sunset

The Royal Marines' last colonial campaigns differed radically from their Victorian predecessors, and from each other: jungle campaigns in Malaysia against local Communist Terrorists (CTs) during the Malayan Emergency 1948–60, and Confrontation 1963–66, contrasted with the barren rocks of Aden. Military solutions seemed to have lost their effectiveness or demanded disproportionate effort. Marines landed from HMS *Mauritius* in the early days of the Emergency found 'bandit hunting is mostly hard work with little to show for it.'[22] Long hours were spent lying in mosquito-haunted swamps, or wading chest deep 'feeling carefully for a footing on smooth rock or else sinking knee deep into mud and rotten vegetation. . . hauled bodily up the far bank of the streams, with water running off in gurgling cascades from trousers and through pouches.'[23] Marines learned to prepare meals without making smoke, to move noiselessly through the forest, and to go without smoking. Locally recruited Iban trackers were 'worth their weight in compasses. Not only will they point north and south, but can choose the easiest route.'[24] 'X' Troop 40 Cdo claimed the Brigade's longest patrol in Malaya: 'twenty-two miles as the crow flies, but as the Marine walks in the jungle, a three week trip.'[25] 'Shake up' operations with 'terrific air strikes, 25-pounder and mortar barrages' drove CTs deeper into the forests, but netted few dead: 'from the point of view of the man on the ground, one day seems much like another.'[26] Progress was gauged from a scoreboard, dead CTs worth three points and a prisoner four, reflecting the importance of intelligence gathering. Competition was fierce, units claiming fractional scores for arms and legs found after air raids.

Aden posed different but equally intransigent problems. The chutes and overhangs of the Radfan Mountains tested Commando Climbing Leaders, with little respite at the top where 'one step out of a sangar in the wrong direction meant a step into nothing.' Ambush patrols using the easy route might take two hours to travel less than 400 metres.[27] In Aden City every doorway and alley presented potential danger or vital cover. Patrols inched along caterpillar fashion, two men at a time, 'to provide the maximum cover for the minimum of movement'.[28] As always professionalism paid off. A radio conversation overheard between two Royal Anglian officers enriched a spell in 'that terrorist infested township' Sheikh Othman:

First Officer: 'Sheikh Othman seems very quiet this afternoon.'

Second Officer: 'Yes they know that the Charlie [Commando] call signs are in the area.'

Enemy weapons were cheap: grenades, antique small arms, pipe mortars and landmines that drew a request for hover boots. Mines varied from undetectable nylon jobs to the home-made 'Jumping Jack', propelled 3 feet into the air before exploding. Their users cost little more. Two would-be bombers detected outside Dhala camp by radar drew fire from everything available, including a Saladin's 76mm gun: 'The only weapons we did not fire were the Wombat and Carl Gustav. As the CSM remarked "Those Gollies haven't had so much spent on them in their whole life!"[29] But the insurgents' main weapon was peculiar to the late twentieth-century and cost them nothing – almost a hundred television and other journalists visited Aden during 1966 when there were three separate investigations into alleged military cruelty. Marines found they were 'players on a stage and that the world is our audience. . . playing out a drama that is currently the focus of world opinion'.[30]

Media intrusion upon the immediate task in hand, the next vehicle to be searched or dark alley to be penetrated would become a feature of future conflicts. It had not arisen during the Malayan Emergency or Confrontation, which might explain their better outcomes, except the outlook there was never so bleak. In Malaya a resettlement programme had separated CTs from the people on whom they depended for food. Within hours of 45 Cdo's arrival in Perak, 'two thirds of the unit found itself in parties of section strength, nursing into life resettlement villages.' It was 'a most uninteresting and dispiriting business', but essential clearing of the battleground.[31] 'Hearts and Minds' policies were transferred to Borneo during Confrontation, patrols: 'treating minor medical cases, giving "gash nutty" to the kids, reluctantly giving much prized cigarettes to the parents, cautiously sipping tuak (local rice wine) and tasting the odious wild pig offered to us in the customary Iban manner'.[32] Dried fish heads were too much, finding their way to the pigs underneath the huts. Other local customs could have serious consequences:

> I wish to inform you that about 4.00 pm on 10.1.51 one of your Dyak trackers boarded a public bus from Kuala Kangsar. On the way the said tracker discharged his rifle, making a bullet hole in the roof of the bus. Two of your Marines were rested on the roof of the bus and one of them had his ammunition pouch grazed by the bullet.
>
> Please advise your men not to travel on the roof of the bus in future for the bus company may be charged for carrying excess passengers.[33]

Marines in Malaya lived close to Nature, eating King Cobra as a change from bully beef. 42 Cdo's 'B' Troop reported 'huge cat like shapes prowling past at night and confirmed their state of sobriety by finding tiger tracks next morning.'[34] In Borneo, where leptospirosis deterred washing, even Iban tribesmen were chary of moving downwind of patrols. Camouflage techniques became so effective that an Iban woman squatted to answer the call of nature within 10 feet of a concealed GPMG team. Primitive conditions in the field contrasted with modern technology installed in fortified bases. These were rat-infested labyrinths lit by generators where: 'Transistorised intercoms to defensive positions conjure up a vision of Sunray taking on the role of a Managing Director seated at his huge desk pressing buttons.'[35]

In Malaysia Royal Marines contributed to a stable and democratic future. When 40 Cdo left their fort at Jambu in 1966 village elders begged them to stay, until pacified by offers of defence stores, leaving only the heads for the Assault Engineers to blow up. The departure from Aden was very different. Confounded by political dithering 45 Cdo stood by as Arab factions tore into one another, and speculated about departing like 'the Cockleshell Heroes. . . paddle out one dark night to a waiting submarine. . . We read the papers, scratch our heads, and get on with the job.'[36] Once more sea power extricated British troops from a hopeless predicament. Still dressed in jungle greens 42 Cdo had brushed up on Internal Security and sailed for Aden in HMS *Bulwark* to cover the evacuation – 45 Cdo flew out on 28 November 1967 by Hercules; 42 Cdo left next day in their helicopters, the last British unit in the colony.

North and South

Despite the crucial part amphibious forces played in the evacuation of Aden, continued pressure upon Britain's position East of Suez raised question marks over the future of a low-technology infantry force within NATO. Denis Healey defended the Corps in Churchillian terms, 'referring to the fact that they fight as well in the jungles as on the beaches', but 43 Cdo's rundown in 1968 underlined the *Daily Sketch*'s headline 'Marines to be Scrapped'.[37] NATO was more than just the North German Plain, however, the fiords and mountains of its Northern Flank making the perfect playground for Commando soldiers. Newly returned from South Arabia, 45 Cdo performed one of the Corps' most startling quick-change acts, deploying 300 Marines for Mountain and Arctic Warfare training in 1969, and a full Commando Group of 900 in 1973. At the end of the decade an exercise in Norway would see the first integrated deployment of a full Commando Brigade since the Second World War.

Preparing for the next war, Royal Marines found themselves fighting post-colonial battles closer to home. Northern Ireland, like other shore entanglements, diverted units from 'proper soldiering', but helped reconcile an Army strapped for trained infantry to the continued existence of four Commandos. As Spearhead Battalion, 41 Cdo was among the first reinforcements when gangster patriotism spread from Palestine and Aden to Ulster in 1969: 'proof if it were needed that 3 Commando Brigade can no longer make any claim to the centre of the stage – the spotlight has shifted West of Suez.'[38] Marines had served in Ireland before, patrolling Dublin in plain clothes after the Phoenix Park murders in 1882, and defending Coastguard stations during the 1920s. Never has a commitment been so thankless or interminable, seeming to an outsider to have 'started from little and ended in nothing, neither solution nor satisfaction'. Thirty years and almost forty Ulster tours by RM Commandos have borne out

41 Cdo's early assessment that 'the problem remains as stubbornly insoluble as ever, the legacy of hate and mistrust one side feels for the other seems unquenched and unquenchable.'[39] Optimism that community relations projects could defuse tension was brutally dispelled as Marines became targets for brickbats, broken glass skimmed along the pavement and Molotov cocktails, the petrol laced with sugar to stick to the body. One Black Friday five of 41 Cdo were injured by blast bombs thrown by 'people we had tried to help, whose children we had taken to the countryside, for whom we had built sandpits, whose friendship we had tried to win. And now this.'[40] As gun battles erupted across 'Peacelines' and the IRA detonated twenty-eight bombs across Belfast on another Black Friday (21 July 1972) military action took precedence over 'de-escalation'. Marines acquired personal armour and CS gas grenades, riding into action in armoured lorries, or Pigs, hung with coils of barbed wire. 'A' Company of 40 Cdo suffered three casualties during their first four-month tour: 'approximately 400 rounds fired at us, and returned 305 during 52 shooting incidents. Twelve explosions have occurred, one of them inside our Camp. We have searched 11,000 cars and 583 houses, found 345 lb of explosive and two rifles.'[41] In July 1972 Operation Motorman against Republican No-Go Areas was the largest British military operation since Suez, with fifteen battalions, two of them commandos. Assault Squadron LCUs discreetly landed AVREs from Lough Foyle for barricade demolition in 'Free Derry'. Despite their pledge 'to pursue the fight with the utmost ferocity', the attrition of nightly gun battles drove the IRA to 'more diabolical and successful tactics', as the battle became one of terror and propaganda.[42] The tempo of operations fell, but threatened a wider field. Terrorist bombs killed eleven RM Bandsmen at Deal and maimed the CGRM. Within Ulster Commandos spent more time patrolling the countryside, to deny IRA access to their sanctuary across the Border:

> At least this is what they all joined for – chasing the baddies across the countryside, protecting the honest homesteaders, and confronting the women.

In a province renowned for rain, there was 'stacks of "Oggin" for Royal to play in'. Support Company 40 Cdo was responsible for 720 square miles of County Fermanagh and 111 miles of border, dealing with double assassinations, culvert bombs, command-detonated booby traps, and car bombs. Troops under command totalled 850, enough on a good night to put 58 eight-man Vehicle Checkpoints on the ground, 'an impressive sight to the travelling gunman'.[43]

The Falklands War of May–June 1982 was the very opposite of Ulster: a crisp, old-fashioned campaign with a beginning, a middle and an end. It came just in time, as further defence cuts, 'driven by short-term politico-economic expediency rather than long-term strategic sense', threatened the landing ships that give 3 Commando Brigade its raison d'être. Inaptly titled 'The Way Forward', the 1981 Defence White Paper supports the view that 'the only element of continuity in [amphibious] policy through the years has been that of neglect.' While 3 Commando Brigade was spared, 'as of high value for tasks both in and beyond the NATO area. . . likely needs did not warrant replacement of the specialised amphibious ships *Intrepid* and *Fearless*', curious logic that would leave the Royal Marines' skilled landing forces with nothing to land from.[44] The decision was reversed only weeks before an Argentine invasion of British territories in the South Atlantic demonstrated the continuing relevance of an amphibious warfare capability, ready to be sent 'the Lord knows where, to do the Lord knows what'.[45]

The subsequent conflict triumphantly vindicated the flexibility and effectiveness of sea power, as the Task Force travelled 8,000 miles to liberate British territory the size of Wales from numerically superior land and air forces: 'Nothing else could have done the job.'[46] Amphibious forces again proved their ability to achieve tactical surprise, sidestepping Argentine defences at Port Stanley to land 3 Commando Brigade in San Carlos Water against light opposition. Finesse was essential as the LVTs and heavily gunned support craft of 1944 were long gone. Scorpion tanks embarked in LCUs were the only available source of close fire support. Crucially, Operation Corporate drew a line under a long period of imperial retreat, associating amphibious warfare with political success rather than evacuation. As the 1940s reformers had intended, Royal Marines acted as the nucleus of the amphibious forces of the Crown, providing landing craft crews and essential expertise, as well as the core of an expeditionary force reinforced with additional infantry, armour and supporting arms. The Commando Logistics Regiment, formed in 1972, was especially significant, landing stores fast enough to maintain political and military momentum, then splitting amoeba-like to support active operations by two Infantry Brigades. The success of the medical arrangements was in striking contrast to early Marine operations, not a single friendly casualty dying once they had reached the Medical Squadron at Ajax Bay.

There were other contrasts with earlier wars. Operations depended to an unprecedented extent on helicopters. Usual rules about seat belts and minimum weather conditions were waived to keep up the 'constant shuffle of ammunition in and casualties out', while night flights from darkened ships convinced RM ground crew of the attractions of being on the ground.[47] The Falklands proved 'a much more intimate war than ever before', the media clamour for immediate news compromising operations and the peace of mind of those left behind, 'Too much of the burden of war was borne by the families at home.'[48] Trench foot and diarrhoea were old enemies, reducing one Troop to 'hobbling wet gremlins with knackered digestive systems'.[49] A night attack looked like 'something out of All Our Yesterdays, hundreds of troops marching to the front, while artillery flashed on the horizon'.[50] During air raids on shipping in San Carlos Water, 'the phrase heard more than any other was "It's just like watching a film" and it was.' 42 Cdo's Mortar Troop put a new gloss on an old adage, 'Time spent on base plate preparation is never wasted'.[51]

Above all else the Falklands justified the intensive training of Commandos and Paratroopers, another invention of the old ISTDC. The loss of *Atlantic Conveyor* with many helicopters compelled most of the infantry to march 84 miles from the bridgehead across East Falkland to Port Stanley, 'The first 17 miles of which were carried out by men carrying Bergens as well as fighting order, a total weight often over 120lbs.' Milan and mortar No. 2s carried 153 and 146lbs respectively. Everyone bore a hand with ammunition. Even 42 Cdo's CO carried two mortar bombs, 'Not so good when you are carrying them, but marvellous when they arrive out of the sky to support your attack.'[52] Fieldcraft honed by decades of active operations gave Marines a crucial advantage over Stanley's more numerous defenders, Argentinian troops 'just bumbling around on the skyline, providing an excellent demonstration of "how to be seen at night"'. Commando patrols, on the other hand, approached within 20 yards, or closer:

> The most successful recce was when a 9 man patrol managed to infiltrate into an enemy position on Two Sisters, reporting back and remaining undetected until they were compromised by an Argentinian looking for somewhere to relieve himself. In the ensuing contact, the patrol successfully extracted itself leaving 9 enemy dead and some wounded, without any own casualties.[53]

Argentine defences around Port Stanley, the islands' main town, were based on a ring of small mountains. While 42 Cdo were tasked with capturing Mount Harriet and 45 Cdo with Two Sisters, 40 Cdo remained in the bridgehead as reserve, a backhanded compliment to their reliability. Two companies reinforced the Welsh Guards at Sapper Hill, but the war was 'not all we thought it might be'. After so many low-intensity operations, 'it was a unique experience to be preparing for a full scale Commando assault on a conventional army in a well prepared defensive position.' In battle 'the Commando policy of hitting hard with everything at our disposal, from rifle to Naval gunfire proved its worth.'[54] Gaining cover on the rocky hilltops, individual sections systematically cleared snipers and machine-gun posts:

> with the assistance of noisy but effective support from a mixture of NGS, Artillery and Mortar Fire. . . just in front of advancing troops. When this had to be lifted the enemy were literally blasted out of the rock strongholds with 84mm and 66mms.[55]

When Captain Ian Gardiner looked back down the Two Sisters ridge, his spine froze: 'the position was impregnable. Had Royal Marines been ordered to defend such a position, they would have died of old age in there.' Two days later, after further assaults by 2 Para and 2nd Scots Guards, over 10,000 Argentinians surrendered. Twenty-five Royal Marines died by enemy action, a measure of the professional skill that even overcame the harsh conditions of the Falklands 'Camp':

> we refined our methods of living in this inhospitable place to such a degree that by the end we were like wild animals, and almost preferred living out of doors. We could have lived in the wilds indefinitely on what we carried in our fighting orders. Never let it be said that we had come to the end of our endurance by the time we reached Stanley, or that the weather would have beaten us. We could have gone on for ever![56]

Epilogue

Twenty years after the Falklands War and 200 since Earl St Vincent obtained their Royal title, Her Majesty's Jollies continue to fulfil their historic function as amphibious infantry within the Royal Navy, together with other special naval roles: landing craft crews, Special Boat Section and bands. Sea service refuses to fade away. Marines carry out seaman duties in patrol vessels, besides military tasks in larger vessels. Air Defence detachments operate Javelin missiles in the Gulf, and Marine protection parties abseil from Lynx helicopters onto ships suspected of breaking UN sanctions. Comacchio Company, heir to 43 Cdo's traditions, has expanded into Fleet Protection Group RM, responsible for naval base defence including inshore security of the Royal Navy's nuclear deterrent. The post-Cold War search for peace dividends has left 3 Commando Brigade largely unscathed, with its associated Artillery, Signals, Engineer and Logistics units. The resumption of normal international politics has encouraged radical thinking about the Royal Navy's strategic purpose: out has gone the deep-water emphasis that removed guns from frigates and scrapped Commando carriers, in favour of renewed appreciation of the political leverage provided by forces like the Amphibious Ready Group:

> deployed complete with its combat and logistics support. . . rapidly diverted to a trouble spot, taking full advantage of the unique access provided by the sea to stand well off a coast without commitment or infringing national sovereignty.[57]

New amphibious ships are coming into service after years of delay. HMS *Ocean* has already shown her usefulness off Sierra Leone. A purpose-built LPH, *Ocean* carries up to 830 Marines, with Sea King helicopters to carry them ashore. Two *Albion* class LPDs, carrying 710 at a pinch, are expected to replace the veteran *Fearless* in 2003. All three ships can accommodate the RAF's big Chinook helicopter, are built to military damage control standards, and will carry new faster landing craft. While Marines clearly remain soldiers, they are perhaps more closely integrated within the Royal Navy than at any time since the Second World War. Absolute numbers of Marines have declined since 1982, but they represent a higher proportion of a greatly reduced Navy.[58]

Historians must resist the temptation to view the present as in some way the culminating point, triumphant or otherwise, of the past. Today is as transient as any other point in time. The temptation is particularly difficult to resist when comparing the well-ordered professionalism of today's Marines with the ill-conceived improvizations of some of their predecessors. The contrast between operations at Cartagena and in the Falklands could not be more striking. The unthinking Victorian neglect of a Corps of proven fighting value contrasts sharply with the conscious pursuit of a distinct rational identity since the 1940s. Elements of continuity remain, however. Royal Marines can no more focus exclusively on their maritime role today than the Duke of York's Regiment could in the 1670s. Recent missions in such unlikely places as Kurdistan and Kosovo have proved that well trained infantry need never lack employment. Amphibious forces, no longer at the mercy of wind and weather, provide a better means than ever of concentrating maximum force at the decisive point, in conditions of speed and security. Marines are an essential component of such forces with their offensive spirit and the flexibility that come from Commando training, and constantly working in an air/land/sea environment. Such troops can no more be improvized now, when every conflict is a brush-fire war, than they could in the slower moving 1740s and 1940s. Across five centuries of peace and war, the history of the Royal Marines demonstrates how down-to-earth preparation and combat effectiveness are inextricably bound together, a unity symbolized by the Corps' badge: the Great Globe itself encircled by the Laurel Wreath.

Appendix I

Marine Establishments 1690–2000

Year	Numbers	Context
1690–98	3,000	Nine Years' War
1702–13	8,000	War of Spanish Succession
1739–48	10,000	War of Jenkins' Ear & Austrian Succession
1755	5,000	Formation
1756–62	15–19,000	Seven Years' War
1763	4,300	Post-war reductions
1776–82	25,000	American War of Independence
1783	4,495	Post-war reductions
1793	9,815	French Revolutionary War
1794	12,115	-do-
1797	22,716	-do-
1802	30,000	-do-
1803	12,000	Peace of Amiens
1804–15	31,000	Napoleonic Wars
1816	6,000	Post-war reductions
1820–53	9–12,000	Small wars
1854–56	15,500	Russian War
1857–65	18,000	Interventions in China and Japan
1866–91	12,500–14,000	Small wars
1892–1913	16–19,000	Naval races
1914–18	18–55,000	First World War: total casualties 12,315
1919	15,000	Demobilisation
1923–35	9,500	Disarmament
1939–45	12–78,500	Second World War: total casualties 7,542
1948	13,000	Harwood Committee proposes disbandment
1960	9,000	Retreat from Empire
1982	7,500	Falklands War
2000	6,500	Peace Dividend

Sources:
1755–1945: Col Markham Rose, *The Story of the Royal Marines* (1935)
Col G.W.M. Glover, *Short History of the Royal Marines* (1948)
1945–2000: J.D. Ladd, *By Sea, By Land* (1998)

Appendix II

Marine Regiments 1690–1747

The Two Marine Regiments 16 Jan 1690–1 Aug 1698

1st   Earl of Torrington
      → Earl of Danby/Marquis of Carmarthen
2nd   Earl of Pembroke
      → Sir Henry Killegrew
      → Lord John Berkeley
      → Sir Cloudesley Shovell

The Four Marine Regiments 1 Aug 1698–20 May 1699

William Seymour
Henry Dutton Colt
Henry Mordaunt
Thomas Brudenell (ex-Carmarthen's & Shovell's)

Queen Anne's Marine Regiments 10 Mar 1702–6 Mar 1713

Colonels	*Quarters 1704*	*Status post-1713*
1) Thomas Saunderson → T. Pownall → Charles Wills	Canterbury	30th Foot (1/East Lancs)
2) George Villiers → Alexander Luttrell → Joshua Churchill → Sir Harry Goring	Exeter/Plymouth	31st Foot (1/East Surreys)
3) Edward Fox → Jacob Bor	Southampton	32nd Foot (1/DCLI)
4a) Henry Mordaunt → transferred to Line 1703	n/a	Disbanded
4b) William Seymour (Queen's Own Marines) → transferred to Line 1710	Exeter/Plymouth	4th Foot (King's Own)

4c) Charles Churchill	Exeter/Plymouth	Disbanded
5) Henry Holt	Chichester	Disbanded
6) Viscount Shannon	Rochester	Disbanded

Source: BSS, i, p. 35 & RM 11/11/7, Abstract of General Orders relating to the Marine Forces #5.

The Ten Marine Regiments 1740–48

The Ten Marine Regiments were numbered 44th to 53rd Foot within the Army.

From 25 Oct 1739:
1st	Edward Wolfe
	→ G. Keightley (1745)
	→ G. Churchill (1745)
2nd	William Robinson
	→ R. Frazer (1741)
3rd	Anthony Lowther
	→ R. Sowle (1745)
	→ H. Holmes (1746)
4th	John Wynyard
	→ James Long (1742)
	→ Byng (1744)
5th	Charles Douglas *
	→ J. Grant (1741) *
	→ S. Daniel (1741) *
	→ James Cochrane (1741)
6th	Hon. Lewis Ducie Moreton *
	→ J. Cotterell (1741)
	→ Hon W. Herbert (1747)
	→ James Laforey (1747)

Added 25 Dec 1740:
7th	Henry Cornwall (Cornwallis?)
8th	William Hanmore (Hammer?)
	→ J. Duncombe (1742)
	→ Lord G. Beauclerk (1747)
	→ James Jordan (1748)
9th	Charles Powlett
10th	J. Jeffreys
	→ Sir Andrew Agnew (1746)

* Died at Cartagena

Source: BSS vol i, pp. 72 & 87.

Notes

Introduction
1. *JRUSI* 1944, lxxxix, p. 28, Brig H.T. Newman RM, 'Functions of the Royal Marines in Peace and War'.
2. *G&L* 1946, lvi, p. 236: reviewing Col G.W.M. Glover RM, *A Short History of the Royal Marines*.

Chapter 1 Overture and Beginnings
1. RM 11/13/10(A), Gunner W. Craig RMA (HMS *New Zealand*), 1905–07, p. 86 & RM 11/13/246, Bombardier D. Wynne, 29 Jun 1882.
2. Burchett, *A Complete History of the Most Remarkable Transactions at Sea* p. 677.
3. Memoirs of Lord Torrington quoted in BSS/I p. 41.
4. Burchett p. 677. The garrison surrendered officially 24 July. Allied losses: 91 killed; 206 wounded.
5. BSS/i p. 41: Journal of Rev Thomas Pocock, Chaplain HMS *Ranelagh*. Dicing with death was a common way of mitigating the severity of seventeenth-century military discipline.
6. Edye MSS/III pp. 154–5, 3 Nov 1704, Adm Sir John Leake/John Methuen (British Ambassador to Lisbon).
7. Edye MSS/III, p. 158, 10 Nov 1704, Leake/Methuen, p. 51; 2 Nov 1704, Council of War, p. 49; 30 Nov 1704, Hesse-Leake, p. 157; 26 Nov 1704, Leake/Methuen & p. 150; 19 Dec 1704, Methuen/Sec. Hedges.
8. 13th and 35th Foot, later the Somerset Light Infantry and 1st Royal Susssex.
9. Quoted in BSS/i, p. 54, *Affairs of the World*, Mar 1705.
10. Quoted in BSS/i p. 56, *Affairs of the World*, Mar 1705.
11. Thomas More Molyneux, *Conjunct Expeditions*, p. 127.
12. Quoted in BSS/i p. 56, *Affairs of the World*, Apr 1705.
13. Edye MSS/III, p. 75, 5 Sept 1704, Harley/Duke of Newcastle.
14. CTB 1709, p. 159, Royal Warrant, 5 May 1709.
15. Edye MSS/III, p. 160, 7 May 1705, Methuen/Hedges, Secretary of State.
16. CTB 1705–6, p. 249, 10 May 1705, Treasury Warrant.
17. S. Martin-Leake, *Life of Sir John Leake, Rear-Admiral of Great Britain*, p. 239.
18. Glover, quoting *Triumphs of Her Majesty's Arms*, 1707.
19. Edye MSS/III, pp. 102–3, Petition of Capt John Mason, 1711 & p. 110, Petition of John Curtis, 1710.

20. Privy Council Register, Ca II vol iv, fol 264, quoted in BSS/i, p. 15.
21. CSPD 1664–65, pp. 54 & 162. The officers included: Sir Chichester Wray (Lt Col); Sir Charles Littleton (Major); Sir John Griffin (i.e. Griffiths), John Legge and Nathaniel Darell (Captains). Field officers at this time commanded companies, so received Captain's commissions also.
22. Edye, *Historical Records*, p. 21.
23. CSPD 1673, p. 414, 1 Jul 1673, Littleton/William Bridgeman.
24. Edye, p. 44.
25. CSPD 1664–65, p. 407, 4 Jun 1665, Sir William Coventry/Lord Arlington.
26. Edye, p. 60, Captain Utber.
27. CSPD 1665–66, p. 561, 21 Jul 1666, Earl of Carlisle/Sir John Williamson (Secretary of State) & p. 572, 24 Jul 1666, Lt Edward Suckley/James Hickes.
28. Edye p. 82, Letters to Williamson 11 & 12 May 1667. Another source gives 2 killed and 10 wounded.
29. CSPD 1667, p. 217, 20 June 1667, Capt Silas Taylor/Williamson.
30. CSPD 1667, p. 207, 18 June 1667, Richard Browne/Williamson.
31. CSPD 1667, p. 259, 2 July 1667, p. 263, 3 July 1667 & p. 266, 4 July 1667, Capt Silas Taylor/Williamson.
32. CSPD 1667, p. 270, 6 July 1667, Richard Browne/Williamson.
33. CSPD 1667, p. 263 & Edye, p. 87.
34. J. Childs, *Army of Charles II* (Routledge & Kegan Paul, 1976), p. 180.
35. CSPD 1667, p. 266, 3 July 1667, Oxford/Williamson.
36. CSPD 1667, p. 299, 16 July 1667, Purser Richard Tyler/Samuel Pepys.
37. Edye, p. 161.
38. CSPD 1672, p. 92, 29 May 1972, Thomas Lucas/Nathaniel Herne. Montague was the Earls' of Sandwich family name.
39. CSPD 1672, p. 104, 30 May 1672, Capt Silas Taylor/Williamson.
40. Edye, p. 151.
41. Edye, p. 152.
42. CSPD 1672, p. 104, Capt Silas Taylor/Williamson, 30 May 1672.
43. Edye, p. 148.
44. CSPD 1673, p. 30, 11 Mar 1673, Note by Williamson.
45. CSPD 1680–81, p. 7, 5 Sept 1680, Charles II/Oxford.
46. CSPD 1680–81, p. 178, 5 Feb 1681, Information of Capt Edward Le Neve.
47. Edye, pp. 242–3, Tangiers Rescue, p. 8.
48. CSPD 1675–6, p. 273, 26 Aug 1675, Taylor/Williamson & p. 284, 4 Sept 1675.
49. BSS/i, p. 24.
50. CSPD 1678, p. 389, 2 Sep 1678, Monmouth/Lord Faversham & 3 Aug 1678, Williamson/Littleton.
51. CSPD 1673–74 pp. 492–3, Dispositions of Garrisons of HRH's Regiment 1674.
52. Gillespie, *Historical Review of the Royal Marines Corps*, p. 1.
53. Edye p. 104.
54. Edye p. 139, 2 May 1672, Darell/Arlington.
55. CSPD 1672, p. 141, 2 Jun 1672, Darell/Williamson.
56. CSPD 1672, p. 191, 10 Jul 1672, Buller/Williamson.
57. CSPD 1672–73, p. 149, 11 Nov 1672 & p. 478, 25 Jan 1673, Darell/Williamson. Nieuport and Ostend were in the Spanish Netherlands, and hence neutral. Zealand was one of the hostile United Provinces.

58. CSPD 1683, p. 103, 12 Jul 1683, Lt Philemon Powell/Littleton.
59. CSPD 1667, p. 246, 29 Jun 1667, Darell/Arlington.
60. CSPD 1682, p. 157, 7 Apr 1682. Information of Edward Roberts, p. 171, 19 Apr, Capt James Wallis/Capt Ralph Widdrington.
61. CSPD 1683, p. 403, 17 Sept 1683. Anonymous letter to the king & p. 409, Secretary Jenkins/Littleton. Also p. 411, 21 Sept, Lt Powell/Jenkins.
62. CSPD 1685 #1159, 6 July 1685, Earl of Sunderland/Earl of Faversham.
63. Edye, pp. 196–7, p. 199 & p. 215.
64. CTB 1679–80, pp. 530–1, 11 May 1680, Henry Guy/Littleton.
65. CSPD 1687–88, p. 1498, 15 Sept 1688, Earl of Sunderland/Littleton & p. 1543, 24 Sept 1688 Warrant.
66. Edye, p. 293, 6 Nov 1688.
67. Edye, p. 294, Littleton/Lady Littleton.
68. Edye, p. 294, n.d.

Chapter 2   False Starts and False Musters

1. CSPD 1690–91, pp. 211–2, Memorandum n.d. & Edye, *Historical Records*, pp. 330–1.
2. See appendices for numbers and regiments.
3. Edye MSS/IX, 2 Aug 1739, Adm Vernon/Newcastle.
4. Quoted in Richmond, *The Navy and the War of 1739–48*, vol I, p. 272.
5. Edye MSS/VII, p. 64, 17 Aug 1709, Capt James Herbert/Admiralty. The Royal Navy regularly pressed men from homeward-bound merchant ships.
6. Edye MSS/VII p. 27, 17 Feb 1710, Commodore Charles Cornwall/Admiralty.
7. CSPD 1694–5 p. 191, 18 Jun 1694, Warrant to Marquis Carmarthen. Recruits would be quartered in public houses until forwarded to headquarters.
8. 1756 Act of Parliament 'for the more speedy recruiting His Majesty's land and marine forces' quoted in *The Gentleman's Magazine*, 1756, p. 146.
9. Edye MSS/III, p. 81, 11 Sept 1705, Memorial.
10. Edye MSS/III, p. 40, *London Gazette*, 4–7 Mar 1709. A 'black man' at this period implied a dark Caucasian.
11. RM 11/28/32, Papers relating to Cottrell's Marines, 15 Nov 1745, Capt George Gordon/Cottrell.
12. RM 11/28/32, 24 April 1743, Capt Richard Webb/Cottrell. General Wolfe acted as an inspector of Marine forces.
13. Edye MSS/VII, p. 69, 28 Feb 1713, Capt William Houlding/Admiralty (annotated).
14. Edye MS/VII, p. 4, 19 May 1707, Capt Aldred/Admiralty.
15. G.R. Barnes & J.H. Owen, *Private Papers of John Earl of Sandwich*, II, p. 104.
16. Edye, p. 98.
17. Edye MSS/III, p. 170, 28 Jun 1703.
18. BSS/i, p. 133, See Appendices.
19. Edye MSS/VII, p. 25, 12 Nov 1707, Capt Matthew Campbell/Admiralty.
20. Edye MSS/XI, 8 Mar 1711, Walker/St John.
21. RM 11/11/7, *Abstract of General Orders,* Item 30: n.d.
22. RM 11/28/32, 24 Apr 1742, Capt Richard Webb/Col Cottrell. Officers were respited 8d a day for every man they were below establishment, although the Government only paid 6d per man mustered, thus making it impossible to subsist the men actually present under arms.

23. CSPD 1664–65, p. 101, 2 Dec 1664, Sir William Coventry/Secretary Bennet.
24. CSPD 1666–67, p. 456, 16 Jan 1667, news item.
25. Edye, p. 43, 11 May 1665, Lt William Gardiner/Pepys.
26. Edye MSS/VII, p. 52, 27 Mar 1706, Capt Lord Archibald Hamilton.
27. RM 11/11/7, *Abstract of General Orders,* Item 43, 14 Jan 1707.
28. Edye, pp. 346–9.
29. Edye, p. 313, 2 Apr 1690, Treasury Warrant.
30. Edye, p. 383.
31. Edye, pp. 589 & 592, petitions to Marquis of Carmarthen and Treasury, and of Mrs Burton, wife of Lt Charles Burton.
32. Edye, p. 459.
33. Edye, p. 590.
34. Edye MSS/III, p. 89, 15 Jul 1709, John Devereux.
35. Edye MSS/XI, 8 Jul 1712, Admiralty/Lord Dartmouth.
36. Parliamentary Commission 1746, App.XLII, p. 210, Proceedings of Court Martial 10–13 April 1742.
37. Edye MSS/III, p. 79, 28 Apr 1705, Jane Dyer.
38. Edye MSS/XI, 11 Mar 1702, Memorial Prince George/Queen Anne.
39. CSPD 1702–03, p. 64, 23 May 1703, Royal Letter. Previously Marines had been on the Land Forces Establishment, except when at sea.
40. See RM 11/11/7, *Abstract of General Orders.*
41. Scouller, *The Armies of Queen Anne,* p. 31, 3 Nov 1703, Paymaster Marines/ Lord Treasurer.
42. Edye MSS/VII, p. 110, 16 April 1708, Capt John Smith.
43. CTB 1709, p. 21, 17 Mar 1709, Royal Warrant to Paymaster of Marines.
44. RM 11/11/7, *Abstract of General Orders,* Item 32, 9 Nov 1706. Chatham Chest paid out small pensions to disabled seamen, and (after the Admiralty assumed control) Marines, in return for stoppages of 6d per man per month.
45. RM 11/11/7, *Abstract of General Orders,* Item 19, 25 Jan 1705.
46. BSS/i, p. 51, *Life and Adventures of Matthew Bishop* (1744) & CTB 1712, pp. 169–70, 26 Feb 1712, Thomas Hanley/Sir Roger Mostyn.
47. Scouller, p. 280, 7 Nov 1706 Petition of 13 officers & the widow of another, deprived of 8 years pay.
48. CTB 1709, p. 300, 8 Aug 1709, Petition forwarded to Auditors of Imprest, & p. 353, 9 Sept 1709, Letter of Direction. Plunkett sold his commission to recoup his debts, i.e. parted with his company.
49. CTB 1709, p. 109, 22 Mar 1709, William Lowndes/Navy Commissioners.
50. Edye, p. 430, 5 Dec 1694.
51. Parliamentary Commission 1746, pp. 155–7.
52. Parliamentary Commission 1746, p. 139, Lt Col Sewell.
53. Parliamentary Commission 1746, p. 155, Capt John Boulton & Lt John Gilbagie.
54. Scouller, p. 135.
55. Parliamentary Commission 1746, p. 145, Capt Robert Shafto.
56. Parliamentary Commission 1746, pp. 141–3, Edward Lloyd, late Agent, and Brigadier J. Jeffreys. Exact amounts were:.

18 Months Off-reckonings assigned:		£4,554 14s 10¾d
2 -do- by warrant:		£ 365 8s 5d
Paid by the Agent:		£1,900 18s 0d
Jeffreys' Profit:		£3,019 5s 3¾d

57. Edye, pp. 477 & 440.
58. Edye MSS VII/16–18, 7 Nov 1706, Capt Thomas Butler & 15 Nov 1706, William Morgan.
59. Edye MSS/XI, p. 64, 19 Dec 1741, Capt Gregory.
60. RM 1/28/32, 9 Apr 1748, Record of Court Martial.
61. Parliamentary Commission 1746, p. 141, John Roberts Clothier.
62. Edye MSS/XI, p. 59, 2 Jan 1741, Admiralty/Duke of Newcastle.
63. Parliamentary Commission 1746, p. 154, Thomas Jones, Surgeon and Paymaster.
64. Edye MSS/VII, p. 71, 9 Feb 1706, Capt James Jesson.
65. Edye MSS/VII, pp. 53–5, 29 Sep 1706 & 6 May 1707, Capt Sir Thomas Hardy.
66. Edye MSS/VII, p. 23, 4 Nov 1707, Capt Philip Cavendish.
67. Parliamentary Commission 1746, p. 143, Capt John Murray.
68. Edye MSS/VII, p. 45, 11 Dec 1712, Capt Richard Griffith.
69. RM 11/28/32, 25 Jun 1745, Cottrell/William Adair.
70. Edye, p. 520, Capt John Price.
71. Edye, MSS/XI, pp. 60–4, various dates, Captains Geddes, Robinson, Fox, and Holburne.
72. Edye MSS/XI, p. 65, 28 Apr 1742, Admiralty/Duke of Newcastle.
73. Edye MSS/XI, p. 59, 2 Jan 1741, Admiralty/Duke of Newcastle.
74. Edye MSS/XI, p. 22, 19 Feb 1747, Admiralty/Duke of Newcastle referring to 'Warrant dated the 28th February last'.
75. Anonymous, *Letter. . . Concerning the Four Regiments Commonly Called Mariners.*
76. *A Short Vindication of Marine Regiments*, Edye, pp. 563–72 reproduces both pamphlets.
77. BSS/i, pp. 323–4, *The Flying Post*, No. 3543, 16–18 Sep 1714.
78. Edye MSS/XI, 28 July 1713, *Heads of Instructions for the Commissioners appointed to Disband and Account the Marine Regiments.*
79. RM 2/8/4(5a), Petitions of Thomas Hoole 1713.
80. Edye MSS/XI, 6 Mar 1714, Abstract of payments. Detachments returning from sea were still being paid off in March 1714.
81. Edye MSS/XI, 24 Dec 1713, S. Hunter & N. Layton/Mr Secy Bromley.
82. Edye MSS/XI, n.d. Humble Petition of the Marine Soldiers Commanded by Major Gen¹ Wills.
83. Quoted in BSS/i, pp. 68–9, 25 Dec 1713, Orders from the Marquis of Ormonde.
84. Edye MSS/XI, 26 Dec 1713, Lt-Col Markham/Mr Secy Bromley.
85. Edye MSS/XI, 5 May 1714, Admiralty/Mr Secy Bromley.
86. Edye MSS/XI, 24 & 31 Dec 1713, Commissioners/Mr Secy Bromley.
87. NC 1805 XIV, p. 50.
88. RM, Extract From His Majesty's Order in Council Dated 3 April 1755.
89. CSPD 1690–91, p. 248, 7 Feb 1691, Home Secretary's direction.
90. Williams, *Documents Relating to Anson's Voyage* p. 49–50, Walter & Robins, *Anson's Voyage.* Sir Charles Wager was First Lord of the Admiralty, 21 Jun 1733–19 Mar 1742.
91. Edye, p. 463.
92. O'Loghlen, *The Marine Volunteer,* p. 122.
93. Nicholas, *Historical Record of the Royal Marine Forces,* I, p. 358.

94. O'Loghlen, pp. 123–4.
95. Nicholas, I, p. 54.
96. Quoted in J.A. Lowe, *Records of the Portsmouth Division of Marines 1764–1800*, p. xix.
97. BM, Add Mss 39190, 28 Dec 1774, Pitcairn/Col Mackenzie.
98. Edye MSS/III, p. 76, 30 Sept 1708, Thomas Pitt/various persons.
99. Edye MSS/XI, 10 May 1711, Bor/Burchett.
100. O'Loghlen, pp. 125–6.
101. Bonner Smith, *Letters of Admiral of the Fleet The Earl of St Vincent*, vol II, pp. 155 & 157.

Chapter 3   Action Under Sail

1. BSS i, p. 26, Memorial in favour of forming two Marine Regiments, 1690.
2. Edye MSS/VII, p. 80, 4 Oct 1709, Capt John Lonen/Admiralty.
3. RM 7/4/1, *Derby Mercury*, 30 Mar 1782, Capt Pole/Admiralty.
4. RM 11/13/061, Capt John Robyns Diary, 19 Feb 1810.
5. RM 11/13/091, Col Richard Swale Diary, 13 Jun 1800, 26 Mar 1801 & Feb 1806.
6. RR, p. 42, Maj Christopher Noble, 1 Aug 1799.
7. RM 11/13/061, Robyns, 10 Nov 1799.
8. RM 11/13/093, Sgt John Howe Diary, 21 Dec 1780.
9. RM 7/9/1–17, Maj Mortimer Timpson, *Memoir*, pp. 16–17.
10. RM 11/13/093, Howe, 9 May 1793.
11. Williams, p. 196; Walter & Robins.
12. Brian Lavery, *Shipboard Life and Organisation 1731–1815*, p. 232, 'Orders for the Officers of Marines on Board HMS Mars', 31 May 1799.
13. CSPD 1664–5, p. 408, 5 Jun 1665, Richard Burges/Williamson.
14. CSPD 1672, p. 94, 29 May 1672, Littleton/Williamson.
15. RM 7/4/1, *Derby Mercury*, 30 Mar 1782, Capt Pole/Admiralty.
16. RM 7/9/1–17, Mortimer Timpson, pp. 15–16.
17. GM 1744 pp. 170–2.
18. *Derby Mercury*, 26 Jan 1759, 9 Nov 1758, Capt Tyrell/C-in-C Leeward Islands.
19. NC xiv, p. 482 & XV, p. 305.
20. NC xxix, p. 295, Letter from 'your obedient servant AN IRON GUN'.
21. RM 7/7/10(24), *Derby Mercury*, 30 Mar 1782, Capt Pole/Admiralty.
22. NC xxx, p. 171, 26 Apr 1813, Capt Black.
23. RM 11/13/093, Howe, 7 Jul 1781.
24. CSPD 1673, p. 490, 10 Aug 1673, P.B./Littleton.
25. RM 11/13/093, Howe, 9 Jul 1781.
26. RM 11/13/155, Lt William Ackroyd, *Notebook*.
27. NC ii, p. 572.
28. CSPD 1673, p. 491, 10 Aug 1673, P.B./Littleton.
29. NC ii, p. 161.
30. NC xxx, p. 161.
31. O'Loghlen pp. 121–2.
32. Williams, p. 48, Nov 1739, Secy at War to House of Commons.
33. Lt J. MacIntire, *A Military Treatise on the Discipline of the Marine Forces etc*, pp. 6–7.

34. BSS/i p. 308.
35. MacIntire, p. 121.
36. O'Loghlen pp. 114 & 119.
37. CSPD 1667–8, p. 393, 15 May 1668, Capt Anthony Langston/Williamson.
38. *Derby Mercury,* 25 Aug–1 Sep 1780, 13 Aug 1780, Capt MacBride.
39. *GM* 1756, p. 506, Action between HMS *Colchester* (50) & *Lyme* (20), and the French *Aquilon* (40) & *Fidele* (24).
40. *Derby Mercury,* 15–22 May 1747, anonymous correspondent.
41. BSS/ii, p. 322.
42. RM 11/13/093, Howe, 16 Mar 1781, describing the First Battle of the Capes.
43. BSS/i, p. 244, Sergeant Thomas Rees.
44. BSS/i, p. 321, from aboard the *Assurance* in the Downs, 3 July 1652. Soldiers from Baxter's, Berkstead's, Ingoldsby's & Pride's Regiments all served at sea.
45. CSPD 1665–6, p. 503, 6 Jul 1666, R. Watts/Williamson.
46. Edye, *Historical Records,* pp. 574–5; Anonymous, *Letter. . . Concerning the Four Regiments Commonly Called Mariners,* p. 10.
47. BSS/ii, p. 324, *The Flying Post or Postmaster,* 16–18 Sept 1714.
48. Edye MSS/VII, p. 31, 11 Aug 1709, Lord Duffins & p. 57, 12 Nov 1707, Capt W. Heriott.
49. D.A. Baugh, *Naval Administration 1715–1750,* p. 49, 15 Feb 1719/20, Admiralty Memorial & *Regulations and Instructions Relating to HM Service at Sea* 1757, p. 199. Minimum complements of small arms men, excluding Marines, ranged from a 1st Rate's 150 to a sloop's 30.
50. RM 11/13/155, Ackroyd & RM 11/13/093, Howe, 16 Mar 1781.
51. MacIntire, p. 113.
52. O'Loghlen, p. 114.
53. BSS/i, p. 240.
54. MacIntire, pp. 104–6 & 119.
55. Edye MSS/VII, p. 64, 27 Jun 1709, Capt Robert Hughes.
56. MacIntire, p. 111 & Brian Lavery p. 232, 'Orders for the Officers of Marines on Board HMS Mars', 31 May 1799.
57. *NC* xxix, p. 256, 22 Mar 1813, Capt Irby.
58. BSS/i, p. 256, anonymous seaman.
59. *Derby Mercury,* 26 Jan 1759; 9 Nov 1758, Capt Tyrell/C-in-C Leeward Islands.
60. BSS/i, p. 256.
61. *NC* xxx, p. 161.
62. Gardiner, p. 26.
63. BSS/i, p. 140.
64. RNM MSS/16, Captain Richard Moubray, *Notebook in HMS Active* 1801–7.
65. BSS/ii, p. 18, Lt Thomas Hurdle.
66. W.G. Perrin, *Boteler's Dialogues* pp. 160–1.
67. Edye MSS/XI, p. 72, 8 Jan 1708, Capt Charles Hardy (HMS *Roebuck*).
68. Edye MSS/XI, p. 72, 4 Oct 1744, Admiralty/Newcastle.
69. Brian Lavery, p. 477, Capt Robert Clarke RM.
70. O'Loghlen, p. 121 & BSS/i, p. 126, 25 Aug 1778, OC Chatham Division/Admiralty.

71. MacIntire, p. 319.
72. D. Bonner Smith, *Barrington Papers,* p. 298, 31 Mar 1761, A Keppel/Hon Capt Barrington.
73. CSPD 1670, p. 362, 3 Aug 1670, Charles II/Master of Ordnance.
74. RM 11/28/32, 20 Dec 1742, *Orders to be observed by the Officers Commanding Any Detachment of Coll Cottrell's Regiment on Board HM's Fleet.* Cf BSS/i, p. 121, Admiralty order 5 Aug 1755 & *Regulations and Instructions Relating to HM's Service at Sea 1808,* p. 423.
75. GM 1744, p. 172.
76. MacIntire, pp. 316–20 & p. 120.
77. *Regulations and Instructions Relating to HM's Service at Sea 1808,* p. 423 & Brian Lavery, p. 227; *State and Condition of the arms and accoutrements of marines serving on board HMS Blenheim,* only 51 out of 74 muskets were complete.
78. Edye MSS/XI, 7 Jul 1741, Capt Ambrose (HMS *Rupert*).
79. O'Loghlen, p. 121.
80. MacIntire, pp. 1 & 11.
81. O'Loghlen, pp. 112–13.
82. RM 11/13/093, Howe, 24 Jan 1781.
83. MacIntire, p. 3.
84. MacIntire, pp. 8 & 214.
85. RM 11/13/152, Lt Edward Wilson, 3 Oct & 18 Mar 1815.
86. A Quondam Sub, *Symptoms of Advice to the Oxxxxxxs of an Amphibious Corps* p. 63.
87. CSPD 1672, pp. 94–5, 29 May 1672, Silas Taylor/Williamson.
88. RM 11/13/093, Howe, 16 Mar 1781.
89. RM 11/12/42, Capt Lewis Roteley RM, Papers.
90. BSS/ii, p. 14.
91. *Derby Mercury,* 26 Jan 1759; 9 Nov 1758, Capt Tyrell/C-in-C Leeward Islands.
92. *Derby Mercury,* 11–18 Jan 1760; 26 Jan 1759, Officer in HMS *Magnanime* after Quiberon Bay.
93. GM 1745, p. 387.
94. GM 1745, p. 387.
95. NC xv. p. 207 & BSS/i, pp. 255–6.
96. MacIntire, pp. 112–13.
97. NC xxix, p. 256.
98. MacIntire, p. 115.
99. BSS/i, p. 31.
100. NC xv, p. 440, Obituary & BSS/ii, pp. 14 & 17.

Chapter 4   Raids and Expeditions

1. RM 2/8/4(5a), Petition 1713. 'Pettyvovas' = Petit Goaves, now in Haiti.
2. BSS/ii p. 311.
3. BSS/i, p. 27 & Edye, p. 326.
4. Molyneux, Pt I, pp. 101 & 109.
5. BSS/ii, p. 311.
6. CSPD 1694–5, pp. 168–9 & 183–4, 8 Jun 1694, Lord Berkeley/Sir John Trenchard & Relation of Capt Nathaniel Green.

7. Molyneux, Pt II, p. 48.
8. Edye MSS/III, p. 171.
9. Edye MSS/VII, p. 105, 9 July 1704, Capt Charles Stucley.
10. BSS/ii, p. 312.
11. Edye MSS/III, p. 75, Thomas Erle, 24 Jul 1708.
12. Edye/III, pp. 57–8, 13 Sept 1705, Paul Methuen.
13. Edye/III, pp. 161–3, 6 Oct 1705, HM Consul Genoa & 13 Oct 1705, Sir John Methuen-Hedges.
14. B. Tunstall, *The Byng Papers,* i, pp. 121–2, 18 Jun 1706, Sir John Leake/ George Byng.
15. Molyneux, p. 132.
16. BSS/i, p. 324, *The Flying Post* No. 3543, 16–18 Sep 1714.
17. CTB 1708, p. 474, 31 Dec 1708, Petition Maj Gen Wills & 23 Mar 1708, Report Dr John Lecaan, Physician to the Forces &c in Spain.
18. Edye MSS/III, p. 139, 28 Dec 1705, Galway/Sec. Hodges.
19. Edye MSS/XI, 28 Mar 1711, Ordnance Office/Thomas Erle & 5 Apr 1711 St John/Admiralty.
20. *Byng Papers,* ii, p. 301, 18 Jun 1708, Stanhope/Earl of Sunderland.
21. BSS/i, p. 324, *The Flying Post* No. 3543, 16–18 Sep 1714.
22. Molyneux, p. 174.
23. GM 1741, p. 235, Brian Ranfft, *Vernon Papers,* p. 620, & GM 1742, p. 352.
24. Molyneux, p. 173.
25. Edye MSS/XI, 23 Dec 1740, Sir Challoner Ogle/Newcastle & BSS/I, p. 75.
26. Edye MSS/XI, 9 Oct 1741, Answer to Sgt Elder's Petition.
27. BSS/i, p. 76, *Roderick Random.*
28. *Derby Mercury,* 11 Jun 1741.
29. Edye MSS/XI, 4 April 1741, Vernon/Wentworth.
30. GM 1741, p. 385.
31. GM 1741, p. 305, Vernon & Wentworth/Newcastle.
32. Molyneux, pp. 177–9.
33. Edye, p. 516.
34. Molyneux, pp. 175 & 181.
35. GM 1741, p. 310.
36. Edye MSS/XI, 18 May 1741, State and Condition of the Transport Ships & *Vernon Papers,* p. 322, 17 Aug 1741, Admiralty/Vernon.
37. GM 1741, p. 557.
38. Edye MSS/XI, 30 Jun 1741, Wentworth/Vernon.
39. Edye MSS/XI, 5 & 9 Aug 1741, Wentworth/Vernon at Santiago.
40. Nicholas, i, p. 24.
41. GM 1742, p. 352, Parliamentary debate.
42. Molyneux, Pt II, pp. 5–8.
43. CSPD 1690–1, p. 212, *Memorandum.*
44. BSS/i, p. 309, Parliamentary views on the Marines in 1740.
45. BSS/i, p. 135 & Gardiner, p. 8.
46. Anon, *Letter to a Member of Parliament Concerning the Four Regiments Commonly Called Mariners,* p. 10.
47. Molyneux, Part II, p. 50.
48. Bonner Smith, p. 180, 20 Sept 1757, Edward Hawke/Hon Capt Barrington.

49. MacIntire, pp. 222–48.
50. *USJ* 1844, *My First Smell of Gunpowder,* p. 556.
51. MacIntire, p. 244.
52. Gardiner & RM 11/13/313, Lloyd.
53. Gardiner, p. 14.
54. Gardiner, pp. 19–20.
55. Gardiner, pp. 26–7.
56. Gardiner, p. 34.
57. Gardiner, pp. 37 & 41.
58. All 1762 refs RM 11/13/313, Robert.
59. Gardiner, pp. 29 & 39.
60. RM 11/13/313, Lloyd, 19, 26 & 31 Jan 1762.
61. BSS, i, p. 139.
62. Molyneux, Pt II, p. 11.
63. BSS/ii, p. 105.
64. Nicholas, i, p. 58.
65. BSS/i, p. 111.
66. BSS/i, p. 105, 4 May 1761, Collins/Mrs Collins.
67. RM 7/4/1, Andrew Rea, *General Orders at the Camp on Bell Isle,* 24 April.
68. BSS/i, p. 108.
69. Maj-Gen J.L. Moulton, *The Royal Marines,* p. 12.
70. BSS/I, p. 115.
71. Molyneux, p. 120.
72. Col J. Davis *The History of the Second Queen's Royal Regiment* (1895), ii, p. 407.
73. BSS/ii, p. 315–6, 24 Jun 1758? Boscawen/Collins & 27 Jul 1758, Collins/Mrs Collins.
74. BL Add MSS 39190, Pitcairn/Mackenzie, Dec 1774; Barnes & Owen, I, p. 58, 14 Feb 1775, Pitcairn/Sandwich.
75. RM 7/7/5(7), 8 Dec 1774, Capt W. Souter/Brother-in-law.
76. RM 7/7/5(7), 22 Apr 1775, Souter.
77. BSS/i, pp. 156–7, 22 Jun 1775, J. Waller/Jacob Waller.
78. BSS/i, pp. 158–9 & 166. Total British losses, 226 killed, 828 wounded of whom Marines – 29 killed, 94 wounded.
79. RM 7/7/3–4, 14 Jul 1775, Lt D. Collins/Lt Col A.T. Collins.
80. RM 7/7/3–4, *Berrow's Worcester Journal,* 10 Aug 1775.
81. RM 7/7/3(5), Letter 15 Aug 1775, D. Collins/Mother.
82. RM 7/7/5(7), 2 Dec 1775, Souter.
83. RM 7/7/3(5), Letter 15 Aug 1775, D Collins/Mother.
84. RM 7/7/1–2, Marine Order Book 1775–77, 5 Dec 1775, 3 Jan & 11 Feb 1776.
85. Nicholas, i, p. 91.
86. Sandwich Papers IV, pp. 122–3, 21 Mar 1777, A.T. Collins/Sandwich.
87. RM 7/7/5(7), 23 Mar 1776, Souter.
88. RM 7/7/5(8), Letter 11 Nov/13 Nov 1776, D. Collins/Mother.
89. RM 7/7/1–2, Order Book, 24 Feb 1777, 17 Jun 1776 & 18 Apr 1777.
90. *Leicester & Nottingham Journal,* 8 Mar 1777; 29 Nov 1776, Major Batt/Lt Col Goreham.
91. RM 7/7/1–2, Order Book 1775–77, 26 Feb 1777.

92. Sandwich Papers II, p. 29, 16 Apr 1778, Keppel.
93. Nicholas, i, p. 99.
94. Sandwich Papers, IV, p. 230, 6 Jan 1782, Rodney/Sandwich.

Chapter 5   Sea Service and Barrack Life
1. Lavery, p. 432 & RM 11/12/42, 1 May 1807, Lt Lewis Roteley RM/Father.
2. Edye, p. 97.
3. Scouller, p. 208, Guardsman John Marshall Deane.
4. A Quondam Sub, p. iii.
5. Pitcairn/Mackenzie, n.d., 1774.
6. RM 11/13/152, 2nd Lt Edward Wilson Diary, 7 Oct 1815.
7. W. Fernyhough, *Military Memoirs of Four Brothers. . .*, p. 57, JF/parents, 3 Jun 1801.
8. RM 11/13/57(A), Lt J. Haverfield, 8 Jul 1847, HMS *Inconstant.*
9. RM 2/8/4(5a), Petition of Thomas Hoole, 1713.
10. RM 11/13/093, Sgt John Howe, 15 Feb 1780.
11. Howe, 2 Jan 1782.
12. Edye MSS/VII, p. 82, 4 Jul 1712, Lt A. Horsman/Capt Thomas Liall.
13. Edye MSS/XI, *Draft Regulations* 1747, #11 & #13.
14. O'Loghlen, pp. 111–12.
15. RM 11/12/42, 14 Aug 1805, Roteley/Father.
16. RM 11/13/152, Wilson, 2 June 1816.
17. Edye, pp. 4–5, Gillespie, p. 1.
18. RM 2/8/4(5a), Petition of Thomas Hoole, 1713.
19. CSPD 1690–91, pp. 211–2, Memorandum n.d. & Josiah Burchett, *A Complete History of the Most Remarkable Transactions at Sea etc.*, p. 615.
20. D.A. Baugh, *Naval Administration 1715–1750*, p. 154; 6 May 1747, Adm J. Stewart-Admy Sec; *Draft Regulations* 1747, #22.
21. *Draft Regulations* 1747, #8.
22. Report 1746, p. 139, Lt Col Sewell (*Leopard*).
23. RNM MSS/118, Capt John Sutton, *Order Book* 1794–1801. The swifter was rigged between the outer ends of capstan bars for additional hands.
24. Lavery, p. 229, Orders for Officers of Marines. . . HMS *Mars.*
25. USJ 1844, *My First Smell of Gunpowder,* p. 407.
26. NC 1803, p. 245.
27. JRUSI 1871, xv, p. 497, Maj-Gen G.A. Schomberg, *Are the Royal Marine Forces a Necessary Auxiliary to the Royal Navy?* (Cmdr Gilmore RN).
28. Edye MSS/VII, p. 111, 17 Feb 1712, Capt Charles Smith (*Oxford*).
29. Lavery, p. 224, Orders HMS *Blenheim,* 1796.
30. MacIntire, p. 139.
31. RM 7/4/1–7/8/1, 25 Aug 1745, Adm Vernon/Capt Windham (HMS *Drake*).
32. GM 1759, p. 496.
33. CHOP 1760–65, #632, 26 July 1762, Samuel Seddon/King George III.
34. USJ 1844, p. 411.
35. RM 11/13/093, Howe, Oct 179.
36. Edye MSS/VII, p. 43, 1 Dec 1711, Capt W. Gray.
37. MacIntire, p. 143.
38. Lavery, p. 220, 15 Aug 1798, St Vincent/Med Fleet.
39. J.S. Corbett, *Fighting Instructions,* p. 37.

40. RAdm H.G. Thursfield, *Five Naval Journals* 1789–1817, pp. 340–1, Capt Cumby's Order Book.
41. Capt Sir Robert Steele RM, *The Marine Officer; or Sketches of Service*, i, pp. 236–7, Maj C Noble RM.
42. RM 11/13/152, Wilson, 18 Mar 1815.
43. RM 11/13/89, Gen John Tatton Brown, *Written Orders. . . Royal George* #18.
44. Capt Basil Hall, *Fragments of Voyages and Travels* (Moxon, 1850) p. 152.
45. Edye, p. 536, Sep 1699, Admiralty/Adm Aylmer.
46. MacIntire, pp. 261–9 & 293 & O'Loghlen, p. 116.
47. Edye, p. 43.
48. Edye MSS/VII, p. 81, 4 Jul 1712, Capt Thos Liell.
49. Edye MSS/VII, p. 103, 27 May 1713, Capt R. Rowzier (*Deptford*).
50. *MM* vi, p. 341, W.S. Neale, *Cavendish or the Patrician at Sea.*
51. *G&L* 1898, p. 160, *RMLI at Inkerman? Yes!*
52. Quondam, p. 61.
53. BSS/i, p. 131, Whitfoord Papers – Cooks held an Admiralty Warrant, and were therefore naval officers.
54. BSS/i, pp. 129–30.
55. RM 11/13/091, Col Richard Swale Diary, 20–26 Dec 1799.
56. Byng Papers ii, p. 198, 3 Jul 1708, Prince George Orders for CM.
57. Howe, 2 Jan 1782.
58. Edye MSS/VII, p. 66, 3 Nov 1712, Capt William Heriott (HMS *Guernsey*).
59. O'Loghlen, pp. 116–17.
60. RM 11/13/89, Tatton Brown, *Remarks on board HM Ship Royal George,* 1811.
61. Lavery, pp. 408–16, *Black List of HMS* Blake.
62. RM 11/13/093, Howe, 7 Jun 1779.
63. Lavery, pp. 465–8, *Journal of Robert Clarke.*
64. RM 7/9/1–17, 18 Sep 1810, Capt F. Liardet/Messrs Charles Fox.
65. Lt J. Urquhart RM, *Hints to Young Marine Officers on their Duties Afloat* (Burrill, Chatham, 1842) p. 28.
66. Edye MSS/VII, p. 83, Nov 1710, Capt John Lowen (HMS *Advice*).
67. BSS/i, p. 129.
68. CSPD 1673, p. 315, 30 May 1673, Littleton/Arlington.
69. Quondam, pp. iii-iv.
70. Lavery, p. 519 & W. Fernyhough, *Military Memoirs of Four Brothers,* 1829, p. 57: JF/parents, 12 Oct 1805.
71. RM 11/12/42, Roteley/Father, 23 Jan 1808.
72. Quondam, pp. 68–9.
73. *NC* xxix, pp. 25–31.
74. RM 11/12/42, 1 May 1807, Roteley RM/Father.
75. C. Field, *Old Times Afloat,* p. 92.
76. RM 11/12/42, Roteley/Father, 9 Sept 1805.
77. RM 11/13/091, Swale, 26 Apr 1799 & 30 Mar 1800.
78. RM 11/13/89, Tatton Brown.
79. Quondam, pp. 1–3.
80. Lt. P.H. Nicholas, *Historical Record of the Royal Marine Forces,* 1845, I, pp. xxx–xxxi.

81. Quondam, pp. 3–4.
82. CSPD 1703–4, p. 392, Declaration of Council, 1 June 1702.
83. RM 11/13/093, Howe, 2 Oct 1780 & 24 Jan 1781.
84. RM 11/13/093, Howe, Jan 1794.
85. RM 11/12/42, 30 Apr 1806, 14 Dec 1806, 1 May 1807 & 15 Apr 1808, Roteley/Father.
86. Edye, p. 576.
87. RM, Extract From His Majesty's Order in Council dated 3rd April 1755.
88. Gen Sir H. Blumberg & Col C. Field, *Random Records of the Royal Marines*, p. 26.
89. Brian Ranfft, *Vernon Papers*, p. 511, 4 Nov 1745, Admiralty/Vernon.
90. CSPD 1702–3, p. 260, 29 Aug 1702, Complaint Catherine Renauf & p. 235, 2 Sep 1702, Lt Col Lewis-Nottingham.
91. RR, p. 205.
92. RM 11/45/3, 10 Sept 1783.
93. RM 11/31/2, 15 Nov 1779.
94. RM 11/31/2, 31 May 1781 & 9 Oct 1781.
95. RM 11/31/2, 10 Sept 1757.
96. O'Loghlen, p. 116.
97. RM 7/7/13, Order Book 3rd Battalion, 1 Aug 1814.
98. Howe, n.d. 1778.
99. L. Becke & W. Jeffery, *A First Fleet Family. . . from the Papers of Sgt William Dew of the Marines* (Fisher Unwin, 1896), pp. 43–4.
100. Perrin, *Keith Papers* ii, p. 28, 20 Nov 1797, Capt J. Elphinstone-Keith.
101. RM 7/7/13, Order Book, 8 Apr, 9 Jun, 22 Jun & 28 Sept 1814.
102. RM 11/13/091, Swale, n.d. 1799.
103. RM 11/31/2, 3 Nov 1780 & 28 Nov 1780; RM 11/45/3, 18 Nov 1783.
104. Edye MSS/XI, 26 Mar 1711, Admiralty/Adm H. Walker.

Chapter 6 The Marines and the Emperor

1. Richmond, i, p. 274.
2. Edye MSS/VII, p. 59, 7 Aug 1707, Capt Francis Hosier (*Salisbury*).
3. RM 11/13/093, Sgt John Howe, Mar 1779.
4. BSS/i pp. 187–8 & 194.
5. Delegates' Reply to Admiralty Offer of 18 Apr 1797.
6. Corbett, *Spencer Papers*, ii, p. 113, 18 Apr 1797, Capt J.W. Payne/Earl Spencer.
7. RM 7/9/1–17, Mortimer Timpson, pp. 6–8.
8. RM 7/9/1–17, Mortimer Timpson, pp. 2–4.
9. *Corbett, Spencer Papers*, ii, p. 113, 18 Apr 1797 Capt J.W. Payne/Earl Spencer.
10. W.G. Perrin, *Keith Papers*, ii, p. 17, 3 Jun 1797, Examination of seamen at Sheerness; p. 28, 4 Aug 1797, Certificate of Good Conduct & p. 27; 5 Jul 1797, Keith/Adm Sir R. King.
11. RM 11/13/061, Capt John Robyns Diary, Jan–May 1797.
12. An Impartial Account of the Proceeding on Board HM Ship *London*, Tuesday, 7 May 1797 & ADM 1/107, Capt Vashon to Bridport, 7 May 1797.
13. ADM 1/107 269, Colpoys to Evan Nepean, 8 May 1797 & RNM/1996 8

19598 6.10.3, 13 May 1797, *The Loyal and Humane Tars of His Majesty's Fleet, at St. Helen's.*

14. *Corbett, Spencer Papers,* p. 399, 4 May 1797 Spencer/Sir John Jervis. Marine rates of pay were now:

	Sergeant	Corporal	Drummer	Private.
To 25 July 1797 on shore	1/6d	1/=	1/=	8d
-do- at sea	1/=	8d	8d	6d

15. RM 7/9/1–17, Mortimer Timpson, pp. 9 & 13.
16. RNM 1996/31(38), Adm Knowles' *Standing Orders* 1796 #10.
17. *Corbett, Spencer Papers,* p. 119, 27 Apr 1797, Capt Parr (*Standard*)/Spencer.
18. J.S. Tucker *Memoirs of Earl St Vincent* (Bentley, 1844), i, pp. 297 & 329, 18 Jul 1797, St Vincent/Capt Duckworth.
19. A Quondam Sub, p. iv.
20. Tucker, i, p. 340, 21 Aug 1798, St Vincent/Evan Nepean.
21. Lavery, pp. 219–22 & RR p. 93.
22. Lavery, pp. 633–4, Adm Philip Patton, *Strictures on Naval Discipline &c.*
23. BSS/i, pp. 207–8, Capt Basil Hall.
24. Lavery, pp. 228–9, Orders for the Officers of Marines, HMS *Mars.*
25. RM 11/13/89, Tatton Brown, #2; Lavery, p. 196, Captain's Orders, HMS *Indefatigable,* 1812.
26. RM 7/7/13 Order Book, 1 Aug 1814.
27. Anonymous, *to a Member of Parliament,* p. 6.
28. NC v, p. 77.
29. J.K. Laughton, *Barham Papers,* p. 190, 1 Jun 1805, Nauticus/Barham.
30. *Regulations and Instructions Relating to His Majesty's Service at Sea,* 1808, pp. 421–2.
31. Corbett, *Spencer Papers,* p. 212, 30 Jun 1797, St Vincent/Spencer.
32. NC vii, p. 528.
33. BSS/i, p. 204.
34. E. Fraser & L.G. Carr Laughton, *The Royal Marine Artillery,* i, pp. 10–12; Col Campbell Dalrymple KDG; Gen Desaguliers RA; 13 Oct 1779, Kempenfeldt/Sir C. Middleton.
35. *Sandwich Papers* ii, p. 119.
36. Fraser & Carr Laughton, i, p. 21, 25 May 1804, Nelson/Capt Sir T. Troubridge.
37. BSS/i, p. 264.
38. Steele, i p. 164.
39. BSS/i, p. 265, Gen Sir Charles James Napier.
40. Fraser & Carr Laughton, i, p. 129.
41. Fernyhough, *Military Memoirs,* p. 11, JF/parents, 3 Jun 1800.
42. BSS/i, p. 242, Sergeant Packwood RM.
43. BSS/i, p. 142, Major T. Oldfield.
44. Fernyhough, p. 35, JF/parents, 4 Jun 1804.
45. BSS/i, p. 242, Sergeant Packwood.
46. BSS/i, p. 143, General Sir John Savage RM.
47. Fernyhough, p. 56, JF/parents, 12 Oct 1805.
48. Moulton, p. 16; Marine detachments 13; 2nd Queens 5; 25th 2; 29th 5; 69th 1.
49. *The Times,* 6 Jan 1873, Rev H.P. Jeston, *A Trafalgar Veteran,* Billyruffian/ Bellerophon.

50. RM 11/12/42, Roteley Journal, 21 Oct 1805 & Speech p. 5, times quoted vary from ship to ship.
51. BSS/i, p. 253, Nicholas.
52. RM 11/12/42, Roteley Speech, pp. 5–6.
53. BSS/i, pp. 253–4, Nicholas.
54. RM 11/12/42, Roteley Journal & Speech, pp. 7–8 & 21 Oct 1805. The French *Achille* blew up at 5.45.
55. *NC* xiv, p. 462 & Laird Clowes, v, p. 142–3 f.n.
56. RM 11/12/42, 4 Dec 1805, Roteley/Father.
57. Comparative losses and numbers engaged were: 432 RM/1,700; i.e. 25%; 2,692 RM/20,000 i.e. 13%.
58. RM 11/12/42, 1 May 1807, Roteley/Father.
59. RM 11/13/61, Robyns, 21–22 Jun 1808.
60. RM 11/13/89, Tatton Brown, 5 Nov 1813.
61. Nicholas, i, p. xxxvi.
62. Fernyhough, p. 140.
63. RM 11/3/45, Lt W. Pridham RM, 27 Jun 1808.
64. Sgt Thomas Rees, *Journal of Voyages and Travels,* pp. 31–4; the 25 Marines present lost 2 killed and 10 wounded.
65. Lavery, p. 471, *Journal of Robert Clarke.*
66. RM 11/13/61, Robyns, 26 Jul 1804 & 2–9 Dec 1813.
67. *NC* xiv, p. 166, 18 Jun 1805.
68. RM 11/12/42, Roteley/Father, 14 Dec 1806.
69. RR, p. 17, *Extracts from My Uncle's Diary* 1796–1820, 3 Oct 1799.
70. RM 11/13/091, Swale, 30 May 1800.
71. BSS/i, p. 277.
72. *NC* xxx, p. 78, 16 May 1813, Capt E. Brace (*Berwick*)/Vice-Adm Sir Ed Pellew; p. 436, 7 Jul 1813, Capt C. Rowley (*Eagle*)/Rear Adm T.F. Fremantle.
73. *NC* xxx, p. 237, 28 May & 10 Jun 1813, Capt J. Tower (*Curacao*).
74. *Keith Papers,* iii, p. 285, 10 Sept 1812, Melville-Keith.
75. *NC* xxx, p. 75, 20 Mar 1813, Capt T. Ussher (*Undaunted*)/Vice-Adm Sir Ed Pellew; p. 239, 24 Apr 1813, Capt B.W. Taylor (*Apollo*)/Rear Adm T.F. Fremantle; p. 436, 18 Aug 1813, Capt R.H. Moubray (*Repulse*)/Vice-Adm Sir Ed Pellew.
76. *NC* xxx, p. 434, 6 Jul 1813, Rear Adm T.F. Fremantle/Vice-Adm Sir Ed Pellew; p. 435, 18 Jun 1813, Cmdr J. Harper/Rear Adm T.F. Fremantle; p. 436, 18 Aug 1813, Capt T. Ussher (*Undaunted*)/Vice-Adm Sir Ed Pellew.
77. RR, pp. 45–7, Aug 1815, Letters of Lts A. Burton & T. Hurdle RM.
78. *USJ* 1836, iii, p. 325, *Economy of a Man of War – The Marine Officer.*
79. *Corbett, Spencer Papers,* iii, p. 345, 23 Jun 1800, Pellew/St Vincent & p. 361, 6 Jul 1800, St Vincent/Spencer; iv, p. 149, 11 Mar 1801, Keith/Spencer.
80. RM 11/3/45, Pridham, 12 Mar 1800. The Marines landed 12 Mar 1801, 38 officers & 589 other ranks strong.
81. Edye MSS, *100 Years Ago,* p. 319. 25 Killed & 35 wounded, just on 10%.
82. *Keith Papers,* ii, p. 341, 31 July 1801 Keith/Hutchinson.
83. RM 11/13/091, Swale, 25 June 1807.
84. Fernyhough, pp. 95–102 & 117–22.
85. *Keith Papers,* iii, p. 284, 10 Sept 1812, Melville/Keith & p. 274, 7 July 1812, Keith/Popham.

86. *NC* xxx, p. 233, 8 Jun 1813, Capt C. Adam (*Invincible*)/RAdm Hallowell.
87. All refs RM 7/7/13 Order Book.
88. RM 7/9/1–17, Mortimer Timpson, p. 31.
89. RM 11/13/61, Robyns, 24 Aug & 12 Sept 1814.
90. *USJ* 1836, iii, p. 325, *Economy of a Man of War – The Marine Officer.*
91. RM 11/13/61, Robyns, 5 Apr 1814.
92. RM 7/7/13 Order Book, 25 Oct 1814.
93. BSS/i, p. 301.
94. RM 11/3/45, Pridham, 12 Mar & 8 Nov 1815.
95. RM 11/13/152, Wilson, 2 April 1816.
96. BSS/ i, p. 217 & ii, p. 4.

Chapter 7   Pax Britannica

1. *JRUSI* 1902, xlvi, p. 890, Sir John Colomb, *Garrisons for Coaling Stations* & 1883, xxvii, p. 122, Capt J.C.R. Colomb RMA, *The Use and Application of Marine Forces; Past, Present and Future* (Maj-Gen Sir Andrew Clarke RE).
2. Nicholas, I, p. xviii.
3. RM 11/3/45, Lt W. Pridham RM, 10 & 27 Sept & 26 Oct 1816.
4. BSS/i, p. 275.
5. RR, p. 196, Blumberg, *Divisional Colours of the Royal Marines.*
6. RM Box 15/4/1 17, Dec 1845, Col J. Owen, DAG/Admiralty.
7. RR, p. 114, *Palmerston's Own* (USJ, 10 Jul 1844).
8. BSS/ii, p. 29, 2nd Lt F.A. Halliday RM.
9. BSS/ii, p. 37. Major Owen was Colonel as CO of a battalion on active service.
10. RR, p. 32, Gen Simon Fraser.
11. BSS/ii, p. 52.
12. RM 11/13/43, Lt Henry Woodruff, 22–23 Nov 1855.
13. RR, p. 80, Gen Simon Fraser.
14. RM box 7/11/2–7/15/1, Lt-Col T. Hurdle/Lord Raglan, 16 June 1855.
15. *G&L*, 1898, p. 160, *RMLI at Inkerman? Yes!.*
16. *G&L*, 1914, p. 28, *Balaklava and the Royal Marines.*
17. *G&L*, 1911, p. 46, Turner Letter.
18. *G&L*, 1898, p. 160, *RMLI at Inkerman? Yes!.*
19. RM 11/13/310, Col Ellis RMLI, 13 Nov 1854 (*sic*).
20. *G&L*, 1914, p. 45, *Balaklava and the Royal Marines.*
21. *G&L*, 1899, p. 170, *On Balaklava Heights.*
22. *G&L*, 1898, p. 134, *In a Blizzard.* Green coffee needed roasting, so required twice the fuel.
23. BSS/ii, pp. 83–7.
24. BSS/ii, pp. 87–8, ILN, 1855, 14 May 1855.
25. RM 11/13/17(A), 2nd Lt Francis Lean RM, 9 Jun 1855.
26. RR, pp. 13–14, C-in-C's Regulations… regarding the Mortar Boats. 20 Jul 1855.
27. All quotes RM 11/13/17(A), Lean, 9 Aug 1855.
28. RR, p. 15, Capt J.M. Wemyss RMA.
29. *G&L*, 1901, p. 128 Henry Derry RMLI.
30. Lady Ellis (ed.), *Memoirs and Services of the late Lt General Sir SB Ellis,* etc (Saunders & Otley, 1866), p. 199 & pp. 288–9.

31. RM Box 7/11/3, n.d., list of troops and equipment.
32. BSS/ii, p. 130.
33. RM 11/13/85, Pvt W. Baker, pp. 8–9.
34. Lady Ellis, p. 231.
35. RM Box 7/11/3 8, Jan 1858, Lt J Cooke/Col Holloway.
36. RM 11/13/85, Baker, pp. 11 & 13.
37. *A&NG*, 1873, p. 593.
38. RMM Box 7/14/9, 2 Aug 1873, Festing/Maj Gen Schomberg DAG.
39. Adm Sir E.R. Fremantle, *The Navy As I Have Known It* (Cassell n.d.) p. 210.
40. *A&NG* 1874 p. 219, Vindicator.
41. RM Box 7/14/9, 2 Aug 1873 & 22 Sept 1873, Festing/Maj Gen Schomberg DAG.
42. RM Box 7/14/9, 8 Oct 1873, J.C. McNeill/Lt P. Hearle.
43. RM 7/14/9(4), Lt Parkins Hearle RMLI, 21 Nov 1873.
44. RM 7/14/9(4), Lt Parkins Hearle RMLI, 23 Jan 1874.
45. *A&NG*, 1873, p. 594 & 1874, p. 169.
46. Lt-Cdr C.F. Goodrich USN, *Report of the British Naval and Military Operations in Egypt*, 1882, p. 206.
47. *A&NG*, 7 Jun 1879, p. 404.
48. BSS/ii, p. 173.
49. RM 7/14/5, 11.9.1882 (sic), Cpl Joseph Love/Father.
50. RM 11/13/14, Lt W.H. Palmer, *Journal*, p. 23. RM casualties at Tel-el-Kebir: 5 killed, 54 wounded & 21 missing.
51. *A&NG*, 1882, p. 790.
52. *HT*, 25 Oct 1882.
53. RM 11/12/13, 20 Sep 1884, Lt A.E. Marchant RMLI/Brother-in-law.
54. Maj-Gen Sir G. Aston, *Memoirs of a Marine* (John Murray, 1919), p. 47.
55. NMM JOD/188, Gunner J.T. Wilkinson RMA, 29 Feb 1884.
56. Aston, p. 49.
57. RM 11/12/13, 20 Sep 1884, Lt A.E. Marchant RMLI/Brother-in-law.
58. RM 11/12/13, 19 Feb 1885, Lt A.E. Marchant RMLI/Brother-in-law.
59. RM 11/13/192, Pvt Thomas Holbrow RMLI, p. 2.
60. *G&L*, 1895, p. 51.
61. RM 11/13/192, Pvt Thomas Holbrow RMLI, p. 3.
62. *LG*, 6 Jan 1891, 1 Nov 1890, Fremantle/Admiralty Sub-Enclosure No. 1.
63. *A&NG*, 1881, p. 143.
64. *A&NG*, 1899, p. 1175.
65. *G&L*, 1902, p. 17, *Indian Mutiny Reminiscences*.
66. *G&L*, 1893 p. 174, Quartermaster F. Butler, *Relief of Bhansi*.
67. LG, 6 Jan 1891, p. 78, 1 Nov 1890, Fremantle/Admiralty.
68. *G&L*, 1894, pp. 162–3, *Experiences of No. 1 Column(By One Who Was There)*.
69. *G&L*, 1893, pp. 183–4, Acting QM Sgt J.L. Hammond RMLI, *The Vitu Expedition*.
70. *G&L*, 1894, pp. 162–3, *Experiences*.
71. *G&L*, 1894, pp. 162–3, *Experiences*.
72. *G&L*, 1897, p. 55, Sgt Ellison RMLI, *Benin Expedition*.
73. *G&L*, 1894, pp. 162–3, *Experiences*.

74. *G&L*, 1897, p. 43, Cpl Rogerson RMA, *The Benin Expedition.*
75. *G&L*, 1897, p. 44, Rogerson.
76. *G&L*, 1897, p. 56, Ellison.
77. *G&L*, 1897, p. 44, Rogerson.
78. *G&L*, 1893, pp. 183–4, Hammond.
79. *G&L*, 1894, pp. 162–3, *Experiences.*
80. *G&L*, 1894, pp. 162–3, *Experiences.*
81. *G&L*, 1897, p. 44, Rogerson.
82. RM 11/13/283, Anon, 26 Jul 1884.
83. RM 11/13/43, Lt H. Woodruff RMLI, 25 Nov 1855, 6–8 Jan 1856 & 5 Feb 1855.
84. RM 11/13/283, Anon 30 Jul 1884.
85. RM 11/13/67, Pvt E. Keep RMLI, 21 June 1902; 7 Jul 1902 & 27 Mar 1903.
86. RM 11/13/283, Anon, 25 July & 5 Aug 1884.
87. RM 11/13/43, Woodruff, 27 Jan & 12 Feb 1856.
88. RM 11/13/67, Keep, 23 Mar 1905 & 6 Sept 1903.
89. *G&L*, 1899, p. 181.
90. RM Box 11/12/–, 29 Jun 1900, Capt H.T.N. Lloyd.
91. BSS/ii, p. 282, Sergeant Gowney RMLI.
92. NMM MS 84/081, Cpl F.G. Smith RMLI.
93. BSS/ii, p. 281.
94. RM 11/13/67, Keep, 3–10 Mar 1903.
95. *A&NG*, 1899, p. 1174.
96. RM 11/12/13, 14 Dec 1899 Capt A.E. Marchant RMLI/Brother-in-law. RM losses: 11 killed & 73 wounded out of 190 i.e. 44%.
97. BSS, ii, pp. 240-2, Lt W.T.C. Jones RMLI.
98. RM 11/12/13, 14 Dec 1899 & 19 Jan 1900, Capt A.E. Marchant RMLI/Brother-in-law.
99. RM 7/16/1, 2 Sept 1900 & 23 Jan 1900 Pvt F.W. Phillips RMLI/Parents.
100. RM 11/12/13, 14 Dec 1899, Capt A.E. Marchant RMLI/Brother-in-law.
101. RM Box 11/12/- n.d., Capt Bruce/Colonel Commandant Eastney.
102. *G&L* 1902, p. 17, *Indian Mutiny Reminiscences.*
103. *JRUSI* 1883, xxvii p. 102: Colomb, *Marine Forces.*
104. *A&NG*, 1884, p. 162.
105. *JRUSI*, 1883, xxvii, p. 90, Colomb, *Marine Forces.*

Chapter 8   The Advent of Steam

1. *JRUSI*, 1883, xxvii, p. 108, Capt J.C.R. Colomb RMA, *The Use and Application of Marine Forces; Past, Present and Future.*
2. RM 11/13/17(A), Lt Francis Lean RMLI, 25 Apr & 14 Jun 1855.
3. Maj W.H. Poyntz, *Per Mare Per Terram*, p. 56.
4. *JRUSI*, 1902, xlvi, p. 890, Colomb, *Garrisons.*
5. RM 11/13/10(A), Craig, p. 36.
6. RM 11/13/30, Pvt E.W. Horton & 11/13/67, Pvt E. Keep, 27 Jul 1904.
7. RM 11/13/17(A), Lean, 11 Feb 1855.
8. RM 11/13/108, Bugler J.W. Carroll RMLI.
9. RM 11/13/10(A), Craig, p. 29.
10. RM 11/13/2, Cpl A.P. Saunders RMA, 30 Apr 1915.

11. RM 11/13/10(A), Craig, p. 51.
12. Poyntz, p. 52.
13. RM 11/13/10(A), Craig, p. 44–5.
14. RM 11/13/283, Anon, 25 Dec 1884.
15. RM 11/13/2, Saunders, 17 Dec 1914.
16. RM 11/13/10(A), Craig, p. 44–5.
17. *JRUSI* 1883, xxvii, p. 98, Colomb, *Marine Forces.*
18. *JRUSI* 1876, xix, p. 626, Capt J.C. Wilson RN, *Seamen of the Fleet, Their Training and How the Employment of Marines Afloat in Peacetime Affects Them.*
19. *JRUSI* 1871, xv, p. 501–2, Schomberg (Rear/Adm Campbell).
20. RR, p. 245–6, Order in Council, 11 Aug 1854, *Rations and Victualling Arrangements. . .*
21. RM Box 15/4/1 20, Apr 1847, Col J. Owen DAG/Admiralty.
22. *JRUSI* 1883, xxvii, p. 98, Colomb, *Marine Forces.*
23. *JRUSI* 1876, xix, p. 604, Wilson.
24. *JRUSI* 1902, xlvi, p. 892, Colomb, *Garrisons.*
25. *JRUSI* 1882, xxvi, p. 187, Capt L. Baine RN, *Prize Essay – The Best Method of Providing an Efficient Force of Officers and Men for the Navy.*
26. *JRUSI* 1876, xix, p. 622, Wilson (Cdr W. Dawson).
27. *JRUSI* 1871, xv, p. 281, Capt J.C. Colomb, *General Principles of Naval Organisation.*
28. *JRUSI* 1883, xxvii, p. 105, Colomb, *Marine Forces.*
29. RM 11/13/43, Woodruff, 1 Jan 1856 & 11/13/283, Anon, 25 Nov 1884.
30. RM 11/13/128, Mne R. McHalliday.
31. *JRUSI* 1871, xv, p. 276, Colomb, *Naval Organisation.*
32. *JRUSI* 1902, xlvi, p. 892, Colomb, *Garrisons.*
33. *JRUSI* 1876, xix, p. 623, Wilson (Cdr W Dawson).
34. *JRUSI* 1871, xv, pp. 502–3, Schomberg (Rear Adm Shadwell & Adm of the Fleet Sir George Sartorius).
35. *JRUSI* 1882, xxvi, pp. 221–2, Baine.
36. *JRUSI* 1871, xv, p. 498 Schomberg (RearAdm Shadwell).
37. *JRUSI* 1876, xix, p. 614, Wilson (Rear Adm Willes).
38. *A&NG,* 7 Feb 1874, p. 81.
39. *JRUSI* 1883, xxvii, pp. 98–9, Colomb, *Marine Forces,* referring to the 2nd Afghan War 1878–80.
40. *Report from HM Commissioners for Inquiring into the System of Military Punishment in the Army* (1836), p. 270, Col R. McLaverty RM.
41. *ILN,* 11 Sept 1847.
42. *Military Punishment* (1836), pp. 275 & 273, Surgeon H. Parkin.
43. RR, p. 3.
44. J.B. Hattendorf & R.J.B. Knight, *British Naval Documents 1216–1961,* p. 721, 10 Dec 1859, Confidential letter to Commanders-in-Chief.
45. RM 11/13/303, E. Taber RMA.
46. *Standing Orders for the RMA* 1876 (Charpentier, Portsmouth), pp. 8, 14 & 114–17.
47. *JRUSI* 1902, xlvi, p. 888, Colomb, *Garrisons.*
48. RM Box 11/12/– Character Reference for Minnie Ackerman & C. Smith/ Mother; gippa = gravy.

49. RM 11/21/30, Colour Sergeant N.J. Hiscock RMLI, *Twenty One Years Service Ashore and Afloat,* pp. 2–3.
50. *JRUSI* 1876, xix, pp. 625 & 622, Wilson, *Seamen of the Fleet* (Maj-Gen G.A. Schomberg & Commander W. Dawson).
51. RM 11/21/30, Hiscock, p. 13 (15 Nov 1911).
52. Poyntz, p. 53.
53. RM 11/13/89 Tatton Brown.
54. *Queen's Regulations and Admiralty Instructions for the Government of Her Majesty's Naval Service,* 1862, p. 136.
55. *USM,* Aug–Sep 1893, vii (NS), p. 1125, Lt J.M. Rose RMA, *The Royal Marine Artillery.*
56. *JRUSI* 1871, xv, p. 283, Colomb, *Naval Organisation* (Capt H.W. Brent RN).
57. *JRUSI* 1871, xv, p. 504, Schomberg.
58. RM 11/13/114 13, Feb 1915, Maj F.J. Harvey RMLI/Maj A.P. Grattan RMLI.
59. Lt Commander P. Kemp, *Fisher Papers,* i, pp. 405–9, Fisher/VAdm Sir W. May, C-in-C Atlantic Fleet; original underlined.
60. Fraser & Carr Laughton, *i,* pp. 673–4.
61. Adm Sir E. Chatfield, *HMS Excellent 1830–1930* (Charpentier, Portsmouth, 1930), p. 4.
62. Fraser & Carr Laughton, *ii,* p. 338.
63. RM 11/13/17(A), Lean, 9 Aug 1855.
64. *JRUSI* 1883, xxvii, p. 99, Colomb, *Marine Forces.*
65. *JRUSI* 1871, xv, pp. 501–2, Schomberg (Capt Balfour RN & Capt Studdert RMA).
66. Fraser & Carr Laughton, *ii,* p. 334, Brigade Order, 28 Dec 1831, RM Office.
67. Hattendorf & Knight, p. 687, Memo 4 Sep 1844.
68. RM 11/13/293, Col A.L.S. Burrowes, emphasis added.
69. RM 11/13/17(A), Lean, 1, 21 & 26 Jun 1855.
70. Fraser & Carr Laughton, *ii,* p. 518, 23 May 1867, Admy Order.
71. *JRUSI* 1883, xxvii, p. 102, Colomb, *Marine Forces.*
72. Fraser & Carr Laughton, ii, p. 516.
73. RM 11/21/30, Hiscock, p. 4.
74. 11/13/10(A), Craig, p. 141.
75. RM 11/12/13(27), 5 Dec 1898, Capt F.M.B. Hobbs RMA/Col F.H. Poore (Eastney).
76. RM 11/21/30, Hiscock, pp. 12 & 9.

Chapter 9   Action Under Steam
1. RM 11/13/2, Saunders, n.d.
2. RM 11/13/2, Saunders, 29 Jul, 4 Aug & 5 Sep 1914.
3. Blumberg, pp. 3–4. RM numbers rose from 19,945 to 56,816 including specialist wartime units such as RM Engineers.
4. *JRUSI* 1871, xv, p. 487, Schomberg.
5. Fraser & Carr Laughton, ii, p. 705.
6. RM 11/13/2, Saunders, 5 Aug 1916.
7. RM 11/13/71, Cpl H.W. Cauchey RMLI, 31 May 1916.
8. J. Swales, *The Life and Music of RMB X1522,* p. 56.

9. RM 11/13/299, D.G. Elmer, RMB X967, *To Be a Musician in the Royal Naval School of Music 1936–48*, p. 17.
10. RM 11/13/2, Saunders, 28 Aug 1914.
11. RM 11/13/277, Pvt W.J. Stevens RMLI (HMS *Queen Mary*), 28 Aug 1914.
12. RM 11/13/114, 9 Feb 1915, Capt A.G.B. Bourne RMA/Col F.T. Phillips RMA & 13 Feb 1915, Maj F.J. Harvey RMLI/Maj A.P. Grattan RMLI.
13. RM 11/13/2, Saunders, 5 Aug 1914, 24 Jan 1915 & 28 Aug 1914.
14. RM Box 7/12/4 3, Jun 1916, Capt Chandos E. Hill RMLI/Capt A.D. Pounds RN & 7 Jul 1916 CEH/Lily (CEH's sister). Times given vary from ship to ship.
15. RM 11/13/2, Saunders, 29 May 1916.
16. *G&L* 1919, pp. 74–5, Capt E. Hughes RMLI.
17. RM Box 7/12/4, n.d., Capt Chandos E. Hill RMLI, *Account of the Action of 29th May 1916*.
18. RM 11/13/199, n.p., Sgt N.V.J. Jago RMLI, *The Battle of Jutland witnessed from the Agincourt*.
19. RM Box 7/12/4, Pvt G. Neasham RMLI, *The Battle of Jutland 31st May 1916*, p. 2.
20. RM 11/13/114 13, Feb 1915, Harvey/RMLI. Cf. Blumberg BSS, p. 53:

	RM Engaged	Killed	Wounded.
Trafalgar	3,690	117	225
Jutland	5,832	538	51

21. H.W. Fawcett & G.W.W. Hooper, *The Fighting at Jutland* (Glasgow, 1921), p. 87.
22. *G&L* 1956, p. 202, Lt Col FR Jones/Editor.
23. RM Box 7/12/4, n.d., Capt A.G.B. Bourne RMA, 'X' Turret Report – Battle of Jutland.
24. Fraser & Carr Laughton, ii, p. 707.
25. RM 11/13/71, Cauchey, 2–3 Jun 1916 & 15 Nov 1915.
26. RM 11/13/2, Saunders, 17 Sep 1914 & 28 Aug 1914.
27. British forces in France 1 Nov 1918 numbered 1,497,198 excluding colonial troops; Marines present at surrender 21 Nov 1918: 86 officers, 44 WOs, 4,818 O/Rs (Blumberg BSS, p. 68).
28. RM 11/13/277, Stevens, 10 Aug 1914.
29. RM 11/13/2, Saunders, 28 Aug & 25 Oct 1914.
30. RM 11/21/30, Hiscock, p. 19.
31. RM 11/13/63(f), n.p., Gunner F.F. Crowe RMA, *HMS Moldava 2nd Cruise* (original punctuation missing).
32. RM 11/13/170, Pvt M.G. Carter RMLI, HMS *King Alfred 1915–16*.
33. RM 11/13/63(f), n.p., Crowe.
34. RM 11/21/30, Colour Sergeant N.J. Hiscock RMLI, *Twenty One Years Service Ashore and Afloat*, p. 26.
35. RM 11/13/170, A.G. Cooper, 21 & 17 Jan 1916.
36. RM 11/13/80(a), Pvt T.H. Haywood RMLI, 6 Apr & 19 Aug 1915.
37. RM 11/21/30, Hiscock, p. 27.
38. R. Rowe, *Sticky Blue! A Boy and a Battleship*, p. 46.
39. RM 2/19/16, Detachment Standing Order HMS *Venerable*, 1944, No.10; the character 'f' appears to have replaced 'g'.
40. RM Box 7/19/20, Orders & Instructions for RMs Borne on Ships' Books on the Mediterranean Station, 25 Jun 1944, para. 30.

41. RM 2/24/17, HMS *Ceylon,* Gunnery Station Bill 1956.
42. RM Box 7/19/20, Sgt A.B. Wilde RM (1st Capt of Turret)- Gunnery Officer HMS *Exeter.* OCRM was killed so reports went to the Lt(G).
43. Swales, p. 79. *Bismarck* sank HMS *Hood* two days earlier with all but three of her 1,419 complement.
44. RM 10/2/King, C/Sgt V.S. King, *My last Commission,* n.p.
45. J. Swales, p. 137.
46. RM Box 7/19/20, Cpl Gibson-Ford, *Scharnhorst Action,* p. 5 & Pvt R. Thompson (*Evening World* cutting).
47. RM 11/13/2, Saunders, 17 Jan 1915 & 17 Aug 1916.
48. RM 11/13/275, Col P. Beeman, *Calcutta and Charybdis with Beeman* 1939–1943, i, p. 32.
49. RM 11/13/292, G.E. Kitchen, *The Most Dangerous Moment – An Account of the Loss of HMS Devonshire,* etc, p. 35.
50. RM 11/13/275, Beeman, ii, p. 5.
51. RM 11/13/275, Beeman, i, pp. 20–1.
52. RM 11/13/275, Beeman, i, pp. 23 & 25.
53. RM 11/13/275, Beeman, i, p. 63.
54. RM 11/13/299, Elmer, p. 24.
55. RM 11/13/305, K.R. MacDonald, *A Bandsman and Barbed Wire,* May 1941–May 1945.
56. RM 11/13/299, Elmer, pp. 25 & 27.
57. RM 11/13/124, Mne B. Knapton, 8 Oct 1940 & 2 Feb 1941.
58. RM 11/13/299, Elmer, p. 23.
59. RM 11/13/275, Beeman, i, p. 47.
60. RM 11/13/275, Beeman, i, pp. 80–2.
61. RM 11/13/275, Beeman, ii, p. 24.
62. RM Box 7/19/20, Cadet Feltham (HMS *Trinidad*) & J. Swales, pp. 107–13.
63. RM 11/13/279, Bandsman J.B. Nicholls (HMS *Dido*), 21 May 1941.
64. RM 11/13/279, Nicholls, 11 Jul 1943.
65. RM 11/13/288, Mne John J. Cook, *The Tragic Years,* p. 7.
66. RM 11/13/279, Nicholls, 26 Sep 1943.
67. RM 11/13/253, Arthur Webster, *HMS Arethusa at Normandy,* 12 Jun. 1944
68. RM 11/13/253, Webster, 24 Jun. Much of the time 'A' and 'B' turrets fired broadsides of four rounds.
69. RM 11/13/253, Webster, 13 Jun. 1944
70. RM 11/13/253, Webster, 6, 9, & 14 Jun. 1944
71. R. Rowe, pp. 164 & 175–6.
72. R. Rowe, p. 185.

Chapter 10   Poor Bloody Infantry

1. RM Box 7/17/10–11, 2 Sept 1914, Reorganising Brigade & 12 Feb 1975, Maj-Gen T.H. Jameson RM.
2. RM Box 7/17/10–11, 20 Oct 1914, Paris/Admiralty.
3. RM 11/13/1(3), E.E. Rowland RMLI, pp. 3–4.
4. RM Box 7/17/10–11, 20 Oct 1914, Paris/Admiralty.
5. Blumberg BSS, p. 122.
6. *G&L* 1914, xxi, p. 190, *One of the Marine Brigade.* RM losses at Antwerp: 2+23 killed; 2+103 wounded; 1+311 missing (Blumberg BSS, p. 124).

7. Blumberg BSS, p. 117.
8. *JRUSI* 1895, xxxix, p. 476, Maj Elmslie RA, *Lessons to be derived,* etc. Generals Amherst and Abercrombie carried out successful amphibious expeditions against Canada (1759) and Egypt (1801).
9. RM Box 7/17/3, 29 Mar 1915, Sgt F. Meatyard RMLI/Parents.
10. RM 11/13/208, Sgt E. Kershaw RMA, 18 Mar & 25 Apr 1915; the regiments were: 1st Royal Dublin, 1st Munster Fusiliers and 2nd Hampshires. They lost 1,200 out of 1,500.
11. Maj A.F. Becke, *Military Operations at Gallipoli* (Heinemann, 1929), i, p. 202.
12. RM Box 7/17/3, *Dardanelles Drivel,* 17 May 1915.
13. *G&L* 1919, xxvi, p. 69.
14. Becke, p. 215.
15. Portsmouth & Chatham, 28 April; Deal, 29 April; Plymouth worked as a beach party at Helles.
16. *G&L* 1915, xxii p. 164, Letters.
17. *G&L* 1916, xxiii, p. 183, *Machine Gun Section at Gallipoli.*
18. RM 11/13/321, Pvt William Brown RMLI, *1915–1917,* n.p.
19. RM 11/13/65, Sgt-Major Edward Bastin, *Deal Battn RMLI,* 12 July 1915.
20. IWM DS/MISC/57, Paris/Mrs C. Pilkington, 28 May & 29 June 1915 in *RND,* pp. 1532 & 1537.
21. *G&L* 1916, xxiii, p. 160, *With the RM in Gallipoli.*
22. *G&L* 1916, xxiii, p. 165, *With the RM in Gallipoli.*
23. *G&L* 1915, xxii, p. 211, *Machine Guns in Trenches.*
24. RM Box 7/17/3, *Albert's Diary while in the Dardanelles,* 16 Nov 1915.
25. IWM DS/MISC/57, Paris/Pilkington, 20 Nov 1915 in *RND,* p. 1542.
26. RM 11/13/65, Bastin, 25 Dec 1915.
27. *G&L* 1916, xxiii, p. 165, *With the RM in Gallipoli.*
28. IWM DS/MISC/57, Paris/Pilkington, 8 Jan 1916 in *RND,* p. 1543.
29. RM Box 7/17/3, *Albert's Diary,* 8 Jan 1916.
30. IWM DS/MISC/57, Paris/Pilkington, 10 Jan 1916 in *RND,* p. 1544.
31. RM 11/13/65, Bastin, 15 Jan 1916.
32. *G&L* 1916, xxiii, p. 31, *RM and the Dardanelles. A&NG* listed RM casualties as: 680 killed, 1402 wounded, 115 missing out of 4,030 embarked (all ranks).
33. IWM DS/MISC/57, Paris/Pilkington, 22 Jun 1916 in *RND,* p. 1546.
34. RM 7/17/9, n.d., *Notes Which Have Been Obtained From Other Formations on the Present Formation On The Somme* & RM 7/17/5 (1), Maj L. Montagu, 20 Nov 1916, p. 2.
35. RM 7/17/5 (1), Maj L. Montagu, 20 Nov 1916, p. 5.
36. D. Jerrold, *The Royal Naval Division,* p. 253.
37. RM Box 7/17/5, *Report on the Operations of the 63rd (RN) Division East of Ypres 24th Oct–5th Nov 1917,* p. 6.
38. RM 11/13/321, Brown, n.p.
39. J. Sparrow & J.N. MacBean-Ross (Surgeons RN), *On Four Fronts with the Royal Naval Division,* pp. 224–5.
40. RM Box 7/17/5, *Report on the Operations of the 63rd (RN) Division East of Ypres 24th Oct–5th Nov 1917,* p. 8.
41. RM 11/13/295, Pvt Walter Stanley Popham, *A Soldier's Diary Nov 1916–*

Mar 1919, p. 43. 1st RMLI losses 13–14 Nov 1916: 47 killed, 210 wounded, 85 missing (all dead) – Blumberg BSS p. 321.

42. *RND,* p. 1117, Capt H, Horn, 6 Jan 1918.
43. *RND,* p. 204, K.D. Tallett, *The RM and the Gavrelle Windmill, 28 April 1917 – Triumph or Tragedy?.*
44. RM Box 7/17/5, *Report on Operations,* p. 7.
45. RM 11/13/295, Popham, p. 48.
46. RM 7/17/5 (1), Maj L. Montagu, 20 Nov 1916, p. 3.
47. RM 11/13/295, Popham, pp. 40 & 47.
48. *G&L* 1918, xxv, p. 125, *Obituary* & Capt C. Falls, *Military Operations in France and Belgium* 1917, (Macmillan, 1940), i, pp. 156–8.
49. Jerrold, p. 205.
50. RM Box 7/17/5.
51. RM 11/13/295, Popham, pp. 1–2, 831 & 34. Cushy was Army/Hindustani implying easy or comfortable.
52. RM 11/13/321, Brown, n.p.
53. *RND,* p. 917–23, PRO WO95/3117, *What the Army High Command Thought of the 63rd (RN) Division.*
54. RM 11/13/295, Popham, pp. 38 & 45.
55. RM 11/13/295, Popham, p. 20.
56. Sparrow & MacBean-Ross, pp. 224–5.
57. RM 11/13/321, Brown, n.p.
58. RM 11/13/295, Popham, pp. 77–8.
59. *RND,* pp. 807 & 811; PRO WO95/3110, Journal of Surg Lt A.L.P. Gould RN attached 2/RMLI.
60. RM 11/13/295, Popham, p. 85.
61. *RND,* p. 812, Gould.
62. Blumberg, BSS, p. 345.
63. RM 11/13/295, Popham, pp. 88–90.
64. *RND,* p. 813, Gould.
65. *RND,* p. 1120, Horn in 2 Apr 1918.
66. RM 11/13/295, Popham, pp. 116, 118, 123 & 130.
67. RM 11/13/295, Popham, p. 133. RM losses at Niergnies: 9 killed, 120 wounded, 14 missing. They captured 2 field guns, 12 machine guns, a German Marine bugle and about 1,000 POWs (Blumberg BSS, p. 376).
68. RM 11/13/295, Popham, pp. 139 & 137.
69. *G&L* 1918, xxv, p. 104, Lt F.J. Hore (QM 4th Battn), *Zeebrugge.*
70. RM Box 7/17/2, Lt (later Maj-Gen) C.R.W. Lamplough, *4th Bn. Royal Marines– Zeebrugge* 1918, p. 1 & Letters, n.d., Sgt H. Wright/Mrs Wright.
71. RM Box 7/17/2, Lamplough, p. 1.
72. *G&L* 1918, xxv, p. 105, Hore, *Zeebrugge.*
73. RM Box 7/17/2, Batt. Order, 8 Apr 1918, para. III.
74. *G&L* 1919, xxvi, p. 63, Anon (Pvt J. Feeney RMLI), *Zeebrugge;* See Holliday, *From Trench and Turret,* p. 66 for the writer's identity.
75. *G&L* 1919, xxvi, p. 63, Feeney.
76. RM 11/73/1, Capt A.R. Chater, *Personal Narrative of the Adjutant 4th Battn RM HMS Vindictive,* p. 4.
77. RM Box 7/17/2, Lamplough, p. 3.
78. *G&L* 1919, xxvi, p. 64, Feeney.

79. *G&L* 1919, xxvi, p. 64, Feeney.
80. Fraser & Carr Laughton, ii, p. 754. Total RM losses: 119 dead; 234 wounded; 13 missing.
81. RM 11/73/1, Chater, p. 5.
82. *G&L* 1919, xxvi, p. 64, Feeney.
83. RM 11/73/1, Chater, p. 4.

Chapter 11   Where Sea Meets Shore
1. Amphibious Warfare Headquarters, *History of the Combined Operations Organisation*, p. 9.
2. *G&L* 1920, xxviii, p. 53, *Some thoughts on the principles on which the Royal marines should be organised and trained*. Also p. 66 M. Filmer Bennett, *The raison d'être of the Royal Marines*.
3. RM Box 7/17/7, letter 7 Feb 1919 in Maj V.M. Bentinck RM, *Indiscipline in the Royal Marines North Russia* 1919, Annexe E1.
4. RM Box 7/17/7, Bentinck, p. 11.
5. *JRUSI* 1927, lxxii, p. 757, Capt E.J. Woodington RM, *Functions and Future of the Royal Marines* in response to 'Classiarius', pp. 56–8.
6. *JRUSI* 1944, lxxxix, p. 22, Newman.
7. K.J. Clifford, *Amphibious Warfare Developments in Britain and America*, pp. 10–16.
8. *JRUSI* 1944, lxxxix, p. 22, Newman.
9. *G&L* 1951, lviii, p. 123, General Sir Alan Bourne. There were two MNBDOs: MNBDO I served in Crete and the Far East; MNBDO II in Sicily.
10. RM Box 7/19/6, Gen Sir Ian Riches/Prof A. Marder, 5 May & 4 July 1974.
11. RM Box 7/19/16–17, SBPO G.K. Hewitt.
12. F.A. Hynes, *LCF 36*, pp. 20–4.
13. RM Box 7/19/6, 15 June 1942, Sturges/Under Secretary of War – Report #6.
14. RM Box 7/19/16–17, *The Story of Fifty Marines*, p. 5.
15. Clifford, p. 80; Capt L.E.H. Maund/Adm Fergusson, C-in-C Norway.
16. RM Box 7/19/19, Mne Peter Bowers, pp. iii-iv.
17. RM Box 7/19/19, Maj H.G. Haslar, 8 Dec 1941, *RM Report on Operations in the Narvik Area in May and June 1940*.
18. RM Box 7/19/19, Capt W. Keen RM (HMS *Hood*), 27 Apr 1940.
19. RM Box 7/19/19, Surg Lt F.A. Henley RNVR, *RM Norwegian Expedition* & Rutter *The Royal Marines – The Admiralty Account of their Achievement 1939–1943*, p. 24.
20. RM Box 7/19/7, *Work of the Royal Marines in Crete*.
21. M. Simpson, *The Cunningham Papers*, i, p. 439, 14 Sept 1941, *Despatch on Crete Evacuation*. RM losses in Crete exceeded 50%: 1,114 out of 1,951, including 900 POWs.
22. RM Box 7/19/7, *Log of Invasion Barge '96'*.
23. RM Box 7/19/22–23 Capt RGS Lang RM 19 Nov 1945: *Report on the Services of the Combined RM Detachments of HM Ships Prince of Wales and Repulse*, p. 7.
24. Rutter, pp. 41–2.
25. RM Box 7/19/22–23, Lang, p. 10; Rutter, p. 41.

26. P.G. Halpern, *Keyes Papers,* iii, pp. 86–8.
27. RM Box 7/19/12, J.F. Kruthoffer, 25 Mar 1986.
28. RM Box 7/19/12, *Summary of Log of Chasseur No. 10,* 19 Aug 1942.
29. *History of COO,* p. 84.
30. RM Box 7/19/12, *Report on Events off Dieppe,* Capt P.W.C. Hellings RM et al.
31. RM Box 7/19/12, W.H.J. Heffernan, 18 Jul 1985.
32. RM Box 7/19/12, J.F. Kruthoffer, 25 Mar 1986.
33. *JRUSI* 1944, lxxxix, pp. 25–7, Newman & RM Box 7/19/20, Orders & Instructions for RMs Borne on Ships' Books on the Mediterranean Station, 25 Jun 1944, Part III. Also Ladd, *By Sea, By Land* pp. 134–7 & *History of COO* pp. 110–11.
34. Hynes, p. 31.
35. *JRUSI* 1945, xc, pp. 213–17, RAdm L.E.H. Maund, *Development of Landing Craft.*
36. LCGFA J. Brewin, LCF(L) 5 & Stan Booth, BPC 1.
37. *History of COO,* p. 114.
38. RM Box 7/19/16–17, *RM in Sicily and Italy.*
39. RM Box 7/19/16–17, SBPO G.K. Hewitt.
40. RM Box 7/19/16–17, *Lessons from Salerno,* 19 Nov 1943.
41. RM Box 7/19/26, Diary of X Tp 40 Cdo, 3–4 Oct 1943, 15 Jan & 14 Feb 1944.
42. RM Box 7/19/16–17, RAdm R.L. Conolly USN/CinC Med, 24 Aug 1943, 'Commendation for a job well done'.
43. RM Box 7/19/26, Lt-Cmr F.R. Arundale RNVR (SNO LCF(L)), Med Report, Dec 1943 & Lt A. Wormald RNVR (Lt-Cmr LCF), 28 July 1943.
44. RM Box 7/19/16–17, *RM in Sicily and Italy.*
45. LCGFA Stan Booth, LCF 37.
46. LCGFA Mne H. Neville, LCF 32, p. 3.
47. LCGFA Gordon Hand, 558 LCA Flotilla RM.
48. LCGFA Mne H. Neville LCF 32, p. 3.
49. LCGFA Gordon Hand, 558 LCA Flotilla RM.
50. LCGFA SubLt R. Browning RNVR, LCF 34, p. 5.
51. RM Box 7/19/5, Recommendations MV *Llangibby Castle,* 10 Jun 1944.
52. RM Box 7/19/5, Maj D.F. Flunder, 48 Cdo, pp. 1–2.
53. RM Box 7/19/5, Anon Signaller, 41 Cdo.
54. RM Box 7/19/5, Capt J.E. Day, 45 Cdo, p. 3.
55. RM Box 7/19/5, Signaller & Lt A.C. Badenoch ASG, p. 3.
56. RM Box 7/19/5, 4th SS Brigade Intelligence Summary, 19 Jun 1944.
57. RM Box 7/19/5, *Their Own Petard.*
58. LCGFA Mne G.W. Foster, LCF 36, *The Second Front,* p. 5.
59. Hynes, pp. 77–85.
60. LCGFA SubLt R. Browning RNVR, LCF 34, pp. 5–6.
61. RM Box 7/19/5, Lt-Col T. Gray 41 Cdo.
62. RM Box 7/19/5, Flunder, p. 4.
63. RM Box 7/19/5, Sgt W. Andrews 47 Cdo, pp. viii–ix.
64. H. StG. Saunders, *The Green Beret – The Story of the Commandos* 1940–1945 (Michael Joseph 1949), p. 281.
65. RM Box 7/19/5, Andrews, p. x.
66. *History of COO,* p. 251; Nos. 7 & 8 Army Commandos disbanded after

heavy losses. 48 RM Cdo replaced 10 Inter-Allied Cdo, making 7 Army and 9 RM Cdos assigned to SS Brigades.

67. Saunders, p. 291.
68. 3 Cdo Brigade, *The Third Jungle Book*, Mar 1946, p. 36.
69. RM Box 7/19/3, K.A. Sellars RN, 14 Nov 1944, *Operation Infatuate*, p. 9.
70. RM Box 7/19/3, Lt-Col Sir N. Tailyour: Quantico Lecture. XXX Support Squadron had, 6xLCG(L), each 2x4.7″ guns; 2xLCG(M), each 2x17pr; 6xLCF, each 2xtwin 4″; 6xLCS(L), each 6pr, 2x20mm, 4″ mortar; 5xLCT(R), each 1,064x5″ rockets.
71. LCFGA R. Leaney, LCF 32 & RM Box 7/19/3, K.A. Sellars, p. 3.
72. LCFGA R. Leaney, LCF 32.
73. RM Box 7/19/3, Anon report (Lt-Col C. Phillips) 47 Cdo, pp. 5 & 10: initial strength 22 officers & 375 O/Rs; casualties 30 killed, 4 missing, 56 wounded. LC crews: 172 killed & 125 wounded out of 1,030.
74. RM *PPL*, 11 Jun 1945, Appendix.
75. RM *PPL*, 5 Aug 1945, p. 5.
76. *History of* COO, p. 112.
77. RM Box 7/19/26, Gen Sir Ian Riches, *Operation Roast*, pp. 6, 3 & 5.
78. RM Box 7/19/26, J. Farmer, n.d.
79. *Third Jungle Book*, Mar 1946, p. 8: Maj-Gen R.G. Sturges, *Special Order of the Day*.

Chapter 12   Survival of the Fittest

1. *Third Jungle Book*, Mar 1946, pp. 8–10, Maj-Gen R.E. Laycock, Special Order of the Day & Speech 24 Oct 1945.
2. RM *PPL*, 8 Oct 1945, p. 7.
3. RM *PPL*, 8 Oct 1945, p. 7.
4. RM 2/21/28, Military Training of 50 Other Ranks from *Belfast*, pp. 2–3.
5. Anon, *Training a RM Detachment Afloat* (1945), pp. 19–20.
6. *G&L*, lvi, Oct 1948, pp. 297–8.
7. RM *PPL*, 11 Jun 1945.
8. RM *PPLs*, 1 May 1945 & 11 Jun 1945.
9. *G&L*, lix, 1951, p. 132.
10. *G&L*, lix, 1951, pp. 58–60.
11. *G&L*, lvi, 1948, pp. 232–3. Haganah was the forerunner of the Israeli Army.
12. RM *PPL*, 1 Apr 1945, Appendix.
13. *G&L*, lxiv, 1956, Capt T.M.P. Stevens, *RM Helicopter Assault*, pp. 243–4.
14. RM Box 15/4/1, Briefing on White Paper.
15. Hattendorf and R.J.B. Knight, p. 805, 6 Apr 1959, Mountbatten/RAdm R.M.J. Hutton.
16. RM 2/24/14, HMS *Bulwark*, *The Detachment – Royal Marines*.
17. *G&L*, lxxiv, 1966, p. 142, *As Others See Us*.
18. *G&L*, lxxiv, 1966, p. 272.
19. *G&L*, lxxv, 1967, p. 194, Capt J.M. Coleby RM & p. 31, Lt Col J.E.J. Lloyd RM; *G&L*, lxxiv, 1966, p. 275, Maj P.G. Davis RM.
20. *G&L*, lxxv, 1967, p. 31, Lt-Col J.E.J. Lloyd RM.
21. *G&L*, lxxiv, 1966, p. 22.
22. *G&L*, lviii, 1950, p. 196.

23. *G&L*, lxxiv, 1966, p. 99.
24. *G&L*, lviii, 1950, p. 259.
25. *G&L*, lix, 1951, p. 166.
26. *G&L*, lviii, 1950, p. 235.
27. *G&L*, lxxv, 1967, pp. 66–7.
28. *G&L*, lxxv, 1967, p. 68.
29. *G&L*, lxxv, 1967, p. 87.
30. *G&L*, lxxv, 1967, pp. 66–7.
31. *G&L*, lix, 1951, p. 137 & lxi, 1953, p. 5.
32. *G&L*, lxxiv, 1966, p. 212.
33. *G&L*, lix, 1951, p. 331, Kuala Kangsar Bus Co/Adj 40 Cdo.
34. *G&L*, lix, 1951, p. 166.
35. *G&L*, lxxiv, 1966, p. 212.
36. *G&L*, lxxv, 1967, p. 198.
37. *G&L*, lxxv, 1967, p. 228 Healey was Defence Minister 1964–70.
38. *G&L*, lxxv, 1967, p. 340.
39. *G&L*, lxxviii, 1970, pp. 336–7.
40. *G&L*, lxxviii, 1970, p. 339.
41. *G&L*, lxxxi, 1972, p. 325.
42. *G&L*, lxxxi, 1972, pp. 203 & 273.
43. *XL Northern Ireland*, Aug 1979 & Jan 1980.
44. *JRUSI* 1982, cxxvii, p. 13, Adm Sir Henry Leach, *British Maritime Forces – The Future* & p. 47 RAdm E.F. Gueritz, *The Falklands – Joint Warfare Justified*.
45. Anonymous, *Letter. . . Concerning the Four Regiments Commonly Called Mariners*.
46. *JRUSI*, cxxvii, 1982, p. 14, Leach & p. 47 Gueritz.
47. *G&L*, xci, 1982, p. 258.
48. *G&L*, xci, 1982, p. 214.
49. *G&L*, xci, 1982, p. 245.
50. *G&L*, xci, 1982, p. 238.
51. *G&L*, xci, 1982, pp. 320 & 325.
52. *G&L*, xci, 1982, p. 325.
53. *G&L*, xci, 1982, pp. 250–1.
54. *G&L*, xci, 1982, pp. 251.
55. *G&L*, xci, 1982, p. 245 84mm=Carl Gustav and 66mm=Light Anti-tank Weapon.
56. *G&L*, xci, 1982, p. 335.
57. Lt-Col Bill Dunham in *Maritime Strategic Studies Institute*, No. 3, Dec 1999.
58. RM Nos 1982–2000: 7,899–6,725; Total RN: 74,687–42,558. IISS *Military Balance* 1982, p. 28 & *Jane's Fighting Ships* 2000–2001, pp. 746 & 765.

Bibliography

Periodicals Consulted, and Abbreviations

A&NG	Army and Navy Gazette
CHOP	Calendar of Home Office Papers
CSPD	Calendar of State Papers Domestic
CTB	Calendar of Treasury Books
G&L	Globe and Laurel
GM	Gentleman's Magazine
HT	Hampshire Telegraph
ILN	Illustrated London News
JRUSI	Journal of the Royal United Service Institute
LG	London Gazette
MM	Mariner's Mirror
NC	Naval Chronicle
RND	Royal Naval Division (periodical)
USJ	United Services Journal
USM	United Service Magazine

Other Abbreviations Used in Footnotes

BL	British Library
BSS	Britain's Sea Soldiers
COO	Combined Operations Organisation
Edye/MSS	Admiralty papers transcribed for Col Edye RMLI (at RM Museum)
f.n.	Footnote
HMSO	HM Stationery Office
IWM	Imperial War Museum
LCGFA	Landing Craft Gun and Flak Association (papers at RM Museum)
n.d.	No Date
NMM	National Maritime Museum
n.p.	No Page
PPL	Policy and Progress Letter
PRO	Public Record Office
RM	Royal Marines Museum Archives
RR	Random Records of the Royal Marines

Where a source appears in several consecutive references, the footnote appears against the last quotation.

Select Bibliography (London publishers unless stated)

Amphibious Warfare Headquarters, *History of the Combined Operations Organisation 1940–1945* (London 1956).

Anonymous, *Abstract of General Orders Relating to the Marine Forces 1702–07* (RM 11/11/7).

Anonymous, *Albert's Diary while in the Dardanelles* (RM Box 7/17/3).

Anonymous, *Letter to a Member of Parliament Concerning the Four Regiments Commonly Called Mariners* (1699).

Anonymous Marine Order Book 1775–1777 (RM 7/7/1–2).

A Quondam Sub, *Symptoms of Advice to the Oxxxxxxs of an Amphibious Corps* etc. (1789).

Capt L. Baine RN, *Prize Essay – The Best Method of Providing an Efficient Force of Officers and Men for the Navy* (JRUSI 1882, xxvi, p. 183).

Pvt W. Baker RMLI, Diary (RM 11/13/85).

G.R. Barnes & J.H. Owen, *Private Papers of John Earl of Sandwich* 1771–1782 (Navy Records Society 1932).

Sgt Major Edward Bastin, *Deal Battn RMLI* (RM 11/13/65).

D.A. Baugh, *Naval Administration 1715–1750* (Navy Records Society 1977).

Col P. Beeman, *Calcutta and Charybdis with Beeman* 1939–1943 (RM 11/13/275).

Gen Sir H. Blumberg & Col C. Field, *Random Records of the Royal Marines* (*G&L* 1936).

D. Bonner Smith, *Barrington Papers* (Navy Records Society 1937).

Gen John Tatton Brown, *Written Orders of Captain A King to the Royal Marines of HM Ship Royal George* (RM 11/13/89).

Pvt William Brown RMLI, *1915–1917* (RM 11/13/321).

J. Burchett: *A Complete History of the Most Remarkable Transactions at Sea, etc.* (1720).

Col A.L.S. Burrowes: *Action with Huascar* (RM 11/13/293).

Bugler J.W. Carroll RMLI, Diary (RM 11/13/108).

Cpl H.W. Cauchey RMLI, Diary (RM 11/13/71).

Classiarius, *The Future of the Royal Marines* (JRUSI 1927, lxxii, pp. 56–8).

K.J. Clifford, *Amphibious Warfare Developments in Britain and America from 1920–1944* (Edgewood, NY 1983) ISBN 533–05370–6.

W. Laird Clowes, *The Royal Navy – A History from the Earliest Times to 1900* (Sampson Low Marston, 1903).

Capt J.C. Colomb, *General Principles of Naval Organisation* (JRUSI 1871, xv, p. 269).

Capt J.C.R. Colomb RMA, *The Use and Application of Marine Forces; Past, Present and Future* (JRUSI 1883, xxvii, p. 122).

Sir John Colomb, *Garrisons for Coaling Stations* (JRUSI 1902, xlvi, p. 890).

Mne John J. Cook: *The Tragic Years* (RM 11/13/288).

J.S. Corbett, *Fighting Instructions 1530–1816* (Navy Records Society 1905).

J.S. Corbett, *Private Papers of George 2nd Earl Spencer First Lord of the Admiralty 1794–1801* (Navy Records Society 1913).

Cottrell's Marines, Miscellaneous Papers (RM 11/28/32).

Gunner W. Craig RMA (HMS *New Zealand*), Diary 1905–07 (RM 11/13/10(A)).

Gunner F.F. Crowe RMA, Diary *HMS Moldava 2nd Cruise* (RM 11/13/63(f)).

Col L. Edye RMLI, *Historical Records of the Royal Marines, etc.* vol i (Harrison 1893).

D.G. Elmer, RMB X967, *To Be a Musician in the Royal Naval School of Music 1936–48* (RM 11/13/299).

Maj Elmslie RA, *Lessons to be derived from the Operations of landing an Expeditionary Force on an Enemy's Coast*, etc. (*JRUSI* 1895, xxxix, p. 437–83).

Col M.H.H. Evans RM, *Amphibious Operations – The Projection of Sea Power Ashore* (Brassey's 1990).

W. Fernyhough, *Military Memoirs of Four Brothers… Engaged in the Service of their Country… by the Survivor* (1829).

Col Cyril Field RMLI, *Old Times Afloat* (Andrew Melrose 1932).

E. Fraser & L.G. Carr Laughton, *The Royal Marine Artillery* (RUSI 1930) vols i & ii.

Richard Gardiner, *Account of the Expedition to the West Indies etc* (1759).

Capt A. Gillespie RM, *Historical Review of the Royal Marines Corps* (Swinney, Birmingham 1803).

Col G.W.M. Glover RM, *A Short History of the Royal Marines* (Gale and Polden, Aldershot 1948).

Lt-Cdr C.F. Goodrich USN, *Report of the British Naval and Military Operations in Egypt* 1882, prepared for the Office of Naval Intelligence, etc (Washington, USA 1885).

RAdm E.F. Gueritz, *The Falklands – Joint Warfare Justified* (*JRUSI* 1982, cxxvii, pp. 46–52).

P.G. Halpern, *The Keyes Papers* (Navy Records Society 1981).

Maj A.P. Grattan RMLI, Transcript letters (RM 11/13/114).

J.B. Hattendorf and R.J.B. Knight, *British Naval Documents 1216–1961* (Navy Records Society 1993).

Lt J. Haverfield, Diary HMS *Inconstant* (RM 11/13/57(A)).

Pvt T.H. Haywood RMLI, Diary of HMS *Baralong* (RM 11/13/80(a)).

Colour Sergeant N.J. Hiscock RMLI, *Twenty One Years Service Ashore and Afloat* (RM 11/21/30).

Pvt Thomas Holbrow RMLI, Diary (RM 11/13/192).

S.M. Holliday, *From Trench and Turret: Royal Marine Letters and Diaries 1914–1918* (RM Museum Eastney n.d.).

Pvt E.W. Horton, Diary (RM 11/13/30).

Sgt John Howe, Diary (RM 11/13/093).

F.A. Hynes, *LCF 36* (Sotheran, Redcar 1994).

Sgt N.V.J. Jago RMLI, *The Battle of Jutland witnessed from the Agincourt* (RM 11/13/199).

D. Jerrold, *The Royal Naval Division* (Hutchinson 1923).

Pvt Edward Keep RMLI, *Journal of the Commission of HMS Sphinx from May 2nd 1902 to March 23rd 1905* (RM 11/13/67).

Lt Commander P.K. Kemp, *Fisher Papers* (Navy Records Society 1960).

G.E. Kitchen, *The Most Dangerous Moment – An Account of the Loss of HMS Devonshire...* 5 Apr 1942 (RM 11/13/292).

Mne B. Knapton, Diary SS *Natia* (RM 11/13/124).

Sir John Knox Laughton, *Letters and Papers of Charles, Lord Barham 1758–1813* (Navy Records Society 1911).

Brian Lavery, *Shipboard Life and Organisation 1731–1815* (Navy Records Society 1998).

Adm Sir Henry Leach, *British Maritime Forces – The Future* (*JRUSI* 1982, cxxvii, pp. 10–15).

Lt Francis Lean RMLI, Diary (RM 11/13/17).

Lt Robert Lloyd, Order Book (RM 11/13/313), photocopy of original at University of North Wales Bangor.

JA Lowe: *Records of the Portsmouth Division of Marines 1764–1800* (City of Portsmouth 1990).

K.R. MacDonald, *A Bandsman and Barbed Wire* May 1941–May 1945 (RM 11/13/305).

Lt J. MacIntire, *A Military Treatise on the Discipline of the Marine Forces, When at Sea: Together with Short Instructions for Detachments to attack on Shore* (1763).

Col Markham Rose RMA, *The Story of the Royal Marines, Lectures for Recruits* (1935).

Lt J.M. Rose RMA, *The Royal Marine Artillery* (USM Aug–Sep 1893 vii (NS)).

S. Martin-Leake, *Life of Sir John Leake, Rear-Admiral of Great Britain,* G, Callendar (ed.) (Navy Records Society 1920).

RAdm L.E.H. Maund, *The Development of Landing Craft* (*JRUSI* 1945, xc, pp. 213–17).

T.M. Molyneux, *Conjunct Expeditions that have been carried on jointly By the Fleet and Army, with a Commentary on Littoral War* (1759).

Captain Richard Moubray, *Notebook in HMS Active* 1801–7 (RNM Admiralty Library Manuscript MSS/16).

Maj-Gen J.L. Moulton, *The Royal Marines* (Leo Cooper 1972).

Brig H.T. Newman RM, The *Functions of the Royal Marines in Peace and War* (*JRUSI* 1944, lxxxix, p. 21–32).

Lt P.H. Nicholas RM, *Historical Record of the Royal Marine Forces* (Boone 1845).

Bandsman J.B. Nicholls, Diary HMS *Dido* (RM 11/13/279).

Lt T. O'Loghlen, *The Marine Volunteer containing the Exercises, Firings and Evolutions of a Battalion of Infantry to which is added Sea Duty and a Supplement (1764).*

Lt W.H. Palmer, *A Short Journal of the Late Egyptian Campaign of 1882* (RM 11/13/14).

Parliamentary Commission 1746, *Report from the Committee Appointed to Consider the State of His Majesty's Land Forces and Marines* (reprinted HMSO 1803).

W.G. Perrin, *Boteler's Dialogues* (Navy Records Society 1929).

W.G. Perrin, *The Keith Papers* (Navy Records Society 1927).

Pvt Walter Stanley Popham, *A Soldier's Diary Nov 1916–Mar 1919* (RM 11/13/925).

Maj W.H. Poyntz, *Per Mare Per Terram: Reminiscences of Thirty-two Years of Military and Constabulary Service* (Economic Printing and Publishing Company 1892).

Lt W. Pridham RM, Diary (RM 11/3/45).

Brian Ranfft, *Vernon Papers* (Navy Records Society 1958).

Andrew Rea, *General Orders at the Camp on Bell Isle* (RM 7/4/1).

Sgt Thomas Rees, *A Journal of Voyages and Travels* (1822 reprinted Cornmarket 1971).

Capt John Robyns RM, Diary (RM 11/13/061).

Capt S.W. Roskill RN, *The Navy At War 1939–1945* (Collins 1960).

Capt Lewis Roteley RM, Papers (RM 11/12/42).

R. Rowe, *Sticky Blue! A Boy and a Battleship* (Devonshire House, Devon 1995).

O. Rutter, *The Royal Marines – The Admiralty Account of their Achievement 1939–1943* (HMSO 1944).

Cpl A.P. Saunders RMA, Diary *Princess Royal* (RM 11/13/2).

Maj-Gen G.A. Schomberg, *Are the Royal Marine Forces a Necessary Auxiliary to the Royal Navy?* (JRUSI 1871, xv, p. 497).

Maj R.E. Scouller, *The Armies of Queen Anne* (Oxford University Press 1966).

M. Simpson, *The Cunningham Papers* (Navy Records Society 1999).

Cpl F.G. Smith RMLI, Lecture notes on the Boxer Rebellion and Siege of Peking (NMM MS 84/081).

Capt William Souter, Letters (RM 7/7/5(7)).

J. Sparrow & J.N. MacBean-Ross (Surgeons RN), *On Four Fronts with the Royal Naval Division* (Hodder & Stoughton 1918).

Capt Sir Robert Steele RM, *The Marine Officer; or Sketches of Service* (Henry Colburn 1840).

Pvt W.J. Stevens RMLI, Diary HMS *Queen Mary* (RM 11/13/277).

Capt John Sutton, *Order Book 1794–1801* (RNM Admiralty Library Manuscript MSS/118).

Col Richard Swale RM, Diary (RM 11/13/091).

J. Swales, *The Life and Music of RMB X1522* (Singing Saw Press, Haverfordwest, 1993).

E. Taber RMA, *My Career since 1870* (RM 11/13/303).

Maj-Gen J. Thompson, *The Royal Marines – From Sea Soldiers to a Special Force* (Sidgwick & Jackson 2000).

3 Cdo Brigade, *The Third Jungle Book* Souvenir Number (Hong Kong 1946).

Rear Admiral H.G. Thursfield, *Five Naval Journals 1789–1817* (Navy Records Society 1951).

Maj Mortimer Timpson RM, *Memoir* (RM 7/9/1–17).

B. Tunstall, *The Byng Papers* (Navy Records Society 1930).

Arthur Webster, *HMS Arethusa at Normandy* (RM 11/13/253).

Gunner J.T. Wilkinson RMA, Diary (NMM JOD/188).

G. Williams, *Documents Relating to Anson's Voyage Around the World 1740–44* (Navy Records Society 1967).

Lt Edward Wilson, Diary (RM 11/13/152).

Capt J.C. Wilson RN, *Seamen of the Fleet, Their Training and How the Employment of Marines Afloat in Peacetime Affects Them* (*JRUSI* 1876. xix. p. 604*)*.

Capt E.J. Woodington RM, *Functions and Future of the Royal Marines; a Prize Essay* (*JRUSI* 1927, lxxii, p. 754–66).

Lt H. Woodruff RMLI, Diary (RM 11/13/43).

Bombardier D. Wynne, Diary 1879–82 (RM 11/13/246)

Glossary

The Julian calendar was ten or eleven days behind the Gregorian calendar used in Europe. I have used Julian dates for events within the British Isles, until September 1752, and fractional Old Style/New Style dates for European events. Years start on 1 January, and appear as whole numbers, e.g. March 1677 not 1676/1677.

Pre-decimal monetary values are expressed in pounds, shilling, and pence:

£1 = one pound = 20 shillings = 100 decimal pence
1/- = one shilling = 12 old pence = 5 decimal pence
1d = 1 old penny = 0.4 decimal pence

ANZAC – Australia and New Zealand Army Corps
ASW – Anti-Submarine Warfare
AVRE – Armoured Vehicle Royal Engineers: Churchill tank with petard mortar
BEF – British Expeditionary Force
BL – Breech Loading
Cable – naval unit of measurement: 200 yards or one-tenth of a nautical mile
CGRM – Commandant General Royal Marines
DAG – Deputy Adjutant General
DD – Duplex Drive: an amphibious Sherman tank
DUKW – American amphibious lorry
ERA – Engine Room Artificer
FRMO – RM Officer with general responsibility for all Marines in a Fleet
Funky – frightened
Gash – leftover
GPMG – General Purpose Machine Gun
Guinea – gold coin worth £1 1s 0d (£1.05)
HE – High Explosive
HO – Hostilities Only
JP – Justice of the Peace
KGV – King George V
LCA – Landing Craft Assault
LCF – Landing Craft Flak
LCG – Landing Craft Gun

LCI(S) – Landing Craft Infantry (Small)
LCM – Landing Craft Mechanised
LCS – Landing Craft Support (Small)
LCT – Landing Craft Tank
LCU – Landing Craft Utility
LCVP – Landing Craft Vehicle & Personnel
Lewis Gun – First World War light machine gun
LPD – Landing Platform Dock
LPH – Landing Platform Helicopter
LSI – Landing Ship Infantry
LSL – Landing Ship Logistics
LVT – Landing Vehicle Tracked: an armoured amphibious personnel carrier
Matross – Gunner's Mate
Milan –Anti-Tank Guided Missile
ML – Muzzle Loading
MNDBO – Mobile Naval Base Defence Organisation
MV – Merchant Vessel
NGS – Naval Gunfire Support
OCRM – Officer Commanding Royal Marines
OP – Observation Post
PIAT – Projectile Infantry Anti-Tank
PO – Petty Officer
Q/F – Quick Firing
RMA – Royal Marine Artillery
RMB – Royal Marine Brigade
RMLI – Royal Marine Light Infantry
RMO – Royal Marine Officer
RND – Royal Naval Division
RNVR – Royal Naval Volunteer Reserve
SNO – Senior Naval Officer
T/S – Transmitting Station
USMC – United States Marine Corps
Very – signal rocket used in First and Second World Wars

Index

Note: Ranks and titles are generally the highest mentioned

Abercrombie, Sir Ralph 149–50
Aboukir Bay *see* Nile, Battle of the
Aboukir, HMS 213
Abyssinian crisis (1936) 253
Ackroyd, Lieut. William 58
Acre 155, 161
Active, HMS 66
Adair, Captain 140–1
Aden 280–3
Admiral's Regiment *see* Duke of York's
  Regiment
Admiralty: administration improves under
  Anson 26, 46; and deployment of
  Marines 32; and payment and
  equipment of Marines 32, 39, 114;
  assumes control of Marines 46; reduces
  RM strength after Napoleonic Wars
  158; and punishment 195; and Great
  War amphibious operations 232
Agamemnon, HMS 128
Agincourt, HMS 206, 209
air power 220–1
Albemarle, George Monck, 1st Duke of 11
Albion, HMS 66–7, 114, 234, 279
Alecto, HMS 182
Alexandria 172–3, 184, 201
Algiers: bombarded and stormed (1816)
  71, 159
Alicante: amphibious attack on (1706) 79
Almanza, Battle of (1707) 80
Althea: landing at (1703) 78
Amazon, HMS 144
Amelia, HMS 65, 73
American War of Independence (1775–83)
  98–103, 129
Amethyst, HMS 137
Amiens, Battle of (1918) 246
Amiens, Peace of (1802) 132
Amoy 169
amphibious operations: Marines in 75–9,
  87–8; organisation and principles of
  86–9; Nelson favours 143; in
  Napoleonic Wars 144–8; in Great War

232–6, 250; inter-war development
  253; in Second World War 254–5, 258;
  in Suez crisis (1956) 278; and use of
  helicopters 278; in Falklands 285
Ancre, Battle of the (1916) 240–1, 244–5
Andrews, Bill 269
Annapolis 97
Anne, Queen 3, 34–6, 120
Anson, Admiral George, Baron 25–6,
  46–7, 54
Antelope, HMS 39
Anthony, HMS 254
Antwerp: in Great War 231–3; in Second
  World War 270–1
ANZACs: at Gallipoli 236–8
Apollo, HMS 147
Arab, HMS 146
Arabica, SS 216
Arethusa, HMS 227–8
Arethuse, l' (French frigate) 65, 73
Argentina: and Falklands War 285–6
Argonauta (French ship) 142
Argyll, HMS 204
Ark Royal, HMS 276
Arlington, Henry Bennett, 1st Earl of 19
Army & Navy Gazette 171, 175, 186,
  194, 239
Ashanti, HMS 276
Ashanti War, Second (1873–4) 170–1
Aston, Major-General Sir George Grey
  232–3
Atcherley, Captain 142
Atlantic, Battle of the (World War II) 223
Atlantic Conveyor (ship) 286
Augusta, HMS 39, 62
Austerlitz, Battle of (1805) 143
Avant, Boy Bugler P.J.M. 223

Balaklava 162–4
Baltimore, HMS 12
Bamford, Captain E., VC 249–50
Bantry Bay, Battle of (1689) 26
Baralong, HMS (Q-ship) 215–16

Barcelona: attacked and captured (1705)
    78–9
Barfleur, Battle of (1692) 57
Barracouta (gunboat) 170
Barrington, William Wildman, 2nd
    Viscount 47
Basra 184
Bastin, Lieut. 239
Bayly, Admiral Sir Lewis 215
Beachy Head, Battle of (1690) 72, 136
Bearcroft, Captain 187
Beatty, Admiral Sir David (*later* 1st Earl)
    210–11
Beaucourt 242
Bedford, HMS 30
Beeman, Lieut. Philip 220, 222, 224
Belfast, HMS 219, 276–7
Belgium: in Great War 231–3
Belleisle, HMS 139–40, 142, 162
Belle Isle, siege of (1761) 94–6
Bellerophon, HMS 72, 156
Bellona, HMS 56, 214, 216
Benin expedition (1897) 178, 180–1
Bennet, Captain Thomas 15
Beresford, Lord Charles 178
Beresford, Colonel William 150
Bertrand, General Count Henri 156
Berwick, HMS 107, 146
Berwick upon Tweed 20
Bethell, Vice-Admiral 232
Bickerstaffe, Philip 57
Bienfaisant, HMS 60
Billinge, William 9
Bismarck (German battleship) 218
Biter, HM Gunboat 166
Blake, HMS 116
Blanche, HMS 61
Bland, Lieut. 145
Blenheim, HMS 69
Blücher (German cruiser) 208
Boadicea, HMS 178
Boer War 186–8
Bomarsund (Aaland Islands) 164–5
Bor, Brigadier Jacob 6, 28, 33, 35, 39, 44,
    49, 79, 80–1, 126
Borneo 281
Boscawen, Admiral Edward 97
Boston, Mass. 99
Bourne, Lieut.-General Alan G.B. 207,
    258, 260
Boxer Rebellion (China, 1900) 185
Boyne, HMS 4, 40
Brace, Captain 146
Branson, Captain 102
Brest: blockaded (Napoleonic Wars) 143
Bristol, HMS 90
Broke, Captain 66
Bromley, Captain 15
Brown, Lieut. Tatton 116, 198
Bruce, Captain 188
Brumpton, Corporal Charles 265
Brunei 279

Bucentaure (French ship) 142
Buckingham, HMS 56, 65
Buenos Aires 150–1
Buller, Captain Anthony 19
Bulwark, HMS 279, 283
Bunker's Hill, Mass. 99–101
Burma 257–8
Burston, Major 80
Busigny, Lieut. 73
Bustle, Private Thomas 116
Butler, Captain 38

Cadiz: attacked (1702) 4; attacked in
    Napoleonic Wars 136, 138
Caernarvon, HMS 197
Calcutta, HMS 220–1, 223–4
Calder, Sir Robert 138
Calliope, HMS 190
Camaret Bay: raid on (1694) 76–7
Campbell, Sir Colin 162
Camperdown, Battle of (1797) 73
Canada: Marine actions in 97
Canton 168–9
Cape St Vincent, Battle of (1797) 138
Capes, Second Battle of the (1781) 58
Capricieuse, La (French ship) 66
Carlos II (el Hechizado), King of Spain 3
Carlos III, King of Spain 79, 81
Carlos, Don 159
Carmarthen, Thomas Osborne, Marquis of
    77, 85
Carruthers, Captain 96
Cartagena (South America): expedition
    (1741) 26, 39, 82–5, 87, 93
Cartagena (Spain): landing at (1706) 79
Castor, HMS 162, 193
Cathcart, General Charles, 8th Baron 82
Cavendish, Admiral Philip 40
Centaur, HMS 279
Charles II, King 10, 18–19, 68
Charybdis, HMS 224
Chatham: as Grand Division HQ 47–8;
    RM barracks 121–3; expands 122
Chatham Chest (charity) 9
Chesapeake Bay 152–4
Chesapeake, USS 59, 66, 68
Chichester, HMS 34, 39
China: wars in (1840s–1850s) 167–9;
    see also Boxer Rebellion
Churchill, Joshua 30
Churchill, (Sir) Winston 232, 254, 258,
    260
Clan Lamont (LSI) 265
Clausewitz, Karl von 240
Cleopatra, HMS 105, 118, 145
Cockburn, Admiral Sir George 154
Codrington, Captain Edward 116
Coghlan, Captain 148
Colchester (transport) 97
Coldstream Guards: troops at sea 11
Collard, Gunner John 136
Collet, Lieut. C.H. 220

Collins, Colonel Arthur Tooker 95–6, 98, 100, 102, 122
Collins, Mrs Arthur Tooker 102
Collins, David 100–2
'Collinson, Sam' (Chinese General) 170
Colomb, Sir John 189, 192–3, 280
Colossus, HMS 208
Colpoys, Admiral Sir John 129–30
Colwell, Major 176
Comacchio, Lake (Italy) 272
Combined Operations Organisation 258
Commando Brigades (*formerly* Special Service Brigades) 269–72, 275
Commando Logistics Regiment 285
Concord 98–9
Constant Warwick, HMS 60
Continuous Service Act (1853) 192
Cooper, Joseph 28
Corgeou (Brittany) 148
Cork, siege of (1689) 76
Cornwall, Commodore Charles 27
Cornwall Lieut. Henry 20
Cornwall, HMS 58
Cornwallis, General Charles, 1st Marquis 58, 134
Cottrell, Colonel 39
Courageux (French frigate) 56
Covey, Marine 73–4
Cracherode, Mordaunt 25
Craig, Gunner 190
Cressy, HMS 213
Crete 222, 226, 256–7
Crimean War (1854–6) 162–7
Cumberland Island, Georgia 154
Cunningham, Admiral Andrew (*later* Viscount) 257, 275
Curacao, HMS 146–7
Curtis, John 9
Cyprus 278

D-Day (1944) 227–8, 264
Daffodil, HMS 248–9
Dakar: attacked (1940) 253–4
Danton (French ship) 205
Dardanelles 234
Darell, Major Nathaniel 14, 18–20, 27, 31
Dart, HMS 182, 184
Deal: Marine depot at 47; RM bandsmen killed by IRA bomb at 284
Defiance, HMS 105, 116, 128, 144
DEMS (DAM ships) 214–15
Dennis, Lieut. 12
Deptford: dockyard 121
Deptford, HMS 78
Derry, Private Henry 168, 179, 188
Devonshire, HMS 38, 49, 80, 126, 220
Dew, William 124
Diadem, HMS 150–1
Dickinson, Sergeant 129
Dido, HMS 226
Didon, Le (French frigate) 63

Dieppe raid (Operation Jubilee, 1942) 259–61
Digby, Captain Francis 15
Dilkes, Rear-Admiral Sir Thomas 4
Dogger Bank, Battle of (1915) 205, 208
Dolphin, HMS 40
Donegal, HMS 54, 214
Dorsetshire, HMS 38
Douglas, Rear-Admiral Sir Charles 63
Dove, HMS 29
Dove, Lieut. Robert 9
Dowell, Lieut. George, VC 165
Dryad, HMS 145
duels 118
Duke of Wellington, HMS 189–90
Duke of York, HMS 219
Duke of York's Regiment (*earlier* Admiral's Regiment): and Commandos 1; formed 10–11; uniform 10, 13, 21; arms and equipment 11, 68; in Dutch Wars 11–16, 62, 70; name changes 11, 21; in Low Countries 17–18; strength and home distribution 18–19; indiscipline 21; disbanded 22–3, 26; payments for 31; inter-service rivalry 114
Duncan, Admiral Adam, Viscount 73, 129
Duncombe's Marines 67
Dunkirk evacuation (1940) 221
Dunn, Sergeant 129
Dutch *see* Netherlands
Dyer, Cornelius 33
Dyer, Jane 33

Eagle, HMS 97, 146–7, 224
Edser, John 20
Edye, Colonel Lourenço 10, 14, 16, 34, 105, 108
Egmont, HMS 66
Egypt: in Napoleonic Wars 149–50, 155; in invasion of Syria (1840) 161; and threat to Suez Canal (1882) 172–5; and 1956 Suez crisis 278
Elisabeth (French ship) 71
Enterprise, HMS 63
Enzheim, Battle of (1674) 17
Euryalus, HMS 141
Evans, Widow 20
Excellent, HMS 197–200
Exeter, HMS 217–18

Faddy, Captain 53
Falklands War (1982) 285–7
Faroe Islands 255
Farrant, Lieut. Dover 200
Faulknor, Captain 56
Fearless, HMS 285, 288
Feeney, Private James 249
Fernyhough, Lieut. John 106, 117, 136, 138, 142
Fernyhough, Lieut. Robert 143
Ferrol, Battle of (1805) 138
Festing, Lieut.-Colonel Sir F.W. 170–1

Field, Cyril 128, 138, 173
Fiji, HMS 222–3
Finch, Sergeant, VC 249–50
Firefly, HMS 202
Fisher, Admiral Sir John Arbuthnot 199
Fisher, Captain 7
Fleet Air Arm 220–1
Flora, HMS 72
Florissant (French frigate) 56, 65
Flushing: bombarded and captured (1809)
  143–4
Formidable, HMS 63
Forster, Matthew 20
Fort Cumberland 203
Forte, La (French frigate) 58
Fortrey, Captain James 16–17
Fougueux (French ship) 65, 140
Four Days Fight (1666) 12
Fox, HMS 168
Frampton, Captain 175
Fraser, Major Simon 161–2
Fremantle, Admiral Sir Edmund Robert
  180
French Revolution 58, 127
Freyberg, Lieut.-Colonel Bernard (*later* 1st
  Baron), VC 240

Gage, General Thomas 99, 101
Galicia, HMS 85, 90
Gallipoli 231, 234–9, 244, 251
Galway, Henri de Massue de Ruvigny, 1st
  Earl of 80
Gambia 180–1
Gardiner, Captain Ian 287
Gardiner, Lieut. 12, 31
Gardiner, Captain Richard 90
Gardiners Bay, NY 53
Gavrelle Windmill, Battle of (1917) 240,
  242
Genoa, HMS 73
Gentleman's Magazine 37
George I, King 43
George II, King 26
George IV, King 158, 159
George V, King 248, 250
George, Prince of Denmark (husband of
  Queen Anne) 21–2, 34–5, 38, 115
George, Prince of Hesse-Darmstadt 4–7,
  79, 85
Germany: in Great War (1914–18) 205–6,
  213, 231–2, 241, 245–7; in Second
  World War (1939–45) 231, 255–6; Fleet
  surrenders (1919) 251
Gerrard, Lieutenant E.L. 220
Gibraltar: captured and held (1704) 3–9,
  76; centrality to RM 3; as RM's battle
  honour 3, 156; strategic importance 8
Gillespie, Alexander 18, 96, 128
Globe and Laurel (journal) 231, 251, 278
Gloucester, HMS 222
Gooch's Marines 82
Gordon, General Charles George 176–7

Goree (West Indies) 78
Gorgon, HMS 161
Goring, Sir Harry 30, 44
Goshawk, HMS 182–4, 193
Gossamer, HMS 204
Graf Spee (German pocket-battleship) 217
Graham, General Thomas (Baron
  Lynedoch) 136
Graves, Admiral Samuel 58, 98
Great War (1914–18) 205–17, 231–47
Greece: evacuation (1941) 221
Greyhound, HMS 62
Griffiths' company (1665) 18
Griffon, HMS 118
Guadeloupe: attacked (1859) 89–90
Gulf, The 184

Hadendoa tribesmen (Sudan) 175–7
Haig, General Sir Douglas (*later* 1st Earl)
  243
Halifax, Nova Scotia 101–2
Halliday, Captain L.S.T. 185
Hampshire Telegraph 174
Hampton, Virginia: sacked (1812) 135
Hardy, Captain Sir Thomas Masterman
  39, 141
Harley, Robert (*later* 1st Earl of Oxford) 8
Harper, Commander 148
Harris, Rear-Admiral Sir Robert 188
Harvey, Major F.J., VC 199, 208, 210–11
Harwich: attacked by Dutch (1667)
  13–14; and Battle of Sole Bay 70
Harwood Committee (1949) 275
Hastings, HMS 195
Havoc, HM Gunboat 167
Hawke, Admiral Sir Edward 88
Hawkey, Lieut. 118
Haydon, Captain Peter 271
Healey, Denis (*later* Baron) 283
Hearle, Lieut. Parkins 171
Heffernan, Sergeant 259–60
helicopters: for landing and supply 278,
  285, 288
Heligoland Bight, Battle of (1914) 205,
  207
Henley, Captain John 9
Henry, HMS 15
Herbert, Captain 13
Herbert, Henry 21
Herbert, Sidney 200
Hermione (Spanish treasure ship) 120
Hero, Le (French ship) 56
Hesse, George, Prince of *see* George, Prince
  of Hesse-Darmstadt
Hewett, Lieut. 152
Hill, Captain Chandos 208
Hindenberg Line (Western Front) 246
Hiscock, Colour Sergeant Nathaniel 204
Hodgson, General Studholme 94–6
Hogue, HMS 213
Holbrow, Thomas 177
Holland Regiment 11

Holt's Regiment 44
Hong Kong: in Opium Wars 168
Hood, HMS 223
Hoole, Thomas 44, 75–6
Hopson, General 90–1
Hoste, Captain 147
Houle, Thomas 106, 108
Howe, HMS 229
Howe, John 28, 54, 57–8, 63, 69–70, 106, 115, 120, 124
Howe, Admiral Richard, Earl 58
Howe, General William, 5th Viscount 101–3
Huascar (Peruvian turret-ship) 201–2
Hughes, Captain Robert 64
Hunt, Corporal 182
Hunter, Corporal Tom, VC 272–3
Hunton, General Sir Thomas 275

Iceland: occupied (1940) 255
Illustrious, HMS 116
Inconstant, HMS 114
Indefatigable, HMS 108, 135, 208
India: North West Frontier 18
Indian Mutiny (1857–8) 179–80
Indomitable, HMS 208, 224
Indonesia 279
Inflexible, HMS 201–2
Ingoldsby, Colonel 62
Inkerman, Battle of (1854) 163
Inter-Services Training and Development Centre (ISTDC) 253, 286
Intrepid, HMS 185, 285
Invergordon Mutiny (1931) 193
Invincible, HMS 107, 210
IRA (Irish Republican Army) 284
Ireland 283
Iris, HMS (converted Mersey ferry) 248, 250
Iron Duke, HMS 206, 211
Isabella, Queen of Spain 159

Jacobs, Captain Maximilian 116, 128
Jamaica 82, 86
Jamaica, HMS 30
James II , King (*earlier* Duke of York and Albany) 11, 13, 19–22, 55, 77
James Francis Edward Stuart ('the Old Pretender') 43, 45
Japan 170, 257–8, 269
Jeffreys, Colonel 37
Jellicoe, Admiral Sir John (*later* 1st Earl) 209
Jenkins, Sergeant 129
Jenkins's Ear, War of (1739–48) 25, 69, 81
Jolley, Thomas 20
Jones, Captain F.R. 210
Juste, Le, HMS 136
Jutland, Battle of (1916) 205–6, 208–11

Katherine, HMS 73

Keigwin, Captain 76
Keith, Admiral George Keith Elphinstone, Viscount 147, 149–51
Kempenfeldt, Admiral Richard 134
Kent, HMS 252
Keppel, Admiral Augustus, 1st Viscount 29, 94–6, 103, 122, 134
Kershaw, Sergeant Edwin 234–5
Keyes, Admiral Sir Roger (*later* Baron) 247, 250, 258
Khartoum 176–7, 204
Killigrew, Colonel Sir William 10–12, 18–19
King Alfred, HMS 214
King George V, HMS 218
Kinglake, Alexander William: *History of the Crimean War* 162
Knapton, B. 223
Knight, Captain 129
Knowles, Admiral Sir Charles Henry 130
Konigsberg (German cruiser) 220
Korean War (1950–3) 277
Kosovo 288
Krabbendyke 136
Kronstadt 165, 202
Kruthoffer, Sergeant 260
Kurdistan 288
Kuwait: 1951 operations in 279

la Boulaye, Lieut. 122
Lambert, Private 211
Lancaster, HMS 30
landing craft: introduced (1750s) 88; developed between World Wars 253; in Second World War 261–3, 270–1; post-Second World War 279
Leake, Admiral of the Fleet Sir John 5–8
Lean, Lieut. Francis 166–7, 200
Leander, HMS 73
Leeward Islands 89–93
Legge's company (1665) 18
Leipzig, Battle (of Nations, 1813) 136
Leopard, HMS 108
Leopold I, Emperor 3
Lerida, Battle of (1707) 80
Lewis, Major George 124–5
Lexington, Mass. 99
Lion, HMS 199, 208, 210, 212
Littleton, Sir Charles 11, 14–15, 17–23, 31, 53, 55, 57, 67, 117, 144, 199
Littleton, Henry 22
Lloyd, Robert 90–1
Loire (French frigate) 54–5
London, HMS 129
London Trained Bands 10
Long, Marine William 265
Louisburg, first siege of (1746) 97
Lowestoft, Battle of (1664) 12, 55
Lowestoft, HMS 78
Lowther, Colonel 38
Loyal Katherine, HMS 12
Loyall Subject, HMS 12

Lumsden, Major F.W., VC 243
Lynn, HMS 110
Lyon, HMS 71

MacDonald, Bandmaster 222
MacIntyre, Lieut. John 68, 88, 112–13
Mackenzie, Colonel James 94–6, 98, 122–3
Mackenzie, General John 48
McKinnon, Lieut.-Colonel William 158
MacLean, Captain 144
Macleod, Lieut.-Colonel 83
Madagascar landings (1942) 254
Madden Report (1924) 252
Magnanime, HMS 56
Mahdi, the 175–6
Maitland, Brigadier Frederick 149
Maitland, Admiral Sir Thomas 202
Malaga, Battle of (1704) 5, 57
Malaya, HMS 193
Malaysia 280–2
Malta: in Second World War 223–4
Mar, HMS 132
Marchant, Captain A.E. 186–8
Marietta, USS 185
Markham, Lieut-Colonel 45
Markland, Captain 148
Marlborough, HMS 56, 138
Marlborough, John Churchill, 1st Duke of:
  shares Barbara Villiers as mistress with
  Charles II 1, 17; commands Marine
  force in France 17; duel with Henry
  Herbert 21; dukedom 22; joins William
  of Orange 22; Marines mutiny 33;
  betrays Camaret Bay plan 76; Marines
  in Spain 81
Marriott, Lieut. R.A. 198
Mars, HMS 129
Marsala, Sicily 226
Martin, Jean 122
Martinique: captured (1759) 89–93
Mary II, Queen 32
Mashobra (depot ship) 255
Mason, John 9
Massey, General Eyre (1st Baron Clarina)
  103
Matthews, Admiral Thomas 68
Matthews, Colonel 235–6
Mauritius, HMS 280
Meatyard, Sergeant Frederick 236, 246
Medway, river: Dutch raid (1667) 13–14
Mehemet Ali 161
Melpomene, HMS 61
Melville, Robert Saunders Dundas, 2nd
  Viscount 147, 151
Merlin, HMS 202
Mermaid, HMS 54–5
Methuen, Sir John 6–7
Methuen, Field Marshal Paul Sanford, 3rd
  Baron 186
Mexico 170
Middleton, Captain Charles 16
Milan, HMS 120

Minden, HMS 70, 106, 112
minelaying 214
mines 202
Minheer, Lieut. 58
Minorca 81
Miraumont, Battle of (1917) 240, 242–3
missiles: nature of 71
Mitchell, Thomas 72
Mobile Naval Base Defence Organisation
  (MNBDO) 253–4, 256, 260, 263–4
Molyneux, Thomas: *Conjunct Expeditions*
  86
Monarch, HMS 188
Moncall, Colonel 7
Monckton, Lord Robert 90, 92
Monmouth, HMS 58, 129
Monmouth, James Scott, Duke of 17–18,
  20–1
Montagu, Captain Lionel 240
Montague, HMS 128–30
Moore, Commodore 87, 90
Mordaunt's Regiment 122
Moresom, Captain 139
Morocco 16
Morris, Lieut. William 21
Motor Landing Craft (MLC): introduced
  253; developed 261
Motorman, Operation (Northern Ireland,
  1972) 284
Mountbatten, Admiral of the Fleet Louis,
  1st Earl: as patron of RM 47; as
  commander of Combined Operations
  258, 260–2; on future of Navy and
  Marines 278
Murmansk: convoys to 223, 225
Murray, Captain John 39
Mutiny Acts 32, 122
Myers, Captain, US Marine Corps 185

Namur, HMS 61
Napier, General Sir Charles 135
Napoleon I (Bonaparte), Emperor of
  France 143, 155–7
Napoleonic Wars 127, 133, 136–8,
  145–51, 157–8; blockade in 142–4
Narvik 255
Nash, Captain 85
Natia, SS 223
Naval Brigades 177–82, 188
Naval Chronicle 46, 109, 132, 146
Naval Defence Act (1889) 203
Naval Gunfire Support (NGS) 226
naval warfare: tactics and manoeuvres
  under sail 53–9
Navarino, Battle of (1827) 157, 159
Nelson, Admiral Horatio, 1st Viscount:
  Trafalgar victory 52, 139; on HMS
  Victory 107, 118; on naval discipline
  for military personnel 134–5; naval
  successes 137–8; shot and killed 141–2;
  understands amphibious forces 143
Neptune, HMS 143

Netherlands: in War of Spanish Succession 4; in Anglo-Dutch Wars 11–16, 18–19, 54–5, 62; alliance with British against French (1678) 17, 72
Newman, Captain 54
Newton, Private David 139, 142
New Zealand, HMS 190, 203
Nicholas, Paul Harris 86, 96, 139; *Historical Record of the Royal Marine Force* 119
Nicholls, Major Edward 155
Nicosian, SS 215
Nigeria, HMS 224
Nile, Battle of the (1798) 53, 137
Nore mutiny (1797) 127–30
Norfolk, HMS 62, 219, 225
Normandy: invaded (1944) 227–8, 264–8
North Africa: 1942 landings 260
North America: Marine actions in 96–103, 152–5; and expulsion of French from Canada 97–8
North Cape, Battle of (1943) 219
Northern Ireland 283–4
Norway: 1940 campaign in 255; arctic training in 283
Norwich, HMS 38
Nymphe (French ship) 72

Obligado, Battle of (1846) 159
Ocean, HMS 288
Okinawa: invaded (1945) 228
Oldfield, Major Thomas 137, 155
O'Loghlen, Lieut. Terence 47–8, 59, 69, 91, 113, 123; *The Marine Volunteer* 91
Orient, L' (French ship) 112
Ostend: garrisoned by Duke of York's Regiment 17; in Great War 232
Ottoman Empire (Turkey) 159, 161–2; in Great War 234–7
Owen, Major J. 139, 142, 160
Oxford, Aubrey de Vere, 20th Earl of 13–14
Oxford, HMS 110

Pacific: in Second World War 228–9
Packwood, Sergeant 138
Palestine: British mandate ends (1948) 277
Paradox, HMS 13
Paris, Major–General Archibald 233, 237–9, 244, 247
Parker, Lance-Corporal Walter, VC 237
Parks, Colonel 40
Passchendaele, Battle of (1917) 240–1
Paterson, Thomas 37
Pearl, HMS 179–80
Pedestal, Operation (1942) 224
Peel, Captain 179
Peiho River (China) 169
Peking 185
Pellew, Sir Edward 149
Pembroke, Thomas Herbert, 8th Earl of 136
Penelope, HMS 224

Peninsular War (1808–14) 151–2
Pepys, Samuel 31
Percy, Hugh (*later* 2nd Duke of Northumberland) 99
Peter Port, Guernsey 122
Peterborough, Charles Mordaunt, 3rd Earl of 79
Phillips, Private F.W. 187
Phoenix, HMS 63
Picton-Phillipps, Lieut.-Colonel 'Tiger' 258–9
Pierce, Captain 58
Piper, Colonel 21
Pique (French ship) 61
Pitcairn, Captain Williams 102
Pitcairn, Major John 29, 48, 98, 100–1, 105
Placentia: amphibious raid on (1703) 76–8, 97
Pleydell, Lieut. 64
Plunkett, Captain James 33, 35
Plymouth: as Grand Division HQ 47–8; RM barracks 121–2
Poë, Major 177
Pole, Captain 52
Pollard, Midshipman 141
Pompee, HMS 129
Popham, Commodore Sir Home 150
Popham, Private Walter 243–4
Port Glasgow, HMS 30
Port Mahon (Minorca) 81
Port R, 147
Port-en-Bessin, Normandy 267
Portsmouth: as Grand Division HQ 47–8; RM barracks 121; reputation 122
Powell, Lieut. Philemon 20
Pownall, Lieut. 52, 55
Poyntz, Major W.H. 167
press (impressment) 27, 40; discontinued 191
Prettyjohn, Corporal John, VC 163
Pridham, Lieut. William 144, 155, 158
Primrose, Operation 255–6
Prince of Wales, HMS 221, 257
Princess Charlotte, HMS 161
Princess Royal, HMS 190, 205, 208
prize money 120–1, 130
Prosser, Captain Samuel 91
Prudente, HMS 66
Puddifoot, Sergeant 218

Q-ships 214–16
Quebec: 1711 expedition to 97; siege and capture (1757) 97
Queen Charlotte, HMS 112, 124
Queen Mary, HMS 207–8, 212
Quiberon Bay, Battle of (1759) 56–7, 71, 73
Quondam Sub, A (pseud.) 117, 119, 131

Raleigh, Sir Walter 112
Ramillies, HMS 254
Ramsey, Private James 195

Ranelagh, HMS 4
Rayo, El (Spanish ship) 142
Redoutable (French ship) 140–1
Rees, Sergeant Thomas 144
Reno, River (Italy) 272
Repulse, HMS 221, 257
Revenge, HMS 65, 139
Richardson, Lieut. 61
Rippon, HMS 66, 68, 90–1
River Plate, Battle of the (1939) 217
Roberts, Field Marshal Frederick Sleigh,
    1st Earl 187
Robyns, Captain John 52–3, 129, 143,
    144–5, 153–4, 157
Rochambeau, Jean Baptiste Donatien de
    Vimeur, comte de 57
Rochefort 88
Rochester, HMS 29
Rodney, Admiral George Brydges, 1st
    Baron 58, 90–1, 103
Rodney, HMS 221
Rooke, Admiral Sir George 4–5, 9
Rotely, Second Lieut. Lewis 107, 117–18,
    120–1, 138–42, 145, 157
Rowe, Boy Bugler 229
Royal Artillery: service with Royal Navy
    134–5
Royal Commission on Manning (1858)
    194
Royal George, HMS 198
Royal James, HMS 15
Royal Marine Artillery: formed 133–5;
    discipline and standards 135–6; in
    Crimean War 164–7; training and
    standards in 198, 200, 202–3; role
    202; amalgamated with RMLI 216
Royal Marine Commandos: link with
    Admiral's Regiment 1; formed 258;
    expanded and reorganised 260–1;
    casualties 262; in Sicily 262–4; in
    Normandy invasion 264–8; in advance
    through Europe 269–71; in northern
    Italy 272; post-Second World War role
    and organisation 276–80; *see also*
    Commando Brigades
Royal Marines: battle honours 3, 159;
    origins 3, 10, 16, 25; reputation 10;
    first use of name 16; formation of
    regiments and enlistment 26–9, 40;
    Grand Divisions formed (1755) 26,
    47–8, 122; administration and payment
    for 30–8, 44; *Rules and Instructions* for
    36; under Army (1740s) 36; inadequate
    clothing 38–9; loss rates and wastage
    39–40; sickness 40–1; regiments
    disbanded and reduced 41–6, 49;
    berthing arrangements 43; disciplinary
    functions on board ship 43, 51, 192–3;
    mutiny over ill-treatment 44–5; Anson
    reforms 46–7; integrated corps
    established (1755) 46–7; Draft
    Regulations (1747) 47; numerical
strength 47, 132–3, 158, 288; status of
    officers 48–9, 198–9; functions and role
    51–2, 60; early training and fighting
    tactics 53–67, 69–70, 136–7; weapons
    and equipment 67–9, 168; casualties in
    battle 72–3, 86, 100, 210, 239–42, 256,
    287; used in amphibious operations
    75–81, 87–8, 144–8, 232–5, 250; deaths
    from disease in West Indies expedition
    76, 81–2, 93; badge 96, 159; shipboard
    service and conditions 105–13, 115,
    117–19; dress and uniforms 107, 131,
    133, 174; enlistment for life 113;
    relations with Royal Navy 113–14,
    198–9; discipline and punishment
    115–17, 123–5, 152–3, 194–6; slow
    promotion 119–20; granted prize
    money 120–1; barracks 121–3; guard
    dockyards 121; officer training 122,
    198; granted 'Royal' title (1802) 127,
    133, 136, 287; and naval mutinies
    127–30; physical separation from seamen
    130–2; gunnery 134–5, 143, 199–204,
    216–17; in action at Trafalgar 138–42;
    in imperial defence (19th-century)
    157–8; new colours 158; post-Napoleonic
    demobilisations 158; in Carlist wars
    (Spain) 159–60; motto ('Per Mare Per
    Terram') 159; VCs 163–5, 210, 237,
    243, 250, 273; Light Infantry (RMLI)
    formed (1855) 167; Horse Marine
    (Vera Cruz) 170; sea duties reduced
    191–2; recruitment to 193–4, 197; good
    conduct badges 196; married men and
    families in 196–7; sports and games
    196; basic and field training 197,
    243–4; esprit de corps 198, 244–5; Band
    Service 206–7, 218–19; and air power
    220; Flying Column (RM Brigade, Great
    War) 232–3; role reviewed after Great
    War 251–3; near mutiny in Russia
    (1918–19) 252; in Normandy invasion
    264; post-Second World War role and
    reorganisation 275–7, 287–9; as
    colonial garrison force 280–3; future
    role 288–9; regiments listed 293–4
Royal Naval Division (63rd, Great War)
    233–4, 237–40, 244, 247
Royal Navy: expanded after Glorious
    Revolution 23, 25; manpower shortages
    27, 51, 108; Marine complements
    29–30; reforms under Anson 46; relations
    with Royal Marines 113–14, 198–9;
    discipline and punishment 115–16, 128,
    194–5; mutinies 127–30, 193; gunnery
    and gunners 134–5, 199–201, 203–4;
    victories in Napoleonic Wars 137–8; sea
    supremacy after Trafalgar 143; inaction
    after Napoleonic Wars 157; first use of
    camouflage 166; defeat at Peiho River
    (1859) 169; in Boer War 188; steam
    power introduced and developed

189–92; manning reforms (1853) 192;
first torpedoes 202; in Great War
(1914–18) 205–14; radio
communications 213; in Second World
War 216–26; admits RM officers to
command commissioned ships 261;
post-Second World War reorganisation
276; *see also* Naval Brigades
Ruby, HMS 51
Ruffane, Captain Henry 71–2
Rupert, HMS 12–13, 69
Russell, Admiral Edward (Earl of Orford)
37
Russia *see* Crimean War; Soviet Union
Rycaut, Colonel 87
Ryswick, Treaty of (1697) 41

St Andrew, HMS 29
St Helena 155
St James' Day Fight (1666) 12–13
St Vincent, Admiral of the Fleet John
Jervis, Earl of 1, 47, 49, 112, 130–3,
149
Salamanca, Battle of (1812) 151–2
Salerno landings (1943) 226
Salisbury, HMS 115
San Estevan, Battle of (1707) 80
San Felipe (Spain) 152
San Sebastian 160
Sandwich, Edward Montague, 1st Earl of
15
Sandys, Duncan (*later* Baron Duncan-
Sandys) 278
San Nicolas (Spanish ship) 138
Santa Catalina (Spanish ship) 55–6
Santiago campaign (1741–2) 39
Santiago de Cuba 86
Santissima Trinidad (Spanish ship) 141
Saracen, HMS 148
Satellite, HMS 190
Saturn, HMS 129
Saumarez, Sir James 134
Saunders, Corporal Albert 205
Sceptre, HMS 111
Scharnhorst (German battle-cruiser) 219–20
Schooneveldt, Battle of (1673) 16, 117
Scipion, HMS 143
Sebastopol 164, 238
Secker, Sergeant 141
Seine, HMS 145
Selborne Scheme (1902) 199
Senior, Captain Guy 188
Serpent, HMS 54
Seydlitz (German battle-cruiser) 209
Seymour, Admiral Frederick Beauchamp
Paget (*later* Baron Alcester) 202
Seymour, Brig.-General 78
Shafto, Captain 33, 37
Shah, HMS 201
Shannon, HMS 59, 66, 68, 179, 191, 200
Sheerness 18–20, 27
Shorte, Major 100

Shovell, Admiral Sir Cloudesley 34–5, 44,
58
Sicily: invasion and campaign (1943)
262–4
Sierra Leone 288
signalling: with flags 58; by radio 213
Simms, Lieut. 130
Simoneseki, Straits of 170
Simoom (troopship) 171
Singapore: falls to Japanese (1942) 257
Smith, Boy Bugler 197
Smollett, Tobias 83
Soissons, Battle of (1918) 246
Sole Bay, Battle of (1672) 15–16, 19, 55,
70, 73
Somme, Battle of the (1916–17) 240–1
Souter, Captain William 98–9, 101
Soviet Union (and Russia): World War II
convoys to 223–6; Allied intervention
(1918–19) 252
Spain: as ally in Napoleonic Wars 144;
Carlist wars 159–60; *see also*
Peninsular War
Spanish Succession, War of (1701–14)
3–5, 25, 26, 28, 78–81
Special Service Brigades *see* Commando
Brigades
Spencer, George John, 2nd Earl 129–30,
134
Sphinx, HMS 157, 183–4, 186, 190
Spicer, Captain 38
Spithead mutiny (1797) 127–30
Spragge, Sir Edward 57–8
Statira, HMS 143
Steele, Lieut. Robert 135
Strombolo, HM Bombship 152
Sturges, General Robert 254–5, 260
submarines: in Great War 206, 214–16
Success, HMS 52, 55
Sudan 175–7, 188, 203–4
Suez Canal: threatened (1882) 172–3;
crisis (1956) 278
Suffren Saint Tropez, Admiral Pierre
André, de 58
Sultan, HMS 202
Sveaborg 165–7, 198, 200
Swale, Colonel Richard 52, 115, 118, 125,
146, 150, 157
Swales, Bandsman Joffre 221
Swallow, HMS 178
Swiftsure, HMS 68, 116, 145
Sybille, HMS 58
*Symptoms of Advice to the Oxxxxxxs of
an Amphibious Corps* 70
Syria 160–1

Taber, Gunner Edward 196
Talmash (Tollemache), General Thomas
77
Tangiers 16–17
Taylor, Captain Silas 15
Tel-el-Kebir 172–3, 175

Temeraire, HMS 65, 73, 139, 141
Test Act (1673) 20, 40
Texel, Battle of the (1673) 16, 57–8
Theseus, HMS 155
Thetis (French frigate) 137–8
Thomas, Private Ralph 219
Tiger, HMS 207, 209, 211, 276
Tigre, HMS 155
Tilbury, HMS 39
Timpson, Lieut. Mortimer 54, 128, 130, 158
Torch, Operation 260
torpedoes 202
Torres Vedras 151
Torrington, Admiral Arthur Herbert, Earl of 16–17, 29, 136
Toulon, Battle of (1744) 56–7
Trafalgar, Battle of (1805) 52, 65, 136, 138–43
Trew, Captain 204
Trinidad, HMS 225
Tromp, Admiral Cornelius van 57
Troy, Captain 65
Tulloch, Captain 172
Tummins, Major 142
Turenne, Henri de la Tour d'Auvergne, vicomte de 17
Turkey *see* Ottoman Empire
Turner, Sergeant William 114, 162–4
Tyger, HMS 60

U-boats *see* submarines
United States of America: War of 1812 59, 103, 145, 152–3; Marine co-operation with British 185, 277; in Korean War 277
Ushant, First Battle of (1794) 61
Utrecht, Treaty of (1714) 81

Vauban, Marshal Sébastien le Prestre de 5, 77, 94, 96
Vaughan, Captain Roger 15, 17, 73
Venerable, HMS 73, 217
Vernon, Admiral Edward 26–7, 82, 84–6, 110, 122, 127, 137
Vernon, HMS (technical training centre) 213
Viborg 165
Victoria, Queen 173
Victoria Cross: awarded to RMs 163–5, 210, 237, 243, 250, 273
Victory, HMS 71, 118, 139–42
Vigo 4
Villeneuve, Admiral Pierre de 142

Villiers' Regiment 33, 120
Vindictive, HMS 248–50
Viper, Force 257–8
Virginia 16, 21, 97
Volcano, HMS 166

Wager, Sir Charles 47
Walcheren 270–1
Walker, Admiral Sir Hovenden 30, 97, 126
Waller, Lieut. J. 99–100
Walpole, Sir Robert 27
War of 1812 59, 103, 145, 152–5
Warrior, HMS 191
Warspite, HMS 193, 226–7
Washington, DC: burned (1814) 153
'Way Forward, The' (1981 Defence White Paper) 285
Weazle, HMS (sloop) 56
Wellington, Arthur Wellesley, 1st Duke of 151–2
Wemyss, Captain 72, 165, 167
Wentworth, General Thomas 82, 84, 86
West Indies: expedition to (1740) 76, 81–2
Western Front (Great War) 239–47
Wheeler, Sir Francis 76
Whitfield, Samuel 35
Wilkinson, Gunner Thomas, VC 164
William III (of Orange), King 22, 41–3, 76
William IV, King (*earlier* Duke of Clarence) 9
Wills, General Sir Charles 80–1
Wills's Regiment 44–5, 80
Wilson, Captain 73
Wilson, Lieut. Edward 155
Wilson, Lieut. 187
Witu 178, 180–1
Wolfe, Colonel Edward 29, 33, 36–7, 39, 85
Wolfe, General James 97
Wolseley, General Sir Garnet 171–3
Woodruff, Lieut. Henry 182–4
World War I *see* Great War (1914–18)
World War II (1939–45): at sea 216–29; on land 231, 255–6
Wray, Sir Chichester 12, 14, 18–20
Wright, Colour Sergeant Harry 223, 248

Yarmouth, HMS 210
York and Albany, Duke of *see* James II, King
Yugoslavia: Special Service Brigade in 269

'Zealand – the Design' (1673 plan) 16
Zeebrugge raid (1918) 159, 247–50